A Dark Inheritance

A Dark Inheritance

BLOOD, RACE, AND SEX IN COLONIAL JAMAICA

Brooke N. Newman

Yale UNIVERSITY PRESS

New Haven & London

Published with assistance from the Annie Burr Lewis Fund.

Published with assistance from the foundation established in memory
of Calvin Chapin of the Class of 1788, Yale College.

Yale University Press books may be purchased in quantity for educational,
business, or promotional use. For information, please e-mail
sales.press@yale.edu (U.S. office) or sales@yaleup.co.uk (U.K. office).

Set in Adobe Garamond type by Newgen North America.
Printed in the United States of America.

Library of Congress Control Number: 2017964207
ISBN 978-0-300-22555-6 (hardcover : alk. paper)

A catalogue record for this book is available from the British Library.

This paper meets the requirements of ANSI/NISO Z39.48-1992
(Permanence of Paper).

10 9 8 7 6 5 4 3 2 1

For my parents, Jane and Mike Newman

Contents

Acknowledgments

It is my pleasure to thank the many generous institutions and individuals who made the publication of this book possible. The seeds for this project were planted long ago and nurtured at the doctoral level by talented and generous mentors, including Deb Harkness, Frances Dolan, Joan Cadden, and John Smolenski. Postdoctoral research fellowships from institutions on both sides of the Atlantic—the Henry E. Huntington Library; the Eccles Centre for American Studies at the British Library and the British Association of American Studies; the Gilder Lehrman Center for the Study of Slavery, Resistance, and Abolition at Yale University; the Rothermere American Institute at Oxford University; the John Carter Brown Library at Brown University; the William Clements Library at the University of Michigan, Ann Arbor; the John Hope Franklin Research Center for African and African American History and Culture at Duke University; the Library Company of Philadelphia and the Historical Society of Pennsylvania; the Massachusetts Historical Society; and the Latin American Studies Center at the University of Florida—enabled me, perhaps recklessly, to shelve my dissertation and fashion an entirely new book project from scratch. I am incredibly grateful to these institutions for their support and indebted to their talented staff members, including librarians, archivists, digital specialists, and researchers, for their invaluable assistance. A long-term National Endowment for the Humanities fellowship at the John Carter Brown Library proved especially formative in shaping the direction this book would ultimately take, and I thank the JCBL staff, especially Val Andrews, Kim Nusco, John Minichiello, and Ken Ward, for their assistance. (Any views, recommendations, or findings in this book do not necessarily reflect those of the National Endowment for the Humanities.)

Additional financial support from the History Department and the Humanities Research Center at Virginia Commonwealth University facilitated multiple archival trips in the United States, Britain, and Jamaica and assisted the research and writing necessary for the completion of the manuscript. My colleagues at VCU have been wonderfully supportive, and I owe particular thanks to Richard Godbeer, Catherine Ingrassia, Carolyn Eastman, Shermaine Jones, and Oliver Speck for their comments on chapter drafts and proposals. Richard Godbeer has long been an enthusiastic supporter of this project as well as a dear friend, and I cannot thank him enough for his mentorship, constructive feedback, and wicked sense of humor. Many thanks also to fellow VCU history colleagues and friends John Kneebone, Leigh Ann Craig, Emilie Raymond, Katy Shively, John Powers, Karen Rader, Bernard Moitt, Peter Stone, Antonio Espinoza, Ryan Smith, and Sarah Meacham for their suggestions, encouragement, and camaraderie, and to Kathleen Murphy and Debbi Price for their helpful administrative assistance.

Academic books are dependent on the work and support of others, and this book is no exception. I have been incredibly fortunate to cross paths with historians whose scholarship I greatly admire and who have, in one way or another, helped shape this project. I would particularly like to acknowledge Trevor Burnard, Jack Greene, Amy Turner Bushnell, Nuala Zahedieh, Dana Rabin, Gretchen Holbrook Gerzina, Kathleen Wilson, Manuel Barcia, David Lambert, Regulus Allen, Justin Roberts, Holly Snyder, Simon Middleton, Nicole Aljoe, Phil Withington, Molly Warsh, Brett Rushforth, Elena Schneider, Alexandre Dubé, Daniel Livesay, Ruth Hill, Simon Newman, Phil Stern, Karin Wulf, Becky Fraser, Ben Schiller, Becky Goetz, Ruma Chopra, Olivia Weisser, Jen Manion, Alan Gallay, Jennifer Morgan, Holly Brewer, Peter Thompson, Marilyn Morris, Jenna Gibbs, Abigail Swingen, and Manisha Sinha for their feedback at conferences, workshops, and other formal and informal venues, productive in-person conversations and e-mail exchanges, or advice on writing and book-related matters. Trevor Burnard, who served as an outside reviewer for the press, provided detailed, astute comments and suggestions that helped to guide my revisions. I am indebted to him for his professional mentorship and close engagement with and enthusiasm for this manuscript since the proposal stage. Thanks are also due to the Omohundro Institute of Early American History and Culture for inviting me to circulate a chapter draft in progress at an institute colloquium in spring 2012 and for organizing two intellectually stimulating conferences: "The 'Political Arithmetick' of Empires in the Early Modern Atlantic World, 1500–1807" in 2012 and "Region and Nation in American Histories of Race and Slavery" in 2016.

At Yale University Press, Erica Hanson and Adina Berk offered encouragement and expert assistance from our first point of contact, and Eva Skewes provided excellent technical support during the production stage. Copy editor Joy Margheim also deserves praise for her discriminating eye and skillful editing. I must also gratefully acknowledge the keen insights and suggestions of the external readers, who provided vital feedback that helped to strengthen the manuscript and clarify its argument. Any remaining faults are, of course, entirely my own. My family and friends have patiently supported me with words of encouragement, phone and Skype conversations, in-person visits, lively dinners and nights out, and more. Special thanks to my parents, Jane and Mike Newman, for their unwavering love and support and for nurturing my passion for books at a young age. Thank you also to my immediate and extended family members, Katelyn, Bryan and Kelsey, Aunt Val and Uncle Charlie, Rosanne and Scott, Aaron and Rachel, and my Australian in-laws, David, Anne, Louise, Sarah, Lachlan, Luke, Sean, Robert, and Penny, for your love and encouragement along the way. Although Anne did not live to see this project come to fruition, I hope the final result would have pleased her. A community of close friends, those both near and far, has carried me through the many ups and downs of life, parenthood, and finishing a book manuscript. Thank you to Brenda and Paul, Brian and Monic, Tracy and Mike, David and Alli, Richard, Emilie, and Craig, Katy, Oliver and Margaret, Bridget and Aaron, Carolyn and Kevin, Karen and John, Kristin and Jason, and Chung and Emily for your friendship, encouragement, and good cheer.

I owe my greatest debt to Greg Smithers for his crucial feedback at every stage of this project and sustaining love and humor. He served as this book's sounding board from the very beginning (whether he liked it or not), helped me to juggle the logistics of residential fellowships in the U.K. and the United States with small children in tow, and read and commented on the entire manuscript on multiple occasions. Thank you, Greg, for making this book possible and helping me to see it through to the end. Finally, and certainly not least, I thank my bold, free-spirited daughters, Gwyneth and Simone, for putting up with international trips and extended absences and hundreds of missed opportunities for adventure so that I could research and write this book, which has lived with us for the entirety of your young lives. At long last, it's finished. Now, let's step outside together and take a moment to enjoy the sunshine.

Introduction

In December 1825, John Campbell, John Manderson, and Thomas Raeburn, prosperous and respectable merchants of mixed ancestry from Montego Bay, a bustling port on Jamaica's northwestern coast, sent a memorial on behalf of the free people of color in St. James parish to William Burge, Jamaica's attorney general, for submission to the Commissioners of Legal Inquiry in the West Indies. Alexander Sympson from the Kingston Committee of People of Colour, a group formed to put pressure on the colonial legislature to grant free people of mixed descent equal rights with whites, submitted an additional memorial claiming to represent "the body of free coloured persons on the island." Appointed by the Colonial Office following the British imperial government's adoption of an amelioration policy in 1823, calculated to improve the moral and physical condition of the enslaved "such as may prepare them for a participation in those civil rights and privileges which are enjoyed by other classes of his majesty's subjects," the commissioners had returned to Jamaica to collect answers to the questions posed to local officials during their first visit in the spring of 1825. As news of the commissioners' arrival circulated through the island, leading free men of color moved swiftly to make known the grievances of those already free and of mixed blood.[1]

Calling the commissioners' attention to the discriminatory colonial laws, "by which that class of His Majesty's subjects are limited in participating in the British Constitution," Campbell and his associates presented Jamaica's free people of color as faithful, law-abiding subjects, unjustly confined to a position little superior to that of the slaves despite their blood ties to whites, allegiance to the Crown, and invaluable contribution to the island's defense. Between 1795 and 1825, they noted, the number of free people of mixed descent increased from approximately ninety-six hundred to twenty-eight thousand (with an additional ten thousand undocumented individuals not included in the latter figure), or from a little over a third to more than half of Jamaica's total free population, accompanied by a parallel rise in compulsory militia service. Colonial officials nonetheless continued to deny free people of color the full liberties and privileges of British subjects, including the right to jury service, public office, and the franchise. Although British Protestant blood flowed in their veins, and free Jamaicans of mixed ancestry routinely displayed "a firm loyalty and devoted love for the country of their birth," that same country "spurned them as spurious outcasts and treated them with the cruelty of a stepmother." Classified in law as a discrete and marginalized racial class, tainted by illegitimacy and the intermingling of European and African bloodlines, individuals of mixed descent had long suffered at the hands of an exclusionary racial system designed to uphold "that custom which had united the idea of degradation with mixture of blood."[2]

To stake a claim to the "undoubted constitutional right of British subjects" by virtue of birthright, Campbell and his fellow memorialists outlined Jamaica's early constitutional history as an English royal colony. In 1661, they explained, King Charles II issued a proclamation to encourage the settlement of Jamaica, guaranteeing all the children of English subjects born on the island the status of free denizens of England. However, rather than establishing a settler colony commenced on Christian principles, chiefly the production of legitimate offspring in wedlock, the first English adventurers in Jamaica embraced an "anti-social system of concubinage" instituted by their Spanish predecessors "as an almost necessary result of that inequality which opinion had long created between the pure and impure of blood." For in Spanish America, a woman "under the taint of Indian or African descent had no political equality, which might enable her to be esteemed as a companion and received as a wife," thus dooming her to the degraded position of the concubine. Free to gratify their passions in a distant territory "where the will of the European adventurer was almost the sole law of the land," Englishmen in Jamaica engaged in carnal relations with enslaved African women, who, as a result of their debasement and codification as chattel, "found no security from a violation of their persons." In time, these pervasive coercive unions gave birth and increase to "a new race of People," partially English by blood, "denominated Mulattoes."[3]

English fathers, the memorials continued, rejected their mixed-descent offspring and "alone concluded their pure offspring in the declaration 'that all children of the natural born subjects of England to be born in Jamaica shall from their respective births be reputed to be, and shall be, free denizens of England, with all the privileges of the free born subjects of England.'" Refuting the common law principle favoring the paternal line, the colonial legislature sanctioned the disinheritance of the illegitimate mixed descendants of Englishmen en masse, "declaring the colored community a distinct people," tarnished and disenfranchised on the basis of "mixture of blood and servility of origin." Near-total legislative autonomy empowered the Jamaica assembly to deviate selectively from English legal practice and block the heritable quality of paternal blood for offspring born to enslaved mothers in perpetuity, thereby depriving mixed individuals with blood ties to Englishmen of their constitutional inheritance. By adopting the prejudicial Spanish designations "Negroe, Mulattoe, Quadroon, and Mestiza" to bar persons descended from slave ancestors from enjoying their common law birthright, English settlers in Jamaica "maintained their exclusive privileges in the very prerogatives of blood."[4]

The injustices articulated by Campbell and his associates, specifically their attempt to expose the unconstitutional basis for the exclusion of individuals of African maternal origin from the rights and privileges of British subjects, provide a level of complexity absent from the commission's final report on Jamaica's free people of color. The published account consisted of nothing more than Attorney General Burge's concise, top-down responses to five questions posed by the commissioners, followed by their own brief comments and suggestions. From the commissioners' standpoint, the memorials submitted by the freemen from Montego Bay and Kingston, voicing grievances "more of political than of jurisprudential matter," fell outside the commission's purview and consequently were omitted from their report and forwarded separately to the Colonial Office. These unpublished memorials, preserved in the British National Archives yet long overlooked, capture rare, unmediated colonial voices excluded from the traditional historical narrative for nearly two centuries. Even now, historians remain inattentive to these documents and to their articulation of a constitutional right to equal treatment under the law predicated on hereditary blood status.[5]

The memorials indicate that, in an effort to stake an equal claim to the inherited liberties of British subjects, free persons of mixed ancestry highlighted their blood link to English fathers and contested colonial doctrines that only purity of lineage conferred access to the common law birthright. Invoking the terms of Charles II's 1661 proclamation as the foundation of their entitlement to the inherited rights and privileges of Englishmen adhered strongly to local tradition; the Jamaica assembly regarded it, as Jack Greene notes, as "'a Magna Charta' that provided a legal basis for Jamaica's claims for English rights and local autonomy." What also emerges from these documents is an explicit connection between early Anglo-Atlantic racial ideologies, which unfurled unevenly in a series of seventeenth-century colonial slavery statutes, and much older discourses concerning the hereditary rights and privileges, and physical, moral, and intellectual characteristics, transmitted through blood.[6]

That the Jamaican freemen of color cited the sexual economy of slavery and the mixture of English and African bloodlines as the evidentiary basis for their claim to inherited common law liberties raises crucial, previously unexamined questions about the relationship between concepts of blood, race, and subjecthood during the slave era. Why, when, and to what extent did sanguinary divisions subsume other considerations to determine official racial classifications and the rights accorded or denied to various classes of colonial subjects in Jamaica? How did early modern notions of inheritable blood and blood purity—concepts strongly associated with Spanish Christian lineages free of Jewish or Muslim admixture and the preservation of the old nobility in France, though likewise pervasive in English legal tradition and Protestant doctrine—become infused with racial significance and assume the force of law in Jamaican slave society? Was the utility of blood lineage as an identity marker tied solely to unique local circumstances, or did the constitutional framework of the British Atlantic empire influence its emergence? Furthermore, in a revolutionary era characterized by mounting critiques of imperial slavery on humanitarian grounds and Enlightenment theories of universal rights, did attempts by free people in Jamaica to lay claim to white privileges as a blood inheritance have any ground to stand upon? In other words, to what extent did the "fantasies of blood" underpinning Atlantic slave regimes and "exercised through the devices of sexuality," to borrow from Michel Foucault, influence evolving definitions of the British imperial body politic and the rights and identities of its subjects at the local level? Answering these questions is the central aim of this book and requires a reappraisal of the multiple meanings of race and subjecthood in the British Atlantic.[7]

A Dark Inheritance traces the centrality of genealogical concepts of hereditary blood in the delineation of legally marginalized racial classes in colonial Jamaica and to their imagined place within a broader imperial polity interlinked by ties of common descent and allegiance to the British sovereign. It demonstrates that claims by Jamaican colonists that English liberties accompanied settlers across the Atlantic as their exclusive birthright overlapped with and facilitated the codification of both slavery statutes and racial classifications designed to preserve the natural-born subject's constitutional inheritance in law. Focusing on the sexual relations between African-descended women and British West Indian white males as the locus of local and transatlantic debates about slavery, interracial intimacy, and national identity, this study argues that the mingled bloodlines of both proved vital to the perceived degeneration or redemption of white racial purity in the British Atlantic world. While the system of hereditary slavery, which became increasingly established in both custom and law throughout early English America and the Caribbean, privileged the maternal line as a determinant of racial status, in eighteenth-century Jamaica a blend of maternal and paternal lineage determined official racial designations and the differential legal treatment of various classes of colonial subjects. *A Dark Inheritance* shows how enduring ideas about the supposed resilience of African bodies and inherited characteristics, as conveyed through the maternal line, wrestled with legal, political, and cultural discourses assigning preeminence to British males in the transmission of the English constitutional and racial inheritance overseas.

Although the scholarly debate on the origins of racial slavery in the early British Atlantic has generated a huge body of literature, the bulk of these investigations are geographically limited to the Chesapeake and framed around the institutional emergence and evolution of African chattel slavery.[8] More recently, standard formulations focused on the development of colonial slave regimes buttressed by racial ideologies that posited the inherent inferiority of Africans have given way to newer, more compelling explanations concerned with how intersecting variables, including class, gender, ethnicity, religion, and international contexts, influenced English slave systems and racial constructs. Attention to fungible notions of genealogical inheritance as the conceptual bridge connecting the emergence of the hereditary institution of slavery to statutory racial classifications assigning either rights or compulsory duties to discrete subsets of the colonial population remains minimal, however. Historians have not yet addressed how legal ascriptions and cultural conventions overlapped to naturalize the notion that racial identities and traits inhered in blood or why, in some Anglo-Atlantic societies but not in others, the successive intermingling of "pure" and "impure" bloodlines held the power to regenerate white subjects in provincial statutes.[9]

Disinterest in the dynamic meanings and possibilities of hereditary status and blood mixture in English colonial discourses stems from a widespread assumption that notions of blood purity held little significance in the Anglo-Atlantic world. "Although the French and the Spanish often spoke about the purity of blood, the English did not," two colonial American historians have recently asserted. "To them blood was not a matter of purity or degrees of impurity (one eighth, one quarter, one drop) but of paternal lineage."[10] While a sweeping statement of this nature might apply to New England, it does not capture the whole climate of English thinking on blood and racial inheritance during this period. Failure to recognize that fictions of blood purity also allowed for the divergent treatment of colonial populations in the British Atlantic, providing a rationale for who could lay claim to a common law birthright and who could not, has limited our understanding of racial classifications and their impact at the local level. As Joyce Chaplin contends, "Arguments for inherited differences that focused on African bodies provided a foundation for emerging ideas about race, that is, the belief that certain corporeal traits were specific to certain lineages." Yet, with notable recent exceptions, it is precisely matters of heredity, blood lineage, and a sense of heritable nationhood that are largely absent from the historiography on race in the early British Atlantic. Localized interpretations of British subject status and the differential distribution of rights and duties in racially ordered colonial slave societies are also underdeveloped, especially for the British Caribbean.[11]

A Dark Inheritance begins, then, by reconsidering the legal and conceptual foundations from which racialized notions of blood lineage and an inherited birthright in rights arose in the Anglo-Atlantic world. It focuses on Jamaica, the largest and most valuable of Britain's Caribbean holdings, analyzing how a genealogical concept of whiteness concerned with ancestral bloodlines came to determine the basis of local eligibility for the full rights and privileges afforded to British subjects. Exploring racial concepts previously overlooked by scholars of the British Atlantic, this study emphasizes how overlapping understandings of birthright, blood, and national belonging led to the demarcation and exclusion of particular classes of colonial subjects from the English constitutional inheritance, profoundly shaping the lived experience of racial definition. The pages that follow interrogate the emergence and evolution of racial classifications at the provincial level, underlining the fundamental interconnectedness of marginalized colonial populations both in Jamaican law and social practice and in the British metropolitan imagination. Tracing the pervasiveness of questions about blood inheritance and mixed lineages to developing legal and cultural articulations of race and nation on both sides of the Atlantic, this book offers a new framework for understanding the varied meanings and interpretations of British subjecthood and its extension to new categories of colonial subjects.

Jamaica, the most important slave society in the eighteenth-century British Atlantic, is the ideal site for a historical analysis of this nature (figure 1). The island's historical significance to Britain and simultaneous failure as a settler society exemplify the inconsistencies and incompatible dualities at the

1. Emanuel Bowen, *An Accurate Map of the West Indies* (London, 1752). Library of Congress, Geography and Map Division.

heart of imperialism: the entanglement of the torrid peripheral zone with the metropolitan core and the vast expanse between these distinct geographic and cultural spaces in British self-conceptions. As the richest, most productive British Caribbean sugar-exporting colony in the mid-eighteenth century, with the largest slave majority and a moneyed, vocal, politically influential white settler and absentee community, Jamaica was, as Vincent Brown remarks, "by no means peripheral to the British Empire; it was the focus of concentrated attention." At the same time, it boasted one of the most savage and brutally exploitative slave systems in the Atlantic world as well as a socio-sexual environment that condoned illicit unions between white men and women of African descent and that resulted in a growing number of enslaved and free people of mixed ancestry. "As economic boon and cultural miasma," observes Kathleen Wilson, Jamaica, like the British West Indies generally, "hinted at the strangeness and hybridity of colonial power and the danger it posed to the honor of the English nation and the virtue and integrity of its imperial project."[12]

While Jamaica is the focal point of this study, attempts by Jamaican colonists to invoke native liberties inherited from paternal forebears did not occur in an intellectual vacuum but partook of a long-standing political tradition celebrating the hereditary birthright of freeborn Englishmen. Long before the American Revolution, settlers throughout the Anglo Atlantic deployed the language of inheritance both to defend their constitutional rights and identities as freeborn subjects and to deny the English common law birthright to marginalized populations whom they sought to subjugate and exploit. As Henry Care explained in *British Liberties; or, The Freeborn Subject's Inheritance,* a widely circulated legal tract first published in 1682, the English inheritance consisted of the rights enshrined in the Magna Carta granting security of life, liberty, and property to "all the freemen in the realm, for us and our heirs forever." Similarly, Edmund Burke referred to English common law "privileges, franchises, and liberties" as an "*entailed inheritance* derived to us from our forefathers, and to be transmitted to our posterity; as an estate specially belonging to the people of this kingdom without any reference whatever to any other more general or prior right."[13] But who could claim the rights and privileges of freeborn Englishmen as the inheritors of a paternal birthright overseas remained a matter of fierce debate. While some colonists interpreted English liberties as rights rooted in natural law and enshrined in the ancient constitution, and therefore potentially universal, others saw the English system of law and liberty in explicitly genealogical terms as the exclusive preserve of the descendants of English (and later British) settlers.[14]

In either case, few welcomed the prospect of extending the inherited liberties and privileges of Englishmen to non-Christian foreigners or enslaved Africans and their descendants. If an Englishman were asked, for instance, "if the like privileges are not the birth-right of a Turk, or a negro slave in Jamaica? 'tis a hundred to one but he hesitates for an answer," wrote John Collier in his *Essay on Charters* (1777); "and when he does answer, the odds are as great, but he replies in the negative." The grounds commonly used to deny "a Turk or Jamaica negro" equal rights with British subjects, Collier clarified, were twofold: "*custom*" and, more importantly, "charter, given by a King, through virtue of his royal *Prerogative*." Indeed, the constitutional relationship between the Crown and the colonies, specifically the capacity for prerogative rule in the king's overseas dominions to permit local practices that diverged from common law, such as hereditary slavery and the legal marginalization of discrete categories of colonial subjects, lies at the heart of the matter.[15]

The memorials submitted by Campbell and his associates, which serve as the entry point into the subject of this book, are included in a thick manuscript volume containing hundreds of documents presented to the commissioners on behalf of British West Indians of mixed descent during the mid-1820s. They offer evidence of collective action on the part of free individuals descended from slave ancestors seeking redress from the imperial center for injustices and legal disabilities long suffered at the hands of colonial officials. Their grievances, though deeply embedded in the Atlantic slave system from which they arose, focused not on the institution of slavery itself but rather on the exclusion of free people descended from white fathers and enslaved mothers from the ancient liberties of British subjects. Such records offer a unique window into the mind-set of mostly urban, educated males of mixed ancestry in an era characterized by imperial calls for the amelioration of slavery. During this highly charged period, British West Indian whites, as Melanie J. Newton points out, "did everything they could to subvert the amelioration process and reinforce the legal apparatus of racial segregation." At the same time, transatlantic debates over amelioration provided free people and slaves "with a new political language in which to articulate claims to equality with the empire's white subjects."[16]

This book argues that the language used by free people and other marginalized subjects in the British Caribbean to press for equal rights was far from new. Rather, it built on evolving definitions of and ongoing uncertainties surrounding British subjecthood and to whom precisely the legal inheritance of freeborn Englishmen applied, both within an expansive, diverse empire and outside British territory. In a period characterized by mounting controversy concerning the nature and extent of British subjectship overseas, the ideology of purity of descent by which Jamaican officials obscured entangled genealogies to draw a line of demarcation between "His Majesty's white subjects" and other demographic groups ultimately exposed fractures between colonial variants of subjecthood born of unique local circumstances and British imperial policy. Departing from the common law tradition that birth within the king's allegiance, or incorporation through naturalization or conquest, conferred the full rights of subject status, legislators in eighteenth-century Jamaica hewed more closely to the Spanish model, separating the colonial population into a hierarchy of racial classes accorded liberties or disabilities on the basis of blood. As in Spanish America, where "attitudes toward peoples of color originally derived from contact with infidels," Jamaica's racial hierarchy became "messily intertwined with religion"; the law held that only white Protestant male freeholders could wield political power and hold positions of public trust.[17]

However, unlike Spanish America, in colonial Jamaica individuals of mixed lineage did not attain the privileges of whiteness by purchasing a *gracias al sacar*, or royal exemption, directly from the Crown. Rather, a small number of men and women of mixed ancestry appealed to the colonial legislature for a private act, which, if granted, was later submitted to the Privy Council in Britain for confirmation. The formal whitening process in Jamaica was thus highly localized and ad hoc, permitted as a result of the extensive autonomy granted to colonial legislative bodies under the prerogative framework of the Atlantic empire. Although the colonial constitutional structure facilitated and sustained Anglo-Atlantic slave regimes and gave rise to Jamaica's lineage-based definition of subject status, such local interpretations began to fall under increasing imperial scrutiny by the latter eighteenth century. As the British government shifted toward a policy of greater centralization, it tightened the reins of control over the empire, collapsing provincial distinctions between white and nonwhite subjects and subjecting both to the rule of the imperial center.[18]

By singling out certain kinds of colonial subjects for differential subjugation, the actions of officials in eighteenth-century Jamaica became enmeshed in multiple disputes taking place in Britain and across the British world to define the terms and obligations of territorial and extraterritorial subjecthood. In metropolitan Britain, confessional status and cultural and ethnic distinctness produced a gradation of differentiated subjects, whereby all those of suspect loyalty, including Catholics, Jews, Nonconformists, Dissenters, Denizens, and, after the Jacobite rebellion of 1745, Highland Scots, found their liberties circumscribed in law.[19] Parliamentary measures aimed at relaxing the legal disabilities imposed upon disenfranchised communities, such as the contentious Jewish Naturalization Bill of 1753, generated national crises, as Britons debated the potential ill effects of extending to religious and ethnic minorities the full "Freedom and Privileges of Englishmen." After 1763, British overseas territorial expansion and the loss of the American colonies greatly amplified such domestic concerns. In an empire largely idealized as "Protestant, commercial, maritime, and free," Britain's acquisition at the end of the Seven Years' War of millions of peoples of non-European, non-Christian, servile, or non-Protestant ancestry in India, Senegal, North America, Quebec, and the Caribbean shattered visions of homogeneity and engendered pressing questions about the legal status of religiously and ethnically diverse imperial subjects.[20]

The indeterminate status of British subjecthood in the eighteenth century is rooted in a long and muddled history of English nationality law dating to the medieval era. Beginning with the 1351 statute *De natis ultra mare* (25 Edward III, c. 1), which likened "birth within the king's allegiance" to "birth within the realm," a conception of English nationality extending the territorial principle of *jus soli* (the right of soil) to encompass the mystic body politic gained widespread acceptance in English common law. In fourteenth-century legal terminology, the mutual bond of "ligeance" between a Christian sovereign and his/her subjects, which began at the moment of birth, determined who could claim legal benefits, specifically the right of inheritance. Unlike those born within the sovereign's ligeance, who owed the Crown obedience by birthright and received certain liberties in exchange for their allegiance, those born outside the Crown's dominion and ligeance were deemed outsiders, or aliens, ineligible to receive the full advantages of subjects. Benefits of subject status included the right to buy, sell, bequeath, and inherit land in England, to sue in English courts, and to trade freely.[21]

For an alien to enjoy the privileges of a subject required either a parliamentary act of naturalization or royal letters of denization, which granted the recipient some of the rights of subjects but not the ability to inherit lands. The parent of a denizen, "being an alien, had no inheritable blood," thus preventing the lineal transmission of real estate. Denizens could transmit property to their offspring, however, "because, by denization, their blood acquired an hereditary quality." A naturalized subject, after receiving the sacrament of the Lord's Supper and taking the oaths of allegiance and supremacy, was legally "restored in blood" and granted equal rights with natural-born subjects. The Tudor break with Rome and the Protestant Reformation that followed infused both naturalization and the restoration of blood after attainder with religious significance, "forasmuch as the naturalizing of strangers, and restoring to blood persons attainted, have been ever reputed matters of mere grace and favour," pronounced the Oath of Allegiance Act of 1609 (7 Jam. I, c. 6), "which are not fit to be bestowed upon any others than such as are of the religion now established in this realm."[22]

Although birth within the Crown's dominion conferred the status and rights of a natural-born subject, a secondary emphasis on parentage indicates that territorial and genealogical notions of nationality overlapped simultaneously. Rooted in the civil law principle of *jus sanguinis* (the right of blood), acquisition of English nationality by descent was adopted in a limited form as a means of transmitting subject status to children born abroad of English, and after 1707, British, parents. A 1541 naturalization act (33 Hen. VIII, c. 25) placed emphasis on paternal rather than parental lineage as the primary determinant of subject status for the first time, declaring that children born abroad of English fathers would still be considered natural-born subjects. Keechang Kim argues that the Tudor preference for the paternal line in cases of foreign birth lacked precedent. This may explain why an explicit emphasis on paternal as opposed to parental lineage did not resurface again in English nationality law until the eighteenth century. Sir Edward Coke's oft-cited judgment in *Calvin's Case* (1608) enlarged upon earlier definitions of nationality combining birth and descent by laying down the general principle that persons "born under the obedience, power, faith, ligealty, or ligeance of the King, are natural subjects, and no aliens," so long as both parents were at the time of birth "under the actual obedience of the king."[23]

In spite of Coke's explication of the principle of birthright citizenship, as the English expanded into the northern Atlantic during the seventeenth century the question of whether the inheritance of English nationality overseas required one or both parents to be natural-born subjects remained unanswered. In addition, the absence of slavery in England at the time of *Calvin's Case* meant that Coke had no occasion to distinguish between those of the king's subjects considered free and those classified as unfree, recently freed, or born free yet lineally descended from enslaved ancestors. This lack of clarification led to exceptional legal questions in the colonial Anglo Atlantic. In mid-seventeenth-century Virginia, ambiguities about the common law status of illegitimate persons of mixed descent enabled Elizabeth Key, an indentured "Moletto" servant reclassified as a "negroe" slave by the overseer of her late master's estate, to sue successfully for her freedom and that of her son based on her status as a practicing Christian and the child of a free Englishman. Consequently, in 1662 Virginian lawmakers exerted their authority to define local statuses, rejecting the English common law principle that a child inherited the condition of the father (*partus sequitur partem*). By applying the civil law concept of *partus sequitur ventrem*—"the brood belongs to the owner of the dam or mother," as Sir William Blackstone put it a century later—to consign the offspring of slave women to perpetual hereditary enslavement, legislators in Virginia, and soon throughout early Anglo America, clarified that Africans and their descendants were not a class of English subjects eligible for rights under common law but merely the *property* of subjects.[24]

Nonetheless, even those born of English parents faced assumptions that their ancestors' bloodlines had degenerated in the Americas, producing offspring of successively lesser stock than those living in the mother country. Fears of creole degeneracy in the New World, which colonists and English commentators shared, stemmed from the predominance of early modern geohumoral theories of human variation: that a people's distinctiveness arose from the land and climate in which they and their ancestors had originated and to which their bodies and bloodlines had grown accustomed. Fears of Anglo-Irish acculturation resulting from repeated English attempts to colonize Ireland, and culminating in the antidegeneracy Statutes of Kilkenny in 1366, had demonstrated the difficulty of safeguarding the "purity" of English bloodlines outside the geographical confines of the nation. The possibility of degeneracy made the preservation of English identity in the wildernesses of the Americas all the more pressing. British nationality laws seemed to confirm contemporary concerns that residency, birth, and upbringing in alien environments would alter the bodies, temperaments, lineages, and, most worrisome, loyalties of English subjects overseas.[25]

Although the short-lived General Naturalization Act of 1709 (7 Ann., c. 5) reiterated that the children of native subjects born overseas would also be considered natural-born subjects, the Act of 4 Geo. II, c. 21 (1731) specified that British nationality and its associated rights inhered exclusively in the male line for up to one generation. The revised British Nationality Act of 1773 (14 Geo. III, c. 14) extended the principle of blood descent one step further, to include two generations born overseas of a legitimate male line, but did not extend the transmission of subjecthood beyond the second generation.

While formal rules regarding the conferral and transmission of British subject status overseas did not crystallize until the late eighteenth century, in the interim Anglo-American legislators took matters into their own hands, assuming, as Marilyn C. Baseler explains, "that the power to confer citizenship was inherent in the rights granted in colonial charters." Moreover, because the legal decentralization characterizing prerogative rule allowed colonial assemblies to operate with minimal oversight, they also assumed the authority to deem segments of the free populace "aliens" unfit to exercise the full liberties of natural-born subjects irrespective of birthplace. This distinction proved critical. As Blackstone clarified, as opposed to the allegiance of natural-born subjects, which he characterized as "natural" and "perpetual," the allegiance of aliens was considered "local" and "temporary," "confined in point of time, to the duration of such his residence; and, in point of locality, to the dominions of the British empire." As such, colonial governments could subject resident aliens to legal disabilities at will.[26]

In Jamaica, colonial officials initiated the legislative exclusion of free persons of servile, non-Christian, and mixed ancestry from the English common law birthright more than half a century after the island's conquest. During the intervening period, the Jamaican legislature parceled out large plots of land to the planter class and imported thousands of African slaves to work them. Compelled by a desire for quick riches, white planters and the managerial staff through which they governed instituted a brutally productive slave-labor regime buttressed by legally sanctioned violence, terror, and sexual exploitation. Jamaican slave law implicitly consigned the offspring of enslaved wombs to permanent hereditary slavery, ensuring, as Jennifer Morgan points out, that "the crucial matter of heredity and the permanent mark of racial inferiority situated enslaved women's reproductive identity at the heart of the matter in ways not always explicated by slave owners and their visible archives." The inability of enslaved mothers to transmit a blood inheritance free of the stain of servility allowed for the preservation of the English constitutional birthright for white Protestant settlers alone, as transmitted along the paternal line and legitimated in the wombs of white women.[27]

While the commodification and exploitation of black female sexuality undergirded the ideology and practices of racial mastery in colonial Jamaica, it also resulted in slave women bearing numerous offspring with unsanctioned blood ties to the minority white settler community. Born of illicit unions between white men and enslaved women of African descent, these lineal connections failed to hold up under legal scrutiny. Not only did the child follow the status of the mother according to local policy, English common law classified children born of illicit unions as "bastards" or "spurious issue"—hence *filius nullius,* "child of nobody"—with no rights of inheritance or maintenance. "Being thus the sons of nobody, they have no blood in them, at least no inheritable blood," remarked Blackstone. What's more, "aliens," or all those born outside the king's allegiance and lacking claims to British subjectship, were also "incapable of taking by descent, or inheriting: for they are not allowed to have any inheritable blood in them." In colonial Jamaica the offspring of illicit unions between white men and enslaved women were born into slavery per provincial statutes, treated as permanent aliens, and regarded as bastards under the common law. However, in time, unofficial paternal ties led to the release of a minute segment of this population from bondage, prompting local statutory limitations on free individuals of mixed ancestry.[28]

Manumitted persons of mixed blood joined an even smaller population of freed blacks, and neither group found that freedom from bondage equated to full subject status. And they were not alone. Jewish men and women, considered a distinct religious and ethnic subgroup, faced a variety of legal restrictions and tax burdens that set them apart from white Protestant settlers. In February 1808, as the white settler population dwindled and several "free negroes" claiming to be "Christian and naturalized" petitioned the Jamaica assembly for the right "to be tried by a jury, as a white man," the colonial legislature began the process of codifying distinctions between white Protestant subjects and categories of free people ("Jews, mulattos, negroes, and Indians") deemed incapable of public trust. Local statutes governing the legal disabilities to which various classes of free people were subject expressed the official view of what constituted a white subject in eighteenth-century Jamaica and also lent legal and ideological legitimacy to the island's racial hierarchy and structures of socioeconomic domination. "Official racial classification served to *demarcate* legal and social divides within the colonial population," suggests Mara Loveman in reference to colonial Latin America, "to group together sets of human beings according to a particular principle of classification, to accord them different sets of rights, responsibilities, and restraints in both law and practice, and thus to *constitute* colonial subjects of particular *kinds.*"[29]

Rooted in a genealogical notion of blood heredity infused with religious meaning, Jamaican racial classifications and differential legal disabilities emerged in tandem with local concerns about demography, colonial self-government, and the preservation of whiteness and British liberties on the frontiers of the Atlantic. By 1720, the white settler population had declined and stabilized at roughly seven thousand, while continual imports from Africa had increased the slave population to around eighty thousand; additionally, by 1730, free people of African and mixed ancestry constituted 10 percent of the island's total free population. These demographic trends worsened dramatically over time and were exacerbated by the presence of independent Maroon communities, whose autonomous existence and conflicting priorities would prove especially troublesome to Jamaican officials over the coming decades (table 1). At stake, then, were not simply the basic liberties associated with freedom and white skin but the constitutional rights and privileges conferred by British ancestry and subjecthood in a colony fast becoming Africanized.[30]

To preserve both the inheritance of freeborn Englishmen and a slave regime characterized by bondage or legal disabilities for the many and rights and privileges for the few, colonial officials in Jamaica redefined British subjecthood to accord with local concepts of blood, lineage, and race. Shaped by white colonial elites, Jamaican racial classifications developed against a backdrop of broader cultural assumptions that bloodlines delineated individual as well as national identity, and that neither remained unchanging. Even "a nation's collective character could improve or decline," observes Andrea Ruddick. "An important concept in connection with the latter outcome was the idea of 'degeneracy': literally, the loss of identity as a *gens*," or race of people. Although the causes of national degeneracy encompassed a wide range of factors, including climate, "racial mixing was held to be the chief culprit."[31] Yet by privileging blood as a racial marker in law, the colonial legislature also rendered the bloodlines of differentiated colonial populations susceptible to alterations through mixture. As this study reveals, Jamaican statutory definitions of race fluctuated during the slave era; the instability of racial categories, and the shifting fates of individuals within Jamaica's racial system, was intimately bound up with the exercise of colonial power. Who could enjoy the privileges of whiteness in accordance with Jamaican law varied remarkably over time, demonstrating the considerable discretionary authority local officials held over racial classifications and the extent to which continual revision of the legal parameters of whiteness could serve their ideological interests. The result was that in eighteenth-century Jamaica, as in Spanish America, genealogical definitions of whiteness, which defined white status through the absence or gradual diminution of African or Indian blood, allowed for the possibility of white racial regeneration, a gradual whitening of the population through mixture over several successive generations.[32]

TABLE 1. JAMAICA POPULATION ESTIMATES, 1661–1834

Year	Whites	Slaves	Free People	Total
1661	2,956	514	--	3,470
1673	7,768	9,504	--	17,272
1693	7,365	40,635	--	48,000
1700	7,300	42,000	--	49,300
1720	7,100	79,600	--	86,700
1730	8,230	74,523	1,012	83,765
1755	12,000	130,000	c. 2,500	144,500
1774	12,737	192,787	4,093	209,617
1788	18,347	226,432	9,405	254,184
1800	27,000	309,000	10,000	346,000
1807	30,000	350,000	c. 20,000	400,000
1825	25,000	330,000	38,800	393,800
1834	15,000	311,070	45,000	371,070

Sources: Richard S. Dunn, *Sugar and Slaves: The Rise of the Planter Class in the English West Indies* (1972; repr., Chapel Hill: University of North Carolina Press, 2012), 155; Trevor Burnard, *Mastery, Tyranny, and Desire: Thomas Thistlewood and His Slaves in the Anglo-Jamaican World* (Chapel Hill: University of North Carolina Press, 2004), 16; David W. Galenson, *Traders, Planters and Slaves: Market Behavior in Early English America* (Cambridge: Cambridge University Press, 1986), 4; 1730 census, CO 137/19/part 2, f. 24; "Governor Knowle's response to queries," 1755, CO 137/28, f. 228; "Stephen Fuller's estimate of free people in 1761," CO 137/75, f. 92; 1774 census, CO 137/70, f. 94; 1788 census, CO 137/87, f. 173; B. W. Higman, *Slave Population and Economy in Jamaica, 1807–1834* (Kingston: University of the West Indies Press, 1995), 62; Great Britain, *The Parliamentary Debates,* vol. 17 (London, 1828), 1243; "Account of the free colored population in Jamaica," 1825, CO 318/76, f. 49; Gad Heuman, *Between Black and White: Race, Politics, and the Free Coloreds in Jamaica, 1792–1865* (Westport, CT: Greenwood Press, 1981), 7.

This book contends that shifting our gaze to the West Indies, and Jamaica specifically, allows us to recognize that English colonial attitudes toward racial mixture and the inclusion of subjects of nonwhite and mixed racial ancestry in the political nation bore a greater resemblance to Iberian and French models than historians have thus far acknowledged. A genealogical definition of whiteness enabled local officials in Jamaica to exercise considerable authority over the rights accorded to different classes of colonial subjects and over the individual racial identities of free men and women of mixed ancestry. Although colonial legislatures throughout the mainland British Atlantic enacted prohibitions against cross-racial sex and marriage, public concerns about and official responses to such unions depended heavily on local circumstances.[33]

In the British West Indies, demographic disparities between white settlers and enslaved Africans, coupled with a skewed sex ratio favoring white males (Barbados excepted), resulted in extensive sexual contact between white men and African-descended women. Colonial law and customary opinion overlapped to classify the mixed offspring resulting from these illicit unions as an inferior, hybrid race, tainted by the enslaved status of their mothers irrespective of white paternity.[34] Like attainted felons dead in English law, their blood metaphorically "stained" or "blackened" and thereby divested of inheritable qualities, African captives in the British Caribbean were cut off from kin, criminalized in slave codes, and renamed "Negroes." "Not only was the slave denied all claims on, and obligations to, his parents and living blood relations but, by extension, all such claims and obligations on his more remote ancestors and on his descendants." "He was," Orlando Patterson insists, "truly a genealogical isolate"—subject to different rules of law. African blood, corrupted by the stain of slavery and heathen ancestry, transmitted "a negative kind of birthright," in the words of Colin Dayan, requiring the colonial legislature to restore its heritable qualities once freed from the institutional confines of slavery. "In the jurisprudence of the colonies as in the faith of the Mahomedan," confirmed Campbell and his associates, "the black drop must first be wrung from the life blood without which cleansing no man can enter into paradise." Consequently, though free people of mixed blood solicited for "all the rights and immunities of the white inhabitants, to which their petition implied they had a natural claim," colonial officials in Jamaica repeatedly informed them "that an enlargement of their few franchises was inconsistent with the established principles of the constitution of the island."[35]

Consigned to a subjugated racial class regarded in part as chattel merchandise, as inheritable realty, as heathen aliens, and as bastards, former slaves and their descendants found themselves in a world in which blood ties, hereditary status, and religious belief determined access to or inhibited socioeconomic opportunities, legal protections, and political rights. In contrast to white Christian adult male British subjects who owned at least ten acres of land or a house with a taxable yearly value of ten pounds in local currency, free men of African and mixed descent were ineligible for the franchise and denied the full property rights of whites unless they also possessed a bloodline purged of "corruption," as defined and recognized in law, and were baptized into the Church of England. "Everyone has the like natural blood, which he receives from Adam," wrote Francis Plowden in his summation of King's Bench Chief Justice Sir Matthew Hale's determination on the legal incapacity or "Non-ability" attending alien bloodlines; "but it is the municipal law, which gives the heritable capacity: so that in England, it is the place of the birth joined with the natural blood, that gives the enabling quality to inherit: yet this natural blood must proceed from such kindred as our law takes notice of."[36]

In a colonial society supported by the coerced labor of slaves, and rigidly stratified along racial lines, provincial law did not take notice of the blood of freed slaves and their descendants following an act of manumission, whether voluntary (being deliberately freed by a master) or involuntary (being granted liberty by law). Although manumission liberated an enslaved "nonperson" from a master's dominion, allowing for "the slave's rebirth into social life," it conveyed neither "freedom as power"—specifically, the ability to shape and wield the authority of the colonial state through the franchise and office holding—nor the qualities of blood possessed by white British subjects. Manumission served the interests of the master class by extending the gift of personhood to newly freed slaves with one hand and, with the other, marking such individuals with the stain of their servile origins. As the representatives of Jamaica's free community of mixed ancestry explained to the commissioners of legal inquiry, the colonial legislature had resolved that "the act of manumission by the owner [constituted] nothing more than an abandonment or release of his property over the person of the slave." Construed as a private act, manumission therefore "did not and could not convey to the object of his bounty the civil and political rights of a natural born subject and the same principle was applied to the issue of freed mothers, until after the third generation from the negro ancestor."[37]

Edward Long, a planter resident on the island between 1757 and 1769 and author of the influential *The History of Jamaica* (1774), captured the rationale underlying the limited freedom following manumission when he remarked, "For they [freed slaves] were not supposed to have acquired any sense of morality by the mere act of manumission." According to Long and other pro-slavery authors, manumitted slaves and their free offspring, though released from a state of wretched degradation, carried the same tainted blood as their enslaved forbearers. In this ideological framework, the wombs of women of

African descent served as polluted vessels, transmitting bloodlines contaminated by slavery to the next generation and inhibiting their offspring's capacity for moral virtue. As a result, saving a few "select persons, of good education and morality," Long contended, even those "descendants of the Negroe blood" born free and unblemished by the blot of slavery, "are not fitly qualified for this enlargement." Capacity for the full rights of subjectship arose not from freedom or property ownership but from a hereditary status viewed as compatible with the adoption of a white Protestant British identity.[38]

In Jamaica, although lineage, faith, and color overlapped, identification as one of "His Majesty's white subjects" turned above all upon blood and unofficial sanguinary ties. Tracking the genealogies of free individuals and the relative purity of their ancestry drew upon a long-standing European legal and religious culture focused on bloodlines—their continuation, stagnation, degeneration, or regeneration. Jamaican colonial law imbued white males with the transformative capacity to overcome the supposed contaminating power of African blood, thereby cementing the hegemonic potential of white male sexuality to regenerate and redeem British racial purity. After a voting act passed in 1733, all persons less than "Three Degrees removed in a lineal descent from a negro ancestor," regardless of servitude status or skin color, were legally classified as "mulattoes" and barred from exercising the full constitutional rights of white colonial subjects. "The descendants of Negroes by White people, entitled by birth to all the rights and liberties of White subjects in the full extent, are such as are above three removed in lineal digression from the Negro venter [womb]," wrote the planter-historian Bryan Edwards. "All below these, whether called in common parlance Mestizes, Quadrons, or Mulattoes, are deemed by law Mulattoes."[39]

By offering individuals of mixed ancestry the possibility, albeit remote, of not just freedom from bondage but rebirth in blood as white colonial subjects, Jamaican officials cemented their dominance. They alone held the power to determine who was a slave and who was free, who was black and who was white, and who could invoke a right to the English common law inheritance and who could not. Moreover, the potential eligibility of their children and subsequent descendants for the rights of white subjects offered strong incentive to free women of African and mixed descent to engage in illicit relations with white men rather than to marry and produce legitimate children with men of African ancestry. As a number of scholars demonstrate, sex and reproduction, and the institutional mechanisms designed to regulate intimate practices and put them into the service of the colonial state, are foundational aspects of colonialism. Interracial sex played a constitutive role in Jamaican slave society: as a means of asserting white male dominance over the enslaved through control of black female sexuality, and as a vehicle for the production of illegitimate mixed offspring whose unsanctioned paternal blood ties could, in extraordinary cases, receive legal recognition and act as a buttress for the colony's socio-racial order.[40]

Because this redemptive process occurred as a result of relationships ineligible for legal sanction, colonial authorities retained full control over its enactment, determining at their own discretion whether or not to include certain individuals within the boundaries of white racial privilege. While other scholarship views illicit interracial unions through "a family lens," arguing that informal blood ties between whites and blacks carved out "spaces of tolerance" in racially polarized slave societies, this study interprets such relations and the official response to the resulting mixed offspring as integral to the articulation of colonial power and white patriarchal privilege. In imperial contexts, Ann Laura Stoler declares, illegitimate mixed-race children born of interracial sexual contact did not pose a threat to colonial communities so much as raise "the possibility that they might be recognized as heirs to a European inheritance." "The point should be obvious," she emphasizes: "colonial control and profits depended on a continual readjustment of the parameters of European membership, limiting who had access to property and privilege and who did not."[41]

Beginning in the 1730s, beset by rebellious Maroons and having failed to attract sufficient European migrants to the island, Jamaican officials bent the law to their own ends, permitting the statutory rebirth of privileged mixed-race individuals within the third generation as white British subjects. Between 1733 and 1802, hundreds of prosperous, well-connected mixed-race individuals took advantage of their blood ties to prominent white men to attain private acts from the Jamaican legislature granting them the legal status, but typically not all of the rights, of free white colonists, "as if they and every one of them were free and Natural Born Subjects of the Crown of Great Britain and were Descended from White Ancestors." Yet far from simply "publicly transforming Negroes into white men," as Winthrop Jordan claims in a seminal essay, colonial officials in Jamaica exercised their own legislative prerogative by enabling select white males to transmit a blood inheritance to their illegitimate descendants of mixed ancestry. By enumerating whiteness as a matter of blood heredity, the Jamaican legislature satisfied two principal local aims: the continuance of white control over property and power despite deeply unfavorable demographic conditions and the potential to augment the white settler population through selective intermixture. After 1760, when a massive slave revolt prompted Jamaican officials to move white status out to four generations removed from an African ancestor, legal exceptions for rich, well-connected mixed-race individuals remained feasible, though more restrictive in nature and increasingly controversial.[42]

Racially exclusive definitions of subjecthood based on ancestry developed hand-in-hand with a colonial gender ideology predicated on the supposition that white women and white men were endowed with different procreative capacities. The former, to reproduce white subjects and preserve the purity of British lineage in the tropics; the latter, to absorb and extinguish servile maternal bloodlines, transmuting the resulting mixed offspring into white subjects over successive generations. But allowing for the regeneration of white British colonial subjects through illicit interracial sexual contact sparked significant debate, both in eighteenth-century Jamaica and in metropolitan Britain. By the late eighteenth century, as abolitionist agitation and revolutionary conflicts throughout Europe and the Atlantic world cast a sinister light on the island's fast-growing, upwardly mobile mixed-race population, colonial legislators in Jamaica struggled to mitigate the unintended consequences of their discretionary whitening policy. Members of Jamaica's white settler community increasingly vocalized their resistance to the extension of common law liberties to free people of African and mixed ancestry. Appeals by white settlers to keep stigmatizing racial classifications and disabilities in place stemmed not only from a desire to maintain white political and socioeconomic hegemony but also due to mounting concerns that their own identities as white British subjects were at risk.[43]

To chart the ensuing transatlantic debate over British racial purity, which reached its zenith during the era of abolition, this study takes what historian David Armitage calls a "cis-Atlantic" approach. It analyzes the local factors that gave rise to particular sexual practices and racial ideologies in colonial Jamaica and situates them within a broader British Atlantic and imperial context. Drawing upon a wealth of archival and published sources, this study integrates the history of the metropolitan core and West Indian periphery by addressing the contested nature of whiteness and British identity in an age characterized by calls to fundamentally reform or eradicate the colonial slave system. It shows how white male settlers' sexual relations with enslaved and free women of African descent threatened to erode both the racial distinctions developed to buttress the slave system and the prominent place of West Indian colonists in the British Empire. Contemporary concerns that the influence of slaveholding, a hot climate, and interracial sex had made white Creoles cruel, debauched, and mongrelized reached their zenith during the abolition period and its immediate aftermath, from roughly the 1780s through the 1820s. Abolitionism led to the articulation of a public proslavery defense that proved fundamental in realigning British attitudes about race and provoked questions about the precise nature and limitations of common law liberties in slave societies. By experimenting with the supposed redemptive power of white male blood to absorb a dark inheritance of maternal origin, Jamaican colonists profoundly shaped both the tone of the slavery debate in Britain and its potential consequences for national identity.[44]

Foregrounding local developments in Jamaica and analyzing them within an Atlantic perspective, the chapters that follow attempt to further realize Trevor Burnard's recent declaration that Atlantic history has "been instrumental in restoring the British West Indies to its rightful position as the most dynamic part of British America." Posing new questions about the way notions of slavery, race, and subjecthood were intertwined, this study aims to demonstrate that the constitutional relationship between the colonies and the Crown, which allowed for extensive local autonomy, gave rise not only to the codification of hereditary racial slavery but also to the legal marginalization of colonial racial classes based on imaginaries of blood. Jamaica's lineage-based racial classificatory system was not an anomaly but one of many ways colonial governments sought to implement British dominion overseas through population management and social engineering. *A Dark Inheritance* concentrates on the central issue raised by the Afro-Jamaican men from Montego Bay and Kingston in 1825: that a shared constitutional and blood inheritance existed in the legal interstice between the Crown's white subjects of British descent and those of African origin. This mutual inheritance built upon the biblical verse favored by monogenesists (Acts 17:26, "that God hath made of one blood all the nations of men") while taking it one step further—by initiating the transmission of the English birthright to a new generation of mixed-race colonial subjects, born as a result of slavery's sexual economy.[45]

The book is organized into two major parts. Part 1, "Blood, Sovereignty, and the Law," concentrates on the local context and its constitutional backdrop, grounding shifts in racial thinking and statutory definitions in Jamaica to the island's particular status as the first conquered colony added to the

English Atlantic empire and to its contentious relationship with the English Crown. Beginning with the English invasion in 1655, chapter 1 documents how Jamaica's unique geopolitical circumstances intersected with the doctrine of prerogative governance, giving rise to the development of both slave law and local racial classifications enabling the social stigmatization, political subjugation, and economic exploitation of marginalized segments of the free population. Chapters 2 and 3 consider the relationship between notions of hereditary blood status and the legal redefinition of whiteness and British racial identity in Jamaica. These issues are contextualized within ongoing demographic crisis, warfare with the Maroons in the 1730s, a major slave rebellion in 1760, and larger cultural concerns regarding colonial security and slave societies in the British West Indies.

In Part 2, "Blood Mixture, Abolition, and Empire," the focus narrows and then broadens as the intimate experiences, whether real or imagined, of white men, enslaved women of African descent, and free people of mixed lineage in late eighteenth- and early nineteenth-century Jamaica are considered within a transatlantic framework. Offering a narrative case study of two families in colonial Jamaica, the Taylors/Tailyours and the Johnstons, chapter 4 shows how customary practice and personal whim regulated the illicit unions between white men and enslaved women and shaped the treatment and future prospects of the resulting illegitimate mixed offspring, at the individual level and beyond. Chapter 5 shifts focus to metropolitan Britain, interpreting comic depictions of enslaved black women from the abolition era in light of growing public concerns about colonial slavery, interracial sexuality, and the integrity of British bloodlines. Chapter 6 draws together the major strands of proslavery thought to demonstrate how mounting abolitionist agitation in Britain triggered a broader defense of hereditary racial slavery rooted in blood inheritance while simultaneously inspiring collective action on the part of free people seeking equal rights with white imperial subjects. The conclusion briefly returns to the constitutional framework of the British Atlantic empire to show why, in a revolutionary age characterized by the politicization of Enlightenment discourse emphasizing universal human rights and equality before the law, the mixed descendants of slaves in Jamaica looked to the past to establish a claim to the common law birthright of their fathers.

PART ONE

Blood, Sovereignty, and the Law

CHAPTER I

The Birthright of Freeborn Subjects

In June 1660 John Dryden hailed the return of King Charles II in *Astraea Redux,* one of many celebratory poems envisaging the restoration of the Stuart monarchy as the dawn of a new era of English overseas commerce and imperial expansion. No longer encumbered at home by faction, discord, and "lawless salvage Libertie / Like that our painted Ancestours so priz'd / Ere Empires Arts their Breasts had Civilized," Dryden proclaimed,

> Our Nation with united Int'rest blest
> Not now content to poize, shall sway the rest.
> Abroad your Empire shall no Limits know,
> But like the Sea in boundless Circles flow.

Dryden's panegyric to the newly crowned king expressed an aspirational English foreign policy shared by supporters of the budding Restoration establishment, yet originating with and built upon Lord Protector Oliver Cromwell's imperial vision: enhanced naval strength, tighter centralized control over the colonies, and the undercutting of continental rivals through the extension of English overseas trade, shipping, and settlement. While the boundless imperial golden age envisioned by Dryden and his contemporaries fell short of expectations, between 1660 and 1700 England rose to preeminence as the leading maritime and commercial power in Europe. England seized new North

American and Caribbean colonies and invested fully in the transatlantic slave trade; improved its commercial capabilities, resulting in enhanced efficiency and higher profits; took steps toward meeting the objectives of the Navigation Acts by creating a self-contained English Atlantic system; and derived national wealth and strength from its revitalized imperial project.[1]

The island of Jamaica, large and strategically located in the central Caribbean, and the first English colony seized from a rival European power, played an integral role in the English Atlantic empire in the decades after the Restoration. Boasting greater total acreage than all the other English islands combined, Jamaica also provided an ideal base for plunder, naval operations, and contraband trade with Spanish America (figure 2). Early promoters, contends Carla Pestana, imagined Jamaica not as a monoculture island colony along the Barbadian pattern but rather as an "agrarian capitalist model for the West Indies," where industrious English colonizers—aided by an unspecified mass of laborers—would produce a prodigious diversity of crops for export and local consumption. The ultimate failure of this initial vision to materialize explains why Jamaica appeared to advance sluggishly toward the predominance of sugar cultivation and African slave labor, lagging a half century behind Barbados and the Leeward Islands.[2]

The island's early experimental years were critical and formative for Jamaica's constitutional development, institutionalization of slave law, and imposition of legal disabilities on colonial subjects of servile or non-Christian lineage, including free persons of African, Indian, mixed, and Jewish ancestries. Blending English legal traditions with colonial statutes and customs unfolding within a pluralistic Atlantic legal framework, Jamaican officials legislated permanent hereditary racial slavery for "Negroes" and their descendants and gradually redefined English subjecthood as a privileged racial and national status reserved solely for white European Protestants. By the early eighteenth century, as the institution of slavery embedded itself firmly in Jamaica's social and economic life, only "His Majesty's white subjects"—negatively defined in law as non-African, non-Indian, non-Jewish, and unmixed—could lay claim to the ancestral liberties of freeborn Englishmen without legislative intervention.

Jamaica's governing elite forged the colony's slavery regime and progressively degraded all those who fell outside a unitary, heritable white identity in the context of pressing imperial debates about colonial jurisprudence and the indeterminate legal status of conquered territories and their subjects. Beginning in the late 1670s, attempts by the Jamaica assembly to legislate for

2. John Speed, Map of Jamaica/Barbados (detail) (London, 1676). Maps and Imagery Library, Special and Area Studies Collections, George A. Smathers Libraries, University of Florida, Gainesville, Florida.

the colony and control local taxation erupted into a constitutional crisis that raised fundamental questions of imperial governance and the extent of the royal prerogative overseas. Did colonists' claim to English law and liberty derive solely from royal grant, or were the rights of subjects an inherent aspect of membership in a wider community of allegiance? Could the Crown exercise royal prerogative at will, modifying a conquered colony's constitutional arrangements and subsidiary powers after according it the right to English law and representative institutions? Further, to what extent could colonial laws diverge from those of England? In accordance with the repugnancy doctrine, the great diversity of local circumstances in the king's overseas dominions necessitated legislative adaptability, so long as colonial laws did not contradict fundamental English legal principles. The laws of England were to be applied insofar as they were applicable to the distinct conditions in each territory, with colonial acts subject to the Privy Council for review and, in extraordinary cases, disallowance. Yet ambiguities over the application of English law in the colonies and the legislative powers of assemblies remained unresolved for some time, as did the precise nature and extent of the common law liberties English migrants carried with them to the king's dominions overseas.[3]

In the face of Crown attempts to bring colonial legislatures to heel in the decades after the Restoration, lawmakers in late seventeenth-century Jamaica maintained that the royal prerogative could not infringe upon their inherited rights and privileges as freeborn Englishmen. Their appeal to an English inheritance in rights was far from exceptional. References to the inherited rights of English subjects served as a handy colonial legal formula, designed to invoke what John Phillip Reid terms "the authority of rights as property." Cast in terms of the fundamental liberties of the subject, derived from reason and custom and enshrined as positive rights in common law, claims to an English inheritance acquired at birth reverberated throughout the Anglo Atlantic. English colonists invoked their birthright liberties as a means of security against arbitrary royal government but also, and equally important, as justification for dominion over those for whom an inherited property in rights did not entail. To safeguard the exclusive birthright of Englishmen while profiting from the exploitation of others deemed unfit for inclusion as rights-bearing subjects, the property owners who dominated colonial legislatures turned to the rule of law. "The law," declared *Style's Practical Register* (1657), a frequently reprinted abridgement of common law practice, "is the preserver of Inheritances."[4]

In Jamaica, the first conquered colony added to the English Atlantic empire, colonial authorities moved swiftly to claim the English system of law and governance as their birthright as freeborn subjects and to exercise legislative power. The assembly, dominated by the planter elite, held that migrants had carried with them their personal liberties and as much of the English legal heritage as applied to their local situation. At the same time, Jamaican assemblymen, like their counterparts in North America and the eastern Caribbean, borrowed readily from other legal orders to shape the laws that would distinguish "outsiders" and mark them as unworthy of the English inheritance. Colonial officials across the Atlantic experimented with Roman civil law, canon law, and English common and statute law, erecting Anglo-American legal regimes fundamentally plural in origin. By tapping into a "larger transatlantic western European legal culture," legislators in Jamaica and elsewhere demonstrated their "broad, Atlantic (rather than specifically English) cultural orientation," particularly with regard to slave law and the differential treatment of marginalized groups regarded as non-Christian aliens.[5]

Jamaican slave law and the classification of colonial subjects based on hereditary blood status emerged hand in glove with the Jamaica assembly's protracted constitutional struggle with the Crown over local legislative autonomy, the bounds of royal prerogative, and the rights of English settlers in a conquered colony. Officials in Jamaica did not allow their own uncertain legal status in the English empire to impinge upon their municipal-level authority to categorize, manage, and dominate colonial populations—slave as well as free. Jamaican statutes developed to accord different sets of rights and restrictions to colonial subjects categorized as nonwhite aliens helped to constitute white Christian (and specifically Protestant) ancestry as the foundational, legally recognizable basis of English subjecthood and its privileges. In contrast to slave law, which remained relatively static during the century following the passage of the comprehensive slave act of 1696, local statutes ascribing disabilities to racialized categories of colonial subjects emerged in response to changing social conditions. Rapid demographic shifts and internal and external threats to the island's security ushered in an era of legislative dynamism during the eighteenth century. Unprecedented statutory restrictions imposed upon free subjects of African, Indian, Jewish, or mixed extraction signified the law's flexibility as a "technology" of power and an instrument of racial classification and domination. Through local legislation, as Christopher Tomlins contends, colonial regimes articulated "discourses of status that defined the legal and political standing of populations in relation to jurisdictional claims on the territories they occupied; discourses, that is, of subjecthood, citizenship, and sojourn, in relation to constituted authority, both local and imperial."[6]

This chapter begins with a discussion of Jamaica's foundations as an English settlement and significance in the broader seventeenth-century Atlantic community, considers the local and imperial circumstances leading to and resulting from its constitutional crisis, and analyzes the development of a slavery regime and racial codification system shaped by notions of blood ancestry. It then traces how demographic catastrophe and instability during the first quarter of the eighteenth century facilitated the first private petitions and acts granting special privileges to particular individuals of African descent, followed closely by statutes ascribing disabilities to subordinate classes of subjects, including free blacks, Jews, Indians, and people of mixed ancestry. In addition to exploring the economic, social, and religious factors that gave rise to the discretionary treatment of non-Christian and/or non-European colonial subjects, this chapter demonstrates that growing concerns about the place of free people of heathen, servile, or spurious origins in English Atlantic colonies played a vital role in turning fluid, customary racial designations into statutory definitions of race based on lineage.

ESTABLISHING ENGLISH JAMAICA

In the immediate aftermath of the Stuart Restoration, the fate of Jamaica as an English colonial possession remained uncertain. Captured haphazardly in May 1655 by a dispirited expeditionary force led by General Robert Venables and Admiral William Penn, whose defeat at Hispaniola the previous month shattered Lord Protector Oliver Cromwell's ambitious Western Design to conquer the Spanish West Indies, the thinly populated island had served as a death trap for the English invaders and successive waves of reinforcements.[7] Between 1655 and 1660, thousands of English soldiers in Jamaica succumbed to disease, starvation, and violent deaths at the hands of Spanish and African-descended refugees who withdrew to the mountainous interior and instituted a relentless guerilla campaign against the English. Spain refused to recognize the English claim to Jamaica throughout the 1660s, prompting Charles II to take steps to force his right of dominion over the island and its inhabitants and to defend Jamaica from an anticipated Spanish attack. Advocates for Jamaica, a "large and fertile" island "seated in the very heart of the Spanish Indyes," as the cartographer Richard Blome observed, argued that it held enormous economic and strategic potential as an English plantation colony and trading and privateering base. Many of the king's colonial advisors also had a personal stake in the West Indies and sought to develop Jamaica in accordance with their own priorities as well as the national interest.[8]

Still, despite its immense prospective value to England, Jamaica remained a distant, unruly settlement in dire need of financial assistance, government support, and civilians. In early September 1660, the king instructed the Committee of the Privy Council for Foreign Plantations to gather information on the state of the island and apprise him on all that it might offer to and require from the Crown. The following month a special committee convened at Whitehall, ordered by Charles II "to consider of the Businesse of Jamaica" and to prepare a commission appointing Colonel Edward D'Oyley governor of Jamaica until further notice. A former New Model Army officer and the last Cromwellian commander of Jamaica, D'Oyley had spent five grueling years on the island facing supply shortages, ill and disconsolate troops, and a continuously high death rate. Although the English press had touted Jamaica's capture as a righteous blow to "Idolaters, Hereticks, and Members of the false Church," and Cromwell promptly issued a proclamation offering Protestant settlers land grants, exemption from custom or excise payments for three years, and the status of free denizens of England, those on the ground painted a bleak picture. Bread, meat, brandy, footwear, clothing, and arms and ammunition were scarce, morale dangerously low, and the men accounted a "poor Army," containing "but few that either fear God or reverence Man." Worse still, this ragtag force shrank rapidly due to starvation and sickness, with "men going daily to the grave." Venables, imprisoned alongside Penn for the failure at Hispaniola in September 1655, claimed that he had no choice but to abandon his post, for Jamaica had reduced him to "nothing but skin and bones."[9]

Venables and Penn saved their own necks by deserting the expedition but left behind troops ill equipped to transform Jamaica into the flourishing plantation settlement envisaged by participants in the invasion force. Henry Whistler, a naval officer who accompanied the West India expedition, captured the prevailing assumption that the Spanish had failed to tap the island's full potential. "At present it is pore, But it may be made one of the riches spotes in the wordell; the Spanish doth call it the Garden of the Indges," he wrote. "But," Whistler added dismissively, "the Gardeners haue bin very bad, for heare is very littel more then that which groweth naterallie." Nevertheless, in the early years following the English occupation, Jamaica was little more than a beleaguered military outpost. Entries in D'Oyley's journal recounted the soldiers' bitter complaints about the miserable conditions in Jamaica and their inability to return home. "The hearts of our souldiery, by reason of sickness and wants, is brought very lowe," Colonel William Brayne concurred in a letter to Secretary Thurloe in March 1656; "most being barefoote, and some scarcely cloathed to cover their nakedness, and some dead by famine." Although Brayne and D'Oyley actively promoted planting, the situation in Jamaica remained grim as officers and soldiers struggled to cultivate the plots of land allocated to them while overcoming persistent hunger and sickness. "We lessen every day, and are in the midst of many enemies," D'Oyley reported in November 1658, "and the planting we have hopefully begun will fall to nothing without some speedy course be taken."[10]

The enemies to which D'Oyley referred consisted of a small guerilla force of Spanish refugees, led by Don Cristoval Arnaldo de Ysassi, in collusion with independent bands of Spanish-speaking enslaved and free people of African descent, whom D'Oyley and others termed "rebellious negroes and mulattoes." Runaway slaves would later augment and merge with the latter of these two groups, giving rising to their collective designation as "Maroons" despite decidedly different origins. The English word *Maroon* probably derived from the Spanish *Cimarrón,* a term with Arawakan/Tiano roots originally used to describe escaped livestock in Hispaniola but increasingly applied to Indian and African runaways in the Americas. Working together to repulse a common enemy until the arrival of reinforcements, Spanish and African guerilla fighters devastated English troops brought low by a dearth of provisions and ill health, thwarting English attempts to secure Jamaica in the early years following the conquest. D'Oyley, cognizant that the Spaniards owed the security of their position chiefly to the autonomous African enclaves, dispatched frequent raiding parties to ferret out their remote and secreted *palenques,* initially to little avail.[11]

Beginning in earnest in the summer of 1657, the Spanish campaign for reconquest pitted English Protestant invaders against Spanish defenders who vowed to recover Jamaica for the king of Spain and the Catholic faith. Ysassi and his men, while awaiting reinforcements from Cuba and Mexico, relied heavily upon the expert local knowledge and survival skills of their African allies. Ysassi may have boasted of holding the "fugitive negroes" under his obedience in a letter to the Duke of Alburquerque, the viceroy of Mexico, in August 1657, but the African bands had their own leaders and agendas independent of European designs. Following the defeat of Spanish forces, first at Las Chorreras in November 1657 and then at Rio Nuevo in May 1658, as well as the discovery of African provision grounds at Lluidas Vale by an English regiment, a group led by Juan Lubola allied with the English in exchange for political autonomy. "The King of *Spains* Affairs do very much fail in these parts, and his Trade is almost brought to nothing," D'Oyley boasted in a letter published in 1658 after the battle of Las Chorreras. Yet the English were far from the "absolute Masters" of the island that an updated edition of John Speed's *Theatre of the Empire of Great Britain* (1676) later claimed. Numerous "Spanish Negroes" remained at large, refusing to treat with the English long after the last Spanish refugees admitted defeat and fled to Cuba in June 1660, their cause dealt a decisive blow, Ysassi lamented to the Duke of Alburquerque, by Lubola's "league with the English."[12]

UNDER HIS MAJESTY'S OBEDIENCE

Once D'Oyley's forces routed the Spanish from the island, and as news of the Restoration broke soon thereafter, whether Charles II would grant English law and a representative assembly to the conquered colony assumed greater urgency, as did Jamaica's legal relationship with the Crown. The constitutional politics of the early Stuart era had given rise to a conventional understanding of the royal prerogative, upheld by Sir Thomas Fleming's lead judgment in *Bates's Case* (1606), as twofold in nature: *ordinary* (that is, powers exercised in accordance with English law and the ancient constitution) and *absolute* (that is, powers exercised at will in areas outside the jurisdiction of common law or in cases when it was silent or unclear). Yet questions concerning the boundaries of common law and the extent of the monarch's discretionary powers remained unanswered and therefore contested. Differing interpretations of the Crown's ability to determine the appropriate scope and content of its rights and privileges in law formed the core of the debate. Sir Francis Bacon, who served at various points in his career as solicitor general, attorney general, privy councilor, and lord chancellor, held that "the King's prerogative is law, and the principal part of the law"; hence the king's royal discretionary authority allowed him to alter or dispense with the law, if necessary, to the benefit of the people. The legal theorist and solicitor general for Ireland Sir John Davies concurred, arguing that English monarchs held many extralegal powers but wisely refrained from using them in all but the most extraordinary circumstances.[13]

Sir Edward Coke, an influential jurist who served as speaker of the House of Commons, attorney general, and chief justice of the King's Bench, took an altogether different line on royal discretionary power. Resolving that "the king hath no prerogative, but that which the law of the land allows him," Coke underscored the primacy of the common law, "which is the most general and ancient law of the realm," and "to the observation, and keeping whereof, the king was bound and sworn." According to Coke, strict adherence to this amalgam of immemorial laws and customs—a legal fiction that contemporaries later referred to as the "ancient constitution"—secured the survival of the English method of governance and the advantages it offered to the subject. "The ancient and excellent laws of England are the birthright, and the most ancient and best inheritance that the subjects of this realm have," Coke explained in the preface to volume 5 of his *Reports*, "for by them he enjoyeth not only his inheritance and goods in peace and quietness, but his life and his most dear country in safety."[14]

Coke's doctrine linking the common law to the ancient constitution informed subsequent legal understandings of the limits of royal authority, but his arguments did not apply to dominions "beyond the seas" in which the common law had no jurisdiction. In dicta in *Calvin's Case* (1608) regarding the subject status of the *postnati* in England (Scottish subjects born after the accession of James I to the English throne), Coke addressed the incorporation of new territories into sovereign domains, establishing a legal point of reference for future acquisitions. According to Coke's formulation, Charles II could institute whatever form of government in Jamaica he saw fit, for "if a King comes to a Christian kingdom by Conquest, he may at his Pleasure alter and change the Laws of that Kingdom." Yet once the Crown gave "the Laws of *England* for the Government of that Country, no succeeding King could alter the same without parliament." Whether Coke meant the consent of the metropolitan Parliament or a provincial representative assembly was open to interpretation. While it is doubtful that he envisioned core common law liberties as specific rights attached to English emigrants crossing the Atlantic, Coke's influential pronouncements nevertheless "escaped their jurisdictional matrix," giving rise to "a jurisprudence of British liberty." "Through Coke's writings," notes Daniel Hulsebosch, "the metaphor of liberty as property—a birthright—circulated through the empire, and wrought consequences he never intended," particularly in the post-Restoration era.[15]

Although confident in the king's prerogative power to govern Jamaica by his exclusive will, Charles II and his ministers recognized that without a civil

government and other enticements in place to attract English settlers and investors willing to lay down capital, maintaining a firm grip on the colony and
reaping financial rewards commensurate with the cost of its retention would
prove exceedingly difficult. The extraordinarily high mortality rate in early
English Jamaica, as compared with other colonies, was no secret. According
to a rough calculation made in 1661, Jamaica boasted a total population of
less than four thousand, even with the nearly twelve thousand Englishmen
(and some women) who had come to the island, whether as reinforcements
or new settlers recruited from other Caribbean colonies, since the invasion. In
addition to concerns about Jamaica's death rate, prospective settlers eschewed
living under military rule, unsure about both the island's future as an English
colony and the security of their rights and liberties. Yet Jamaica's capacity to
generate vast wealth captured the imagination of English entrepreneurs, merchants, government officials, and planters eager to topple the Spanish from
their hitherto unassailable dominance in the Caribbean. Edmund Hickeringill, a captain sent to the island in the late 1650s, freely admitted in his
book *Jamaica Viewed* (1661) that it "was rather the Grave than Granary to the
first *English* Colony (seated there, after their inauspicious Enterprize, upon
Hispaniola)," but "to describe *Jamaica*, is to praise it," he emphasized. The
climate, fruitful soil, and inviting flora and fauna boded well for a thriving,
ecologically diverse plantation settlement. Jamaica simply needed planters,
accompanied by their families and servants, to populate the island and har-
vest its agricultural potential.[16]

To pave the way for the island's transition from undermanned military
outpost to royal colony, Charles II ordered the special committee of the
Privy Council to issue a royal commission confirming D'Oyley as governor
of Jamaica. D'Oyley's commission, dated February 8, 1661, transformed the
former protectorate commander into an instrument of royal authority, dele-
gating to the new governor certain judicial, military, and economic powers as
the Crown's representative in Jamaica. D'Oyley was instructed to disband the
army, to call assemblies and make laws with the advice of an elected council of
twelve persons, to establish courts of law and administer civil justice, to command the island's military forces and defend Jamaica from insurrection or
invasion, and to encourage commerce and allocate land. News that Charles II
had selected Thomas, Lord Windsor, a royalist army officer and Lord Lieutenant of Worcester, to succeed D'Oyley as the first royal governor reached Jamaica that fall, though Windsor's arrival was delayed for another year. In the
interim, D'Oyley's commission ordered him to, among other things, facilitate

the planting and improvement of the island and "encourage negroes, natives, and others that will live under His Majesty's obedience." Seeking to impose royal authority over the conquered colony and its peoples, Charles II commanded D'Oyley to bring non-Christian aliens, regarded as "heathen savages," into submission. While autonomous groups of African, Indian, and mixed descent might assert dominion over sections of the island, "in English colonizing legal theory a savage could never validly exercise sovereignty over land, for sovereignty, by its very definition, was a power recognized to exist only in civilized peoples whose laws conformed with the laws of God and nature." Furthermore, as non-Christians incapable of swearing an oath of allegiance that required Protestant faith to be binding, "negroes, natives, and others" fell into the latter of two distinct categories of colonial subjects: those who could lay claim to English liberties and those who owed obedience.[17]

Few of the island's original native inhabitants, the Western Tainos, who lived in Jamaica, central Cuba, and the Bahamas, survived the early sixteenth-century Spanish conquest under Juan de Esquivel to submit to the English Crown. In 1656, following close on the heels of Cromwell's Western Design, John Phillips published *The Tears of the Indians,* the second English translation of Bartolomé de Las Casas's 1552 narrative, *Brevissima relación de la destruyción de las Indias,* which effectively supplanted the earlier English translation, *The Spanish Colonie* (1583). Recounting in lurid detail the Spanish slaughter of the New World's indigenous peoples, *The Tears of the Indians* highlighted how "scarce two hundred" Jamaican natives out of a population of many thousands (but probably not six hundred thousand, as claimed) survived the onslaught of Spanish raiders. Jamaica emerged as an important Caribbean entrepôt for the Indian slave trade in the later seventeenth century, though scarce records survive documenting the extent of this trade, particularly from North America. "The Indians are of diverse nations brought hither as of Suranam, Florida, New England, etc., and are sold here for slaves," noted one contemporary in the 1680s; but "nott many are here found because they are subtill and by some means or other geet of the island or else murther themselves, for they will not work." Richard Ligon's *True and Exact History of the Island of Barbados* (1657) described "Indians" in similar terms as "much craftier, and subtiler then the *Negroes;* and in their nature falser." Such observations helped shape English assumptions that Indians, subsumed under the same conceptual framework as Africans and other hereditary heathens subject to permanent bondage, made poor slaves.[18]

By instructing D'Oyley to bring heathen aliens under Crown authority, Charles II implemented Christian just-war principles first formulated by Augustine of Hippo in the fifth century, extended by thirteenth-century theologians including Thomas Aquinas, and sanctioned by papal directives during the age of European overseas discoveries. For Christian writers and political thinkers, the fundamental criteria of a justly waged war included endorsement by a legitimate authority, sufficient cause, and right intention. The view of just warfare promulgated by Augustine equated justice with righteousness and crimes against the law with sins against the divine order. "Seen in this light, any violation of God's laws, and, by easy extension, any violation of Christian doctrine, could be seen as an injustice warranting unlimited violent punishment." Notions of just war warranted European rulers with papal permission to invade, vanquish, and enslave all nonbelievers who contravened Christian doctrine. A series of important bulls issued in response to Portuguese maritime discoveries along the West African coast in the mid-fifteenth century— *Dum diversas* (1452) and *Romanus pontifex* (1455), both issued by Pope Nicholas V, followed by Pope Calixtus III's *Inter caetera* (1456)—provided moral justification for European expansion into Africa and the enslavement of non-Christians. The papacy authorized the king of Portugal to "invade, search out, capture, conquer and subjugate all Saracens and pagans whatsoever and other enemies of Christ," to confiscate and profit from their lands and material possessions, and to "bring their persons into perpetual slavery." In 1493, after Christopher Columbus claimed previously unknown inhabited islands in the Caribbean for the Spanish Crown despite Portuguese objection, Pope Alexander VI issued three bulls confirming Spain's title. His *Inter caetera divinai* of May 1493 granted King Ferdinand and Queen Isabella ownership rights over newly discovered non-Christian lands and peoples. It also provided a legal and discursive model for other European nations seeking to possess inhabited lands and exploit their human and natural resources with just cause.[19]

A European doctrine of discovery legitimating the confiscation of nonbelievers' property, sovereign rights, resources, and personal freedom by a discovering Christian prince was thus fully formulated well before the English established a stake in the Americas. According to the ideological framework underpinning this doctrine, grants of sovereignty in newly discovered or known heathen territories were grounded in spiritual claims and bestowed by the Catholic Church. From the outset, then, the perceived need to protect infidels from ill usage and steer them toward Christian conversion and civilization under papal guidance justified European domination of non-believers. Secular rulers who oppressed or waged war on non-Christian peoples without papal license did so unlawfully. Emphasis on papal authorization as a prerequisite for European interference in infidel societies led to intensified efforts on the part of Charles II to cast himself as a higher authority responsible for the governance and spiritual well-being of all souls throughout England's overseas dominions. It also encouraged the king to promote the spread of Protestant Christianity to subject peoples of heathen ancestry as a means of securing their allegiance.[20]

On the island of Jamaica, plenty of non-Christians remained at large for D'Oyley to attempt to subdue in the name of the English Crown, including some whose ancestors had perhaps arrived as early as 1517, when Spanish settlers brought the first parcel of African slaves to Jamaica to replace the decimated native laborers. The previous year Las Casas had advocated for the introduction of African slaves in place of Indians, a suggestion he came to regret publicly as the vast extent and exploitative nature of the growing transatlantic slave trade came into sharper focus. Las Casas's subsequent qualms fell on deaf ears. Beginning in 1518, Charles V granted the first of a series of *asientos* ensuring the annual supply of thousands of enslaved Africans to Spanish New World possessions. The demand for and importation of African slave labor continued to swell as the century progressed, supplied almost exclusively by Portugal until the Dutch supplanted the Portuguese on the West African coast in the early seventeenth century and became major players in the transatlantic slave trade.[21]

Between 1618 and 1660, a handful of chartered English companies and private traders pursued a limited trade with Africa for material and human commodities. Of the 244,516 African slaves documented by the Trans-Atlantic Slave Trade Database as embarking for New World destinations during this period, 19,510, or 7.9 percent, boarded English ships. The vast majority of slaves who survived the Middle Passage in English ships disembarked first at Barbados, one of the key gateways for the Anglo-American slave trade, before reaching their final destination. Many other enslaved Africans disembarked in Virginia and the English Caribbean prior to the Restoration, but from vessels flying Portuguese and Dutch flags. Desire for swift profits, together with the absence of well-developed transatlantic networks and ready English markets for slaves, detracted from the appeal of slaving for the early Stuart Crown and the English mercantile community. English entrepreneurs set their sights principally on the West African bullion trade and left the trafficking of African captives in the hands of continental merchants. Responding on behalf of the Guinea Company, the first joint-stock company granted a monopoly over English trade with Africa by King James I in 1618, Richard Jobson declined an offer to purchase "young blacke women" while traveling up the Gambia River in 1621. "We were a people who did not deale in any such commodities, neither did wee buy or sell one another, or any that had our owne shapes," he insisted. Although Jobson's oft-quoted assertion accurately captured his expedition's stated goal of locating "that rich gold" rumored to abound in the "inward parts of *Affrica*," the claim itself is misleading.[22]

Since the 1560s, Elizabethan and Jacobean merchants, albeit sporadically and in small numbers, had engaged in the illicit trafficking of precisely "such commodities" with a view to flouting the Iberian monopoly of the trans-atlantic slave trade. While the first early slaving expeditions, led by Sir John Hawkins, ended in defeat and capture by a Spanish fleet in 1567, tales of Hawkins's daring attempts to "obtaine some Negrose" by force or otherwise along the West African coast, and grant of an official crest bearing a bound African, embodied the glory and potential perils of slave trading. The validity of the slave trade as a lucrative English mercantile endeavor received official support in January 1663, when Charles II exercised his royal prerogative by granting a charter to the Company of Royal Adventurers of England Trading into Africa. Pursuant to the company's charter, the Stuart government directed the Royal Adventurers, headed by the king's brother, James, Duke of York, to buy or barter for "any Negroes" available along the West African coast, to the benefit of the Crown, wealthy subscribers, including many members of the royal family, and the English nation. Hawkins and the Royal Adventurers' mutual commercial aim of indiscriminately tracking down "some" or "any Negroes" ripe for sale and transport to New World markets suggests a broadly shared understanding of *Negro* as a synonym for *slave* nearly a century before the restored Stuart monarchy attempted to monopolize the shipment of enslaved Africans to its Caribbean plantations. Skin color was but one of several factors that prompted Christian Europeans to pronounce sub-Saharan Africans suitable for enslavement. Of paramount importance was their classification as barbarous heathens inhabiting an uncivilized landscape ruled by infidels. In the eyes of Christians, sub-Saharan Africans' acceptance of false doctrines and sinful customs made them especially susceptible to the influences of Muslims and other "enemies of Christ."[23]

Reflecting on his experiences in West Africa as a member of John Hawkins's doomed 1567 slaving expedition and in Mexico as a prisoner of the Spanish,

John Hortop characterized Guinea as a savage wilderness ruled arbitrarily by "naked kings" in a constant state of warfare. Their kingdoms consisted not of loyal subjects with rights and liberties guaranteed under the law but rather of "Negroes," "bought and solde for commodities" and transported like brutes to the Indies, an equally barbarous land "inhabited by none but *Negroes* and wilde people." The question was not whether it was morally acceptable for Englishmen to buy "Negroes," an alien people unfamiliar with civil governance and commonly sold as slaves among Christians and non-Christians alike, but rather where and to whom to sell "such commodities" once purchased. While Jobson and other Englishmen may have felt "a certain queasiness with the idea of buying and selling human beings," as Michael Guasco maintains, it is also apparent that the English conceptualized "Negroes" as uniquely set apart from civilized Christian society. Insufficient capital investment, coupled with a lack of political support and demand for slave labor in the Anglo-Atlantic colonies, precluded the English from capturing more than a sliver of the international slave-trading market prior to the Restoration.[24]

The accession of Charles II to the English throne ushered in a new era of commercial growth as African slavery and slave trading aligned closely with English imperial designs. Indeed, gaining control of a larger share of the transatlantic slave trade was at the top of the Restoration government's agenda. Voracious demand for plantation laborers in the Anglo-American colonies coincided with a decrease in English overseas migration, due primarily to population decline and rising wages in England, opening up lucrative new avenues for trade in African slaves. Moreover, the Restoration government's renewal of the Navigation Acts, first passed in 1651, specified, "That no Alien or Person not born within the Allegiance of Our Soveraign Lord the King, his heirs and Successors, or naturalized, or made a free Denizen, shall from and after the first day of February, 1661, exercise the Trade or Occupation of a Merchant or Factor in any of the said Places." By restricting colonial trade to English merchants and ships, and altering the earlier language of the 1651 act to specify "aliens" born outside the king's allegiance rather than merely "strangers," the Navigation Acts put a high premium on English subjecthood and the privileges arising from allegiance to the English sovereign, just as the traffic in and reliance upon African slaves began to accelerate.[25]

Charles II and his ministers envisaged an English Atlantic empire characterized by direct royal oversight over the colonies, state involvement in the transatlantic slave trade, and potentially rebellious heathen laborers converted into obedient Protestant subjects. All of these activities—overseas colonization, trade, slavery, and conversion efforts—offered the prospect of riches and glory for the English Crown. Yet the restored Stuart monarchy's vision of a profitable and benevolent Protestant empire controlled directly from London departed significantly from that held by English colonists. Throughout the later Stuart Atlantic world, and in Jamaica particularly, English colonial statesmen asserted their right to legislative autonomy and sought to impose European Christian hegemony over subordinate populations to their own rather than the Crown's advantage.

THE CODIFICATION OF HEREDITARY RACIAL SLAVERY

As the seventeenth century unfolded, the elite freeholders who controlled local assemblies throughout the Anglo Atlantic set hereditary systems of racial slavery in motion. Whether as servants, slaves, or, more rarely, independent householders, individuals of African and Indian ancestry found their lives constricted by colonial legislators seeking to draw clearer connections between European Protestant origins and the freedom and liberties of the subject. Exploiting the labor of nonbelievers and bringing them into the fold, while at the same time preserving the integrity of the white Christian community, proved challenging for colonial legislators from the outset. According to English writers, the extension of the Protestant faith to Indians and Africans would eradicate heathenism and stem the global spread of false doctrines—specifically Catholicism. Christianizing and civilizing the indigenous peoples of the Americas constituted one of the central tenants of the English colonial project from its inception. Since the Elizabethan era, promoters had argued that by planting colonies in the Americas, England would transform "remote, heathen, and barbarous lands" into civilized bastions of Protestant Christianity and thereby, in the words of the minister Richard Hakluyt, "inlarge the glory of the gospel, and from England plante sincere religion."[26]

The diversity of religious opinions at home and the dearth of institutional and financial support for the Church of England in the colonies complicated this task. Profiting from the labor of baptized Indian or African slaves also presented thorny theological problems. Christian tradition had long frowned upon the enslavement of coreligionists. Additionally, sexual relationships between Christians and non-Christians exacerbated the challenge of consigning nonbelievers and their descendants to permanent hereditary bondage. As doubts arose about the legal status of the illicit mixed progeny of Christians and heathens and the potential enslaveability of new converts, assemblies throughout the Chesapeake and Caribbean colonies responded by acknowl-edging only those born into Christianity and descended from Christian an-cestors as coreligionists. Beginning with the Virginia burgesses, colonial law-makers declared that baptism did not exempt slaves from bondage, with the implicit assumption that Christian faith, like subjectship, was a hereditary status. Thereafter colonists largely set aside conversion efforts, notes Rebecca Goetz, in favor of the redefinition of Christianity "as a religion of white peo-ple." English colonial thought regarding the religious status of slaves over-lapped with Spanish understandings of Christianity as an exclusive identity transmitted through blood, and both perspectives grew out of a broader ideo-logical world concerned with bloodlines and birthright.[27]

The notion that heredity determined religious disposition was a familiar, if controversial, concept in early modern Christian thought. Catholics and Protestants hotly debated whether religious membership was a matter of birth status or choice. Yet theologians in both camps tended to interpret the bibli-cal emphasis on Abraham's "seed" in the narrative promises of Genesis ("And in thy seed shall all the nations of the earth be blessed; because thou hast obeyed my voice" [Gen. 22:18]) in genealogical terms. Saint Paul's explana-tion of the meaning of Abraham's seed in Galations 3:16 reinforced notions of Christian exclusivity: "Now to Abraham and his seed were the promises made. He saith not, and to seeds, as of many; but as of one, And to thy seed, which is Christ." According to this line of reasoning, Christians, as believ-ers in Christ, the corporeal embodiment of Abraham's seed, constituted the true spiritual heirs to God's promises to Abraham and his descendants. Jews, Muslims, and other nonbelievers were thus excluded from the Abrahamic inheritance and their sufferings "proof of divine rejection."[28]

Protestant theologians such as Richard Hooker and Thomas Becon, two of the most influential religious authors in Elizabethan England, argued for the legitimacy of infant baptism as a means of incorporation into Christ's mystical body yet also insisted that Christian infants who died prior to bap-tism would still receive salvation. "For we are plainly taught of God, 'that the seed of faithful parentage is holy from the very birth,'" wrote Hooker; "seeing that to all professors of the name of Christ, this pre-eminence above infidels is freely given; the fruit of their bodies bringeth into the world with it a present interest and right to those means wherewith the ordinance of Christ is that his church shall be sanctified." Consequently, "it is not to be thought that he which, as it were, from heaven hath nominated and designed them unto holiness by special privilege of their very birth, will himself deprive them of regeneration and inward grace, only because necessity depriveth them of outward Sacraments." Becon was rather more explicit, opining that while the covenant of grace descended to the children of the faithful at birth as Abraham's seed, the offspring of heathens held no such assurances. "Forasmuch as they [heathens] belong not to the household of faith, neither are contained in this covenant, 'I will be thy God, and the God of thy seed;' and, 'I will pour out my Spirit upon thy seed, and my blessings upon thy buds;' therefore leave them to the judgment of God, to whom they either stand or fall." "With the children of the faithful," in contrast, "God hath made a sure an everlasting covenant, that he will be their God and Saviour, yea, their most loving Father, and take them for his sons and heirs." As Hooker and Becon saw it, Christian infants, as the inheritors of Abraham's covenant, were assured salvation because of their lineal membership in the "baptized race"; whereas children descended from heathen parentage remained excluded, unless integrated into God's mystical body through conversion.[29]

For Charles II, baptism held the power to bind the heathen residents of his overseas dominions to the English Crown by securing their allegiance as an act of faith to the king. Baptizing and catechizing Indians and Africans, particularly young children, would not only bring them into the fold but obligate them to obey the king as head of the Church of England. As the *Book of Common Prayer* (1662) instructed, "go teach all nations, and baptize them in the Name of the Father, and of the Son, and of the holy Ghost . . . sanctifie this water to the mystical washing away of sin, and grant that *this child* now to be baptized therein, may receive the fulness of thy grace, . . . and that *this child* may be virtuously brought up to lead a godly and a Christian life." In practice, enslaved Africans could lead a "godly" life by approaching both their daily tasks and their superiors like good Christians, with a "humble, lowly, penitent, and obedient harte." "The Church of England's teaching that one is born to obey those in authority (and their heirs) was key to Charles II's thinking about slavery and hereditary status," Holly Brewer observes. "For him, justifying slavery meant bringing slaves not only to Christianity but especially to his version of Christianity, which meant obedience." Moreover, for a sovereign to instill a habit of obedience in his enslaved subjects, as H. L. A. Hart argues, "suggests deference to authority and not merely compliance with order backed by threats." Yet inculcating deference depends, to some extent, on recognition of the rules conferring power—in this case, the validity of an authority structure, as endorsed by the Church of England, in which the highest level of power emanates from the Crown at the top and flows downward to subordinate lords or masters. "The dutie of Subjectes unto the hie powers," Becon's *Principles of Christen Religion* (1560) admonished readers, "is, honourably to speake of them, hartely to looue and reuerence them, [and] humbly to obey them for conscience sake in all things."[30]

While baptism could create new, and ideally biddable, Christian subjects, hereditary status determined who had access to the inherited liberties of Englishmen and to what extent. By wedding the rights and privileges enjoyed by freeborn English subjects to English birth or European Protestant lineage rather than to baptism, colonial lawmakers throughout the seventeenth-century Anglo Atlantic laid the foundation for slavery as a permanent, inheritable racial status. A critical first step in the process of authorizing lifelong slavery for non-Christian aliens took place in 1636, when Governor Henry Hawley and the Barbados Council resolved "that Negroes and Indians, that came here to be sold, should serve for Life, unless a Contract was before made to the contrary." The Barbadian resolution represented a move to institutionalize what was already customary practice in the Chesapeake, although perpetual hereditary slavery had not yet taken root. Colonial lawmakers had, however, begun to identify Africans and Indians, regardless of their birthplace or religious affiliation, as "aliens," a term derived from the Latin *alienus* (strange) and signifying, as Coke recounted, "one borne in a strange Countrie, vnder the obedience of a strange prince or Countrie." That "Negroes and Indians" had a long history as the slaves of England's Iberian Catholic rivals and were "the familiar 'other's' 'Other'" made their hereditary bondage more palatable in both conception and practice.[31]

Resolutions that Africans and Indians should remain slaves for life, and thus never become rights-holding free subjects, occurred in tandem with legislative declarations confirming English liberties for Christian settlers. In 1639 Maryland fixed indentures for all Christian inhabitants at four years and passed an "Act for the liberties of the people." The law specified that "all the Inhabitants of this Province being Christians (Slaves excepted) Shall have and enjoy all such rights liberties privileges and free customs within this Province as any natural born subject of England hath or ought to enjoy by force or virtue of the common law or Statute Law of England," denying such legal rights and privileges to the enslaved and thereby marking them as distinct and inferior.[32] That same year the Virginia burgesses took the first step to identify Africans and their descendants as a separate, subordinate group by requiring that "all persons except Negroes" be armed at the public expense. Propertied elites throughout the Anglo Atlantic took advantage of their distance from the mother country to modify English legal traditions to better suit local circumstances and their own agendas. Accordingly, colonial acts privileged settlers of European Protestant ancestry and granted significant power to free-holders while subjecting Africans and Indians to legal disabilities on the basis of hereditary blood status.[33]

English colonial lawmakers' statutory stigmatization of "heathens" and "Negroes" did not reshape social practices instantaneously. Laws classifying colonial populations and regulating interactions between Christians and hea-thens thus included public components demanding settler complicity and penalizing the refractory. Although such acts may have met with lax and un-even enforcement, early colonial statutes established a formal legal framework for the forced separation of the enslaved from the English settler commu-nity. Gender and sexuality played a central role in this process. In 1643, Vir-ginia lawmakers classified "negro women" as "tithables" subject to taxation like adult male field laborers, setting them apart from women of European descent who were not taxed. In 1644, Antigua passed an "Act against Car-nall Coppulation between Christian and Heathen," stipulating a range of fines and prison terms for married and unmarried Christians who engaged in sexual relations with heathens. Offspring resulting from these forbidden unions would serve a Christian master until age twenty-one, with the penalty increased to lifetime slavery in 1672.[34]

Seventeenth-century colonial statutory innovations focused on maintain-ing the financial and material benefits African slavery afforded to masters by restricting paths to freedom. Denied the inherited rights and liberties of Englishmen and women, and contaminated, according to law, by their servile and heathen origins, "Negroes" were subject to permanent exploitation as resident aliens. In 1662, in the wake of the Restoration and legal suits brought forward by individuals of mixed ancestry with paternal blood ties to the white community, the Virginia burgesses attempted to assuage uncertainties regard-ing the status of "children got by an Englishman upon a negro woman." Turning to a European customary tradition favoring matrilineality in cases of slavery, the burgesses resolved that all children "shall be held bond or free, onely according to the condition of the mother," and that any Christian who fornicated with "a negro man or woman" would pay double the fines im-posed on fornicators. Similarly, the following year Bermuda sought to restrain the "insolent carriage of Negroes, Molattoes & Musteses" by declaring, first, that they were not "free to all national priviledges" regardless of their state of bondage and, second, that freeborn subjects who presumed to marry or copulate with "any Negroes, Molattoes or Musteses" would face banishment or some other punishment at the colony's discretion.[35]

Throughout Anglo America, colonial assemblies assured masters that in matters relating to slavery English law did not apply—unless it proved beneficial to slaveholders. In a sweeping act passed in 1664, Maryland sought to prevent slaves "p[re]tending to be Christned And soe pleade the lawe of England" or intermarrying with English settlers to escape bondage. The act provided that all "Negroes," whether already in the colony or imported in the future, would serve "Durante Vita" (for life); all children born of "any Negro or other slave" would be "Slaves as their fathers were"; freeborn Englishwomen who married slaves "to the disgrace of our Nation" would serve their husband's master during their husband's lifetime; and the children of marriages contracted after the passage of the act "shall be Slaves as their fathers were." Maryland adopted the common law rule of patrilineal heritability due to a growing concern that intimate relations of any sort, whether illicit or legitimate, between English serving women and enslaved Africans would erode the boundary between free subjects and legally marginalized slaves. Boundary crossing also extended beyond the realm of the intimate to encompass a constellation of social practices decried as detrimental to the colonial order. In 1675, for example, lawmakers in Nevis threatened white settlers with corporal punishment due to the "many mischiefs [that] arise by the unchristian-like association of white people with negroes," such relationships "being much to the dishonour of God, and the Scandall of Christianity."[36]

The stain of permanent bondage the enslaved transmitted to their descendants proved fundamental to the emerging ideologies that sustained colonial slave regimes and racial classifications in the seventeenth-century English Atlantic. Midcentury observations that Barbados was inhabited by "Indians and miserabell Negors borne to perpetuall slavery thay and thayer seed," or that "slaves and their posterity" were entirely distinct from Christian servants, "being subject to their Masters for ever," suggest that established local customs stipulating perpetual slavery for Indian- and African-descended individuals had indirectly legitimized lifelong bondage as a matrilineal inheritance. If these early customary practices, later acknowledged and codified in provincial statutes, presented a radical departure from the common law's silence on the subject of slavery, as a body of English colonial laws they unfolded in an unmethodical, incomplete, and sporadic manner. From the outset, the English institution of hereditary slavery emerged, as Jonathan A. Bush observes, "*ex nihilo*," assumed and cited in local statues but "nowhere justified, explained or systematically described." Slavery in the English Atlantic evolved as a set of piecemeal, regionally specific customary practices that in due course received statutory recognition—primarily in the form of "reactive and penal" public policing measures. Colonial statutes specified who was a slave, outlined potential slave crimes and consequences, and to a limited extent, prescribed relations between free and slave but left a wide range of concrete legal problems unresolved.[37]

In 1661, the Barbados assembly passed its first set of servant and slave "codes," setting forth the regulations and punishments that would guide the treatment of coerced laborers throughout the Anglo Atlantic. Calculated to refine the legal parameters governing relations between propertied masters and a labor force of European indentured servants and African slaves, the Barbadian statutes offer insight into the process by which English colonial assemblies innovated in response to the perceived insufficiencies of traditional social divisions and labor classifications. These acts represented a conscious attempt on the part of Barbadian legislators to push beyond antiquated categories of unfreedom permitted by the common law (such as villeinage—long since lapsed into desuetude), with the intention of dispelling any uncertainties attending the simultaneous use of servant and slave labor. Planters in Barbados, Simon Newman points out, had a "fast-developing sense of bound laborers as a new kind of workforce, inferior and contemptible, composed of commodities to be utilized rather than freeborn individuals." They also recognized that while servants from the British Isles would expect to receive basic rights as Christian subjects, African slaves were entitled to no such assurances. Still, the influential slave "code" first promulgated in Barbados in 1661 remained incomplete, demonstrably punitive, and analytically insufficient. Rather than erecting a systematic law of slavery in the vein of the adherents of Roman law, upon which the Portuguese, Spanish, French, and Dutch had instituted their colonial slave systems, the Barbadian code relied overwhelmingly on the threat of violence to keep slaves in line and maintain status barriers tacitly present since African laborers arrived with the first wave of English colonizers.[38]

Exhibiting a preoccupation with punishment that bears a strong resemblance to the concerns of the colonial administrators charged with codifying existing slave laws in the French Caribbean prior to the drafting of the *Code noir* two decades later, the framers of the Barbadian slave code focused on establishing a punitive slave regime. Declaring prior slave laws "imperfect and not fully comprehending the true constitution of this Government in relation to their slaves," the Barbados assembly asserted its power to enact "punishionary Lawes for the benefit and good of the plantations not being contradictory to the Lawes of England." Barbadian officials sought to establish a stark legal distinction between "Christian servants," who as English subjects and Christians possessed positive, if limited, rights under common law, and "Negro slaves," who as "an heathenish brutish and unsertaine dangerous kinde of people" did not. Although Edward Rugemer argues that historians have incorrectly read the surviving manuscript copy of the Barbadian 1661 slave act, transcribing "pride" as "kinde," careful examination of the script used throughout the text suggests that the traditional interpretation is likely the correct one. The Barbadian slave law provided a conceptual framework for denying enslaved Africans, a criminalized alien people, access to the legal protections afforded to English subjects. Instead, the proper government of "Negroes" entailed "mature and serious considerations of the punishes thought good to rendure and revive" in former laws as well as the introduction of new punitive measures. Anglo-Atlantic legal innovations ascribing an innate incapacity for subjectship to enslaved Africans and their descendants signaled the growing influence of theories of hereditary exclusivity. "Negroes," Barbadian legislators declared, were a particular "kinde of people," too barbarous to exercise the inherited common law rights of Englishmen.[39]

JAMAICAN SLAVE LAW AND THE CONSTITUTIONAL CRISIS

As lawmakers in Barbados articulated religious and racial rationales for the differential treatment of an enslaved labor force of foreign, heathen extraction, the Restoration government set its sights on peopling Jamaica and initiating agricultural production. On December 14, 1661, Charles II issued a proclamation to encourage the settlement of Jamaica, which Thomas Lord Windsor carried with him when he arrived in August 1662 to assume the governorship. In addition to disbanding the army, the Crown offered two primary incentives to encourage migrants to try their fortunes in an island colony anticipated to become "the most eminent plantation of all his Majesty's distant dominions": a thirty-acre headright to every settler, plus thirty additional acres for each household member, including servants, and the assurance that settlers would carry English liberties with them to Jamaica. In a clause subsequently construed as both a conferral and a confirmation of the rights and privileges accompanying English migrants as their birthright,

Charles II declared that children of native English subjects born in Jamaica would be considered free denizens of England with the same privileges as his majesty's subjects at home. Cromwell's 1655 proclamation contained a similar pledge, as had all of the earlier charters granted to courtier-explorers or companies of adventurers, such as the London-based investors who sponsored the colonization of Virginia. The Crown's authority to license the departure of English subjects seeking to plant new settlements overseas, an official practice dating back to at least the twelfth century, remained critical to the hereditary transmission of the full rights of subjectship. Children born to unlicensed parents outside the king's allegiance would be accounted aliens and not inheritable in England. Furthermore, as a conquered territory and one of only two colonies (including Virginia) under royal control, Jamaica did not possess an inherent right to the privileges of English law. The Crown's prerogative capacity to determine who counted as a subject worthy of royal protection beyond the confines of the kingdom bolstered the constitutional significance of Charles II's proclamation.[40]

The first and subsequent generations of English settlers in Jamaica held that Charles II's proclamation, rather than the governor's commission and instructions, guaranteed colonists the right to English legal protections and an equal claim to the liberties enjoyed in the mother country. They regarded themselves as freeborn English subjects in possession of inherited rights and legal safeguards that, once validated by "Charter or Commission under the great Seal of *England*," subsequent royal directives could neither alter nor revoke. If English birth served as the wellspring from which liberty flowed, colonists across the Anglo Atlantic saw the law as its guardian. "By a Freeborn Subject, is meant a person that is born under the Protection of the Law," emphasized Sir Robert L'Estrange in *The Free-Born Subject* (1679), "and thereby entitled to certain known Immunities and Privileges, as his Birthright." Similarly, William Penn urged colonists to acquaint themselves with the law in order to gain a "true understanding of that inestimable inheritance that every Free-Born Subject of England is heir unto by Birth-right." The laws of England, he explained, were "bedeckt with many precious Priviledges of Liberty and Property, by which every man that is a Subject to the Crown of England, may understand what is his Right, and how to preserve it from unjust and unreasonable men." Of these prized liberties, the most fundamental included the right to trial by jury, representative government, and due process. For Jamaican colonists, benefits of membership in the English imperial body politic consisted chiefly "of assimilating their laws to those of *England*, being governed by known Laws, without which no mans Liberty or Freehold is to be taken away."[41]

Jamaica's founding settlers looked to the law not only to preserve their national inheritance from arbitrary royal power but also to regulate subordinate populations whom they sought to master, including European indentured servants, enslaved Africans, and autonomous bands of African descent. Subduing and clarifying the subordinate status of the latter was one of the first orders of business, and it proved much more challenging than anticipated. At least three different groups of Spanish-speaking Africans remained on the island after the Spaniards fled: those based in the hills above Guanaboa and led by Juan Lubola; another band known as the Varmahaly "Negroes," located at Los Vermejales under the command of Juan de Serras; and a third, more elusive group based in the valley between the Mocho Mountains and Porus. If Sir William Beeston's account is correct, colonial authorities in Jamaica initially assumed that the subjugation of the outlying Africans would be a brisk affair. As Beeston recounted, after Lubola's party surrendered in exchange for political autonomy, a raiding expedition captured the bulk of the Varmahaly group, excepting "thirty out Negroes left in the Country who by Degrees were all Pikt up & the Island left quiet to the English." However, Beeston greatly exaggerated the strength of the English position. The island was far from quiet. Two years later, colonial authorities came to an agreement with Lubola: members of his palenque would receive "the Same State and Freedome as the English Injoy," as well as a thirty-acre headright, if they agreed to instruct their children in the English tongue. Colonial authorities appointed Lubola colonel of the black regiment of the militia and guaranteed other "outlying Negroes" who submitted "the same privileges benefitts and Imunityes."[42]

If Lubola's actions suggested to colonial officials that they could win the remaining independent groups of African descent over by acknowledging a freedom they had already claimed for themselves, local authorities were sorely mistaken. The Varmahaly band proved far less amenable to negotiation. They also deeply resented Lubola's attempts to hunt them down for his English allies. In dispassionate prose, Beeston recounted how in November 1663 "the outlying Negroes met with Juan de Bola and Cut him to pieces else all things were quiet in the Country." Beeston's anticipated atmosphere of peace did not last long. Members of the Varmahaly group attacked and killed English hunters and settlers who strayed into their territory, much to the dissatisfaction of Sir Charles Lyttelton, the deputy governor, and his council, who attributed the violence to "negroes that haue had too much of their own Libertie." Two years later, in response to the Varmahaly band's continued resistance to English expansion, authorities convened a council of war to put the island "in a posture of Warr." But this war would be neither quick nor definitive. Groups of autonomous Africans proved a source of aggravation to the English in Jamaica for decades to come. Their conspicuous presence on an island with a heavily wooded, mountainous interior served as a beacon of freedom, encouraging runaway slaves to flee in pursuit of other African-descended peoples living outside the enforceable boundaries of English dominion.[43]

The presence of autonomous African communities in Jamaica hastened the establishment of an institutional and legal structure designed to clarify who could exercise the full rights of an English subject and who could not. In January 1664, Jamaica's first assembly, led by Speaker Samuel Long, asserted its claim over lawmaking and the levy, audit, and use of all taxes raised on the island, setting the stage for a battle with the royal executive over legislative authority. Months after asserting in sweeping terms that "all the laws and statutes heretofore made in our native country, the kingdom of England, for the public weal of the same, and all the liberties, privileges, immunities, and freedoms, contained therein, have always been of force, and are belonging to his majesty's liege people within this island as their birth-right," the second assembly indicated that a different set of laws would regulate the governance of bound laborers. While the king's free liege people in Jamaica enjoyed a "mutual, and reciprocal obligation between the Liege Sovereign and his Subjects," slaves and servants owed obedience to their masters as the Crown's subvassals. Members of the assembly envisaged the relationship between a free colonial subject in Jamaica and the king in terms of "liege homage," "in which allegiance was sworn without any reservation, and was therefore due only to the sovereign," and cast the relation of slave or servant and master in feudal terms as a vassal discharging an obligation to a superior. In November, following the arrival of the new governor, Sir Thomas Modyford, accompanied by a thousand Barbadian settlers, the assembly passed an "Act for the Better Ordering and Governing of Negro Slaves" and an "Act for the good Governing of Servants, and ordering the Rights between Masters and Servants," both copied from the Barbados slave and servant codes of 1661. The differing titles of these borrowed laws made plain the colonial legislature's intentions: African slaves would be treated as infidel captives and compelled to labor under threat of violence; servants would possess rights and obligations as fixed by law.[44]

Subtle alterations to the Barbados slave code suggest that Jamaica's ambiguous position as a conquered colony inspired deft maneuvering on the part of Modyford and the assembly to clarify the legal status of Jamaican settlers and their future descendants. Rather than preserving the Barbadian division between "subjects of England," entitled to English liberties, and "Negroes," expected only to obey, Jamaica's first slave act demarcated "Slaves" or "Negro Slaves" from "freemen of England." Legislators dispensed with references to subjecthood and instead privileged colonial masters' status as freemen—a term that in England "denoted access to economic resources and privileges and was enjoyed by all enfranchised inhabitants." Formulating a blueprint for the colony's social and political structure based on preexisting models, the Jamaica assembly placed propertied freeholders at the apex, Christian servants and laborers in the middle, and African slaves at the bottom. Yet even while Charles II had affirmed that he would account the children of native subjects born in Jamaica "free denizens of England," the phrasing of the proclamation of 1661 underscored the difference between natural-born subjects in England, who derived their rights at birth, and denizens of a conquered colony reliant upon the grace of the king. The distinction between the two turned on birthplace rather than blood, and it was thus to their hereditary status as freeborn Englishmen that Jamaican colonists repeatedly turned when grappling with the Crown for local autonomy.[45]

In the 1670s, following the Anglo-Spanish Treaty of Madrid and diplomatic recognition of English holdings in the Caribbean, factionalism descended on the island and a war of wills ensued between the large planters who controlled the Jamaica assembly and authorities in England. After Charles II recalled Modyford in 1671 for licensing privateers to raid Spanish commerce without royal permission, Sir Thomas Lynch administered Jamaica as lieutenant governor and promoted the interests of the island's largest planters. Fearing the king would exercise his prerogative arbitrarily in Jamaica, the assembly moved preemptively to seek greater local autonomy over matters it considered of purely local concern, including the institution of slavery. On no account did assemblymen want the Crown to meddle with slave law or undermine slaveholder power over bound laborers. Broadening access to enslaved Africans and regulating slave labor with minimal oversight from England was key to promoting settlers' financial advantage, "for the planter accounts himself rich according to the number of blacks he is master of," noted Sir Charles Lyttelton, the deputy governor, as early as 1664.[46]

After an initial period of ambiguity regarding the colony's future labor pool, African slavery rapidly became indispensable to Jamaica's economic development and to the wealth of its propertied inhabitants, prompting new measures of control intended to suppress enslaved captives and harness their labor. By the 1670s, African slaves predominated on the island. According to a rough census taken in 1673, 7,768 whites held 9,504 Africans in bondage, and shipments of new captives arrived regularly from West African trading posts. Between 1674 and 1680, the Royal African Company delivered to Jamaica, on average, 1,000 slaves per year, with deliveries rising to a yearly average of 3,674 during the 1680s. On an island as extensive as Jamaica, with its densely wooded, mountainous interior, runaways posed a serious problem, as did communication among the growing numbers of enslaved Africans housed on different estates. In anticipation of slave unrest, the 1664 Slave Act borrowed from Barbados had emphasized that enslaved Africans required swift, brutal punishments to keep them in check; the need for immediacy meant that such punishments could not fall within the "due and formal Process of Law." Fears of insurrection were borne out in Jamaica in 1673 and in 1675, when slaves revolted on remote plantations on the north side of the island, and these were the first among a half dozen rebellions that rocked Jamaica over the next two decades.[47]

In consideration of the steady number of slaves pouring into Jamaica as well as the island's size and terrain, the Jamaican legislature revised the slave code in 1672 and in 1674. The updated versions encouraged the baptism and catechism of African captives, as Charles II had long urged, as a means of inculcating Christian obedience among the enslaved population. The conversion of heathen slaves to Christianity—a fundamental canon of European colonialism—would, the legislature hoped, "Civilize and binde them more to our Service and interest, as we see our neighbours the Spaniards and other nations doe who nonetheless keepe them as Slaves." At the same time, Jamaica's 1674 slave code constructed African chattel slavery as a permanent, inheritable condition, implicitly transmitted along matrilineal lines: "All negroes Lawfully bought or borne slaves shall here continue to bee soe, and further be held adjudged and taken to bee goods and chattels . . . their Christianity or any law Custome or usage in England or else where to the contrary notwithstanding." While the Jamaica assembly appeared to embrace Charles II's reasoning that exposure to Christian doctrine would transform African slaves into loyal and docile workers, there is no evidence that slaveholders put this conversion policy into practice. Instead, fear and violence governed relations between masters and slaves, as slaveholders in Jamaica adopted a punitive rather than benevolent concept of mastery that corresponded with the classification of "Negroes" in colonial law as heathen aliens denied the basic protections retained by English Atlantic subjects in return for their allegiance.[48]

Due to the complex legal status of enslaved Africans as resident aliens, internal enemies, and chattel, the Jamaican legislature accorded masters a significant measure of power over slaves with very few restrictions. Efforts on behalf of Jamaican authorities to claim and delegate sovereignty to private individuals at the municipal level without royal oversight soon led to discord between the Crown and the assembly. For his part, Charles II did not intend to stand idle in Whitehall while Jamaican colonists wrested control of a prominent piece of his Atlantic empire and delayed submitting revenue to the Crown and local legislation for royal approval. By promoting the planting of English colonies in the Americas, Charles II aimed to prevent his subjects from traveling overseas and conducting trade in strange lands, where, as one of his advisors argued, they "forthwith become Aliens to their own country and by degrees contract an interest and affection that is foreign." Therefore, while a vocal proponent of colonial self-government in Jamaica such as Speaker Samuel Long argued that he "desired nothing but his rights and privileges as an Englishman and that he ought to have and would not be contented with less," the king and his ministers viewed the Jamaica assembly as motivated solely by personal advantage rather than the promotion of "the name, honour, strength and magnificence of the Nation."[49]

In 1676, the Lords of Trade, a subcommittee of the Privy Council newly appointed to oversee colonial affairs, began its review of laws sent from Jamaica the previous year by Lord Vaughan, the new governor chosen to replace Lynch. Vaughan, an outsider, had met with a cool reception upon his arrival in Jamaica in 1675. The assembly, claiming legislative and taxing powers in excess of those enjoyed by the House of Commons, asserted its authority to pass legislation and appropriate local tax revenue and royal quitrents for use of the island with no mention of the king, frustrating Vaughan's attempts to defend the Crown's interests in Jamaica. Determined to restrain the irrepressible Jamaica assembly, the Lords of Trade referred the laws of Jamaica to Sir Philip Lloyd, the attorney general, "for his opinion how far they are agreeable to the laws of England and His Majesty's right of dominion in those parts." They also instructed Lloyd to "prepare a Bill like Poyning's law in Ireland, directing the manner of enacting laws in Jamaica." As in Ireland, Jamaica's governors would henceforth refrain from calling assemblies without Crown approval (except in emergencies), and all legislation would originate in England before the Jamaica legislature received it for approval.[50]

When the Jamaica assembly met in September 1678, it refused to ratify any of the laws brought over by the new governor, Charles, Earl of Carlisle, including a perpetual revenue act and laws governing servants and slaves. The assemblymen viewed the Crown's attempt to alter the island's constitutional arrangements as a violation of colonists' inherited rights as Englishmen and vehemently upheld their deliberative power to make and amend laws. For their part, the Lords of Trade held that the colony's constitution stemmed from the governor's commission and instructions, which the Crown could modify at will at any time. Unless the legislators consented to the new arrangement, the king would "reduce all things to the first principles of that Government" and dispense with the Jamaica assembly entirely.[51]

In 1681, after several tense years during which the assembly refused to fund the treasury and Carlisle returned to England in defeat, the Lords of Trade conceded and reappointed Lynch to the governorship. The Lords had uncovered no legitimate legal basis for revoking subordinate legislative powers once granted to a colonial body, and the income from Jamaica was far too valuable to tarry with any longer. In 1683 Lynch struck a deal with the assembly: in exchange for passing a twenty-one-year revenue act guaranteeing fiscal support for the governor, the assembly received confirmation of a large number of acts as well as the right to enact legislation subject to Privy Council review. Although the constitutional crisis had ebbed in favor of the Jamaica assembly, important legal matters remained in limbo. Jamaican colonial officials insisted they had an inherent right to claim English law for themselves and to wield nearly unchecked discretionary authority over subordinate alien populations, particularly African slaves, through the implementation of provincial legal mechanisms. As Governor Handasyd put it in 1711, the royal proclamation of 1661 "granted all the Emunities and priviledges of his Native Subjects of England to all those that would come and settle here, which was the main Encouragement for the Settling this Island, since which time all the English Laws (Excepting some few that has been made for the better Management of Slaves, &c.) has been Constantly observed and followed in all Courts of Justice here, as also an Act passed in this Island for the Statute Law, and Common Laws of England to make them in force here, which was never Repealed."[52]

Yet *Blankard v. Galdy* (1693) in King's Bench had shown that imperial lawyers in England viewed the matter rather differently: the inhabitants of Jamaica, a distant colony conquered from the Spanish, a Christian people, were "governed by their own laws, and not by the laws of England." Jamaica, unlike heathen-occupied territories that the Crown claimed by right of "first discovery, occupation, and possession," had no automatic right to English law or liberties. Robert Raymond and Phillip York, the attorney and solicitor general, later advised the Lords that introducing "the whole Body of English Laws (in cases not particularly provided for by laws of their own)" in Jamaica would be improper; local cases might arise "to which the English laws are by no means consistent" or, if applied, "might do great mischief." The assembly nonetheless continued to assert that Jamaican colonists were, unlike their slaves, "freeborn subjects" and thus "governed by the law of England." Not until the passage of a permanent revenue act in 1728 after years of legal wrangling did the assembly receive confirmation of the English legal privileges Jamaican colonists claimed as their exclusive birthright and that the English inhabitants in "discovered" colonies already enjoyed.[53]

From the beginning, Charles II voiced his disapproval of Jamaica's evolving slave law, and the extensive level of sovereignty extended to individual slaveholders, and demanded a stricter clause to restrain the violence of masters. "A fine is imposed on all such as wilfully and wantonly kill a negro," wrote the Lords of Trade to Governor Lynch in 1683. "The King will not confirm this clause, which seems to encourage the wilful shedding of blood. Some better provision must be found than a fine to deter men from such acts of cruelty." But placing legal restraints on masters to discourage the brutalizing of African slaves did not suit the assembly's agenda. Without license to commit violence against a majority population of disorderly slaves imported from a heathen land, how else would English colonists retain control of Jamaica? In an attempt to attract white settlers, the assembly ameliorated conditions for Christian servants and improved their status in relation to enslaved Africans. In 1681 the revised servant code replaced *Christian* with *white* and prohibited the whipping of naked white servants. It also introduced a deficiency clause requiring masters to employ one white servant, tradesman, or overseer for every five slaves. Settling on the island white males willing to mete out violent punishments to maintain the slave system trumped considerations of Christian humanity. Consequently, in 1683, when legislators considered the appropriate sentence for "willfully, wantonly, and bloody-mindedly, killing a negro," they deemed three months' imprisonment sufficient.[54]

By the 1696 iteration of Jamaica's slave code, which remained in effect until 1781, the principal legal division on the island had shifted to that between a "Negro Slave" and a "white Person." The explicitly racialized legal distinction between free whites and black slaves provided those whose freedom fell short of full independence, such as laborers and indentured servants, with "a property in their whiteness." While the binary division between black and white may have captured the economic, political, and ideological goals of slaveholders in colonial Jamaica, a more complicated range of statuses emerged alongside these racial extremes. The island's policy of religious tolerance attracted an ethnically and religiously diverse population of settlers, and its slave system and troubled demographics also gave rise to free people of African and mixed ancestry. In the early eighteenth century, as authorities coped with the aftermath of the Port Royal earthquake, a plummeting white population, the French invasion, and depredations of the Maroons, members of subordinate groups asserted their rights as free subjects and challenged their treatment as aliens of non-Christian extraction. But their actions did not broaden access to the English legal inheritance. Attempts by Jews and free blacks to attain recognition as rights-holding subjects before the law led to the first statutes ascribing legal disabilities to classes of racialized "others" deemed unfit for the full liberties and protections of natural-born English subjects.[55]

A PRIVILEGED INHERITANCE

On January 20, 1708, during Queen Anne's War (1702–13), fought to prevent French and Spanish hegemony in Europe and the western Atlantic following the accession of Phillip of Anjou, the grandson of Louis XIV, to the Spanish throne, Moses Jesuran Cordoza and Jacob Correa petitioned the Jamaica assembly to relieve the heavy extra tax burden laid upon "the Hebrew Nation inhabiting this Island." Since the passage of an act in 1695, the assembly had imposed a yearly discriminatory tax on Jamaica's Jewish community over and besides the tax paid by all colonists in an effort to raise additional funds. Although members of the Jewish community repeatedly protested against paying a separate tax, the varying sums demanded of them at the will and pleasure of colonial administrators signified the uncertainty of their legal status. Jamaica had served as one of several Caribbean destinations for Jewish migrants after the Portuguese retook Brazil from the Dutch in 1654 and expelled its Jewish population. In 1656, millenarian calls for the conversion of Jews to hasten the Second Coming, coupled with arguments in favor of Jewish economic utility, led to their de facto readmission to England for the first time since their expulsion in 1290, though their status as foreign-born aliens enabled the English government to restrict their political and economic activities. In 1663, the Charter of Rhode Island, which granted colonial subjects liberty of conscience and extended limited rights to non-Christians, served as an important first step on the path toward the expansion of Jewish participation in the Anglo-Atlantic world. By the 1680s, as a result of Charles II's liberal issuing of patents of endenization, Jewish communities engaged in long-distance trade had sprung up in Barbados, Jamaica, London, and New York. The overlapping interests of these close-knit communities, as well as their links to agents in Amsterdam and elsewhere, diminished risks and enabled Jewish merchants to trade at lower prices.[56]

Early English Jamaica offered a wealth of business opportunities for Jewish merchants and retailers, and so, too, did the island's contraband trade with Spanish America for alcohol, cloth, iron goods, flour, silver bullion, and slaves. As they did in Barbados, Jews gravitated to the colony's towns, particularly bustling Port Royal, where they became affluent merchants and traders and built a synagogue. Although the non-Jewish population tolerated Jamaica's Jewish community, economic hostilities mounted between English and Jewish merchants beginning in the 1670s. In 1672, Christian merchants in Port Royal presented a petition to the assembly protesting against the influx of Jews on the island and their alleged engorgement of commerce. They "eat us and our children out of all trade," the merchants complained. Jews were permitted to remain in Jamaica but political currents increasingly moved against them. By 1693, Jamaican law prohibited Jews from keeping Christian indentured servants and required them to bear arms on the Sabbath. Two years later, the assembly passed an act to raise money for the island's defense through a tax on slaves and livestock and imposed an additional sum of £750 Jamaican currency on the Jewish community. If the Jews failed to raise the sum, they faced a £250 fine. "In those days of ignorance, and long after," Edward Long, author of *The History of Jamaica* (1774), reminisced a century later, the Jamaican government "obliged [the Jews] to raise among them a certain tribute, which the assembly varied at pleasure."[57]

While the financial oppression of Jamaica's Jews continued apace, the community as a whole grew in strength. An estimated one thousand Jews resided in Jamaica by the early eighteenth century, with most urban based and engaged in commercial activities, including participation in the slave trade. As far as the Jamaican government was concerned, if the Jews paid their additional tax and did not press for the full liberties of English subjects, they would be allowed to go about their business unmolested. However, in 1702 the assembly received reports that Jewish men had attempted to vote at elections. This breach of protocol stirred debate, but the matter died down rather quickly as members directed their attention to the passage of new legislation requiring the Jews to pay an additional duty of £1,000. In December 1706, an unspecified number of "planting Jews" petitioned for an exemption from exceptional taxation, but the assembly chose to let the petition lie on the table. By the time Cordoza and Correa petitioned for financial relief in January 1708, Jamaica's Jews had held a second-class status and paid a discriminatory tax for some time. As David Eltis aptly notes, "The Jewish presence was a privilege advanced rather than a right recognized."[58]

The same could be said for Jamaica's small but growing community of freed African slaves and their descendants. Some individuals of African descent were now born free, educated, and baptized into the Church of England, yet none possessed the rights and privileges of English subjects. Their legal incapacity as freemen descended from slave mothers encouraged a handful of free blacks to attempt to obtain individual exemptions from the Jamaican government. Ten days after the assembly received Cordoza and Correa's petition, John Williams, "a free negro," presented a petition seeking a private bill enabling him "to be tried by a jury, as a white man." According to Jamaica's slave code of 1696, all freed slaves charged with committing an offense, whether criminal or capital, were to be tried in the slave courts and subject to the evidence of slaves. Williams petitioned for the legislature to waive this restriction on the basis that he had been "set free for his fidelity and good service, and had by his industry gained some small interest in the world, and, although a Christian and naturalized, yet both himself and what he hath are liable to utter ruin, on the evidence of slaves that may witness against him on any occasion." The assembly responded to Williams's unprecedented request in the affirmative and drew up "An act to prevent slaves being evidence against John Williams, a free negro," the first private bill granting special privileges to a former slave in colonial Jamaica.[59]

Other free blacks hastened to follow in John Williams's footsteps. On February 6, 1708, the day Williams's privilege bill passed the house, Manuel Bartholomew also petitioned the assembly, "setting forth that he was born a free negro" and equally liable to ruin unless the legislature prevented slaves from giving evidence against him in court. The council approved the private bills passed in favor of both Williams and Bartholomew but requested one amendment: that the words "as an Englishman" be struck from the final acts, to which the assembly agreed. While the legislature might exempt individual free blacks from the indignity of slave testimony, such an exemption did not signify an equivalence in law between former slaves or their free descendants and freeborn Englishmen. Moreover, freed slaves were never the intended recipients of Jamaica's naturalization act, first passed in 1684, permitting the governor to extend the immunities and privileges of "his Majesties natural born Subjects" to "any alien or aliens, foreigner or foreigners, being already settled in this Island, or such as shall hereafter come settle and plant in it." As the assembly clarified long before the law's passage, "the act intends to naturalize none but such as are qualified to plant and settle"—in other words, those with capital—for "the interest and stock they bring with them is the best security foreigners can give for their allegiance." Such a strategy loosely aligned with Britain's General Naturalization Act of 1709 (6 Ann., c. 5), favoring the extension of the rights of natural-born subjects to "Strangers of the Protestant or Reformed Religion" as a means of augmenting the nation's wealth and strength. After public outcry following the arrival of thousands of impoverished Palatine immigrants in London, Parliament repealed the controversial Naturalization Act in 1712. Few favored extending subject status and its associated privileges to undesirable foreigners, who "did seem to take away their *English* Birthright" and give very little in return.[60]

Jamaica's reliance on African slave labor and conquered status drastically amplified similar concerns about sharing the birthright of Englishmen with free people of non-Christian or servile ancestry. After a session punctuated by unprecedented requests from Jews and free blacks for legal exemptions, including a third bill on behalf of John Callender, "a free negro" distinguished by his "signal services to this island in discovering an invasion intended by the French, and being a Christian," the legislature resolved to send a clear message that English liberties and franchises were reserved for white Protestant male freeholders alone. On February 12, 1708, the same day the Jamaica assembly deemed Williams, Bartholomew, and Callender worthy of special consideration, members resolved to bring in a bill for regulating elections so that "no Jew, mulatto, negro or Indian, shall have any vote at any election or members to serve in any assembly in this island." One week later, following a petition by Robert Bass, the fourth free black to seek exemption from the slave courts based on his industry and Christian status, the assembly declared a moratorium on hearing petitions "of this nature."[61]

With Governor Handasyd's approval, and Crown confirmation on June 27, 1708, Williams and Bartholomew became the first freemen of African descent granted the right to trial by jury in Jamaica. Governor Handasyd balked at granting free blacks special privileges for required militia service, however, and refused to assent to Callender's bill. In his letter to the Lords of Trade, dated March 31, 1708, he explained that the legislature had "passed all Laws that were necessary," including "two private Acts in relation to two free Negroes," and made no mention of Callender or Cordoza and Correa. The grievances voiced by individuals of Jewish and African ancestry had unsettled the island's wealthy assemblymen and councilors; these men had no intention of sharing their rights, wealth, or power with members of alien groups whom they viewed as inferior. Three years later, in an "Act for regulating fees," the first legal clause directed specifically at limiting political participation to white Christian male freeholders went into effect, barring "mulattoes, negroes, Indians, and Jews" from holding public office.[62]

Early requests by Jewish settlers and free blacks for additional rights laid the foundation for future legislation that would classify colonial subjects in Jamaica by racial lineage and accord to them a different set of obligations and restrictions. After 1711, the Jamaican legislature steadily curtailed the civil and political liberties and financial prospects of former slaves and their free descendants. The law prohibited free people from: voting or holding public office, irrespective of property qualifications; driving coaches, navigating boats, or holding supervisory positions on estates; wearing arms, except during periods of active militia duty; or living in or near a town without a license. Freed persons descended from enslaved mothers also remained subject to the slave courts, until granted equal rights with those born free in 1748. Statutes marking free people of African and mixed ancestry as outsiders assigned to an inferior legal status conformed to broader Anglo-Atlantic legal trends. Massachusetts Bay, South Carolina, Virginia, Barbados, Pennsylvania, and Bermuda all passed acts restraining the liberties, franchises, and movements of freemen and freewomen of African, Indian, and mixed ancestry.[63]

White colonial elites in Jamaica considered free blacks untrustworthy as a whole, believing their houses were "often times receptacles of rebellious, and runaway slaves" and their lives "idle and indolent." But singling out known individuals for special favor set an example of good behavior for other freed slaves and their descendants to emulate. In November 1715, the free black merchant John Williams, for instance, petitioned that his wife, Dorothy, and

three sons, John, Thomas, and Francis, "brought up in the Christian religion," might have the same legal advantages he had received by private act in
1708. The assembly agreed to honor his request but the bill stalled in the legislature and did not become law for another year, after Williams submitted a
follow-up petition on September 28, 1716. When the private bill passed in favor of the Williams family arrived in England for royal approval the following
year, Attorney General Sir Edward Northey made no objections, "for that it
is reasonable that a slave converted to the Christian religion and being made
free should be admitted to the same privileges with other freemen." Still, what
common law privileges could freemen of English birth or lineage in overseas
colonies legitimately claim? In 1720 Richard West, counsel for the Board of
Trade, ruled that settlers carried the common law with them across the sea
but did not flesh out any specifics: "Let an Englishman go where he will, he
carries as much of law and liberty with him as the nature of things will bear."[64]

Despite the indistinctness of British legal opinion regarding the precise
nature and extent of the rights Englishmen carried overseas, whether colonial
slave regimes could withstand the extension of English liberties to individuals of alien, heathen ancestry did not give West pause. In 1724 West echoed
Northey's opinion on a clause in an act passed in Virginia stating that "no
free negro, mulatto, or Indian whatsoever" could vote at elections. "Altho' I
agree that Slaves are to be treated in such as manner as the proprietors of them
(having a regard to their number) may think necessary for their security,"
he wrote to the Lords, "yet I cannot see why one *Freeman* should be used
worse than another meerly upon account of his Complexion." In West's view,
distinctions of color should not prevent propertied freemen from the full
exercise of their rights. If "several Negroes have merited their Freedom and
obtained it and by their industry have acquired that proportion of property
so that the above mentioned incidentall Rights of liberty are actually vested
in them," West opined, "for my own part I am perswaded that it cannot be
just by a general Law without any allegation of Crime or other demerit whatsoever to strip all free persons of a black complexion (some of whom may
perhaps be of considerable substance) from those rights which are so justly
valuable to every Freeman."[65]

The perspective adopted by the learned attorney in London was far too
inclusive for the Jamaica assembly. Extending the full liberties of natural-
born subjects to freemen of African or mixed ancestry would encourage the
free descendants of slaves to aspire to a status to which they could never be
entitled in a slave society: to be upon an equal footing with British subjects

descended from white ancestors. Francis Williams, the youngest son of John Williams, was one such assertive free black. A freeborn, well-educated man of property, Williams held a truly exceptional position in colonial Jamaica as a result of special privileges granted to him as a child by private act. As local officials saw it, the problem with Francis Williams was not his propertied status but his blatant lack of humility toward his supposed racial superiors. On November 19, 1724, William Broderick, a colonial official, presented a petition to the assembly in which he alleged that Francis Williams had publicly insulted him and that "if such a precedent should pass by uncensored, it might be of ill consequence to the island in general." After examining Broderick's allegations, an assembly committee reported that Williams had struck Broderick and torn his shirt and neck cloth. Worse still, Williams "had called the said William Broderick 'white dog' several times, and many other opprobrious words, and said he was as good a man as ever stood on Broderick's legs" and exempt "from such trial as other negroes."[66]

Although the house committee found that Broderick had "called Williams 'black dog' several times, and that Williams's mouth was bloody," the assembly determined that Williams's behavior, not Broderick's, posed a threat to the colony's social, political, and racial order. "Williams's behavior is of great encouragement to the negroes of this island in general, and may be attended with ill consequences to the white people thereof," it concluded. To prevent Williams's deplorable actions from encouraging notions of racial equality among the island's free blacks, the assembly resolved to bring in a bill "for rendering free negroes more serviceable to the island . . . and for reducing Francis Williams, a free negro, to the same state of trial and evidence as other negroes." While the proposed bill to distinguish, marginalize, and police free people did not go into effect until 1730, Broderick's allegation of Williams's haughtiness sparked the passage of restrictive legislation that would impact the status of all freemen and freewomen descended from slave ancestors across the island.[67]

The case of Francis Williams offers insight into the Jamaican legislature's standpoint that while granting select individuals the benefits of whiteness could prove useful, permitting former slaves, racial others, and non-Christians access to the full range of economic, political, and legal benefits enjoyed by white subjects threatened to undermine the slave system and erode the liberties that colonists claimed for themselves by virtue of English blood. It had taken many years for the Crown to concede that Jamaican colonists were in fact entitled to the benefits of English law and the right to self-legislate over

matters of local concern. Sharing this hard-won legal inheritance with segments of the population long considered alien, barbarous, and inferior ran
counter to colonial interests and posed a grave impediment to the perpetua-
tion of the racial hierarchies underpinning Jamaica's slave order. Furthermore,
if Jamaica permitted freed slaves and their descendants to lay claim to a constitutional inheritance to which they were not entitled by right of blood inheritance, such an act would challenge the racial exclusivity of the birthright
of freeborn Englishmen and thus imperil English identity itself. Throughout
the 1720s, the assembly also ignored or rejected the complaints of Jewish
petitioners seeking relief from discretionary taxation stemming from their
inferior legal status.[68]

As Jamaica's constitutional crisis had demonstrated, colonists understood
the English birthright and inheritance as legally binding and distinctively
English, rooted in the ancient doctrine of the common law. The English legal
inheritance was not held by sufferance or royal favor but rather an undoubted
right acquired by freeborn subjects at birth and passed down over the generations. Although Richard West and government officials in metropolitan
Britain may have used the language of "complexion" to characterize distinct
classes of privileged or disabled freemen in the Atlantic colonies, a far more
complex and supple system of racial classification rooted in notions of blood
lineage had long since shaped laws and attitudes in colonial Jamaica and elsewhere in the Anglo Atlantic. Beginning in the 1730s, lawmakers in Jamaica
would draw explicitly on fictions of blood ancestry to codify English liberties
as the intrinsic right of white settlers and to naturalize colonial racial classifications based on distinct lines of descent. The uncertainty over the precise
definition of "mulatto" status in particular would lead to the articulation of
the legal parameters of whiteness and give rise to a new racial order.

CHAPTER 2

Blood of the Father

On March 28, 1730, nearly six years after first resolving to draw up a bill to suppress free blacks, specifically Francis Williams, the Jamaica assembly passed an "Act for the better regulating slaves, and rendering free negroes and free mulattoes more useful." Despite its lengthy gestation period, the act followed closely the measures first outlined in 1724 but with attention now directed at both "free negroes" and "free mulattoes." The law required members of these classes to wear distinctive badges and apply for a license to live in or near any of the island's three towns; to register with their local parish vestry and join parties in pursuit of rebellious slaves whenever summoned—or face fines, imprisonment, loss of freedom, and transportation off the island; and to forgo employing white indentured servants, wearing swords or using arms except on active militia duty, working with gold or silver, or keeping a shop within five miles of any town (unless in possession of a freehold worth at least ten pounds per annum).[1]

The shift in focus from containing the threat posed by slaves and free blacks to controlling the activities of all African-descended people underscores the serious dilemma facing colonial officials in Jamaica, as the island's white population continued to decline while the numbers of imported African slaves and their free descendants expanded. Although local administrators redoubled their efforts to attract white Protestant settlers, Jamaica remained deeply vulnerable to attacks by foreign nations and uprisings by internal rebels. To provide for the security of white slaveholders, the assembly therefore turned to the most important tool at its disposal: the leverage it held over legally marginalized colonial subjects, including the island's emergent population of free blacks and individuals of mixed heritage as well as prosperous Jewish merchants and planters. Members of these groups would be identified, classified, and made to serve local needs to the benefit of the ruling white order. First, however, colonial policy makers resolved to address the ambiguity surrounding the racial status and rights and responsibilities accorded to free persons of mixed heritage, generally referred to as "mulattoes." By what measure would the legal boundary between colonial subjects descended from white Protestant ancestors, who held the full rights of British subjects, and those of servile and mixed origins deemed unworthy of full membership in the community of allegiance be determined? The central issue at stake in the debate over racial classifications in Jamaica was the following: at what point would sexual mixture between British males and African-descended women efface the "stain" of maternal slave ancestry, qualifying the resulting offspring to claim the exclusive and hereditary privileges enjoyed by freeborn British white subjects under the law?

This chapter explores the interplay between the specific local conditions and broader historical processes that gave rise to two interrelated legal developments in Jamaica between 1730 and 1760. First, the use of hereditary status, or blood, as a means of determining who qualified for the rights of white colonial subjects; and, second, the privileging of select individuals of mixed ancestry with informal blood ties or other intimate connections to the white settler community. Focusing on blood and lineage was a conscious political choice by colonial authorities seeking to exercise unrestricted authority over the assignment of racial categories within which particular classes of people or individuals fell and the differential rights and responsibilities associated with these designations. Given its geographic isolation, enslaved African majority, and autonomous Maroon communities, Jamaica desperately needed—but failed to attract—sufficient white Protestant settlers capable of defending the island against foreign invaders and mitigating the damage and instability triggered by rebellious slaves. Consequently, Jamaican officials determined to press into service free persons belonging to subordinate classes within the colonial population, including free blacks, free mulattoes, and Jews, in accordance with their presumed inherited characteristics. The legislature would command African-descended peoples to take to the woods to pursue Maroons and runaway slaves, grant the illegitimate mixed offspring and concubines of wealthy white men who embraced Protestantism equal rights with white subjects as a means of augmenting the settler population, and require members of Jamaica's thriving Jewish trading and planting community to contribute to the island's welfare and security through additional taxation.

By the 1730s, Jamaica's critical demographic situation, exacerbated by an atmosphere of panic as a result of conflicts with the Maroons, crystallized once-ambivalent support for the extension of limited rights to loyal free blacks and individuals of mixed blood. However, differential incorporation arrived in the form of racial restrictions designed to enhance the public utility of freed slaves and their descendants while also limiting their prospects for social and economic mobility. Allegedly predisposed physically to better withstand the rigors of a hot climate than European colonists or soldiers, free people of African and mixed descent were compelled to demonstrate their allegiance to the British Crown by fighting slave rebels and securing the island to the benefit of His Majesty's white subjects, or they would forfeit their freedom. The dearth of white settlers also provided openings for elite individuals of mixed ancestry to achieve a more desirable racial classification for themselves, and frequently their family members, in exchange for supporting the white colonial regime. In these exceptional cases, physical attributes proved of marginal value to the attainment of legal whitening through private acts. The legislative grant of white status centered upon unsanctioned ties to prominent white men, a Christian upbringing, and wealth in land and slaves, all of which were supposed to dilute the negative and inferior traits associated with servile African origins.

By codifying in law racial distinctions among free persons based on lineal ancestry (e.g., the degree of distance from an African ancestor), the Jamaican legislature privileged blood as a material and symbolic conduit through which parents transmitted inherited qualities of character, mind, and temperament to their offspring along a line of descent. Unlike slave status, where the customary rule was matrilineal heritability (statutorily defined as those "borne slaves"), racial inheritance was traced bilineally, transmitted through both the patriline and the matriline over multiple generations. As intended, this policy made legal whiteness virtually unattainable for the descendants of slaves. In rare instances, however, colonial administrators implemented an adaptive ad hoc whitening procedure whereby acknowledged paternal blood ties and continued patronage proved determinative for select illegitimate mixed-race individuals seeking to attain legal whiteness. Emphasis on the blood of the father loosely followed the logic of 4 Geo. II., c. 21 (1731), an act that clarified, after centuries of ambiguity, that the transmission of subjecthood to foreign-born offspring occurred solely through the legitimate male line. While many enslaved and free people of African and mixed ancestry in Jamaica were native born by the eighteenth century, the Jamaican legislature continued to regard them as aliens. The centrality of sanguinary inheritance and unofficial ties to prominent white males foreclosed the possibility of racial advancement for the vast majority of free people of mixed parentage, only a fraction of whom possessed the requisite paternal connections, wealth, and education to warrant legislative intervention and a change of racial status in law.[2]

The question of how to determine the legal status of freed slaves and persons of mixed ancestry had plagued colonial officials in the Anglo Atlantic since the mid-seventeenth century. Unlike Spanish, French, and Portuguese colonial administrators, who drew upon legal models issued from Europe and rooted in Roman law—*Las siete partidas* for the Iberian territories and the *Codes noir* of 1685 and 1724 for the French colonies—English authorities received no guidance from the mother country concerning the transmission of slave status, manumission, or the legal position of freed slaves or freeborn individuals descended from enslaved ancestors. Endowed with substantial legislative powers, although subject to the protracted judicial review process—whereby colonial laws repugnant to the laws of England could be disallowed, but only on rare occasions—Anglo-American and Caribbean legislatures were largely left to their own devices to fashion slave laws and assign legal disabilities to colonial populations on the basis of religion, heredity, or other factors. As a result, in the English and, after 1707, British Atlantic, racial classifications and their meanings in law varied considerably by region and were determined as much by political expediency as by ideological motivations. In eighteenth-century Jamaica, attempts to resolve the legal uncertainty over the boundary between "white" and "mulatto" (a catchall category customarily used to identify the offspring of European and African admixture) revolved around discourses of blood and heritability. Legal recognition as one of "His Majesty's white subjects" hinged on a set of underlying assumptions regarding the presumed characteristics, intellectual, moral, and physical, intrinsic to certain bloodlines and the potential for sexual contact to facilitate either degenerative or regenerative changes in distinct lines of descent.[3]

A FRAGILE FOOTHOLD

The Jamaica assembly's inclusion of all free people of African and mixed heritage in the act "rendering free negroes and free mulattoes more useful" unintentionally laid bare the indeterminate nature of whiteness and its legal formulation within the colony's existing system of racial classification. The act provoked a new set of questions about the formal conferral of white status and its associated privileges and the possibility for racial mixture to move segments of the population in the direction of whiteness. Although the law targeted free mulattoes for legal disabilities, as had previous legislation, the assembly recognized that the boundaries of this racial category remained strictly informal, bound by customary practice rather than law. In June 1730 it called for a committee to draft a new bill "for the better regulating negroes" with a proviso tacked on to "explain therein who shall be deemed a mulatto within the intent and meaning of the 'Act for the better regulating slaves, and rendering free negroes and free mulattoes more useful.'" Before members could settle on a legal definition of *mulatto,* John Golding, a prosperous planter and slaveholder of Vere parish, and an individual of known mixed lineage and Protestant faith, petitioned the house "that he, since the making that law, being deemed a mulatto, his white servants were not allowed for deficiencies, though he provided them to that end; and praying relief." Local officials were well acquainted with Golding; his deceased father, also named John Golding and categorized as a "mulatto" according to island custom, had helped to defend Jamaica during the French invasion in the mid-1690s. Preventing an affluent, light-skinned slaveholder such as Golding from benefiting from the use of white servants did not fit the intent of the act. The assembly thus resolved to let "John Golding, his family, and servants, be allowed to pass for deficiencies, as usual," and to omit the section of the law related to mulattoes employing white servants.[4]

Meanwhile, Francis Williams, perhaps Jamaica's only free black of substance, had opted to circumvent the local power structure and appeal directly to London to have the 1730 act overturned by the Crown. He objected to the law on both general and personal grounds, arguing that "several severe Clauses are laid on all free Negroes" and on his family particularly, although the Williamses "were always considered and treated in Jamaica on a Level with the rest of his Majesty's Subjects there." He trusted that sustained attention to the clauses to which he objected would lay bare the unreasonable nature of the act and serve as evidence that the Jamaica assembly had grossly abused its powers. First, Williams objected to the clause requiring free blacks to register with their local parish or, upon failing to do so, face loss of freedom by summary judgment followed by transportation and sale. This clause was "very Improper," he explained, "as it directly takes away those Libertys and Priviledges given the family of the Williams's" by private acts, imposing upon them "a method of Tryal no Englishman is subject to." Unable to avail themselves of the protection of the law, the Williamses would inevitably lose their estate, which, he pointed out, "amounts to above £20,000 which is too great a Temptation." Williams also opposed the provision compelling all free people to pursue runaways, arguing that the act neither permitted sending in suitable replacements better fit for the task "than persons Educated in England as the Free Negroes are" nor contained exemptions for women or the sick. Finally, Williams objected to the clauses restricting free blacks from wearing arms, employing white servants, working with gold or silver, or keeping shops. Such restrictions increased his individual chances of "being assaulted by every one," including "Ignorant Slaves"; prevented his family from complying with the terms of the deficiency act; and crippled the financial prospects of all free people of African descent.[5]

The arguments put forward by Francis Williams proved persuasive to Francis Fane, legal adviser to the Board of Trade, which had replaced the Lords of Trade in 1696 and held the authority to recommend either the confirmation or disallowance of colonial laws. Fane reported unfavorably, noting that the act should have made an allowance for the Williams family considering their exceptional position as wealthy free blacks "and the Hardships they must necessarily lye under in case this Act passes into a Law." In this particular case, Fane was not convinced that local conditions warranted such an extensive divergence from English legal principles. Although Governor Hunter wrote in support of the act—maintaining that as "the number of free mulattos, and free negroes dayly increase," the legislature thought it critical to "render them more usefull to ye country" by compelling them to pursue, rather than fraternize with or supply, the rebellious slaves—the board chose to set aside such considerations. In November 1731, after dismissing protests by Jamaica's agent in London, the Privy Council acted on Fane's report and the board's recommendation, disallowing the act that had stripped free people of any semblance of common law rights and provoked so much controversy. Five months passed before anyone on the island became aware of its repeal, but local officials by then had far more pressing matters on their minds. The same year the assembly sought to bring free people into line and clarify racial distinctions in law, a long series of disputes between British settlers and the Maroons coalesced into an intensive, prolonged conflict that would last until 1739. Indeed, the deteriorating Anglo-Maroon relationship acted as a catalyst to stimulate Jamaican authorities to act on the long-overdue bill to put free blacks and mulattoes to use by pressing them into emergency service against the rebels.[6]

Since 1655, Jamaica's inaccessible mountain ranges and dense, impenetrable forests had enabled groups of Spanish-speaking Africans to avoid capture and carve out autonomous communities that served as a constant source of inspiration for runaway slaves. Beginning in the 1670s, slave rebels and deserters routinely took to the hills and joined these preexisting African communities, augmenting their size and strength. Hybrid bands of Spanish-speaking Africans and newly escaped slaves, later known as "Maroons," were divided into two main groups according to location, windward and leeward, and further subdivided into settlements centered on a town. The larger Windward band was located in the northeastern section of the island and headed by Cuffee at Nanny Town in St. Thomas. The Leeward band, led by a principal chieftain named Cudjoe and his brothers, occupied the central region of the island and their main settlements included Trelawny Town in St. James and Accompong in St. Elizabeth. The Maroons, divided into politically autonomous bands, shared a common goal of retaining the self-government they had acquired after the English invasion and serving as a buffer against further European expansion into territories they claimed as their own.[7]

Over the first quarter of the eighteenth century, as the numbers of slaves in Jamaica rose markedly through annual importations and the Maroons picked up new recruits, the white settler population declined precipitously due to extraordinarily high mortality rates. After the 1690s, marriages among European settlers became less likely and more precarious in colonial Jamaica; very few marriages lasted long enough to produce children, and many survivors never remarried. Land engrossment contributed to the yearly decline of the settler population, as prospects for property and advancement faded for newcomers. According to a census conducted in 1730, approximately 7,648 whites oversaw a reported 74,525 African slaves, with fewer than 3,000 white men fit to bear arms, and the majority of these "hired and indented servants who have no property in the county" and were "scattered from one end of the island to the other." By 1730 free people of African, Indian, and mixed ancestry composed roughly 10 percent of the island's total free population, making their participation in the struggle against Jamaica's "internal enemies" of critical importance notwithstanding their small numbers. In 1729, recognizing the weakness of the white settler community vis-à-vis both the enslaved population and the Maroons, the assembly called for immediate consideration of "the most effectual methods for strengthening and securing the island, and encouraging white people to come over and become settlers, and protecting and defending our rights and liberties." If white colonists sought to keep British liberties exclusively for themselves, they would need to defend them.[8]

The Maroons' uneasy coexistence with the British entered a new phase in the 1720s when planters, having reached the limits of the southeastern plains, began to push into Jamaica's northeastern section, aware that the island held "land uncultivated sufficient to make sugar to serve all of Europe." The Maroons reacted by attacking newly established settlements in Portland parish, particularly at Port Antonio, and the situation became especially critical from the British perspective after repeated armed campaigns to subdue the rebels failed. Fearing that the presence of growing Maroon communities discouraged new settlers sorely needed for the island's defense, the assembly called for additional troops to secure Jamaica from the twin threats of insurrection and external invasion. Rumors abounded that the Maroons had received supplies and assistance from free blacks and communicated with the Spanish, to whom it was feared they would readily turn over the island in exchange for assurances of political independence. "The Slaves in Rebellion are so Numerous and so well provided with Arms and Ammunition," wrote Governor Hunter to the Board of Trade in December 1730, "that I am perswaded they must have some Intelligence with and Encouragement from some either without or within this Island, which is in so weak and defenceless a Condition that 'tis no Vision to suppose they may one day become a prey to their own slaves."[9]

As Jamaica's colonial militia possessed nowhere near the manpower, skill, or motivation needed to quell the mounting resistance, local administrators deemed outside assistance absolutely critical. Although the colonial government brought in a force of Mosquito Indians from Honduras to fight the Maroons, and the British imperial government dispatched two foot regiments from Gibraltar, the parties sent to subdue the rebels failed to achieve their objectives, and a great many succumbed to disease in the process. To make matters worse, when eight hundred British troops arrived in February 1731, they discovered a colony wholly unprepared to receive them, with inadequate barracks in place and a dearth of provisions. Local officials had failed to devise any strategies to bring the war with the Maroons to a close—other than dispersing the newly arrived British troops to remote, inaccessible corners of the island "where," as Colonel Cornwallis exclaimed, "they would not venture to let their new Slaves to go till they had been thoroughly seasoned here, and places where there never was a Rebellious Negroe heard of." Indeed, an exasperated Cornwallis reiterated ten days later, "new Negroes were never used in so ill a Manner as we are." The troops sent to Jamaica had every reason to complain, he argued, for "had they a Fair Enemy to Contend with there's a Chance but the Climate is too Inveterate an Enemy for them." By October 1731, Governor Hunter reported that half of the soldiers had died from either drink or disease, while many of the survivors languished in sickness.[10]

To the dismay of Jamaican colonists, local militia efforts as well as outside assistance proved inadequate to quell the Maroon rebels, with the consequence that a swift resolution to the crisis grew increasingly out of reach. Fighting the war to a successful conclusion warranted an innovative strategy. In an effort to suppress the Maroons before their depredations engulfed the entire island, the colonial government mobilized groups customarily regarded with suspicion to defend Jamaica's slaveholding regime. Yet their defensive role was not voluntary. Time and again local authorities turned to the law to compel free people of African and mixed ancestry into the woods in pursuit of the rebels or into thinly populated areas of the island to erect defensive fortifications and new settlements. The Jamaica assembly branded as unfaithful traitors the free descendants of slaves who refused to prove their loyalty to the ruling white order by defending the latter's interests. At the same time, the assembly allowed an elite subset of free people of mixed blood to demonstrate their allegiance to the British Crown and their affinity with white colonial subjects by "passing" formally as white.

RACIAL INHERITANCE AND THE CORRUPTION OF BLOOD

On March 30, 1733, the assembly received a complaint that stimulated new debate over whether to extend the rights and privileges of British subjecthood to persons of mixed parentage. The legislature had not yet determined under what circumstances or whose discretion the mixed descendants of slaves might be treated as if they had originated from "pure" white ancestors. Yet two Goldings, officials learned, "both being mulattoes," had claimed the full rights of white subjects and attempted to vote at an election in Vere parish. When confronted, they "insisted on their right of voting, at the said election, against a positive law and a resolution of this house." Voting constituted an exercise of political power, ideologically as well as legally, and the enfranchised occupied the highest position in the colonial hierarchy. The wealthy mixed-race Goldings, by boldly exercising the most coveted constitutional right of white male freeholders, had flouted Jamaican law and customary practice. But the question of whether their action demonstrated contempt of the house divided the assembly. While governing elites refused to brook mixed-race in-dividuals attempting to claim the full liberties of white freeholders without official authorization, the Goldings' misconduct raised a critical issue: in a colony frantic for additional white settlers to help preserve white rule and the institution of slavery, who would be accounted a white subject according to Jamaican law?[11]

Although the assembly chose not to punish the elite Goldings, it moved swiftly to draw up a bill regulating elections and setting forth the qualifica-tions for voting and office holding as well as the legal parameters of whiteness. Passing a motion "that it should be ascertained who shall be deemed mulat-toes and how far their corruption of blood should extend," members decided the matter by the end of the same session: "to the third generation, inclusive, only." Less than a week later, at the second reading of the "Bill to secure free-dom of elections . . . and determine who should be deemed mulattoes," a com-mittee of the whole house reconsidered the number of lineal degrees sufficient to transform a mixed individual into a white subject in the eyes of the law. The house concluded that "the three degrees, in the clause mentioned, should be exclusive of the father and the mother." Although cleansing mixed blood-lines of their original "corruption" by means of sexual intercourse between white men and African-descended women constituted the first and most important step in the whitening process, a Protestant Christian upbringing played an equally critical role. As the final wording of the statute clarified, "no person who is not above three degrees removed in a Lineal Descent from the Negro Ancestor Exclusive shall be allowed to Vote or Poll in Elections and no one shall be deemed a Mulatto after the third generation as aforesaid but that they shall have all the Priviledges and Immunities of his Majesty's white Sub-jects of this Island provided they are brought up in the Christian Religion." The symbolic world upon which such a racial definition rested envisioned the transmutation of black into white in terms that capture the tension at the heart of the 1661 Barbadian slave code. Colonial officials regarded "Negro slaves" as akin to "other goods and Chattels" but also unique, "being created Men though without the knowledge of God in the world." In the absence of conversion and its attendant moral consequences, or what Wayne Meeks calls the convert's "consciousness of having turned around," the free descendants of slaves would remain subject to the dominion of Christians.[12]

Classifying individuals descended from a "negro" ancestor to the third generation as "mulattoes," the 1733 act clarified that hereditary blood status determined eligibility for the privileges inhering in white subjects. The assembly's curious use of the phrase *corruption of blood*—a common law doctrine signifying the extinction of hereditary blood resulting from attainder following a sentence of treason—in its discussion of racial terminology invites further analysis. Medieval and early modern people understood blood as a vital physical element in human generation and nourishment (both sperm and breast milk were deemed "nothing else but blood whitened"), as a metaphor to represent ties of kinship and nation, as a spiritual substance of religious and occult significance, and as a line of descent, transmitting property, nobility, and qualities of character from one generation to the next. Reliance upon blood imaginaries as a means of constructing difference, though pan-European, is most notably associated with the Spanish concept of *limpieza de sangre* (purity of blood), whereby the bloodlines of Christian converts with ties to Judaism or Islam were deemed tainted, and with French aristocratic notions of purity, both of which underwent significant reconfiguration in the Americas and gave rise to colonial racial hierarchies based on descent.[13]

Of course, the English also understood religious and ethnic differences, and notions of aristocratic and national rights and privileges, in terms of blood. Inherited blood connections were central to family titles and property claims, to membership in a Protestant Christian community, to understandings of national identity, and to the birthright liberties of English subjects. Severed blood ties could trigger disinheritance and civil death. In English law, the blood of an attainted criminal was adjudged corrupted, or extinguished, in consequence of which his title, lands, and chattels were forfeited to the Crown and his heirs barred from deriving a title or property through him. Metaphorically and in the eyes of the law, corrupted blood ceased flowing vertically, both upward and downward, and obstructed the channels of hereditary descent; an act of Parliament alone restored inheritable qualities to a bloodline corrupted by attainder. Edward Phillips, in *The New World of English Words* (1658), defined "Corruption of the blood" as "signifying in law an infection of the blood, growing to the estate and issue of a man tainted with treason, whereby he looseth all to the Prince, and both he and his heirs are made ignoble." In a separate section Phillips also defined a "*Mulato*" as "one whose father is a Blackamore and his mother of another nation or contrarily."

Corruption of blood, then, deprived an attainted felon's blood of its heritable qualities, punishing the offender as well as his progeny; *mulatto* signified a person of African parentage, along either the patriline or matriline.[14]

The metaphorical imagery of the attainted criminal as one degraded and blackened under the law, civilly dead and his bloodline corrupted, helped set the template for a colonial racial ideology rooted in fictions of blood. John Cowell's handy guide to English legal terminology for the uninitiated explained "that the Children of a Person attainted of Treason, cannot be Heirs to him, or any other Ancestor; and if he were Noble and Gentile before, thereby his Posterity are Degraded, and made Base; and this corruption of Blood cannot be salved, but by an Act of Parliament." The mark of degradation thus fell equally upon the attainted felon and his posterity, as did the stripping away of lawful inheritance into perpetuity unless an attainted bloodline was restored by Parliament. Corruption of blood, as a legal and intellectual construct, transferred readily to a colonial slave regime that had long positioned African captives as debased human chattel whose activities were always already criminalized. Colin Dayan rightly observes that there is "a continuum between being judged a felon, being declared dead in law, and being made a slave," and the legal incapacity accompanying corruption of blood could assume new meanings in a slave society as "tainted blood itself, now no longer under legal quarantine, was transmitted through the generations." Slave codes and statutes assigning disabilities to free individuals of African and mixed ancestry cut off slaves and their posterity from the community of English subjects. English colonists, notes Carla Pestana, "declared themselves to be 'Englishmen of as clear and pure extracts as any,' and they expected their pure English blood to warrant them a certain place in the political community." Indeed, while a white colonist convicted of wantonly killing a slave might face a fine, imprisonment, or, after 1751, execution for a second offense, the assembly ensured that a white offender's punishment did not work corruption of blood, forfeiture of property, or disinheritance of heirs. In contrast, colonial law assigned African-descended individuals an inferior status by virtue of servile lineage and tainted blood even after the attainment of freedom. As the early 1668 act continuing the tax on freed women in Virginia had emphasized, "Negro Women, though permitted to enjoy the Privilege of their Freedom, yet ought not in all Respects to be admitted to a full Fruition of the Exemptions and Immunities of the *English*." As long as the taint of black ancestry justified perpetual enslavement and perpetual alien status, individuals of African descent would transmit the legal fiction of black blood and its associated incapacities to their offspring.[15]

Richard Ligon hinted at the presence of an outward sign of hereditary corruption in his remarks on African slaves in mid-seventeenth-century Barbados. He commented that "there be a mark set upon these people, which will hardly ever be wip'd off," though he questioned the strength of its influence on the characters of all black slaves in equal measure. In contrast, governing elites in Barbados explicitly associated "Negro Slaves" en masse with baseness, degradation, and criminality, particularly in the revised and updated slave code of 1688. The act took the stance that "many heinous and grievous Crimes" were routinely committed by "Negroes," who, "being brutish Slaves deserve not for the baseness of their Condition to be tried by the legal tryal of twelve Men of their Peers or Neighbourhood which neither truely can bee rightly done as the Subjects of England are, nor Execution to be delayed towards them in case of such horrid Crimes committed." Virginia governor William Gooch's remarks nearly half a century later explaining why the burgesses sought "to fix a perpetual brand upon free negroes and mulattos by excluding them from that great privilege of a Freeman (e.g. voting)" were similarly unequivocal. Free people descended from slave ancestors had not yet achieved the requisite moral or intellectual fitness associated with common law rights. The day might come, Gooch reasoned, when the House of Burgesses would see fit "to consider to what degree of descent this incapacity shall extend, but at present there is a necessity of continuing it on the foot it is."[16]

The principle of corrupted blood grew out of English legal constructs related to criminality, attainder, and the forfeiture of property, yet the hereditary defilement of blood had long informed European theories of the genesis of religious and bodily differences among the earth's peoples. If, as most Christians assumed, all mankind originated from the same blood ancestor (Adam), what else but an alteration of blood could explain the emergence of distinct human lineages and their associated characteristics? During the early modern period, dozens of European authors cited the scriptural Curse of Ham—originally Noah's curse upon Canaan, the son of Cham, as "a servant of servants to his brothers" in Genesis 9—as a possible explanation for the diversity of alien cultures, beliefs, and physical appearances. The curse grew in popularity in seventeenth-century European intellectual circles as reliance upon African slave labor intensified and lawyers, travel writers, and theologians searched for biblical justifications for hereditary racial slavery. Fringe interpretations of the curse establishing a link between sin, blackness, and contaminated bloodlines portended the ideological foundations upon which eighteenth-century racial constructs would later build.[17]

In the late sixteenth century, George Best, a captain of one of the vessels in Martin Frobisher's 1577 expedition to locate the Northwest Passage, published what would become the most familiar and widely repeated early English conjecture on the origins of human physical variation. Best's rumination on the blackness of Africans—a mere side note to his focus on the Arctic—gained wide circulation by its inclusion in Richard Hakluyt's enormously influential *Principal Navigations* (1598–1600). In his speculations on human difference, Best recounted a tale of an Ethiopian man and an Englishwoman producing a son as black as his father, "although England were his native countrey and an English woman his mother." This led Best to suspect that "blacknesse proceedeth of some naturall infection of the first inhabitants of that countrey," rather than from climatic causes, "and so all the whole progenie of them descended, are still polluted with the same blot of infection." Best then deployed an altered version of the Curse of Ham as a theological explanation for "the first originall of these blacke men, and how by a lineall discente they have hitherto continued this blacke," erroneously linking the curse to Chus (or Cush), the son given to Africa in Genesis 10, and to black skin. Taking significant liberties with the biblical text, Best detailed how Ham's sexual misbehavior on the ark so enraged God that he willed that "a sonne shuld be borne whose name was Chus, who not onely itselfe, but all his posteritie after him, should be so blacke and lothsome that it might remaine a spectacle of disobedience to all the worlde. And of this blacke and cursed Chus came all these blacke Moores which are in Africa." The English had nothing to fear from overseas exploration and colonization in alien climes; for the cause of blackness, Best concluded, is "the curse and natural infection of blood" resulting from forbidden sex, "and not the distemperature of the clymatee."[18]

MIXED BLOODLINES AND BIRTHRIGHT SLAVERY

Using the language of hereditary contagion, George Best characterized blackness as a visible symptom of an underlying moral and genealogical disorder, one impossible for African-descended people to dislodge due to its (grossly misguided) scriptural origins. His hypothesis certainly held limited currency among the laboring classes in the colonial Chesapeake and Caribbean, who routinely mixed socially as well as sexually with Africans. However, growing concerns about the public consequences of unlicensed intimacy occurring outside the confines of dominant patriarchal sexual mores motivated some colonial assemblies to erect a bar to interracial marriage and to render illegitimate any offspring resulting from the intermingling of English and African bloodlines. Legislators adopted a variety of approaches to accomplish these ends. In 1663, Bermuda imposed a policy of banishment on colonists convicted of marrying or copulating with persons of African or mixed lineage, whether bond or free. The following year, Maryland employed the common law rule of patrilineal descent to deter Englishwomen from marrying black slaves to the detriment of slaveholders and the confusion of distinctions between freeborn settlers and the enslaved. The law subjected Englishwomen who married slaves to lifetime service and their legitimate mixed offspring to permanent bondage, "as divers freeborne English women forgettful of their free Condicon and to the disgrace of our Nation doe intermarry with Negro Slaves by which also divers suites may arise touching the Issue of such women and a great damage doth befall the Masters of such Negroes."[19]

Virginia's adoption of the civil law doctrine of partus sequitur ventrem to define slave status in 1662, two years prior to Maryland's ruling, occurred in response to local developments that threatened to undermine slaveholders' control over the productive and reproductive labor of enslaved women. In the two decades preceding the burgesses' decision, a handful of individuals of mixed lineage sued for their freedom on the basis of paternal links to freeborn Englishmen. By privileging matrilineal heritability in the case of slavery, the burgesses followed a standard procedure of Roman law and a custom widely practiced throughout the Americas. According to the *Institutes of Justinian,* the third part of the *Corpus iuris civilis,* the sixth-century codification of Roman law ordered by Byzantine emperor Justinian I, one became a slave "on being captured by enemies or by birth to a female slave"; furthermore, in cases of dishonorable birth outside wedlock, "one begotten at large follows the mother." *Las siete partidas,* a thirteenth-century Castilian legal code observed by most Spanish and Portuguese slave colonies, took the same line, defining the offspring of a female slave and a freeman as slaves. Similarly, the French *Code noir,* first issued in 1685 for France's Caribbean colonies and later revised in 1724 for French Louisiana, instituted matrilineal heritability for slavery. In 1706, the colonial government in New York likewise turned to the doctrine of partus sequitur ventrem to legislate permanent hereditary slavery, declaring that children "born of any Negro, Indian, Mulatto, or Mestee" assumed their mother's status, as did South Carolina much later in its slave code of 1740.[20]

On the question of slavery's heritability, prominent theologians and jurists alike agreed that the maternal line predominated. Thomas Aquinas provided a powerful intellectual framework for those seeking to legislate slavery as a heritable condition passed down through the mother. In his enormously influential thirteenth-century *Summa theologica,* Aquinas espoused the principle that offspring should follow the womb in all matters relating to lower bodily conditions, including slavery and unsanctioned or dishonorable births. Although Aquinas supported the general rule that "in generating the father ranks above the mother," he pronounced slavery "a condition of the body, since the slave is to the master a kind of instrument of working." It followed therefore that "the seed received by the mother should be drawn to her condition" rather than to the father's more elevated position. Additionally, in an analogy between domesticated animals and man, which later commentators would apply to persons of mixed ancestry in Europe's slave colonies, "in animals born from different species the offspring follows the mother rather than the father, wherefore mules born of a mare and an ass are more like mares than those born of a she-ass and a horse. Therefore it should be the same with men." The influential Dutch jurist Hugo Grotius, whose works, particularly *De jure belli ac pacis* (*The Law of War and Peace,* first published in 1625), enjoyed significant popularity in Stuart England, argued that slaves are made either "by Covenant or transgression" and "also their posterity for ever." "The reason why this dominion was extended to the Children, is," he explained, twofold: first, "because otherwise, if the Takers should use their highest right, they would not be born"; and second, "because servile copulations were neither regulated by Law nor by certain custody, so that no sufficient presumption could shew the Father." Consequently, "*The Law of Nature is this, that he which is born without lawfull Matrimony, should follow the Mother.*"[21]

While lawmakers in seventeenth-century Virginia embraced the civil law maxim of partus sequitur ventrem and Maryland implemented common law procedure, in both cases as a pragmatic solution to local concerns, neither measure immediately transformed Anglo-African relations. Authorities continued to receive complaints from English landowners about marriages and illicit unions between white settlers and blacks and mulattoes. In 1681, Maryland placed heavy fines on ministers who married English people and slaves and masters and mistresses who allowed, or compelled, their female servants to wed slaves and indulge "lascivious and lustful desires" in order to augment their labor force. A serving woman would be released from service following such a marriage and her offspring instantly manumitted. Ten years later, following Bacon's Rebellion, Virginia enacted a law to prevent "that abominable Mixture, and spurious Issue, which hereafter may increase in this Dominion, as well by Negroes, Mulattoes, and Indians, intermarrying with English or other White Women, as by their unlawful accompanying one another." Colonial officials pledged to banish all whites, male or female, who married nonwhites from the colony within three months of conviction. The legislature threatened to fine a white woman who bore "a bastard child by any Negro or Mulatto" fifteen pounds or, in lieu of payment, to bind her into service for five years and her child until age thirty. This act also prohibited manumission, unless the owner paid to transport the newly freed slave out of the colony within six months. In a 1692 measure relegating free blacks to lifetime bondage for marrying white women, Maryland also criminalized marriages that threatened the institution of slavery and white patriarchal dominance over Englishwomen.[22]

In 1705, Virginia provided a statutory definition of *mulatto* for the first time in an act prohibiting any "negro, mulatto, or Indian" from holding public office. Those "accounted a mulatto" included "the child of an Indian, and the child, grandchild, and great-grandchild of a Negro." This definition persisted until 1785, when the legislature classified as mulatto "every person who shall have one-fourth or more Negro blood." In the early eighteenth century, concerns about persons of African lineage fornicating or intermarrying with white Christian settlers and producing "spurious and mixt issue" also spread beyond the Chesapeake to Massachusetts Bay and North Carolina, prompting authorities to enact statutory restrictions. Although Massachusetts's 1705 act targeted all whites, male and female, who married or engaged in sexual relations with African-descended or mixed individuals, colonial officials later explained that "complaints that several negroes had lain with white women" had compelled them to action. In practice, prosecutions were limited to black/mulatto male and white female transgressors. That same year, the Virginia burgesses passed a law fining any minister who married a white person to an individual of African or mixed descent and releasing the Christian servants of white settlers who married infidels from their master's or mistress's service. In 1715, a North Carolina statute preventing intermarriage between whites and "any Negro Mulattoe or Indyan," aimed primarily at black men and white women, "codified a growing intolerance for cross-cultural unions and strengthened definitions of racial difference—a difference that found its articulation in a concern over intermarriage and mixed-race children." The criminalization of sexual encounters between white women and men classified as "nonwhite," on the one hand, and the lax censuring of white men who engaged in illicit interracial intercourse, on the other, allowed for the consolidation of white patriarchal authority over all women's bodies and the continual expansion of the enslaved labor force.[23]

Early critics of slavery challenged what they saw as the moral hypocrisy and sexually exploitative practices of masters in the English Atlantic. Thomas Tryon, a London merchant who published scathing critiques of colonial planters in the late seventeenth century, found the entire system of hereditary racial slavery appalling, including the matrilineal rule for slave status. Donning the voice of an aggrieved slave, Tryon confronted slaveholders who claimed a natural right to hold Africans in bondage and use female slaves at their pleasure. "But pray," he demanded, "have you this Prerogative from your Descent or Pedigree? Or from some different Fabrick of your Bodies?" If planters truly cared about the dignity of their bloodlines or the tenets of their faith, they would discontinue the practice of taking enslaved women as concubines, "upon whom they beget mongrel Children, that are neither White nor Black, but between both, which therefore are called *Molatto's*." For Tryon, begetting such offspring was the least of the planters' sins. After the birth of these "mongrel Children," "the Fathers, being without natural Affection, though they are their own Seed, do expose them, and make them perpetual Slaves, both they and their Posterity." Consigning one's own blood to perpetual hereditary slavery struck Tryon as particularly horrifying and unnatural. "Now what can be more hellish Cruelty, or greater Baseness, then for men to afflict their own Seed . . . and instead of providing for, and well Educating them, to enslave and tyrannize over them, and leave them in that wretched condition to all Generations." No better evidence existed of English degeneration in the Americas, Tryon suggested, than colonists' callous disregard for blood kin.[24]

EXPANDING THE PARAMETERS OF WHITENESS

Few attended to Tryon's concerns about the sexual transgressions of colonial slave society or the immorality of consigning individuals with English blood to hereditary slavery. While Tryon's account offered a critical outsider's perspective on the racialized sexual economy wrought by African slavery, others entertained the possibility that the "spurious" byproducts of colonial slave society could prove expedient in periods of crisis. When, in March 1715, the Board of Trade asked several Jamaican planters then in London how best to settle the island, Richard Rigby, the secretary and provost marshal, proposed an unconventional measure. Given that there were fewer than fourteen hundred white men left in Jamaica fit to bear arms, the government should declare all "Mulattoes and Indians" free to speed the peopling of the island. Rigby's proposal was never put into effect, though the Jamaica assembly received and rejected similar proposals to free mulattoes at the public expense and settle them in underpopulated parishes in 1732 during the Maroon conflict. Colonial authorities did approve encouraging already free individuals of mixed blood to settle in the northeastern section of the island in exchange for land and provisions. At the time, more than half of the free population lived in the parishes of Kingston and St. Catherine, clustered in and around Kingston and St. Jago de la Vega, or Spanish Town, where whites regarded them as a nuisance. Dispersing members of this class to remote, underpopulated corners of the island offered far greater utility to the white colonial regime.[25]

In the spring of 1733, as the elections bill to demarcate mulattoes from whites worked its way through the legislative process, John Golding preemptively petitioned the house for an exemption for himself and his family. He requested, "as he had descended from mulatto ancestors, leave to bring in a bill to entitle him and his children to such rights, privileges, and immunities, as free and natural-born subjects of the crown of Great Britain, descended from white ancestors, enjoy." Golding had reason to anticipate a favorable response to his request. No ordinary individual of mixed stock, Golding held substantial wealth in land and slaves. At his death on December 16, 1758, his estate was valued at £32,036.6.¾, including 334 slaves worth £13,158. The legal whitening of Golding, his seven children, and their future mixed descendants would serve the goals of Jamaica's leading elites. By bestowing the privileges of whiteness upon the Golding family, the legislature would effectively increase the white population and demonstrate to others of mixed descent that British Protestant values, beliefs, and practices produced material rewards. As the assembly underscored, Golding "hath not only by his own Labour and Industry acquired a good fortune in this Island but hath at all times so Distinguished and behaved himself both as a good and Loyal Subject and a Good Protestant as that it were much to be wished that others of the Like Extraction would be Induc'd to Imitate or follow his Example." The Goldings served as a test case for a new system of personal preferment and patronage permitting the racial elevation of well-behaved free people of mixed blood as a rare favor. While the elections bill impeded racial mobility overall, individual exceptions demonstrated the patriarchal power of British male blood and Protestantism to convert the mixed offspring of heathens into loyal and industrious subjects. Critically, the passage of private acts also enabled the assembly to assume a determinative role similar to that of Parliament, adjudging at pleasure whether or not to "purify" supposedly corrupt bloodlines and restore an individual's capacity for inheritance as a white British subject.[26]

Free people of non-European or non-Christian ancestry could also do their part for the colony while still retaining their subordinate racial and religious status. From the perspective of the elite planters who sat on the Jamaica assembly, the exploitation of subordinate racial classes permitted the survival of the colony's hierarchical social and political order. To raise a large sum of money in support of the Maroon War, the assembly levied an emergency tax on "Jews, negroes, cattle, trades and offices." Although Jamaica's Jewish population had long protested their treatment by the Jamaican government and unfair separation "from the rest of His Majesty's Most Dutiful Subjects there," the Crown exerted very little effort to intervene in island affairs on their behalf. Colonial officials demanded that Jamaica's Jewish community pay a yearly discretionary tax, typically £750 or £1,000; singled Jews out from white Christians and barred them from saving deficiencies, except upon their own estates; prohibited Jewish men and women from purchasing white Christian servants; and prevented Jewish migrants from partaking of the material incentives offered to attract white settlers to the island (along with convicts and Quakers). Colonial authorities treated Jewish men, women, and children as white subjects in certain contexts, such as censuses, and as unwelcome and suspect foreigners outside the community of allegiance in most others. That persons of non-Christian lineage, such as Jews or free blacks, could be trustworthy, loyal subjects did not seem plausible, and planters assumed both groups supplied runaway slaves with arms—one for financial motives, the other due to an innate affinity.[27]

While some assembly members considered relaxing Jewish legal disabilities in response to petitions presented by representatives of the Jewish community, even the turmoil engendered by the Maroons could not convince the house to waive the restrictions placed upon the Jews. In 1735, British-based merchants trading with Jamaica submitted representations on behalf of Jamaica's Jewish population to the Board of Trade, pointing out that the discriminatory treatment of the Jews constituted poor imperial policy. In an island colony facing intense demographic, economic, and sociopolitical pressures, they pointed out, "not any the least Discouragement should be given to any People, or Nation, who do not hold Principles destructive to the

British Constitution and Government, from going to, and becoming fixed Inhabitants in, Jamaica, or from exercising Commerce and sending Goods and Merchandise to it." Yet, as a distinct class of colonists regarded by Jamaica's governing elites as wealthy, foreign, and untrustworthy regardless of their place of birth or professed loyalty, Jews were expected to perform their customary duties and empty their purses for the greater good.[28]

Colonial administrators required free blacks to prove their utility in ways more in keeping with their presumed natural propensity for hot climates, uncivilized environments, and punishing physical routines. In late 1734 a motion was made to manumit the enslaved wife and children of Sambo, a free black, who had proven himself "very serviceable to the country" in the armed struggle against the Maroons. Sambo had actively pursued the rebels and helped lead a number of expeditions through remote, wooded areas. When the bill for the manumission of Sambo's and other free blacks' family members was presented to the house, a member interjected that, owing to the enormous public expense incurred in purchasing their freedom, "all the males of their families should be at all times obliged to attend and go out in parties, under penalty of forfeiting their freedom." The assembly agreed and inserted a clause to this effect in the bill to reward Sambo and other free blacks for their service. Freedom as a reward for military service remained contingent upon continued military service. Sambo's bill received local approval on April 14, 1733, the same day a private act declared that John Golding and his wife and children and their future issue "begotten on White Women shall be deemed and taken to be Free and Natural Born Subjects of this Island" and treated henceforth at law "as if they and every one of them were free and Natural Born subjects of the Crown of Great Britain and were Descended from White Ancestors." The act passed in the Goldings' favor thus explicitly tied the benefits of subjecthood to British ancestry and gestation in a white womb.[29]

The striking simultaneous passage of these two private acts for the families of John Golding and Sambo indicates colonial administrators' willingness to experiment with innovative solutions to Jamaica's pressing demographic and defensive crises. It also reveals their assumptions regarding the fitness of particular racialized categories of colonial subjects for specialized tasks. The climate of Jamaica, commentators universally held, "is better adapted to the negroe constitutions." This geohumoral and environmental logic figured centrally in calls for "making free negroes and mulattoes more serviceable"—if they could be trusted. Officials in Jamaica also regularly argued that "the free negroes are in sympathy with the rebel negroes who get their supply of arms and ammunition from them" and did not deserve the island's trust; consequently, "nothing but numbers of white people can save us." In lieu of white settlers, however, administrators entertained the possibility that free people of mixed ancestry might pick up the slack, one way or another.[30]

It was widely assumed that the intermingling of European and African bloodlines resulted in offspring better equipped to withstand the rigor of a tropical climate. In rare cases, affluence and intimate ties to elite whites could expand the utility of mixed-race individuals beyond the confines of defense to the augmentation of the white community itself. Thus at the same time colonial officials in Jamaica tasked men of African descent to hunt rebellious slaves and secure the island for further white settlement, they positioned certain wealthy, well-connected individuals of mixed parentage as legally white. When Jamaica's statutory measures placing restrictions on freemen based on blood ancestry, granting the privilege of whiteness to persons of mixed descent, and extending freedom to enslaved Africans in exchange for military service reached the Board of Trade for approval the following year, they did not stir controversy. Francis Fane considered the freedom of elections act defining "mulatto" status and its associated incapacities and the acts passed in favor of John Golding and Sambo for the Crown and found "no objections in point of law." With Crown sanction, Jamaican authorities now exercised complete discretionary authority over who received freedom and why, and which individuals or groups acquired some or all of the rights and liberties associated with British subject status and which did not.[31]

MAKING COLONIAL SUBJECTS SERVICEABLE

As the 1730s wore on authorities in Jamaica achieved little progress in their efforts to bring the Maroon War to a conclusion. Colonial officials compelled many to fight, but few received sufficient recompense to warrant their sacrifice on behalf of the island's slaveholding planters. In March 1733 the assembly rewarded nineteen "party negroes" who had "acted with resolution, bravery, and fidelity" with small cash rewards (ten pence per head for each male killed or taken, eight pence for each female, and four pence per child) to encourage them to participate in future expeditions. Yet eight months later Governor Hunter admitted that matters had deteriorated and the militia was in a lamentable state; "the foot consisting chiefly of hir'd servants and free Negroes who have no obligations either of honor or interest for the defence of their Master's propertys." The next month planters in outlying Portland parish petitioned the council, desperate for relief. In addition to living in daily fear of a Maroon attack, they worried that "our negroes begin to lose that servile submission they have hitherto been subject to," hence "we dare not correct them as usual." The slaves "do frequently without any evident cause absent themselves and retire to the rebels," refusing to acquiesce to white authority.[32]

Following the death of Governor Hunter in March 1734, Jamaica's temporary governor, John Ayscough, a fellow planter and president of the council, urged the assembly "immediately to think of some more effectual remedy than what has hitherto been taken" to suppress the rebellious slaves. All agreed, as the speaker of the house reported to the secretary of state, that the steps taken to suppress the Maroons, who numbered around two thousand in total, had failed "owing to cowardice and treachery of the parties, raised from time to time out of the militia, which mostly consisted of tradesmen and indented servants, who are unacquainted with arms and military discipline, and are not to be depended on, or from arming our slaves, who, we are convinced, have betrayed us." Governor Ayscough emphasized his particular wish "that some method could be found to make the free Negroes and Mullatoes more useful," and the assembly responded by offering to do whatever lay in its power to compel the free descendants of slaves to serve. In 1734 and 1735 colonial forces dealt a decisive blow to the Windward Maroons, wiping out Nanny Town and dispersing its inhabitants, but the Maroons regrouped and established a new settlement, later named Moore Town, eight miles away. The war continued to drag on at great expense and with no end in sight.[33]

On June 20, 1735, just as the assembly made good on its promise to Governor Ayscough, introducing a new bill "for making free negroes, free Indians, and free mulattoes, more serviceable," the house received word that numerous free blacks and mulattoes had absconded to avoid fighting the rebellious Maroons. The palpable lack of enthusiasm for the ongoing war permeated across all classes of colonial subjects. Meanwhile, local authorities continued to argue that nonwhites should shoulder the main burden of the island's defense based on pragmatic grounds. Free people of African and mixed ancestry were "fittest for the woods" and, if "encouraged to do their duty," the new temporary governor and president of the council, John Gregory, claimed, "would effectually secure us against intenstine enemies at an easier expence, and a much more equal and expeditious way than by raising of parties." Whites, Jamaican authorities insisted, would not readily prevail in the conflict with the Maroons, "as they are seated in vast rocky mountains, full of thickets and woods, and many of them inaccessible to white men, who are not accustomed thereto, and are unable to traverse them." This theory helped to explain the poor performance of the British regiments. Still, the Mosquito Indians, enslaved Africans, free blacks, and men of mixed ancestry proved little better than white soldiers at overcoming the guerilla tactics of the rebels. New proposals to bring in Chickasaw or Creek Indians from mainland North America, "a hardy warlike people" accustomed to rocky and mountainous country, bore too heavy a cost for the already overtaxed colonial government to implement and were abandoned.[34]

Fearing the loss of one of the empire's most valuable colonies, British merchants in London, Bristol, and Liverpool with interests in Jamaica petitioned the Crown to enlarge the number of white settlers and strengthen the island's defenses before it fell to the rebellious slaves—or worse, the Spanish or French. With one hundred thousand African slaves and foreign nations on all sides, they observed, "the Island must unavoidably fall a prey, sooner or later, to a foreign or intestine enemy." Proposals to attract white settlers to the struggling colony centered on the availability of positions for white laborers and the importance of prohibiting black tradesmen and ship pilots from engaging in skilled labor for the future. White settlement and hegemony in Jamaica would remain fragile if free slaves and their descendants took the place of white laborers, as enslaved Africans had replaced white servants at the end of the previous century. Only a native-born, naturally reproducing white settler population promised to keep Jamaica safely in British hands for the long term.[35]

In the interim, war with the Maroons offered confirmation of the vital importance of free people of African descent to the colony's immediate safety and long-term survival. In addition to their defensive uses and alleged suitability to the tropical climate, persons of mixed lineage held the potential, over successive generations of mixture and acculturation to British Protestant norms, to pass as white, claim the liberties of whites, and ultimately reproduce white subjects. Illicit sexual relations between white men and enslaved and free women of African ancestry were both socially acceptable and unhampered by legal restrictions. White male colonial elites in Jamaica, many of whom fathered illegitimate children through multiple short- and long-term relationships with black women, increasingly weighed the risks and benefits of racial mixture in accordance with shifting local circumstances. On the one hand, colonial officials could never fully incorporate free people of mixed parentage into Jamaican slave society on equal terms with British subjects, open to all manner of employment opportunities and positions of public trust, or prospective white settlers would avoid the island entirely. Extending the rights and privileges of natural-born British subjects to large numbers of illegitimate persons of mixed blood would result in Jamaica's permanent castigation as a breeding ground for Creole degeneracy, akin to the Spanish territories. On the other hand, sanctioning the formal inclusion of select mixed-race individuals and families, like the Goldings, into white society could infuse the colony with loyal white subjects, as the law "cleansed" their mixed bloodlines of the stain of African origins. In this way, local authorities reasoned, sexual relations between white men and women of mixed ancestry would abet the colony's survival rather than contribute to its decay.

Whether the bloodlines of British male colonists could overcome a tainted maternal inheritance in order to whiten the population, and thereby accomplish the seemingly impossible proverbial task of washing an Ethiop white, held local as well as imperial significance. Colonial and imperial officials expressed reservations about the extent to which the mixed descendants of African slaves and British settlers retained inherited heathen moral and intellectual traits through their blood link to a distant "negro ancestor." In the case of a mass insurrection, would the descendants of slaves remain loyal to the Crown and white settler community or revert to their ancestors' former presumed barbarity and side with their enslaved brethren? The question of blood inherency would link arguments about the birthright of Englishmen abroad and the inherited rights and privileges of British subjects to developing understandings of race. British commentators considered blood and birthplace key factors underpinning allegiance, with neither factor wholly divisible from religious faith or cultural practices. To place non-Christian aliens such as Africans, Indians, mulattoes, and Jews—all of whom allegedly possessed distinctive physical, cultural, and psychological traits—on an equal footing with natural-born subjects, or to merge with them sexually, held the potential to raze Jamaica's English character. The mixing of bloodlines in Spanish America carried deeply negative connotations for English commentators, negatively impacting Anglo-Caribbean and Anglo-American views of racial mixture; "for however brave their ancestors may have been," as one English official claimed in 1689, the Spanish "have degenerated into a dastardly and mongrel herd of mulattos, mustees and other spurious mixtures, and are now certainly become the very scum of mankind." Blood mixture, many feared, inevitably led to decline for the more "civilized" partner, not improvement.[36]

Colonial legislators across the slave societies of British America grappled with pressing questions related to racial heritage and political participation in the early eighteenth century. In 1721, in response to concerns about "sham Free-holders" voting in violation of "the freedom of Elections, and of the liberty of the subject," Barbados passed an act specifying the qualifications for "*bona-fide* freeholders" capable of voting, holding public office, or serving on a jury. The act permitted only white Christian male subjects, either natural born or naturalized, above age twenty-one with a minimum of ten acres of land to vote or serve as an assemblyman, vestryman, or juror. Clause 8 further clarified that "no person whatsoever shall be admitted as a Free-holder, or an Evidence in any case whatsoever, whose original extraction shall be proved to have been from a Negro." Barbados further determined in 1739 to receive the testimony of a slave "against any free negro, Indian, or Mulatto, where baptized or not" in court, because persons manumitted or descended from slaves were "continuing their baseness" rather than distinguishing themselves from the enslaved population. Similarly, an earlier Virginian law of 1723 stipulated that "no free Negro, Mulatto, or Indian whatsoever, shall hereafter have an vote at the Election of Burgesses, or any other Election whatsoever." This policy contradicted the perspective of the Board of Trade's legal counsel, who argued that no such rule existed in England allowing for the disparate treatment of freemen who met the property qualifications for suffrage. Nonetheless, the burgesses passed additional restrictions the following decade to prevent "Negroes, mulattoes, and Indians who professed themselves to be Christians" from giving evidence in court "forasmuch as they are People of such base and corrupt natures, that the Credit of their Testimony cannot be certainly depended upon," except in slave trials.[37]

When, in 1735, the Board of Trade asked colonial officials in Virginia to explain the rationale of their earlier statute disenfranchising free blacks and people of mixed descent, Lieutenant Governor William Gooch issued a remarkably forthright and illuminating response. Shortly before passing the act of 1723, he explained, the Virginia burgesses had uncovered a conspiracy among the slaves, and "such was the insolence of the free negros at that time, that the next Assembly thought it necessary to fix a perpetual brand upon free negros and mulattos by excluding them from that great priviledge of a Freeman, well knowing they always did, and ever will adhere to and favor the slaves." "And 'tis likewise said to have been done with design," elaborated Gooch, "which I must think a good one, to make the free negros sensible that a distinction ought to be made between their offspring and the descendants of an Englishman, with whom they never were to be accounted equal." Gooch assured the board that while the exclusion of freeholders of African and mixed ancestry from voting might seem severe "to such as are unacquainted with the nature of negros," without restrictions in place to preserve white privilege, a freed slave would regard himself as the equal to his white neighbors—"especially if he is descended of a white father or mother, lett them be of what mean condition soever." Therefore, Gooch concluded, "it seems no ways impolitick, as well for discouraging that kind of copulation as to preserve a decent distinction between them and their betters, to leave this mark on them until time and education has changed the indication of their spurious extraction, and made some alteration in their morals." The Board of Trade, apparently persuaded by Gooch's arguments, agreed to "let that Act ly by" indefinitely. When it came to colonial divergence, the board's point of view aligned with Matthew Bacon's general approach to local customs: "Of such Customs as are against the Rules of the Common Law, yet not being unreasonable in themselves, are good, and from the Conveniency of them bind in particular places." For English colonists to deny the common law birthright of Englishmen to the free descendants of slaves was presented as a matter of political expediency.[38]

Other Anglo-American colonies avoided legislating political rights on the basis of racial heritage during the early years of settlement, preferring to banish manumitted slaves and thereby curtail the growth of a free nonwhite population. A 1722 law in South Carolina required all freed slaves to leave the colony within twelve months or face re-enslavement, as did a Bermudian act for "Extirpating all free Negroes," first passed in 1674 and repeated in 1730 but with a revised time frame of six months. In Jamaica, however, colonial administrators sought to exploit free people for the benefit of the island, putting immediate defensive needs ahead of the long-term goal of white settlement. Attempts to increase the number of white settlers had proven ineffective time and again, and the ever-expanding black-to-white ratio, which rose dramatically from 6.4 to 1 in 1703 to 9.9 to 1 in 1739, posed a major security risk to an isolated slave-powered colonial possession. Local authorities were anxious both to vouchsafe the English constitutional inheritance in Jamaica and to protect the island's heavily outnumbered white settlers. They engaged in this balancing act by developing strategies to co-opt the free descendants of enslaved women as a means of strengthening the slave regime.[39]

In March 1739, the long-delayed resolution of the conflict with the Maroons culminated in the signing of articles of agreement, representing a first hopeful step toward lasting peace and the next phase of Anglo-Maroon relations. Governor Trelawny informed the board in London that the pacification of the Maroons constituted "a critical conjuncture to settle this Island better than it ever yet has been, and consequently to render it more beneficial to our Mother Country." Not only had hostilities ceased in Jamaica, paving the way for new white settlements throughout the island, but the Maroons had also agreed henceforth to hunt runaway slaves and return them to their owners. Colonial officials sought and obtained redress from the Maroons by demanding their assistance in the suppression of enslaved Africans. No longer would their numbers expand to the detriment of British slaveholders. The "perfect state of freedom and liberty" assured to the Maroons in exchange for their services to the colonial government came with strings attached.[40]

Jamaican Jews also suffered the consequences of their classification as outsiders who offered nothing but financial utility to the colony. The legislature was loath to relinquish the additional revenue provided by extra levies imposed upon the Jews both long before and during the Maroon War. After a group of Jewish traders in Jamaica petitioned the British government in January 1737 asking for equal rights with the island's natural-born Protestant subjects, specifically release from additional taxes, the Crown instructed Governor Trelawny not to assent to any such financial impositions on the Jews. Yet even after the conclusion of the Maroon treaty, the assembly and council badgered Trelawny into ignoring his instructions and assenting to another tax, because the Jews "are a very wealthy body; their gains considerable, and acquired with great ease and indolence," though "of little or no advantage to the public." Most importantly, "as an English colony, and by the declarations and charters of government granted to us by His Majesty and his royal predecessors, we have a right of making our own laws, and must be supposed to know our best necessities, and the justice and equality of our taxations." Taxing the Jewish community was yet another example of a necessary colonial divergence to the benefit of public welfare. Jews retained their subordinate status in Jamaica long after the imperial government nixed the partial tax imposed on them and passed the Naturalization Act of 1740 (20 Geo. II, c. 44), waiving for Jewish colonial subjects the naturalization oath required of foreign-born Protestants. At the municipal level, the Jamaica assembly remained committed to its mission of exercising legal authority to the sole benefit of the island's white Protestant settlers.[41]

RACIAL TRANSMUTATION AND WHITE SETTLEMENT

Beginning in the 1740s, sugar plantations spread rapidly along Jamaica's north coast and African slaves poured into the island as land opened up for settlement. Yet the sudden reversal of demographic trends envisioned by Tre-lawny did not come to fruition. The white population remained stagnant. Charles Leslie, among others, underscored Jamaica's reputation as a death trap in his history of the island in 1740. "Our political Arithmeticians imag-ine once in seven Years there is a Revolution of Lives in this Island, that as many die in that Space of Time as presently inhabit it," he mused; "and no doubt the Multitude that dies would soon leave the Place a Desart, did not daily Recruits come over from *Great Britain*." As Leslie acknowledged, "notwithstanding their vast Numbers, the Island but slowly settles." Ongoing and intractable numerical pressures thus inspired white elites to use the law instrumentally for social engineering purposes, chiefly by granting limited legal privileges to the mixed progeny of prominent white men, when the lat-ter served colonial interests. While distinctions of blood remained in place over multiple generations, subject to the gradual processes of mixture and dilution, private acts effectively collapsed the number of degrees required to attain whiteness in law. Adopting a more flexible approach to white status enabled colonial officials to authorize passing such acts, but only for certain elite individuals with strong ties to the white community and a major finan-cial investment in the colonial order.[42]

Susanna Augier, the illegitimate "mulatto" daughter of a white man and an enslaved black woman, was one such remarkable individual. Her father, John Augier, a planter who died in 1722, freed five of his natural mixed-race daughters—Susanna, Mary, Jenny, Frances, and Jane—from slavery in his will and left each of them a share of his estate. Soon after her manumission, Susanna Augier became the mistress of Peter Caillard, a prosperous merchant in Kingston, and bore him three children, Mary, Peter, and Susanna Caillard, in rapid succession during the mid-to-late 1720s. In 1728 Peter Caillard died, leaving Augier a lifetime interest in an estate probated for £26,150.8.1, includ-ing several properties in Kingston and St. Jago de la Vega, a livestock pen in St. Catherine, and mountain property near the Wag Water River (or Agua Alta) in St. Andrew, with Peter and Mary as residuary legatees. Caillard's be-quest transformed Augier, an illegitimate former slave, into an extraordinarily wealthy woman. Less than a year after his death she became the mistress of Kingston merchant Gibson Dalzell and bore two children, Frances and

Robert, both of whom later accompanied their "natural" father to London and settled in Britain. In 1738, five years after John Golding paved the way for the legal whitening of elite free people of mixed lineage, Susanna Augier petitioned for white privileges for herself and her two surviving daughters, Mary and Frances. On July 19, 1738, in recognition of her wealth and elevated status, the assembly passed a private act entitling Augier and her daughters "to the same Rights and Privileges with English Subjects born of White Parents." This act granted Susanna, Mary, and Frances Augier, as well as "their Issue hereafter born in this Island and begotten by white men," limited civil liberties and the legal right to pass as white subjects. Accordingly, both the women and their future offspring fathered by white men would be tried for crimes, misdemeanors, or offences and allowed to give evidence at civil and criminal trials "as if they and every of them were free and natural born subjects of the crown of Great Britain and were descended of and from White Ancestors . . . any Law Custom or Usage to the Contrary notwithstanding."[43]

When Gibson Dalzell died in 1755, he too devised a significant share of his personal estate, valued at £6,854 1s. 3d., to Robert and Frances Dalzell, "his reputed children by [a] Mulatto Woman named Susanna Augier." Robert Dalzell attended Christ Church College at Oxford and married an English-woman; his sister, Frances, married George Duff, son of the first Earl of Fife, and entered the ranks of Britain's landed aristocracy. Susanna Augier died a "spinster" five years later in Kingston, on January 28, 1760, leaving behind expensive furnishings, including marbled tables, armchairs, a bedstead and mahogany dressing table, and china, as well as livestock, a carriage and pair of horses, and seven slaves, valued at a total of £1,097 14s. 8 ½d. Susanna's siblings also did very well for themselves, not merely in their attainment of material privileges, which, as Marisa Fuentes argues, serves as a problematic touchstone against which to measure the "success" of women of African descent in a slave society, but in terms of their legal transformation into colonial subjects with recognized, hereditary rights. The legislature passed private acts in May 1747 privileging Augier's two sisters, Jane and Mary, as well as eleven other illegitimate family members of mixed ancestry. These included four of Jane's surviving children with John DeCumming, four of Mary's children with the Kingston merchant William Tyndall, and two additional siblings, Jacob and Elizabeth, as well as Elizabeth's son. Consideration of bills to whiten more than a dozen persons in one fell swoop generated debate in the house, prompting a motion "to end consideration of enlarging mulatto privileges due to all the other important business." The motion failed. For the time being, the majority of assemblymen supported granting white status as a rare privilege to individuals and entire families projected to uphold the colonial racial order by bolstering the white population.[44]

Official grants of limited white privileges to elite persons or families of mixed blood were nonetheless incredibly rare, accorded only to those with wealth and personal connections. Even with the automatic path to legal whiteness extended by the 1733 voting acting, few individuals of mixed descent could muster the genealogical background or documentation required to meet its terms. Overall, the assembly approved 128 private bills granting white status to roughly six hundred men, women, and children of mixed lineage between 1733 and 1802, only 4 of which granted the recipient all of the liberties of white male freeholders, including the right to vote and hold office. Nearly all petitioners, though they lobbied for all of the legal, economic, and political privileges enjoyed by white colonial subjects, received limited and specific exemptions, and the assembly ensured that each private bill contained wording to that effect. The recipients of privilege bills were thus not fully "white" in the eyes of the law but rather legally *whitened,* on the path toward whiteness. The majority of these remarkable cases involved the illegitimate offspring of the enslaved or free mistresses of white Creole men. Edward Long later noted that officials chiefly made exceptions for the natural offspring of white men "who were inheritors of large estates in the island, bequeathed to them by their white ancestor."[45]

Officially blanching illegitimate persons of mixed ancestry, and thereby permitting the descendants of slave mothers to enjoy a paternal constitutional inheritance to which they had no lawful claim, certainly made Jamaica exceptional in the British Atlantic. But such individuals held social and economic positions of extraordinary rarity compared to nearly all other free people of African or mixed ancestry in Jamaica. William Cunningham Jr., the illegitimate mixed son of assemblyman William Cunningham, who operated a profitable slave plantation in Westmoreland parish, was one of the select few whom the assembly approved for full rights and privileges after some controversy. When the assembly submitted his act for approval in July 1738 to the council, Jamaica's upper legislative chamber amended the wording of Cunningham Jr.'s private bill so that it would not "confer upon the said William Cunningham junior, any power, capacity or ability, of sitting or voting either in the council or assembly of this island, or of holding or enjoying any office of magistracy; but that the said William Cunningham junior shall be totally excluded therefrom."[46]

The assembly responded that the council had acted "in violation of his majesty's prerogative," preventing it from exercising a power akin to Parliament's by, in essence, restoring Cunningham Jr.'s bloodline in law to the benefit of one of the assembly's own members. The council defended their responsibility to advise the Crown "to refuse such favours to the son of a negro woman, as the laws of Great Britain advise him to refuse to all foreigners, though of the most illustrious extraction." Assembly members protested that the disabilities traditionally placed on foreigners in England were designed to prevent large numbers of aliens from flooding the country and "overturning the constitution," a situation not applicable in this case. Moreover, Cunningham Jr., they asserted, was native born and attached to the island, and "the number of persons in the circumstances of Mr. Cunningham, and recommended to his majesty's favour, are inconsiderable." Later developments confirmed William Cunningham Jr.'s highly exceptional circumstances: in 1750 he was appointed sole executor of his father's estate, valued at nearly £46,000. In purely financial terms, Cunningham Jr. belonged to the upper echelons of Jamaican plantation society; he held as strong a stake in the slave system as any substantial man of property.[47]

Colonial officials took great care to prevent the overwhelming majority of persons of mixed ancestry from sharing the British constitutional inheritance with white settlers. By the eighteenth century, the birthright of Englishmen in Jamaica, which colonists had long fought to preserve against Crown encroachments and the machinations of internal and external enemies of foreign extraction, had become firmly wedded to whiteness. White settlers alone had inherited the constitutional right to self-govern in the interest of preserving their lives, liberties, and properties. Yet meanings of whiteness remained fluid; whiteness, as both an ideological and legal construct, responded flexibly to changing times and political needs, broadening and contracting as local conditions dictated. In colonial Jamaica, whiteness, as Warwick Anderson observes generally, "was a variable signifier of difference, not an assertion of fixed qualities." "Whiteness thus was both a sovereign category and a flexible one." Persons of mixed blood could not claim a share of the English common law inheritance while they remained nonwhite subjects in the eyes of the law. Yet the patchwork nature of the British Atlantic empire vested colonial administrators with the legislative power to define and extend the legal parameters of both whiteness and subject status at will.[48]

Favoring the transmutation of a subordinate population regarded as "barbarous" into that of a dominant "civilized" group as a prudent strategy of conquest was not without precedent in the annals of English colonizing experience. During the Tudor era, English officials and reformers attempted a similar strategy in their efforts to assert English authority over Ireland and renew earlier, partially successful colonization efforts initiated by the Anglo-Normans. Beginning in the twelfth century, English commentators contrasted the "savage, rude and uncouth" Irish, whom they hoped to subdue, with the "civil English." While the adoption of English practices, language, and law allegedly evinced civilizing effects, capable of making "the Irish grow civil and become English," in the words of Sir John Davies, Irish barbarity was also assumed to contaminate the body politic, so that "the body that before was whole and sound, was by little and little festered, and in manner wholly putrified." Hence the long-standing presence of great and lesser landowners of distant Anglo-Norman extraction in Ireland, known as the "Old English," offered little confidence to English administrators bent on civilizing Ireland. It had become clear to officials in England that, despite the presence of Irish lords with English blood in their veins, Ireland remained in a state of "barbarous savageness."[49]

Tudor reformers claimed that the Old English had degenerated in the intervening centuries following the Anglo-Norman wave of colonization, giving rise to descendants virtually indistinguishable from the native Irish. To make Ireland English, then, required a fresh colonization strategy focused on "repeopling" Ireland with newly transplanted English-born inhabitants. These "New English" settlers, their bloodlines untainted by centuries of intermixture with Irish natives, would ensure that English colonizing goals in Ireland were achieved. Edmund Burke later recounted that belief in the transformative power of unpolluted English blood prompted the Crown to place native English governors in Ireland, "which first gave rise to that famous distinction between the English by blood, and the English by birth." The Old English responded by arguing, as Sir Nicholas White stressed in a letter composed to the Crown in 1581, "what a strong garrison without pay the seed of English blood hath made to her crown since their first planting, which are easier reformed than supplanted."[50]

English proponents of demographic manipulation in Ireland continued to make their case over the next century, claiming that transplantation and mixture could rectify the population imbalances faced by the Old English. The seventeenth-century political economist Sir William Petty, for example, in his discussion of the impediments to England's greatness as a colonizing power, focused squarely on problems of demography. Petty claimed that governing a colonial empire of geographically distant islands and countries, whereby small numbers of Englishmen attempted to subjugate much larger populations of foreigners, placed too heavy a burden on the administrative center and threatened English rule. Proposing a shift in the demographic balance of power, Petty argued that to maintain control over a conquered territory like Ireland, English colonial policy should concentrate on "the transmutation of the Irish into English," specifically through the exchange of Irish women for English-women. According to this logic, by forcibly removing poor Irish women and substituting English brides in their place, "a natural and firm union" would occur between Irish men and Englishwomen and hence between Irish interests and English colonization goals. Once in Irish households, Englishwomen would take charge of domestic management, occasioning the wholesale acceptance of English legal and cultural customs, manners, religious beliefs, and language in Ireland. Population control, and the biological and cultural reproduction of Englishness, would alleviate the need to maintain English dominion in Ireland through force alone.[51]

Enacting such a policy of demographic manipulation and transmutation in eighteenth-century Jamaica, a slave society short on women of European ancestry, presented a significant set of challenges. For a woman of mixed lineage and illegitimate birth to pass into the sanctified realm of white femininity and reproduce legally recognized white subjects was a deeply provocative issue. White women held a place of unparalleled importance in Jamaican slave society; their wombs served as a mechanism through which white power, privilege, and identity flowed to the next generation. Emphasis on white womanhood as a standard for genealogical purity and legitimacy provided for the smooth intergenerational transfer of both property and whiteness, ensuring the continued Anglicization of the colony. Moreover, a colonial society that allowed for a fungible approach to racial classifications also necessitated the reproduction of white subjects whose ancestry, untainted by mixture with African slaves and their free descendants, conformed to the definition of whiteness in Britain. White women's most crucial task in Jamaica therefore was to reproduce legitimate white children who could preserve white British hegemony and cultural identity despite the brutalities and demographic realities of colonial slavery. Accordingly, as bearers of British blood and white purity, white Creole women were increasing desexualized.[52]

Such was the significance of white female virtue that an unsubstantiated rumor of improper familiarity with "negroes" could devastate a white Creole woman's reputation. During legislative deliberations over the infamous

Edward Manning divorce case from 1739 to 1741, an Irish maidservant, Mrs. O'Hara, accused her former mistress, Mrs. Manning, of inviting slaves into her bedchamber during her husband's absence. O'Hara's allegation that she had witnessed "negro fellows" slinking into her former mistress's chamber and "heard them kiss and smack, and said she believed the negro fellows had lain with Mrs. Manning," permanently altered the tenor of the Manning divorce proceedings. Public opinion branded Mrs. Manning a racially defiled woman, although the original cause of her husband's ire stemmed from her open affair with Ballard Beckford, a member of the assembly. When Francis Fane considered the legality of the act passed in Jamaica to dissolve the Manning marriage for the Board of Trade in May 1740, he regarded the flagrant intimacy between Mrs. Manning and Beckford as sufficient "provocation" to justify the divorce. He nonetheless expressed doubt regarding the validity of the Irish servant's claim that Mrs. Manning engaged in sexually transgressive behavior with black slave men, "for such circumstances would have been the highest aggravation of the offence and consequently the stronger inducement with the crown to consent to the law."[53]

Despite the indispensable role of white women for the biological, social, and cultural reproduction of whiteness in colonial Jamaica, respectable women descended from white ancestors remained in short supply. If, however, colonial officials attempted to remedy the situation by incorporating the mixed descendants of cross-racial pairings into white society as a stopgap measure, they risked raising questions about the very essence of whiteness, British femininity, and the immutability of British bloodlines in the tropics. It was one thing to transplant Englishwomen of little to no consequence into Irish households to civilize Ireland and quite another to expose the offspring of white British males to the reputed corruptive influence of African blood and customs. As Jean Feerick points out, in an era in which differences of blood "could describe differences *internal* to a polity," such as those of rank, and also "support identifications across national and political lines for people of similar social location," the prospect of exchanging blood—or a blood product, such as breast milk—with members of alien groups generated considerable unease.[54]

Contemporaries also held misgivings regarding the prospect of transplanted settlers imbibing inferior manners and physical characteristics through social and sexual mixing with foreigners, a two-way process of exchange that tended to benefit one group to the detriment of the other. Avoiding the ill effects of mixture demanded the erection of firm institutional, physical, and sociocultural boundaries as well as constant vigilance on the part of allegedly more civilized peoples. Edmund Spenser, in *A View of the Present State of Ireland* (originally written in 1596), highlighted the positive aspects of cultural exchange in support of his own program of English transplantation in Ireland. Although the ancient English had cast off the yoke of their allegiance and "are so much degenerate from their first Natures, as to grow wild" in Ireland, Spenser dismissed the first wave of Old English settlers as a failed attempt at colonization during a "very rude and barbarous" period of the nation's history, "for it is but even the other Day since *England* grew civil." Now sufficiently civilized and cognizant of the perils associated with Irish language, customs, wet nurses, and marriage partners, English colonists would not let down their guard. Settling the heedful New English alongside the barbarous Irish and Old English and instituting English law would, in his view, significantly improve the latter two groups while safeguarding the cultural and heritable integrity of the former.[55]

PERMANENT ALIEN-BORN SUBJECTS

As Spenser's comments suggest, not all early modern commentators emphasized the dangers posed to the English through intermixture with natives of other soils and climes. Political aims largely shaped these more positive approaches to biological and cultural hybridization. But the presumed degenerative threat inherent in mixture with aliens retained its rhetorical power and gave rise to new racial meanings and consequences in the context of colonial slave societies and an expanding British imperial world. Jamaica's ruling elite bolstered their efforts to control the labor and movements of former slaves and their descendants and to circumscribe their freedom within narrow limits. African-descended individuals who questioned white authority could find themselves arrested on a slight charge and detained in prison indefinitely, forcibly re-enslaved and sold, or transported off the island. In September 1756, for instance, Benjamin La Cruise, a free-born black, petitioned the assembly after languishing in Spanish Town gaol for five months following the end of his sentence. Originally arrested in February 1752, Cruise was released in December 1755 but attacked and blinded in one eye by Deputy Marshal Charles Baker. Baker then arrested Cruise for breaking the peace and imprisoned him, ostensibly for a term of three months; but, according to Cruise's account, Baker swore that "he would be in danger of his life" if ever released. In the end, the assembly opted to release Cruise from prison but immediately conscripted him, against his wishes, into the Royal Navy without pay.[56]

While free blacks held few options for economic or social advancement, free people of mixed lineage with links to wealthy white males sought to benefit from unofficial blood ties. Elites of mixed parentage who presented private petitions to the assembly, or those who petitioned on their behalf, followed a set model when asking for white privileges. They referenced their allegiance to the Crown, baptism and instruction in the Christian religion, property holdings in land and slaves, inheritance prospects from filial benefactors, and liberal educations. Some petitioners, particularly those set to inherit their white fathers' estates, cited expensive educations received in England. Rare exceptions, like Sarah Shreyer, "a free mulatto woman, the wife of Godfrey Shreyer the elder, of the parish of St. Mary, in the said island, planter, a white man," exhibited their marital status as proof of exceptionality. By midcentury, as more white men devised real and personal property to illegitimate children born to enslaved mothers, and freewomen began asking for white privileges of their own accord, concerns mounted that the mixed descendants of slaves possessed too large a share of land and other property in Jamaica. White men of various backgrounds had facilitated an increase in the number of petitions before the assembly asking for private bills on behalf of "reputed" mixed-race offspring, a development that did not sit well with a segment of freeholders and administrators. Members of the assembly debated whether or not it was sound policy to share white property, racial identity, and consequently power with men and women lineally descended from enslaved African ancestors. Their misgivings illustrate the lingering doubts associated with the fluidity of whiteness as a legal and social construct.[57]

On April 23, 1747, the assembly received simultaneous and conflicting petitions that brought the matter of white privilege and its preservation to the fore. Shortly after Foster March, a lawyer residing in St. Catherine parish, petitioned to expand the rights and privileges of "Foster, Charles, John, William, and Ann March, his reputed sons and daughter, by Elizabeth Rogers, a free mulatto," Elizabeth Rogers, a "free mulatto woman," also petitioned on behalf of herself and her daughter, Mary. Other petitions were presented as well. A group of "inhabitants and freeholders" submitted a formal counterpetition "against any bill or bills before the house for granting to free mulattoes the like privileges and advantages of the laws and liberties of this island, as the petitioners, freeholders, natural born white and liege subjects, enjoy, and have enjoyed since the conquest of this island." A debate immediately ensued in the house, but less than two weeks later the committee appointed to examine March's case reported that the mother of his reputed children, whom March intended to provide for and educate, was classified as a quadroon. Therefore, members concluded, "as these children are three removes from their negro ancestor, and have already so large a share of property, and are likely to have much more, that it would be good policy to open the benefits of His Majesty's laws and government to them." Opinion nonetheless remained divided. "If the said bills should pass into law," argued a group of freeholders opposed to the notion of individuals of mixed blood descended from slaves being put on the same legal footing as white settlers, "sundry mulattoes would be entitled to the same rights and privileges with his majesty's English subjects, free born, of white parents, with such exception as in the bills mentioned." Irrespective of troubling demographic trends and the prudence of an intermediate buffer group between whites and the enslaved, even the limited privileges granted to elite free people appeared to undermine the exclusivity of British subjecthood and white racial superiority. In response to such fears, the assembly offered a compromise: it agreed to repeal specific sections of previously passed private privilege bills "which enable or qualifie the said mulattoes, or their respective issue, to serve on juries in this island."[58]

Such legislative concessions worked temporarily to appease white colonists concerned about the extension of English liberties to nonwhites of servile ancestry but did not halt the growth or upward mobility of Jamaica's free population of mixed descent. Middling whites in particular disapproved of the island's upwardly mobile freed community, the members of which appeared to hold ambitions well above their intended station. In October 1753 tradesmen and artificers in Kingston and Spanish Town protested what they saw as the engrossment of employment by "free mulattoes and negroes carrying on the same trades with the petitioners" and aided by slave apprentices. In addition to potentially taking jobs away from white tradesmen, a rising class of motivated free people sought to attain the same social and economic footing as laboring whites, to the detriment of the colonial racial order and future white settlement. In other words, white Jamaicans would tolerate the existence of free people of African and mixed descent, but only if they remained poor and subservient. They would never accept the descendants of slaves as fellow subjects capable of partaking of the birthright inheritance of freeborn Britons. In the eyes of white settlers, African-descended people, like members of the Jewish community, retained their inherited identity as heathen aliens, even if native born, Christianized, or declared legally white.[59]

The public response to a petition presented by Abraham Sanches to the assembly several years earlier, on October 4, 1750, shows how closely these two subordinate colonial populations were linked in the minds of white settlers. Sanches, a Jewish freeholder in St. John parish, attempted to cast his vote at an election, arguing that in 1742 he was "duly naturalized, and has taken the usual oaths, and therefore humbly apprehends he is entitled to all rights and privileges of the rest of His Majesty's subjects." After colonial authorities printed and distributed Sanches's petition, probably to rouse the public "in support of the custom of not admitting Jews to give their votes at elections," a group of "Christians, freeholders, and other inhabitants" from Kingston submitted a counterpetition. "The people called Jews are a transient people, so widely differing in their religion, laws, and ceremonies, and so abhorred for their behaviour, that they have not been able to obtain a share in the leg of any country upon earth," the petitioners asserted. For this reason, the colonial legislature had wisely placed them "on the foot of mulattoes and negroes," who could ultimately enjoy the rights and privileges of His Majesty's white subjects, but only after their bloodlines were expunged of the taint of African ancestry over many generations and if "brought up in the Christian religion." If Jewish men or non-Christians were granted full suffrage and obtained a share of the government, "Christianity itself may be brought into contempt, and Christian people forced from this island to seek shelter elsewhere." "The Jews are a foreign nation, and of a different religion from us," agreed a separate group of Spanish Town petitioners; Christian inhabitants would "have no safeguard for their religion, liberty, lives, and property" if Jewish hands grasped the reins of power.[60]

The concurrent approval of the Jewish Naturalization Bill (27 Geo. II, c. 1) by the House of Lords in the spring of 1753, modifying statutory requirements to permit Parliament to naturalize "persons professing the Jewish religion," sparked comparable opposition in the Commons and among London merchants. The people of Britain must have "been guilty of some heinous offence," proclaimed William Northey, a tory M.P. for Calne, during a debate in the Commons, for Parliament to consider "depriving them of their birthright" in an era when "the birthright of Englishmen is become much more valuable." "Attempts have formerly been made to rob them of their birthright as Englishmen, but this Bill I must look on as an attempt to rob them of their birthright as Christians." Indeed, Northey reiterated, "extending this birthright to Jews is like saying it should be abolished." Naturalization schemes to enrich the nation worked "provided the people be unanimous, and all ready to cooperate for the public good, or for the defence of the country" and not merely to satisfy one sect's desire "to claim the privileges of Englishmen, and the protection of this crown." "I am persuaded," agreed Sir Edmund Isham, "their numbers will increase so fast in this country, and they will get considerable part of our land-estates into their possession, that will soon contend for power as well as property." Lord Dupplin, who supported the measure, disagreed. Englishmen would not suffer an injury by sharing their birthright with "a rich Jew"; besides, "it is now generally agreed, that a man born in the British dominions, let his parents be of what nation you will, and let himself be of what religion you will, is a natural born subject, and entitled to all the rights and privileges of an Englishman." "As to the unanimity of our people, I believe it can never be expected, whilst we preserve our liberties: in free countries there will always be free parties and divisions; but religion now has less concern in our divisions than it ever had heretofore," Dupplin insisted. The controversy over the "Jew Bill" did not die with its passage but rather spread like a cancer throughout the kingdom, inciting a widespread chorus of disapproval from the metropolitan public and the bill's swift repeal.[61]

The debate over Jewish naturalization in Britain exposed the religious underpinnings of the English constitutional inheritance and its implications for more inclusive understandings of British subjecthood. Colonial authorities and white settlers in Jamaica also took a hard line against extending the English birthright to Jews and nonwhites and increasingly pushed for the greater influence of British values, norms, blood, and culture on the segment of the free population born of mixture between Europeans and Africans. Fear of alien influence and the loss of white hegemony in a colony dominated by a small number of powerful whites excited apprehensions regarding the full inclusion of individuals assigned to subordinate racial classes in Jamaican slave society. As with the idealized vision of Britain as a country of "unanimity," shared by members of Parliament and the public, white colonists of all ranks envisioned Jamaica as a flourishing British settler society in which neither Jews nor the vast majority of free people of African or mixed ancestry were permitted the full exercise of the inherited liberties of freeborn Protestant subjects.

Middling and elite whites in colonial Jamaica strove to relegate members of subordinate racial groups to the margins of slave society as outsiders detrimental to the Anglicization of the colony, though of potential utility for defensive or economic purposes. On the issue of legal incapacity attached to specific mixed-race individuals, the assembly continued to entertain requests for ad hoc exceptions. It would take a major slave rebellion to push colonial officials in Jamaica to reconsider their racial assumptions regarding the proper line of distinction to be maintained between whites and the mixed offspring of Europeans and Africans, whether bound or free. While racial mixture had accelerated the "whitening" of the island through the perceived dilution of African blood, the elite planters who dominated the assembly increasingly questioned whether the process of racial transmutation would ultimately move in reverse, blackening rather than whitening the island. Intermixing with and incorporating the descendants of slaves into the white body politic appeared destined to transform Jamaica into a colony fit for none but "Negroes and Mulattoes."

CHAPTER 3

Whiteness and Hereditary Blood Status

In the early morning hours of Easter Monday, April 7, 1760, shortly after the redeployment of British troops stationed on Jamaica during the Seven Years' War, enslaved men and women in St. Mary parish rose up against their masters, initiating the first of a series of coordinated uprisings intended to overthrow the colony's white ruling order. Known as Tacky's Revolt after one of its principal African instigators, the rebellion resulted in over five hundred deaths and unleashed a wave of turmoil in Jamaica as the colonial establishment found itself in serious jeopardy for the first time since the Maroon War of the 1730s. So devastating was Tacky's Revolt that years later the planter-historian Edward Long pronounced it "more formidable than any hitherto known in the West Indies." At the time, however, authorities in Jamaica regarded the first spark of rebellion ignited in St. Mary as an isolated, containable incident. Immediately upon hearing of the uprising, the Jamaican-born lieutenant governor, Henry Moore, declared martial law, dispatched the local militia and soldiers from the Seventy-Fourth and Forty-Ninth Regiments, and called upon the Maroons at Crawford Town, Nanny Town, and Scotts Hall for assistance. Less than two weeks later, Moore reported confidently to the Board of Trade that the colonial counterinsurgency had "totally suppressed" the uprising. In July, British news coverage of the slave revolt repeated Moore's claim and, relying upon the same "Extract of a letter from a

Gentleman at St. Mary's," depicted the rebels as savage and querulous Africans, their ill-begot design doomed to failure.[1]

News reports in Britain trailed well behind events on the island. On May 25, 1760, a much larger revolt broke out in Westmoreland parish involving slaves from multiple plantations. Although colonial forces defeated the rebels and dispersed them from their encampment at the base of a small mountain range, survivors trekked north into Hanover parish and east across the mountains as far as Clarendon parish, attacking colonists' estates and burning cane fields along the way. By August 1760 coverage of the rebellion in Britain had shifted in response to these fresh developments. "The insurrection, it is now thought, was intended to be general," reported the *Universal Magazine*, "and their plan appears to have been a total massacre of all the Whites, and to make the island a negro colony." In addition to reassuring metropolitan readers that the rebellion would be swiftly suppressed and "the negroes reduced to their former obedience," British newspapers underscored the immense value of Jamaica's slave-produced exports to the nation. Discussion of the rebellion assumed a sharper tone as word of shocking white brutality reached Britain, confirming contemporary concerns that Jamaican planters, "in their indolence and fond desire for more and more Negroes," were like children "playing with Edge-Tools, which they cannot manage" and doomed to cut themselves. Twenty years earlier Governor Trelawny had reported that ten thousand white settlers held one hundred thousand black slaves in bondage, a situation, he feared, headed inexorably toward bloodshed. The disproportionate number of slaves on the island, and the horrific levels of violence needed to maintain white authority, placed the island in a permanently perilous position. If an anticipated joint French-Spanish invasion materialized, Jamaica would fall to the enemy and the jewel of the British Atlantic empire would be forever lost.[2]

Over the following year, as rebellious slaves wreaked havoc on some of the most profitable sugar plantations in the British Caribbean, killing dozens of whites in the process, colonial officials in Jamaica resorted to ever more spectacular displays of brutality. Rebels' ears and heads were cut off and displayed on poles; ringleaders were shackled in irons and hung up alive on gibbets erected in the parade of Kingston, where they languished for over a week before perishing; hundreds were shot, hanged, whipped, or burnt at the stake; others committed suicide; and an additional five hundred rebels were forcibly exiled to Roatán, Britain's prison island off Honduras. "The murders and outrages they committed were thought to justify the cruel punishment inflicted upon them *in terrorem* to others," Long later noted, "but they appeared to be very little affected by it themselves; behaving all the time with a degree of hardened insolence, and brutal insensibility." British newspapers described these atrocious punishments in gory detail, and metropolitan commentators expressed a growing awareness that Britain's hold on Jamaica was remarkably tenuous—a troubling realization at a time when the arrival of an enemy fleet appeared imminent. "For as the negro slaves of that island, of which there are about one hundred thousand, their merciless masters know too well the cruelties they have practiced upon those miserable wretches, to expect any other return than betraying them to an enemy, or cutting their throats," observed the *Caledonian Mercury* in March 1762; "and of this there hath been such recent experience, by an open rebellion of the negroes in various parts of Jamaica for many months, that the only chance this nation hath of preserving it, if attacked, seems to be that of preventing the enemy from effecting a land."[3]

Tacky's Revolt, with its strategic aim to erect a new order from the ashes of the old slave system, profoundly altered British colonial discourses and policies toward enslaved Africans and their free descendants in Jamaica. As white colonists became more apprehensive of the vast numbers of African slaves upon which their livelihoods depended, the legislature called for close scrutiny of slave movements and harsh punishments for the slightest infractions. White attitudes toward free blacks and people of mixed ancestry in general also hardened, though the colonial government continued to grant exemptions to exceptional mixed-race individuals with blood and social ties to influential white men and extensive property in land and slaves. Meanwhile, in Britain, the brutal atrocities committed in Jamaica in the rebellion's aftermath, and sanctioned by the colonial government, cast doubt not only upon the justness of colonial slavery, but also upon the legitimacy of an imperial system that permitted divergent local practices antithetical to English legal principles. Metropolitan commentators called into question the civility and shared Britishness of Anglo West Indians, dismissing colonial arguments that the brutalization of slaves benefited private masters as well as the collective national interest. Jamaica in particular appeared poised on the brink of destruction, its colonists willing to jeopardize themselves and the British Atlantic empire in their single-minded pursuit of profit. The rupture of Tacky's Revolt magnified the emergent gulf between a distinctively British ideology of benevolent mastery, compatible with Protestant humanitarian principles, and West Indian slaveholding regimes predicated on white racial superiority and slaveholders' virtually limitless power to punish (figure 3).

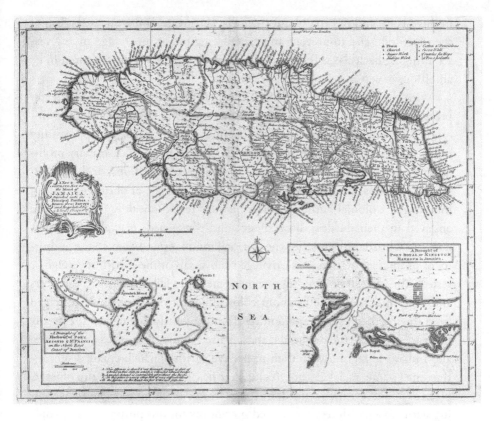

3. Emanuel Bowen, *A New and Accurate Map of the Island of Jamaica*
(London, 1752). Library of Congress, Geography and Map Division.

RESTORING WHITE RULE

In response to the near disaster of Tacky's Revolt, the Jamaican colonial
government reassessed its existing security provisions and policies toward the
island's majority population of African and mixed descent, both slave and
free. In October 1761, the same month the flames of rebellion appeared to
flicker out, the assembly initiated measures to suppress and deter slaves as well
as free people, with the dual intent of averting another mass insurrection and
buttressing the white colonial order. The proposed "Act to remedy the evils
arising from irregular assemblies of slaves, and to prevent their possessing
arms and ammunition, and going place to place without tickets; and for preventing the practice of obeah; and to restrain overseers from leaving the estates
under their care on certain days; and to oblige all free negroes, mulattoes, or
Indians, to register their names in the vestry-books of the respective parishes

in this island, and to carry about them the certificate, and wear the badge, of their freedom; and to prevent any captain, master, or supercargo of any vessel, bringing back slaves transported off the island," was unprecedented in its ambitious sweep and coverage.[4]

With this new statute, the colonial legislature aimed to track with greater precision the movements of slaves and free people of African and mixed lineage, depriving all potential internal enemies of the means and opportunity to conspire collectively against white settlers. In addition to customary prohibitions against unsupervised movements, group congregations, or the possession of weapons, the assembly also forbade the practice of obeah, or African folk magic. Colonial authorities and planters feared obeah emboldened the enslaved in their reckless disobedience and threatened to rival the preeminence of Christianity and thus the spiritual foundations on which the authority of propertied masters—as privileged subvassals of the British sovereign—rested. The burden of carrying out these measures fell primarily to overseers and other managerial staff, whom colonial authorities strongly discouraged from leaving their estates unattended. To more clearly distinguish the legally free and scrutinize their conduct, the act also required free blacks, mulattoes, and Indians to register with their respective parishes, which entailed submitting one's name, racial category/color, certificate of freedom and site of issue, place of abode, nature of freedom (born free or manumitted), and christening status to a parish register created specifically for this purpose. Free people were also instructed to carry proof of their free status and display a distinctive badge (a cross) on their persons at all times.[5]

By seeking to bring an end to British rule and institute an African kingdom in Jamaica, or so colonial authorities assumed, Tacky and his compatriots had left in their wake a legacy of fear and uncertainty not easily dissipated. The assembly viewed the growing masses of enslaved Africans and free blacks and persons of mixed ancestry with increasing distrust. Despite high mortality rates, the slave population had exploded to over 130,000 by 1755 as a result of continuous imports; the white population, in contrast, held steady at roughly 12,000, with less than half of white settlers fit to bear arms. By comparison, a 1761 estimate calculated a total of 3,408 free people of African and mixed lineage in Jamaica, with about 900 "fencible men" and steadily increasing numbers. An island-wide census conducted in 1774 underscored how poorly the white population had fared in comparison to imported slaves and manumitted or naturally reproducing free communities of African and mixed descent: 12,737 white settlers maintained a precarious grip over 192,787 slaves and 4,093 free blacks and mulattoes, roughly 1,200 of whom composed 20 percent of the colony's total militia corps. Between 1702 and 1775, an estimated 497,736 African captives disembarked at Jamaican ports, and around 360,622 remained on the island until their untimely deaths.[6]

After 1760, the hazards posed by the majority slave population to the white colonial order refocused attention on the ambiguous place of free people descended from enslaved ancestors in Jamaican plantation society. Rather than doing their duty and remaining willfully subordinate in a "useful" intermediate position between white settlers and the enslaved, free people had emerged as a class of colonial subjects with their own economic and political aspirations. Contemplating future domestic crises, colonial officials speculated whether, in all likelihood, the greater part of free blacks and people of mixed lineage would turn on the mass of slaves—their "natural brethren"—to support white settlers with whom they shared no, or only a partial and unofficial, blood connection. Concerns mounted that the servile, heathen heritage of freed slaves and their descendants had polluted their bloodlines. In mixed-race individuals, "black blood," colonial elites feared, would prove determinative—unless greatly diminished through multiple generations of mixture with white males and acculturation to Anglo-Protestant values and cultural norms. In later eighteenth-century Jamaica, perhaps more than anywhere else in the British Atlantic, the apparent preponderance of African blood among the island's inhabitants served as the discursive backdrop that shaped the contours of the political debate about the appropriate status for free people of African and mixed origin.

Accordingly, on the same day the assembly introduced the comprehensive "Act to remedy the evils arising from irregular assemblies of slaves," a committee of the whole house pronounced that affluent white men had devised and bequeathed too many large estates, real and personal, to their black/mulatto mistresses and "natural" mixed offspring. To remedy the perceived bastardization and Africanization of the island, members resolved to draw up a separate bill "to prevent the inconveniencies and mischiefs that may arise, from gifts and devises to mulattoes and negroes, who are not already entitled by law to the same rights and privileges with English subjects born of white parents." Disabling affluent free black and mixed-race individuals from protecting their property interests in court was central to the efficacy of such a measure. The following month, in response to a private petition seeking white legal privileges for Jane Harris, a free mulatto woman, and her adult children John and Dorothy Elletson, reputed offspring of John Elletson, a deceased planter and former member for St. Thomas in the East, the assembly moved to alter all future private acts to prevent the beneficiaries from testifying against whites—except in cases of assaults to their persons. Now even the most elite free people of mixed blood granted the "same rights and privileges of English subjects, born of white parents" would hold these privileges "under certain restrictions." The assemblymen also refused to consent to the bill favoring the Elletsons until they struck Harris, the mulatto mother, from the petition.[7]

Although the Jamaican colonial government passed a total of twenty-five private acts between 1733 and 1760, granting around ninety-one mixed-race individuals some of the legal privileges of whiteness, after Tacky's Revolt the assembly deemed the provisions of these prior bills far too liberal. Private acts had enabled a small number of illegitimate men and women of mixed blood to inherit enormous wealth from white elites and to defend their property in civil suits. Both Tacky's Revolt and the growing prosperity of a minority of the nonwhite free population exacerbated fears that white settlers were losing ground to the descendants of slaves. While private acts granted individuals of mixed ancestry the right to enjoy some of the legal benefits of whiteness, the official grant of white status did not make the recipient, or his or her immediate family members, white by blood. It simply allowed the recipient to act *as if* she or he were white and descended from white parents in certain circumstances. This critical legal distinction embedded in the language of the bill assumed greater importance after 1760, as colonial authorities deployed the rule of law to fashion a more exclusive definition of British national and racial identity.[8]

On December 19, 1761, the assembly formally denounced the customary practice of transmitting property to illegitimate offspring born of African-Anglo sexual relations. In language that cast the entire free population as an inferior and spurious class of servile and tainted lineage, members passed an "Act to prevent the inconveniences arising from exorbitant grants and devices to negroes, and the issue of negroes" (also known as the Devises Act). Redefining and contracting the legal parameters of whiteness, the Devises Act specified that the legislature would recognize as white under the law only persons with sufficient documentation proving they were four degrees removed, rather than three, from an African ancestor, making it much more difficult for individuals of mixed lineage to pass officially as white subjects. Critically, the act barred all persons of illegitimate birth who fell outside the revised boundaries of whiteness, and had not yet received privilege bills exempting them from legal disabilities, from inheriting property from white settlers in excess of £2,000 Jamaican currency (£1,200 sterling). By the time the Board of Trade approved the act in Britain seven years later, after much controversy, the assembly had dispensed with the concession for those with preexisting privilege bills; the inheritance cap was now retroactive.[9]

RACIAL INHERITANCE AND CONSTITUTIONAL RIGHTS

The 1761 Devises Act constituted a remarkable policy shift for the lower house of the Jamaican legislature. After a century of defending their liberties and right to self-legislate as natural-born Englishmen, and progressively accepting the notion that the dilution of African blood through admixture with elite white males could whiten Jamaica, colonial policymakers changed their tune. For the first time since Jamaica's foundation as an English colony, the assembly moved to curb the constitutional right of colonists to dispose freely of their real and personal property, in the interest of the public welfare. When Sir Matthew Lamb, the successor to Francis Fane as legal counsel to the Board of Trade and an M.P. for Peterborough, perused the 1761 racial inheritance cap the following year, he opined that the act conflicted with fundamental English legal principles and the Crown should therefore disallow it, unless "the Publick Good of the Island requires it." "Nothing else can Justify such an Act which takes away the Right of Persons in Giving and Disposing of their own Estates and properties according to their own Wills and Intentions," Lamb emphasized. Surely unconstitutional restrictions placed on the entailment of private property constituted a case of colonial repugnancy.[10]

In response to the Board of Trade's request to clarify the rationale underlying the act's passage, the assembly asked Lovell Stanhope, the island's London agent, to forward to the board the results of an inquiry recently conducted by the legislature into the "exorbitant grants and devises [that] have been made to Negroes and Mulattoes or the illegitimate issue of the Negroes or Mulattoes within the fourth degree." The inquiry included a list of thirteen estate inventories and wills naming illegitimate, mixed-race offspring and/or women of African origin as principal beneficiaries of the estates of deceased white men. Here was material proof of the pressing need to stay the hand of white devisees, who had already transferred nearly a quarter of a million pounds in real and personal property to illegitimate persons of African and mixed lineage. Included were a number of prominent white men well known to the assembly, such as Gibson Dalzel and Peter Caillard, both of whom devised their estates to illegitimate mixed-blood children born to the mulatto woman Susanna Augier, whose property holdings they also augmented;

John Elletson, a former member of the assembly who bequeathed his estate to his two illegitimate mulatto children, John and Dorothy Elletson, whom the assembly had approved for a private bill the previous year; and the very wealthy William Foster, whose mulatto daughter, Anna Petronella Woodart, had received a private act passed in her favor and currently resided in Britain.[11]

According to a committee charged to investigate the extent of property held by nonwhites in Jamaica, multiple factors offered confirmation of the "Complexion and Illegitimacy" of the legatees of exorbitant grants and devises. These included public hearsay, or "Notoriety of the Fact"; private acts previously passed on behalf of the recipient(s); the application of the parties themselves for special exemptions; or the terms and language of the wills in which they were named. The assembly presented a handful of specific cases as evidence of the excessive and potentially dangerous stake free people of color held in Jamaica, and it is safe to assume that the men and women named in the list sent to London were not the primary targets of the inheritance cap. The island's free population of mixed ancestry was large and flourishing, and the bulk of this community lived, worked, and socialized in spheres well outside the surveillance of the colonial legislature. By restricting the ability of free people of African and mixed lineage from inheriting large estates, the assembly could halt the upward mobility of middling free people, nearly all of whom operated outside the direct interests and intimate circles of the white colonial regime.[12]

Stanhope, the voice of Jamaica's most elite freeholders as the island's agent in London, submitted an impassioned defense of the act to the Board of Trade. In his view, placing limits on inheritance for illegitimate persons descended from African slaves "is a Matter of such Consequence to the very existence of that Colony" that Stanhope emphasized his willingness to argue his case in person if necessary. For the only way to halt "the degeneration of a People, and the ruin of a Country" was "to prevent the illegitimate Issue of Slaves attaining a Superiority in Rank, Riches, and, in the Consequence, Power, over free men and their unmixed Descendents." Jamaica, a Caribbean slave colony wholly reliant upon captive African laborers and beset with an ever-worsening demographic crisis, differed strikingly from the mother country, Stanhope explained. Proposals to increase the white settler population had thus far failed, white women remained in short supply, and, moreover, "from the extream heat of the Climate [white women] are worn out sooner or become less amiable than they would be in a colder." The island's considerable demographic and gender imbalance had encouraged white men to indulge their basest appetites, leading "to a most scandalous degree, an unlawful commerce with Negro Slaves; which habit reconciles, and numbers sanctify."[13]

Stanhope wrote in defense of the 1761 Devises Act in an era when sexual unions between white men and slave women were commonplace, expected, and legally permissible. Yet illicit interracial intercourse had begun to take on more sinister connotations. As the numbers and wealth of the mixed-race community increased, colonial administrators resolved "to prevent their posterity from being overpowered by Mulattoes, the Descendents of their Slaves." Unconcerned with long-term consequences beyond the immediate gratification of their desires, white men, Stanhope argued, had seeded "a spurious Progeny, subjected by the Wisdom of the Law to many Disabilities" in the wombs of black women. Offering further proof of societal decay in Jamaica, Stanhope noted that some white men had devised large portions of their estates to illegitimate mixed-blood offspring who, due to their inability to vote, hold civil or military office, testify against whites in court, or command white obedience in any capacity, would never be anything but "useless members of Society." By refusing to devote themselves to "the legal propagation of Children by Marriage, and by that means to transmit property and power to a pure and legitimate race," white Creole males had placed Jamaica's "landed and other real property . . . in the hands of a spurious and illegitimate breed of Mulattoes." "Power ever follows property, and whenever they shall become possessed of the largest share of the Property, then it will be absurd and impossible to keep them out of Power," Stanhope stressed; "the Laws against them must be repealed, the Power will then be in their hands, and the Island become a Colony of Negroes and Mulattoes." Without local measures in place to prevent the descendants of slaves from claiming the birthright of Englishmen, specifically the right to political participation and civic engagement conferred by property ownership, Jamaican colonists would become "like their neighbours the American Spaniards"—"the most degenerate and dastardly People upon Earth."[14]

Not all middling or elite whites in Jamaica shared Stanhope's concerns or saw eye to eye with the assembly on the issue of racial inheritance. The debate surrounding the Devises Act became framed as a contest over the applicability of English law in a slave colony in which white men undermined the moral fabric of society by transmitting wealth to illegitimate, mixed-blood offspring. In the spring of 1763 three unnamed members of the council wrote to the Board of Trade in opposition to the inheritance cap, arguing that it violated "our most happy Constitution, by limiting and restraining the Power of

His Majesty's Subjects in disposing of their Estates at their own Pleasure . . . even when such Estates have been entirely the Acquisition of their own Industry and Economy." Stanhope considered the councilors' protest article by article and dismissed their claims out of hand. "The Constitution of a Colony like this is attended with peculiar Circumstances, which make a set of Laws very necessary there, that would be totally inconsistent with the System to be observed in the Mother Country," he asserted. As such, it was incumbent upon the legislature to restrain those who would dispose of their property to the detriment of society, especially men "so degenerate as to give or devise their real or personal property to Savages or their Bastard progeny." Furthermore, although the common law had wisely placed bastards "under severe disabilities," the treatment of bastards in England was beside the point. Stanhope took particular exception to the repugnancy principle for positioning the Crown as the ultimate authority on the constitutionality of colonial laws: Jamaican statutes might contradict English legal principles from time to time but such measures were essential to the interests of the colony.[15]

In his defense of the Devises Act, Stanhope privileged the primacy of local legislative authority over internal colonial matters. Deviations from English law, he stressed, were imperative in a distant slaveholding colony:

> There is so manifest and necessary a difference in the Policy of the Mother Country and the Colonies, as Slavery, distinction of Colour and disability to the fourth degree, that if the violation of our happy Constitution is to be applied to Jamaica, there is no law of that Country violated; on the contrary strengthened by this law. The Colonies are to conform as nearly as they can to the Laws of the Mother Country but in numberless instances their situation and policy points out the contrary. If they pass Laws for promoting Trade, Commerce, Cultivation, and civil policy, founded on experience necessity & sound local policy, tho' they are contrary to laws of the Mother Country they are to be supported.

Therefore, if local circumstances dictated that the colonial legislature should pass measures to restrain men's appetites, "to prevent the Son of the Bound Woman from being Heir with the Son of the Free Woman," then neither the councilors nor the British government should stand in the way. The authority to determine legislation for the public good of the colony lay not in the hands of private individuals easily swayed by their lusts or affections or even at the center of empire but with the elected members of the assembly.[16]

For council members opposed to the Devises Act, the debate over colonial lawmaking and constitutional authority could not be separated from provincial racial definitions, ties of blood, and the birthright of British subjects overseas. Since 1733, colonial policy in Jamaica had specified that informal ties of consanguinity between white men and African-descended women and their offspring, though outside the law, nonetheless transmuted the mixed descendants of African slaves into white subjects over three successive generations. It contravened Jamaican law, then, these councilors insisted, for the assembly to prevent freeborn British colonists from making sufficient provision for their natural offspring, "even tho' they sho'd be removed *three Degrees* from the Negro Ancestor, and consequently are seven eights White, and not distinguishable from white Persons, and altho' the Ancestors of such Offspring, on the Mother's Side, have been free for many generations." Enforcing distinctions of blood between white settlers and their mixed offspring—distinctions that would no longer exist in law after one or two more generations—seemed to these critics both needless and unconstitutional. What threat did mixed-race individuals with all the advantages of white paternal benefactors and a Protestant upbringing pose to whites in Jamaica? Such individuals stood to lose as much from a slave insurrection as the white landowners whose behavior, culture, faith, and bloodlines they had imbibed.[17]

The overwhelming majority of influential Jamaican politicians and planters, both those resident on the island and absentees in London, supported the law, prompting others who might have spoken in opposition to remain silent. In May 1763, the Board of Trade reached out to Rose Fuller, a member of the House of Commons with strong interests in Jamaica. Thirty years earlier, Fuller had inherited his father's estates on the island; he was elected to the assembly in 1735, joined the council in 1737, and soon thereafter was appointed judge of the Jamaica supreme court. After a period of absence from the island in the 1740s due to a factional dispute with Governor Trelawny, Fuller returned to Jamaica in 1752, when Governor Knowles succeeded Trelawny, and took up an appointment as chief justice of Jamaica. Three years later, upon the death of his older brother, Fuller settled permanently in England, now a very wealthy man with extensive property in Jamaica and an eye toward running for higher political office. As a result of Fuller's stature and vocal support for Jamaica in Parliament, the Board of Trade frequently consulted him on West Indian affairs.[18]

On this occasion the board desired, as Fuller detailed in his response, "to know the Sentiments of the Principal Gentlemen of Jamaica and my own upon the Act passed in that Island in 1761 Intitled an Act to prevent the Inconvenicencys arising from exorbitant Grants and Devises made by White Persons to Negroes and the Issue of Negroes." Fuller immediately scheduled a meeting at his centrally-located house on Gerrard Street, known for its coffeehouses and taverns, inviting "several Gentlemen of large Property there, to know their sentiments thereupon." John Morrant and Florentinus Vassall, who together owned multiple Jamaican plantations, attended Fuller's meeting, as did several members of the wealthy Pennant family: John Pennant, eldest surviving son of Edward Pennant, a Clarendon planter and former chief justice of Jamaica; Henry Pennant; and Richard Pennant (later Lord Penrhyn). All expressed themselves "unanimously in opinion for the Act." Fuller also sent a copy of the act to William Beckford, twice lord mayor of London, M.P. for the city of London, "and the most powerful of the absentee planters in the capital." Beckford authorized Fuller "to declare he thought it unnecessary, and that is my own sentiment," Fuller added. His personal opinion aside, Fuller informed John Pownall, secretary to the Board of Trade, that he had "no thoughts of making a formal Opposition to the Confirmation of the said Act, and, as the Majority of those to whom I have communicated about it are for it, I decline stating in writing any objections against it." Gentlemen with interests in Jamaica deemed it expedient to present a united front. Proponents of the Devises Act and their allies favored curtailing settlers' personal liberties if such measures prevented Jamaica from becoming, as Stanhope prophesized, "a Colony of Negroes and Mulattoes."[19]

PRESERVING THE BRITISH RACIAL INHERITANCE

In the aftermath of Tacky's Revolt the assembly instituted a blanket moratorium on the socioeconomic mobility of illegitimate mixed-race people in Jamaica by cutting off their ability to inherit substantial property from white patrons. At the same time, it strategically exhibited a permissive attitude toward ad hoc exceptions. After the passage of the 1761 Devises Act, greater numbers of free people with intimate ties to elite, politically influential white men petitioned for legal exemptions, and the majority of these requests for additional privileges were granted. While relatively few individuals of mixed lineage, or their poor or middling white male patrons, possessed the resources or connections to initiate such procedures on behalf of themselves or their family members, those with claims to large estates and wealthy white benefactors continued to do so. To achieve their public policy objective of permanent white hegemony, Jamaica's governing elites aimed to disinherit the colony's "spurious and illegitimate breed of mulattoes" whose existence, they argued, prevented white men from marrying white women and propagating pure and legitimate heirs. Exceptions to the general rule remained possible for the blood kin and mistresses of prominent white men. However, by linking the rights and privileges associated with British subjecthood more firmly to white racial identity, while simultaneously retaining legislative loopholes for select individuals of mixed heritage, colonial administrators inadvertently underscored the elasticity of the British racial inheritance in Jamaica.

In December 1763, Sarah Morris, a well-to-do free quadroon woman of Kingston, twice petitioned the assembly on behalf of herself and her four-year-old daughter, Charlotte Stirling, requesting that a private bill be introduced granting each of them "the privileges and immunities of a white woman in this island." Claiming that she "was seized and possessed, in her own right, of houses, lands, and slaves, to the value of £4,000 and upwards," Morris pressed the legislature to confer on herself and her daughter the legal privileges that wealthy whites alone possessed.[20] Her only child, Charlotte, she explained, was the "reputed daughter" of the late Robert Stirling, a successful Kingston merchant and owner of one of the largest slave forces in Jamaica. Stirling had left Scotland in 1742 and began his career in Jamaica as a successful trader before purchasing Frontier Plantation in St. Mary parish in 1748 and, with his brother James's assistance, Hampden Estate in the parish of St. James in the 1750s. Although Stirling's expertise as a trader trumped his planting skills, after his death Stirling's estate probated at £76,343, including 750 slaves, though he owed substantial debts to creditors. Baptismal records confirm that Charlotte Stirling was born in Kingston on October 23, 1759, and baptized the following month as "the daughter of Sarah Morris a free Mulatto woman by Robert Stirling Esq." Until Charlotte came of age, Morris intended to provide her with a genteel education in England, "or some other place, as might qualify her to enjoy the privileges and immunities of a white woman in this island."[21]

At first glance, there is nothing unusual about Sarah Morris's request for a private bill granting her legal exemptions. Between 1733 and 1802, fifty-four women of varying degrees of African ancestry—and one woman of mixed Indian and European descent—petitioned the assembly for the privileges of white subjects, in some cases repeatedly, and most justified their appeal by emphasizing their affluent status, Christian upbringing and education, and personal connections to prominent white men. Forty-five British male settlers also presented private privilege petitions during this period, primarily on behalf of their own or others' illegitimate mixed offspring and less frequently for their African-descended mistresses or, in a few exceptional cases, wives. Yet Morris was the first woman of mixed lineage to use gender-specific terms and petition on her own behalf explicitly for "the privileges and immunities of a white woman in this island." Female petitioners of varying degrees of African ancestry, or those white men who presented their petitions, typically requested a bill entitling themselves and their family members "to the same rights and privileges with English subjects, born of white parents" or to "the like benefits allowed to other free mulattoes." There was more than one way to ask for rights. But in all of these cases the white mother, and the white womb through which passage would have entitled the petitioner to white status at birth, remained a shadowy presence in the background. Petitioners born of African-descended mothers never formulated direct claims to legal and social equality with white women. Nor did they openly evoke or otherwise encroach upon the privileges of white femininity in Jamaican slave society.[22]

A closer look at Sarah Morris's life and petitions offers evidence of her keen awareness of the material and social value of both British blood and white womanhood in colonial Jamaica. In the 1760s, when Morris first requested legal exemptions, she resided in Kingston, the largest and wealthiest metropolis in the British Caribbean, with approximately nine hundred households and thirteen thousand residents. The Kingston parish tax list for 1765 records Morris as owning a residence valued at thirty pounds on lower King Street in the East Division and paying two pounds, five shillings in yearly taxes. According to the tax list, Morris lived alongside a small community of free women, including four "free negroes" and two "free mulattoes," clustered together on lower King Street. Her residence was valued at a much higher rate than those of the other women, who owned or leased property valued at twelve pounds on average. In the early nineteenth century, Simon Taylor, one of the richest and most influential planters in Jamaica, remarked that "in the year 1760 there were only three Quadroon Women in the Town of Kingston." While Taylor's claim is difficult to verify, Morris did indeed hold pride of place as Kingston's sole tax-paying quadroon on the 1765 parish tax list. Free blacks, followed by free mulattoes, composed the largest subset of Kingston's nonwhite taxpaying community (around one hundred people total), and a significant share of these individuals resided in the East Division, where they paid 3.2 percent of the overall parish tax for their division that year. These individuals no doubt ran in far different social circles than the 60 percent of the town's population who were enslaved.[23]

Mid-eighteenth-century Kingston was a bustling, populous urban space where, for many migrants, the prospect of sizeable financial success outweighed the substantial risk of an early death (figure 4). It was no secret that Kingston's churchyard, as one commentator wrote, "is perhaps one of the most *greedy Graves* in the whole Earth." The town's location adjoining several swamps, which bred mosquitoes carrying malaria and yellow fever, contributed to the high mortality. Despite as much as a one in five mortality rate during especially sickly years, Kingston was better situated than its rival Port Royal to survive hurricanes and earthquakes and allow for urban expansion. After the bulk of the mercantile community abandoned Port Royal in the 1710s, Kingston flourished, becoming not only the island's commercial hub and major port of entry for African slaves but also a center of white society, free black and Jewish life, and female social and economic activity.

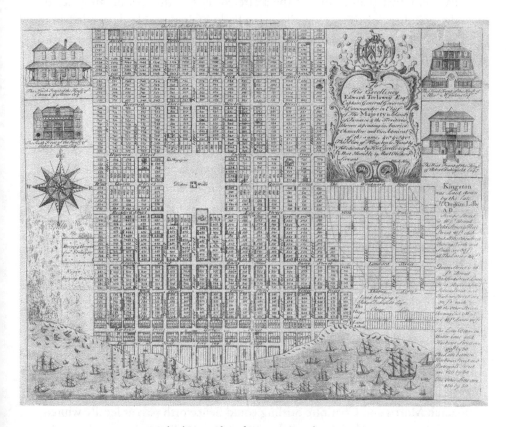

4. Michael Hay, *Plan of Kingston* (London, c. 1745).
Library of Congress, Geography and Map Division.

Contemporaries considered it "a fine Town, well situate, and large; here the most considerable Merchants reside, and this makes it a Place of vast Trade." "Kingston," noted a British officer who visited the island in June 1764, "is now the most trading and only very considerable town in the island." "It is large and very well inhabited, the streets spacious and regularly laid out, cutting one another at right angles, and in the upper part of the town, called the Savannah, there are many sumptuous houses with gardens and offices in proportion." By the late eighteenth century, over one-third of white women and more than half of free women of African and mixed ancestry lived in Kingston, many making their living renting out rooms and charging, in the eyes of visitors, "extravagant" rates.[24]

Morris resided within Kingston itself, in the densely populated south central area, bounded by Church Street, Harbour Street, Orange Street, and the Parade, rather than in one of the scattered huts in the "periurban zone" on the periphery of town with the main body of free people descended from slaves, or on the far southeastern edge of town where free people of means tended to cluster. As a wealthy quadroon woman with ties to a deceased white slaveholder of substantial property and with a daughter classified as "mestee," whose future children with white men would automatically attain white status at birth, Sarah Morris held an extraordinary position. Her actions signpost her intention to use Jamaica's unofficial patronage system as an opening to force recognition of her own and her daughter's blood connection to whiteness as a means of improving their legal standing and future prospects. For the assembly, the central issue of consideration was whether to recognize these unofficial blood ties and grant the moneyed Morris some of the legal advantages afforded to white settlers, but certainly not the full privileges accompanying white womanhood. The assembly responded favorably to Sarah Morris's petition, but the wording of the final bill passed in her favor was standard for those granted after 1761, when the provisions of private acts to expand the rights of free people became strictly limited. The legislature entitled Morris and her daughter, Charlotte, to receive "the same rights and privileges of English subjects born of white parents, *under certain restrictions,*" including the inability to testify against whites in court except in cases of assault, to receive significant grants or devises from white persons, or to inherit real or personal property valued above two thousand pounds from whites. Sarah Morris and Charlotte Stirling could henceforth pass as legally white— and Kingston tax lists indicate that Morris eventually lost her quadroon designation—but neither woman received license to claim the "privileges and immunities of a white woman in this island." In other words, although both women could enjoy a lesser version of white status, the legislature did not erase their servile African origins.[25]

In November 1784, over twenty years after Sarah Morris first petitioned for the privileges associated with white womanhood, she again appealed for legal exemptions. Passing now as a white woman on Knight Street in Kingston's Upper West Division, where increasing numbers of middling and wealthy whites migrated during the late eighteenth century for the salubrious air, Morris petitioned specifically in the interest of her twenty-five-year-old daughter, Charlotte. Her daughter, Morris claimed, "hath long been, and now is, in Great-Britain, where she has received a very liberal education, under the immediate care and patronage of William Stirling, esq, of Keir, her uncle." Both women were already entitled to some of the privileges of white subjects, but Morris now sought the permission of the legislature to dispose of her "very considerable estate" in favor of her British-educated daughter. Morris needed official permission because the assembly had approved Morris's original private privilege bill after passage of the 1761 act preventing all nonwhites from inheriting large estates. The timing of her earlier request for white legal status placed Morris and her daughter at the losing end of the Jamaican legislature's harder line toward people of mixed ancestry's social mobility. In light of Morris's remarkable circumstances, the committee appointed to consider her petition decided to grant her request, noting "that a bill should be brought in, to remove every incapacity in the said Sarah Morris, to grant and devise her estate and effects to her daughter, as she may think proper, and to enable her and her issue to have, hold, and enjoy the same, notwithstanding the said act."[26]

Sarah Morris emerged in Kingston parish tax records in 1791 for the last time, before disappearing from the historical record entirely. Listed as the owner of a residence worth forty-five pounds on Mordant Street, still in the West Division, Morris also leased a nearby property to William Cleland for forty pounds per annum and served as the executrix for Robert Young. She had come far since first petitioning the assembly nearly thirty years earlier. Although much remains unknown about Morris's life and the fate of her daughter, her remarkable climb up Kingston's race-based hierarchy demonstrates that whiteness had transformative social symbolic and economic value in eighteenth century Jamaica. Access to white status and legal privileges enabled a tiny proportion of women of mixed ancestry to gain a share of wealth and social mobility unimaginable for the overwhelming majority of men and women descended from slave ancestors. Individual, and soon collective, attempts by free people such as Morris to attain the benefits and legal protections afforded to white settlers suggest a growing awareness of the disabilities suffered by particular classes of colonial subjects based on assumptions about ancestry and the superiority of European Protestant bloodlines. While white lineage, or the diminution of African blood through mixture with white males over successive generations, determined access to the rights and privileges of British subjects by law in Jamaica, informal whitening practices that predated and paralleled official grants enabled whiteness to remain a malleable social and legal category. Indeed, the enduring pliability of whiteness as a socio-legal construct could lead to uncertain outcomes for individuals of questionable antecedents.[27]

Following the passage of the 1761 Devises Act, the integrity of the white female body took on heightened significance, as only the progeny of white women's wombs could inherit substantial wealth and property. Thus while certain light-skinned individuals continued to pass as white, the legal repercussions for doing so without formal authorization held the potential to impact the property claims and financial welfare of entire families. The impecunious Robert Cooper Lee, for example, arrived in Jamaica in 1749 and, with the assistance of Rose Fuller, a family friend, began training as a lawyer. He was admitted to the Inns of Court in London two years later and by 1764 had risen to the position of crown solicitor. Lee remained on the island another seven years before returning to England and marrying his Jamaican-born, long-term mistress, Priscilla Kelly, in October 1771. As the "natural" daughter of Chief Justice Dennis Kelly, Kelly was illegitimate and of debatable racial ancestry, though apparently of sufficient fairness to pass as white. She may have been originally baptized under the name Margaret, daughter of Dennis Kelly and Ann Right, on November 12, 1738, in Kingston, and born on October 3, 1738. In his will, Dennis Kelly left her a £500 legacy at age eighteen or whenever she married.[28]

For Lee to have married an illegitimate mixed-race woman descended from slave ancestors was highly unusual. Their union would not have increased Lee's standing among Creole elites in Jamaica. By then, the couple had already produced four children, Frances, Robert, Richard, and Matthew, and three more soon followed. Lee was eager to legitimize his family and secure their inheritance as soon as they arrived in England. In metropolitan Britain, the Lees' illicit background and mixed origins could fade quietly into the backdrop. Therefore, on November 16, 1776, Lee petitioned the assembly, by means of his attorney, Richard Welch, for authorization to devise his estate as he wished. Legislative permission was critical, Lee explained, due to the uncertain legal status of his wife, with whom he "hath several children, who, though now considered as not affected by, or within the intent and meaning of the said act; yet, as doubts may hereafter arise from lapse of time and want of evidence, when the witnesses may be dead who could prove the same, and the right of such children to take any estates, real or personal, by deed or will, may be contested." As the committee to which Lee's petition was referred for consideration observed in their report, although "the children of the said Robert Cooper Lee were born of the body of a reputed white woman" and thus "not within the intent and meaning of a certain act," racial status by evidence of hearsay was a shaky foundation upon which to base property claims. Consequently, the committee contended that "to remove any such doubts, and to prevent any evil or mischief that may attend such children, by attempts hereafter to bring them within the intent and meaning of the said act, a bill should be brought in, agreeably to the prayer of [Lee's] petition." Lee's bill passed the house less than a week later and received Crown confirmation the following year in London. Henceforth, the Jamaican legislature would account the mixed-blood children of Robert Cooper Lee and his wife of questionable antecedents white subjects in law, authorized to inherit property without restriction.[29]

African-descended Jamaicans did not passively accept the inferior and alien identity consigned to them under the law but actively advocated for civil rights by invoking their status as British subjects with blood ties to the white community. However, as the 1761 Devises Act intended, very few obtained positions of high social status or acquired substantial wealth from whites or otherwise. By 1784, in addition to Sarah Morris, only nine other individuals—all white men, two of whom made their case to the assembly more than once, acting on behalf of their mixed offspring—had skirted the financial limitations imposed upon them by the inheritance cap. Those elite few who did acquire wealth, education, and connections desired legislative confirmation of their elevated social status above the common class of free people. Others of lesser means joined with free blacks to protest their increased tax burden under the deficiency acts, which penalized them for not employing enough white men and thereby put their families in an intractable situation. Petitioning the assembly in 1773, a group of "sundry quadroons, mulattoes, and free negroes" explained that when they hired white men, they were "obliged to submit themselves to the humour of every white man they so employ, who oftentimes take advantage of the situation of the petitioners, not being on an equal footing with them, and treat the petitioners with great incivility." Denied common law protections, free people existed in a defenseless state of legal liminality.[30]

During the same period that Sarah Morris petitioned for additional privileges, three men of mixed lineage—the wealthy quadroon planter John William Hicks; Dugald Clarke, a mulatto inventor; and John Donaldson, a mulatto overseer of Clarendon parish—petitioned the assembly for pre-1761 privileges. Clarke asked for the right to vote and hold public office and to give testimony against whites in all cases, citing his careful study of "the principles of mathematics," which he believed rendered him "useful to the public." Donaldson requested the same waiver on the basis of his management position on a sugar plantation, and even received support from the committee appointed to examine his case, but was ultimately denied. None of the petitioners specifically requested or required exemptions from the property restrictions imposed by the 1761 Devises Act, however. That white men alone petitioned for the right to bequeath property to their illegitimate mixed-race children makes Morris's personal appeal to the assembly to waive the inheritance cap in favor of her daughter all the more exceptional. Moreover, even requests for exemptions made by prominent white men—such as William Patrick Browne, a member of the assembly in the mid-1760s for St. John and later a council member, and the planter George Brooks of St. Elizabeth parish—while granted, generated debate. A faction in the house opposed lifting the property restrictions imposed upon illegitimate mixed-race children as a matter of racial principle but were continually overruled by the majority in favor of personal exceptions.[31]

REPRODUCING WHITE COLONIAL SUBJECTS

In the decades after Tacky's Revolt, attempts to encourage marriage and the reproduction of legitimate white children failed to alter Jamaica's decidedly African demographic makeup. As the number of whites declined, the enslaved and free population of African descent showed a strong and steady uptick. In October 1773, colonial officials appointed a committee to inquire into the exact numbers of "free negroes, free mulattoes, and free Indians, registered in the vestry books, or residing in the several parishes in this island." The results of the inquiry confirmed how little influence colonial officials held over the free population; with the exception of free people in Kingston and St. Catherine, relatively few had obeyed the law and registered with their local parish. Two months later, a committee of the house presented a report of even greater concern, demonstrating that the slave population had increased from 99,239 in 1740 to around 200,000 in the early 1770s. Yet only 3,000 new settlers had augmented the white population, which grew from 13,000 to 16,000 during the same period. Another 1773 report submitted by the governor, Sir Basil Keith, to Stephen Fuller, Jamaica's London agent and the brother of Rose Fuller, presented an even bleaker outlook. Governor Keith listed a slave population of 202,787, a white population "by the best calculation" of only 12,737, and 4,093 "Free Negroes and other casts." Fuller was floored by Keith's figures: "Whites 12,737 and Slaves 202,787. Which is within a trifle of 16 to 1, being 15.9 to 1. And if you reckon the free Negroes as above, they will be 16.24 to 1 White." The situation in Jamaica had passed the point of no return. With the island completely overrun with African slaves and their free descendants, and stable white families in short supply, Jamaica appeared dangerously unsuitable for whites—particularly white women and children. By choosing the path that led to the greatest wealth combined with the utmost risk to their own and their children's safety, British settlers in Jamaica had imperiled the long-term future of white settlement on the island.[32]

In his 1774 history of Jamaica, Edward Long included a general estimate of the island's population surveyed in 1762–63. Long counted a total of 3,408 "free Blacks and Mulattos" on the island, of whom 1,093 resided in Kingston and 872 in St. Catherine, but he also admitted that these numbers were based on official certificates of freedom granted after 1761 and not careful census data. "They increase very fast," Long concluded, and "are since increased to upwards of three thousand seven hundred, principally in the towns; and, I think, we may reckon one thousand five hundred of them for serviceable men, fit for able service in the Militia." As Long indicated, the free community had already begun to expand rapidly by the 1760s and this trend continued. The planter-historian Bryan Edwards estimated that ten thousand "persons of mixed blood, and native blacks, of free condition" resided in Jamaica in 1791, forming 25 percent of the total free population on the island. According to Gad Heuman's calculations, by the final decades of slavery free people numbered roughly forty-two thousand in Jamaica, well over two and half times the white population and 11.4 percent of the total population.[33]

As Jamaica's failure to become a white settler society seemed more and more certain, it is perhaps unsurprising that colonial lawmakers proposed a number of measures to combat both the rising numbers of free people of African extraction and the morbid decline of the white population. The assembly proposed a bill to limit manumissions and considered placing a discretionary tax on white bachelors above the age of twenty-one. The latter measure provoked controversy and split the house, as many of the members were bachelors and would thus be subjecting themselves to financial penalties. The legislature also seized on rare opportunities to declare mixed-race families with respectable white patriarchs, whose members hovered just outside the legal parameters of whiteness, white in law. On November 18, 1774, for example, Thomas Ross presented a petition on behalf of Mary Stott, "a free quadroon woman," and their five illegitimate "mestee" sons. Ross had baptized and raised them as good Protestants and intended to educate them, he said, "to qualify them for business, and to earn their bread in a reputable way." Members of the assembly responded positively to Ross's petition and introduced a motion that his reputed children, being "persons so near to the degree of white persons," should receive privileges "beyond those of late usually granted."[34]

Permitting the generation of new white settlers through the bodies of women legally classified as one step away from whiteness also occurred on rare occasions during this period. On November 18, 1782, for example, Thomasina Ross Ewers, "a free mustee woman" educated in Britain and possessed of property in land and slaves, petitioned on her own behalf for the privileges of a white subject. In response to her petition, the assembly agreed that Ewers, "being within one remove from white people, and whose children, by a white man, will be white children according to the laws of this island, a committee should be appointed to bring in a bill, granting the said Thomasina Ross Ewers the privileges of giving testimony in all cases whatever." The lightening of Ewers had occurred through mixture between African-descended women and white males over multiple generations, precisely as the 1731 act defining "mulatto" status had anticipated. As the assembly saw it, Ewers's genealogy embodied the linear upward progression from black to white, and members sought to facilitate the legal process by which her descendants would move closer still to whiteness.[35]

Increasing reliance upon companies of rangers composed of African-descended men willing to pursue runaway slaves through wooded and mountainous areas that white men were unwilling to traverse also led to unconventional proposals. Due to a shortage of white men able to bear arms, freedmen composed over 25 percent of ordinary troops by 1788, a number that continued to expand as the century wore on. Finding that "where rangers have been raised, and the captains have resided with their men, and kept them in due obedience, they have greatly added to the security of the parish, and sundry runaways have been taken up," the assembly determined to offer the greatest encouragement to convince free men to enlist. Consequently, "all free negroes and mulattoes, who shall faithfully serve in the said companies for three years, and upon obtaining a certificate thereof . . . shall be entitled to the same privileges as white people, under the usual restrictions in acts passed for giving such privileges to free negroes and mulattoes." Proponents of such measures assured the colonial government that free men of African and mixed blood were "inured by nature to this climate" and possessed "intimate knowledge of the woods and defiles of this county." Enlisting their defensive aid in exchange for limited liberties "would render the defence of the island so perfect, that the preparations of an enemy, however, apparent against Jamaica, need not disturb the tranquility of its inhabitants."[36]

For the Jamaican legislature, maintaining control over the grant of white privileges to persons of mixed lineage proved an effective mechanism for fulfilling the pragmatic aims of white elites, despite growing ideological concerns about race and sexuality. Although colonial officials desperately sought to bolster white settlement on the island, they had also long assumed that that the bodies of Africans and people of mixed blood were better suited to a harsh tropical climate. Sexual mixture with nonwhites, then, while far from ideal, did have its uses—particularly if it led to the birth of white offspring of hardier stock over multiple generations. Two divergent strands of thought regarding racial mixture vied for dominance in late eighteenth-century Jamaica: one pragmatic and driven by demographic necessity, viewing the legal whitening of free people as the lesser of two evils; the other fearful of the prospect of white settlers degenerating as a result of admixture with individuals of African blood. Without an indisputable claim to white racial ancestry, Jamaican colonists risked imperiling their exclusive identity as freeborn white Britons. Many in Jamaica would have agreed with Benjamin Franklin's contention that "the number of purely white people in the world is proportionably very small." In a sea of black, tawny, and swarthy peoples, he mused, "the Saxons only [are] excepted, who with the English make the principal body of white people on the face of the earth. I could wish their numbers were increased." In colonial Jamaica, the question, as always, was *how.*[37]

Thomas Jefferson, another influential Anglo-American who pondered the problem of heterogeneous populations, dismissed racial mixture as a means of productively peopling a nation. In *Notes on the State of Virginia* (1787) he decried the intermingling of whites with free people of African descent,

who "whether originally a distinct race, or made distinct by time and circumstances, are inferior to the whites in the endowments both of body and
mind." Emancipating Africans, and inviting manumitted slaves and their
descendants to join the political community, threatened efforts to keep the
races "as distinct as nature has formed them." The Romans, Jefferson argued,
enslaved fellow whites; thus "emancipation required but one effort. The slave,
when made free, might mix with, without staining the blood of his master.
But with us a second is necessary, unknown to history. When freed he is
to be removed beyond the reach of mixture." But, once "removed," where
should free persons of African descent dwell? Jefferson imagined the American republic's ideal future as unambiguously white and homogenous, "with a
people speaking the same language, governed in similar forms, and by similar
laws," free from "either blot or mixture on that surface." The West Indian islands, in contrast, seemed an ideal repository for unwanted, tainted peoples.
"Inhabited already by a people of their own race and color; climates congenial
with their natural constitution; insulated from the other descriptions of men;
nature seems to have formed these islands to become the receptacle of the
blacks transplanted into this hemisphere." Yet it was precisely the projected
future of the colonial Caribbean as the "receptacle of the blacks" that white
West Indians railed against.[38]

RACE MIXING AND BRITISH BLOODLINES

Multiple conflicting discourses regarding racial mixture existed simultaneously during this period, and colonial and metropolitan opinions on the
topic could differ dramatically. Mixture was associated with the alteration
of a race, or stock, of people over time—for good or ill. Whether the mixing of two separate races produced negative consequences for one or both
groups depended on the perceived nature of the peoples in question. Since
the medieval period, a number of chroniclers and historians had emphasized
the hybrid pedigree of the English as a defining feature of national identity.
Mixture with one or more mythical or newly arrived alien nations—Trojans,
Romans, Normans, Saxons, and Danes—underlay the various iterations of
the English origin myth. Mixture with foreign peoples over successive generations gave rise to "one stocke and nation" whose "native barbarism" had
been purged and "mollified and civilized with Religion, and good Arts." The
superiority of English civility, temperament, culture, language, and law owed
its distinctive character to the mixture of native and foreign bloodlines. As

Edward Chamberlayne observed in his popular *Angliae Notitia; or, The Present State of England* (originally published in 1669), "English blood at this day is a *mixture* chiefly of *Norman* and *Saxon,* not without a *tincture* of *Danish, Romish,* and *British* Blood." If the nation's collective character as embodied in discourses of blood had achieved a harmonious balance, further mixture with alien peoples would destabilize British bloodlines, leading to racial degeneration.[39]

Eighteenth-century political theorists, as the comments of Franklin and Jefferson attest, typically conceived of an ideal national community in terms of racial homogeneity, eschewing the realities of increasing ethnic diversity. But in a slave society like Jamaica with a nominal white settler community, the dominant presence and character of the colony was African rather than British. Sexual mixture between white colonists and African slaves and their descendants, while it might improve the latter, some insisted, would steadily lessen the purity of British bloodlines in Jamaica, to the permanent detriment of the colony and the British Empire. Moreover, racial mixture and illegitimacy went hand in hand, and by the mid-eighteenth century, British authorities and reformers were already concerned that sexual license had led to an increase in nonmarital unions and high levels of bastardy throughout Britain. These concerns, while not universal or uniform, produced numerous plays, poems, and novels focused on illegitimate children and foundlings and contributed to the passage of the Marriage Act in 1753. Interracial sex in Jamaican plantation society was prefigured as a perversion of the natural order on a scale far more heinous than illicit or adulterous sex between unmarried men and women in Britain.[40]

Metropolitan cultural representations of depraved West Indian Creoles flourished during the second half the eighteenth century, tapping into growing concerns that the debauchery of slaveholders had diluted British racial purity and power in the Atlantic empire. A variety of interrelated factors connected to concerns about whiteness and national security, and the deteriorating position of British West Indians in the expanding empire after the Seven Years' War and following the losses of the American Revolution, influenced this shift. In the latter decades of the eighteenth century, condemnatory language directed at Creoles represented the culmination of several centuries of discourse critical of migrants who ventured beyond the geographic boundaries of the kingdom, subjecting themselves and their descendants to unfamiliar soils, climes, and sexual relations that could potentially transform, or even denature, English bloodlines. British commentators chastised white

West Indian men for refusing to master their lusts and took white Creole women to task for their supposed failure to at once reproduce Anglo-Protestant moral standards and satisfy white male sexual needs in colonial slave society.[41]

Like their female counterparts at home, white Creole women's value lay primarily in their role as the biological reproducers of natural-born British subjects and in their sociocultural reproductive capacity. Idealized as delicate, maternal, and unspoiled within their own culture, white Creole women were also expected to emulate the norms of metropolitan polite society and exert a civilizing influence on British West Indian males. Notwithstanding the secure position of white women in West Indian slave society, the burden to imitate imported gender conventions and reproduce whiteness in culturally hybrid colonial spaces served to underline white Creole women's insufficiencies and the general disorder of the Caribbean colonies. As Mary Fissell points out, for early modern English people, the gender order served as a fundamental organizing principle that "provided a wealth of metaphors for disarray and disorder"; gender norms and relations were "fragile, always in need of being re-enacted and reinforced."[42]

A wide variety of popular British media produced during the 1760s and 1770s exhibited negative attitudes toward white Creoles and singled out Anglo-Jamaicans for particular attack. Ranging from farcical plays and operas, such as Samuel Foote's *The Patron* (1764), Isaac Bickerstaff's *Love in the City* (1767), and Richard Cumberland's *The West Indian* (1771), to poems, including John Singleton's *A General Description of the West Indian Islands* (1767), and novels, like Sarah Scott's *History of George Ellison* (1766) and Elizabeth Bonhote's *Rambles of Mr. Frankly* (1773), unflattering depictions of white West Indians had far-reaching consequences. Foote's *The Patron* introduced the character of Sir Peter Pepperpot, a buffoonish Creole who prefers a woman "sweet as a sugar-cane, strait as a bamboo, and her teeth as white as a Negro's." When Elizabeth Bonhote's Mr. Frankly encounters "A West Indian!" in the capital, he muses that, "He seems to forget he has left a land of slaves. He never was in England before—That is an excuse for him." In Cumberland's *The West Indian,* Belcour, a Jamaican "West-Indian, fresh landed, and full of cash" is depicted as a gullible, reckless character too "accustomed to a land of slaves" to navigate metropolitan social norms. His adverse experiences in London prompt him to declaim, "O my curst tropical constitution! Wou'd to heaven I had . . . never felt the blessed influence of the Sun, so I had never burnt with these inflammatory passions!" Yet while an "egregious coxcomb" such as Pepperpot or Belcour may have amused British audiences, Creole women's exposure to slavery proved far more disturbing and problematic.[43]

The History of Sir George Ellison offers a strikingly repellent image of white Creole womanhood as cruel and unfeeling. In the novel, the English-born George Ellison faces reduced circumstances upon his father's death and opts to leave his native country and become a merchant in Jamaica. Once on the island, he meets and marries a wealthy white Creole widow with a slave plantation. Ellison, a British male of refined sentiments, quickly discovers that slavery is "abhorrent to his nature" and seeks to ameliorate conditions for the slaves on his estate—to the horror of his disgusted Creole wife. Mrs. Ellison, a native Creole removed from and hostile to metropolitan gender codes, considers "that however it might be in other families, in their's woman was certainly not the weaker vessel, since she was above those soft timorous whims which so much affected him; had always kept her slaves in as good order as any man in the island, and never flinched at any punishment her steward thought proper to inflict upon them." Although utterly devoted to her favorite lap dog, Mrs. Ellison "had from her infancy been so accustomed to see the most shocking cruelties exercised on the blacks, that she could not conceive how one of that complexion could excite any pity." Mrs. Ellison's lack of human empathy offered confirmation that daily exposure to shocking cruelties, particularly the whipping of half-naked slaves (figure 5), had transformed white Creole women's sensibilities, twisting the British feminine inheritance into something unrecognizable.[44]

Accustomed to their tropical world of unmitigated violence, such degenerate Creole women appeared incapable of adapting to polite standards of femininity. In February 1767, audience members at the Theatre Royal in Covent Garden watched as Priscilla Tomboy, a crude and debauched Creole orphan from Jamaica, swore, abused her slave, and attempted to run away with her lover in Isaac Bickerstaff's comedic opera *Love in the City*. Priscilla's English relatives inform her that despite "the breeding you got in the plantations," expulsion from Hackney boarding school for "beating the governess" was unacceptable. "You think you have got among your blackamoors—But you are not got among your blackamoors now Miss," the family of her guardian, Old Cockney, caution her. Priscilla's physical separation from slave culture and prolonged immersion in metropolitan society make no dent on her manners. She repeatedly unleashes her uncontrollable temper on her black domestic, Quasheba, threatening to have her "horse-whipp'd till there is not a bit of flesh on your bones."[45]

5. Richard Newton, *A Forcible Appeal for the Abolition of the Slave Trade* (London, 1792). © The Trustees of the British Museum.

The "Creolian" also refuses to marry Old Cockney's son, Young Cockney, preferring to ensnare a young captain and elope with him to Scotland. Priscilla's wild behavior prompts Old Cockney and his middling relations to fret and wring their hands. "I allow you cousin *Cockney*," advises Miss Molly Cockney, "her fortune is very considerable?—but she has not more breeding than a rhinoceros." Old Cockney subsequently sets aside his plans for trouble-free social advancement, resolving to return Priscilla where she belongs: Jamaica. Rather than despairing his missed opportunity to attain wealth through marriage to a white West Indian heiress, Young Cockney congratulates himself on his near miss:

> What lose I?
> Plague of her negers, her sugar and rume
> False, fly,
> She's for the devil a chum.
>
> . . .

The man who for nothing should buy her,
Too dear his bargain would pay;
But where's the need of orations?
E'en send her back to her relations;
She's fitterer for the plantations.
Than here with the Christians to stay.[46]

In an age when articulations of British national identity rested on assumptions about the superiority of British bloodlines, Protestant faith, and
cultural practices, Creole women's aberrant femininity not only endangered
the future of white settlement in the Caribbean but also subverted gender and
racial hierarchies increasingly considered crucial to the expansion of British
imperium. For the depraved and racially dubious white West Indian woman,
supposedly an eager participant in the culture of violence required to maintain the slave system, demonstrated the physical and moral breakdown of English womanhood overseas. The inability of white women to exert a civilizing
influence on white Creole males and rein in their illicit passions imperiled
Anglicization. John Singleton, author of a popular quarto-volume blank-
verse poem, *A General Description of the West Indian Islands,* first printed in
Barbados in 1767 and later reprinted twice in Britain, depicted Creole males
as eagerly succumbing to their passions due to the constant accessibility of
enslaved women. "Shun the false lure of Ethiopic charms," he urged white
West Indian men, in favor of legitimate matrimonial connections with white
Christian women:

Or, can the frightful negro visage charm
Thro' vague variety, or wanton lust,
Whilst the blind fool an angel's bosom quits,
To pillow in a fiend's unnat'ral arms,
Where the fond master oft succeeds his slave?

For Singleton, nothing but degenerate lust could prompt civilized men to
engage in sexual relations with slave women of "fearful" appearance and
"fiend[ish]" temperament. By recklessly pursuing enslaved women, slaveholders
engaged in a dangerous circumstance of "traded identity," whereby master
and slave, Briton and African, became "exchangeable figures," thereby weak-
ening white moral authority. Indeed, sexual contact with women with any
degree of African ancestry threatened the British racial inheritance:

> Tho' the lewd spark the tawny shou'd prefer
> To shining jet,' for
> 'Alas! that tawny draws
> Its copper hue from such an odious source.[47]

Singleton also averred, however, that marriage to distasteful white women encouraged men to seek "looser joys abroad," for an unfaithful husband was "sinful made by an impetuous wife."[48]

In colonial Jamaica, white men rarely married, owing to the absence, as a number of commentators claimed, of eligible white female partners as well as their own inclinations. Writing in 1774, Edward Long argued that white Creole men preferred "to give loose to every kind of sensual delight" than to enter the matrimonial state with unsuitable brides. While stressing that Jamaican colonists had not "converted into black-a-moors," as commonly supposed in metropolitan Britain, Long held that white West Indian women had imbibed negative traits due to their "constant intercourse from their birth with Negroe domestics" and thus offered little in the way of civilized refinement to prospective husbands. J. B. Moreton, a former bookkeeper in Jamaica, agreed with Long that white women raised in a Caribbean colony such as Jamaica, surrounded by slaves, could not possibly conform to metropolitan gender standards. Most Creole women remained on the island for their instruction, he explained, where "they receive their education amongst negroe wenches, and imbibe great part of their dialect, principles, manners, and customs." Moreton advised white Creole parents to send their daughters as well as their sons to Britain for education. Safely ensconced in the mother country, they would be prevented from engaging in "any intercourse, if possible, with any of the black or tawny race." Only degradation resulted for the white female confined to the Creole household, in which one often discovered, "a group of white legitimate, and Mulatto illegitimate, children all claimed by the same married father, and all bred up together under the same roof," Long maintained.[49]

Moreton, Long, and other authors of colonial histories held that many of the ills of Caribbean society resulted from its tolerance of coerced sex and intimacy between white men and women of African descent. By allowing sexual relations between the master class and female slaves to progress unimpeded by law or custom, the Jamaican legislature had implicitly sanctioned the proliferation of mixed progeny with some portion of British blood. Long lamented the ubiquitous presence of white men of every rank "cohabiting with Negresses and Mulattas, free or slaves." Nothing beneficial to colonial society or the British imperial polity resulted from these "goatish embraces," which gave rise to "a vast addition of spurious offsprings of different complexions." People of mixed blood, Long argued, were a "tarnished train of beings," who "for their own parts, despise the Blacks, and aspire to mend their complexion still more by intermixture with the Whites." The prospect of legal whitening for the mixed descendants of slave mothers and white men after three successive generations encouraged the intermingling of British and African bloodlines. For mixed-race men and women three degrees removed from an African ancestor "are called English, and consider themselves as free from all taint of the Negroe race." That Jamaican law permitted the mixed descendants of slave ancestors to assume a white British identity disturbed Long, whose ideas, though exceedingly virulent for the era, were nonetheless highly influential. He associated racial mixture with degeneracy and feared it inevitably resulted in the decline of nations. Pointing to Spanish America, Long characterized the entire region as a failed colonial experiment, whereby the inability of lustful Spaniards to control their passions had resulted in "a vicious, brutal, and degenerate breed of mongrels." With this example in mind, it would be "much better for Britain, and Jamaica too, if the white men in that colony would abate of their infatuated attachments to black women," Long concluded, and "perform the duty incumbent on every good citizen, by raising in honourable wedlock a race of unadulterated beings."[50]

The prospect of degenerative decline loomed particularly large in late eighteenth-century Jamaica, as evidenced by the repeated attempts of those with strong ties to the island to counter charges of Creole degeneracy. In the context of colonial Jamaica's hot climate, perpetual demographic crisis, morbid disease environment, and increasing population of mixed ancestry, the potential perils of racial degeneration and contamination proved especially disconcerting. In addition to the perceived threat posed by the natural and climatic environment of the Caribbean on British bodies, white settlers could also succumb to the influence of the enslaved Africans who surrounded them. As Moreton put it, "Even men from other countries, when [they] get inured to the West Indies, how imperceptibly, like wax softened by heat, they melt into their manners and customs." Once on the island, the heat and heady atmosphere of slavery transformed Britons "into children of the sun, fostered and invigorated beneath his celestial rays, eternal votaries to the revels of Bacchus and Venus, luxuriously and voluptuously spend their few days and nights in dissipations dear delightful downy lap, whilst African manners and customs are native and congenial to their hearts!" That the inherent barbarism and infections presumed to run through the veins of African slaves and their mixed descendants could infect whites through blood or blood products, such as breast milk, seemed indisputable. "These Negroes are few of them exempt from the venereal taint," recounted Long, "and very many have, at the time of their arrival, that dreadful disorder, the *yaws,* lurking in their blood."[51]

Lurking in Africans' blood were other, more dangerous taints as well, commentators insisted. Edward Long and his fellow defenders of colonial slavery expressed misgivings about the contaminating prospect of black-white mixture, particularly in the plantation household, due to their low opinion of African physical appearance, cultural practices, and moral character. Intermingling with "Negroes in a state of slavery" or "persons of mixed blood (usually termed *People of Colour*)," in the words of Bryan Edwards, resulted in worsening consequences for whites over time. According to these authors, domestic familiarity with black slaves exposed white women and children to the savage qualities and distempers harbored in African blood. Creole women's refusal to suckle their own infants appalled contemporary observers. "They give them up to a Negroe or Mulatto wet nurse," exclaimed Long, "without reflecting that her blood may be corrupted, or considering the influence which the milk may have with respect to the disposition, as well as health, of their little ones." The assumed connection between breast milk and cross-racial contamination was particularly poignant in an era in which breast milk was thought of as women's highest, or purest, form of blood. Understood this way, drinking milk from an African wet nurse obliged white Creole children to imbibe African blood, contaminating future generations of settler descendants. Critics of the Jamaican-born lord mayor "Creolian Beckford," for example, attacked him by claiming that he "sucked ideas of government from the breast of his nurse, who was a blackamoor Princess" and as a young man had "black princes for his menial servants and *princesses* for his concubines."[52]

Conversely, authors of colonial tracts argued that African-descended individuals, owing to the deeply negative traits and distempers attending their "black blood," would improve themselves through intermixture with whites and consciously sought to do so. As Long explained, people of mixed blood, and women of color specifically, disdained contact with blacks and other mixed-race persons, striving instead to "mend their complexion still more by intermixture with the Whites." "The pride of amended blood is universal," he concluded. Edwards agreed, noting that one should distinguish between "those people who, having some portion of Christian blood in their veins, pride themselves on that circumstance, and to the conscious value of which it is probable that some part of what is commendable in their conduct is owing" and "the free Blacks [who], not having the same advantage, have not the same emulation to excel." As Long and Edwards saw it, persons of mixed European and African lineage envisioned the dilution of their black blood and dark physical features as a one-way linear process, not to be compromised through mixture with the bloodlines of other Africans. Long firmly believed that "no free or unfreed Mulatto ever wished to relapse into the Negro. The fact is, that the opulent among them withdraw to England." In the metropole, the wealthy and illegitimate mixed descendants of white men attempted to pass as white Creoles and intermarry with native-born Britons, thereby shedding a racial past tainted with the stain of servile black ancestry. It disturbed Long and others that the presence of mulattoes masquerading as white West Indians in Britain had resulted in enhanced metropolitan scrutiny of the racial purity of all Creoles.[53]

To alleviate metropolitan accusations of Africanization, British West Indian whites strove to disassociate themselves from people of suspect racial ancestry, and these attempts at disassociation are evident in the literature of the period. In Hellena Wells's novel *Constantia Neville; or, The West Indian* (1800), for instance, the central female heroine is a white West Indian woman sent to Britain, where she finds herself appalled to make the acquaintance of wealthy colonial elites who are in fact mulattoes or "Afric Creolian[s]." To preserve their white daughter's cultural and racial integrity in the British Caribbean, Constantia's parents had kept her distanced from the enslaved due to a "fear of contamination from the negroes." Her father had also warned Constantia "on no pretext to converse or associate with mulattoes; they commonly possessed, in his opinion, the predominate bad qualities of both Europeans and Africans." As a result, Constantia's anxieties about racial contamination and repeated exposure to suspected nonwhites in Britain torment her throughout the novel.[54]

Other authors accounted black blood a permanent stain and pronounced persons of mixed blood as incapable of achieving whiteness no matter how many generations removed from an African ancestor. While sexual unions between whites and blacks produced "innumerable gradations," Moreton strongly held that, "in my opinion, Mongrels, though thirty generations distant from blacks blood, cannot be real whites." If mixture with white men failed, as some observers concluded, to dilute completely the stain of African ancestry from servile maternal bloodlines, then what to make of white Creole males who nonetheless continued to sire offspring with women of African descent? Long explained that Jamaican Creoles took offense when metropolitan Britons wrongly assumed that all children born of white parents in Jamaica would succumb to the barbarous, Africanized environment of the torrid zone. "But the genuine English breed, untainted with these heterogeneous mixtures, is observed to be equally pure and delicate in Jamaica as the mother country," Long contended. Natural-born white subjects, he suggested, could maintain the British racial inheritance as easily in Jamaica as they could in England, so long as they avoided mixing their blood with that of Africans.[55]

Even those writers who deplored the sexual practices of slavery and promoted a future of white settlement in the colonial Caribbean free of racial mixture were forced to contend with demographic realities and long-held social customs. Illicit encounters between British white males and women descended from slave ancestors remained the norm in an island colony in which enslaved Africans and their free descendants composed over 90 percent of the population and many white men remained bachelors. Women of African and mixed ancestry, irrespective of widespread assumptions about black inferiority and degenerative influence on white society, retained their place as white men's preferred sexual partners. Still, only a minute fraction of the offspring born of such unions adopted their reputed fathers' racial identity and successfully claimed the legal, socioeconomic, and political privileges reserved for white British subjects. As illegitimate progeny born of allegedly distinct yet unnaturally intermingled bloodlines, men and women of mixed ancestry occupied an internally liminal position in Jamaican colonial society. Such individuals were destined, as Long envisioned, "to form the centre of connexion between the two extremes, producing a regular establishment of three ranks of men, dependant on each other, and rising in a proper climax of subordination, in which the Whites would hold the highest place."[56]

PART TWO

Blood Mixture, Abolition, and Empire

CHAPTER 4

❖——◦∞☼∞◦——❖

Blood Ties in the Colonial Sexual Economy

On March 19, 1783, twenty-eight-year-old John Tailyour, the latest in a long line of enterprising Scots drawn to the British Caribbean by the prospect of riches in the late eighteenth century, arrived in Kingston to salvage what remained of his transatlantic mercantile career. Born in 1755 to Robert and Jean Tailyour of Kirktonhill, Scotland, near the east coast village of Marykirk, Tailyour had apprenticed with a firm of tobacco traders in Glasgow before heading to Virginia in 1775 to work as a factor in the Glasgow-Virginia tobacco trade. The disruptions of the American Revolution forced Tailyour to return to Scotland the following year, and though he tried twice more to establish himself as a trader in North America, in 1777 and in 1781, both attempts failed. In 1782, with no home left in Scotland to which he could return, due to the sale of the family estate after his father's untimely death, Tailyour resolved to settle in Jamaica under the tutelage of his wealthy and influential cousin Simon Taylor.[1]

Within months of his arrival in Jamaica, Tailyour's prospects began to improve dramatically. Tapping into his cousin Simon's extensive business network on the island and his own contacts in Scotland, Tailyour established himself in the commission business as a town factor in Kingston specializing in the importation of plantation supplies. He altered his last name to match his powerful cousin's and formed the merchant house of McBean, Ballantine, and

Taylor. In 1785, the partners began working as "Guinea factors," selling thousands of enslaved Africans to Jamaican planters, and Tailyour amassed a sizeable fortune as a result. Profits from slave trading enabled Tailyour, unlike so many of his fellow Scotsmen who failed to build colonial fortunes, to return to Britain in 1792 and marry Mary McCall, the daughter of his former employer in Glasgow, with whom he had ten children. In the late 1790s, Tailyour retired to Scotland, purchased his family's former estate at Kirktonhill and several other properties, and spent the remainder of his days enjoying a life of respectable affluence, amid repeated bouts of ill health, before his death in 1815.[2]

John Tailyour's brisk accumulation of wealth in late eighteenth-century Jamaica confirms the critical importance of kinship networks to the success of transatlantic business ventures and at the same time reveals why Jamaica, despite its health risks and overwhelming slave majority, proved enticing to Scottish men on the make. But Tailyour did not spend all of his time in Jamaica engaged in business pursuits. Soon after his arrival in Kingston, Tailyour began cohabitating with Mary "Polly" Graham, an enslaved woman of mixed ancestry owned by his cousin Simon. Graham served as Tailyour's housekeeper throughout his stay on the island and bore him four children, three of whom technically belonged to Simon Taylor as his chattel property from the time of their birth. Enslaved and free women of African and mixed descent routinely assumed the role of housekeeper for white bachelors in Jamaica. "Housekeeping" entailed the performance of a variety of domestic and intimate services for white men, including nursing, cleaning, cooking, washing, sexual intercourse, and frequently, the bearing and raising of children. In exchange, the women of African descent who performed these services could likely anticipate receiving some form of recompense from the white men with whom they cohabited. Compensation varied depending on the status of the partners—free or bound for the woman; lower class, middling, or elite for the man—and the nature and extent of their relationship. Customary gifts to enslaved and free housekeepers, also known as "kept mistresses," included clothes, furniture, and other household items; money, houses, and slaves; release from the most laborious tasks in the fields; deeds of manumission for themselves and their enslaved offspring; and in the most extraordinary cases, a formal education in Britain for select children with blood ties to wealthy white male benefactors.[3]

For many British bachelors in colonial Jamaica, the system of housekeeping constituted a far more appealing and convenient situation than matrimony. Suitable white women were in scarce supply. More importantly, ambitious Britons such as John Tailyour and his ilk aspired to acquire a comfortable independence and return to the metropole as soon as possible, before their bodies succumbed to the ravages of Jamaica's tropical climate. Once safely ensconced in the mother country, returning colonists could start a lawful, church-sanctioned family with a bride of suitable ancestry, free of the taint of African blood, and fulfill their uppermost ambition of becoming landed gentlemen. While in Jamaica therefore they set their sights squarely on the pursuit of two interrelated objectives: business and pleasure. The colonial phraseology of "housekeeping" served as a discursive sleight of hand, characterizing in polite terms deeply exploitative relationships between men and women who occupied asymmetrical racial, social, and gender positions. Because conjugal and other sexual interactions between white men and African-descended women occurred outside the reach of the law, the men never made formal commitments to the enslaved or free women who shared their beds. They could easily cast their housekeepers aside at a moment's notice and move on to respectable marriages with white women of far greater social and economic value. That some men did not do so was in keeping with the perceived conveniences and minimal obligations associated with these relationships as well as the difficulty of living long enough in Jamaica to earn a sufficient income to return home and marry. British men who did marry white Creole women for purposes of social and financial advancement often continued to engage in sexual relations with enslaved women of African descent, thereby reinforcing the gendered and racialized hierarchies of power integral to slave society.[4]

So regular a presence were black and mixed-race female housekeepers in the homes of white bachelors in the colonial Caribbean, abolitionists later used them as an example of the degrading influence of slavery on white men, "nearly the whole of whom live in a state of open and acknowledged, and even boasted, fornication." In the records that have survived, Tailyour and other British males who spent time in Jamaica rarely spoke of their conjugal relations with enslaved or free women to anyone outside of their intimate circles. References to Polly Graham and the children she bore Tailyour occur primarily in letters written by Tailyour's friends and family rather than in comments made by the man himself. Graham's voice, moreover, is mediated through the white men with whom she dealt. Metropolitan observers and moral reformers nonetheless understood the "notorious fact that very few of the white men in the West Indies marry, except a few professional men." Instead, "the merchants and shopkeepers in the towns, and the whole of the deputy planters, (namely overseers), in all parts of the country, have what is called a housekeeper, who is their concubine or mistress, and is generally a free woman of Colour; but the book-keepers, who are too poor and too dependent to have any kind of establishment, generally take some Mulatto, or Black female slave from the estate where they are employed, or live in a more general state of licentiousness."[5]

The "general state of licentiousness" enjoyed by the lower-level white staff on slave plantations could breed a culture of nonchalant sexual exploitation that implicated elite British males to an extent perhaps inconceivable even to abolitionists. In 1799, for instance, Isaac Grant, overseer of James Stothert's Jamaican estate in St. James parish, wrote to Stothert, now an absentee proprietor in Edinburgh, "respecting your daughter Rebecca, at present my house keeper." Although Stothert's natural daughter by blood, Rebecca remained enslaved, compelled to provide all manner of domestic and sexual services for Grant and other white managerial staff on his plantation. Grant, who sought sole possession of Rebecca, offered Stothert an exchange: "I'll give you a good and picked new negro upon condition that you'll give me, say cause and authorize your attrny here, to give me a Title to her, for five years, then to have her freedom as from me." Stothert's own daughter had become yet another commodity exchanged between white men in Jamaica's sexual economy of slavery.[6]

Grant's sexual relationship with Rebecca, the enslaved daughter of his absentee employer, represented one example of a range of possible unions between white men and enslaved and free women of African and mixed decent in colonial Jamaica. Virtually all of these relationships lacked legal sanction and proceeded according to social convention rather than law. White men, both those directly involved in such unions and those whose property rights were invoked when one partner was free and the other enslaved, exercised ultimate discretionary power over the bodies of female slaves and the terms and material outcomes of their sexual engagements. Evidence strongly suggests that while norms, attitudes, and practices surrounding interracial unions remained fairly consistent across lines of social division in eighteenth-century Jamaica, individual male responses to the sexual culture of slavery varied widely. Some engaged in long-term cohabitation and ultimately manumitted their lovers and/or mixed-race offspring; others fulfilled what they saw as their customary paternal obligation by educating, supporting, or leaving bequests to their "natural" children; still others—the greatest majority—sired offspring with slaves and abandoned them to the same hereditary state as their mothers.[7]

Irrespective of individual outcomes, interracial sex in the context of Jamaican slavery produced blood ties not only between women of servile, heathen ancestry and white male colonists but also between Africans and Britons. However real these ties might have been for the men and women involved, they were informal and unsanctioned—and deliberately so. Upwardly mobile white males understood that such relations, if widely known at home, would result in detrimental social and professional repercussions as a result of developing concerns about legitimacy, blood ancestry, and the place of enslaved Africans and their mixed descendants in the wider British imperial world. Drawing on the letters, journals, and personal experiences of multiple white men—mostly Scots—in eighteenth- and early nineteenth-century Jamaica, this chapter demonstrates how British attitudes and discourses surrounding blood lineage and the sexual practices of slavery shaped the lived experience of racial definition in colonial as well as metropolitan sites. British males readily engaged in illicit short-and long-term liaisons with women of African ancestry and fathered illegitimate mixed offspring while resident in Caribbean slave society. Yet, at the same time, there is much to suggest that these same men recognized the significant value placed on legitimacy, blood purity, and whiteness, both in colonial Jamaica and in metropolitan Britain. Personal sensitivities to these issues continued to rise against the backdrop of an escalating national dialogue about the immorality of slave trading and colonial slavery and the inevitability of white racial pollution.

THE TAILYOURS/TAYLORS

When John Tailyour set sail for Jamaica in 1783 with few prospects and little capital, he had "no doubt of getting into some line of business" with the assistance and protection of Simon Taylor, a wealthy cousin he knew by reputation alone. Taylor, "a man of property and influence equal to any in the island," was the ideal kinsman for an enterprising young man newly arrived in Jamaica and determined to get "into a profitable line." Taylor's clout and ties to powerful Jamaican mercantile and planting families enabled his younger cousin to realize his business objectives in short order. Taylor, who hoped to benefit from the younger Tailyour's presence in Kingston and entrust a share of his business affairs to a family member, readily facilitated Tailyour's professional success in Jamaica. He also offered a blueprint for acceptable masculine behavior in Caribbean slave society. "You will easily see," Tailyour told his brother Hercules less than three months after his arrival in Kingston, "that

I must be entirely governed by the opinion and directions of Mr T[aylor]." Taylor's accumulation of significant wealth meant that he was a man worth emulating.[8]

Born in Kingston in 1740, Simon Taylor was the eldest son of Patrick Taylor (originally Tailzour), a Scottish emigrant who left his home in Burrowfield, Forfarshire, to trade in Jamaica. The elder Taylor quickly made business contacts among the island's biggest planters and amassed a generous income, enabling him to marry Martha Taylor, daughter of Jamaican planter George Taylor, whose surname he assumed. As a youth, Simon Taylor was sent to Britain and educated at Eton; he returned to Jamaica in 1760—in the midst of Tacky's Revolt—to inherit the family estate at Lyssons, near Port Morant in St. Thomas in the East, following the death of his father in 1759. Taylor soon added to the family's property holdings, purchasing additional sugar plantations in St. Thomas in the East, St. Ann, and Hanover and earning a lucrative side income as an attorney for absentee owners, including Chaloner Arcedeckne, owner of Golden Grove estate and an M.P. for Wallingford and Westbury during the 1780s. As Tailyour noted, his cousin's position as an attorney "brings him in 3 or 4 thousand pounds per annum." Taylor served continuously as a member of the assembly from 1768 to 1781 and from 1784 to 1810. "In short," concluded Tailyour soon after his arrival, Simon Taylor "is a man of fortune equal to any person residing in Jamaica and I think he is of greater influence than any man in it."[9]

Like many white men who spent their entire lives in colonial Jamaica, Simon Taylor never married. A man of Taylor's wealth and stature would have attracted any number of potential brides from among the most affluent Creole families on the island, but he chose a life of purposeful bachelorhood. Matrimony, both its disappointments and its rewards, was an ever-present and contentious topic of conversation on the island. Although leading Jamaican colonists encouraged fellow white males to marry, finding the right partner, one with property in land and slaves, honorable familial connections, and an irreproachable lineage, could prove exceedingly difficult. Illicit unions or informal relationships with black or mixed-race women, whether slave or free, offered an acceptable alternative for white males, but the white settler community considered marriages between whites and persons of African or mixed blood socially unacceptable. In September 1765, Taylor mentioned hearing a rumor that Rose Price had married "one Miss Patrick a Writing Master's Daughter at Spanish Town and without a Shilling but that Rose sett out the next day for the Red Hills with his Black wife." Taylor lamented the fact that Price, who had recently quarreled with his father, should marry a woman without wealth, status, or a pure bloodline and "play the fool so egregiously." He predicted that Price's actions "will so much incense the Old man that he will disinherit him."[10]

Taylor found the prospect of matrimony dull and unwelcome. He nevertheless frequently urged the marital state on other propertied white men, such as his friend and employer Chaloner Arcedeckne, in order to foil the schemes of collateral family members seeking to inherit their relatives' hard-earned plantation fortunes. In a letter to Benjamin Cowell, Arcedeckne's brother-in-law, dated July 25, 1768, Taylor expressed his personal disinterest in marriage in terms that cast matrimony as a restrictive institution unbefitting a man in a hot climate. "In reguard to Matrimony I have as yett no thoughts of it. You that are in so fair a Climate must want a wife more than one who has been so long in this Hott Country and consequently excessively relaxed." In other words, Taylor preferred the looser social norms and moral codes of a tropical slave colony. "Tho as I am on the Subject," he continued, "there has been the Devill to pay between two disbanded Councillors Viz Bayly and Kennion, about the latters having debauched the others Quadroon Girl. Bayly says he is very glad that he did not catch them in Bed together or he would have been under the necessity of putting him to death." White men in Jamaica may not have been bound by strict moral conventions, but they were still motivated by sexual jealousy. Taylor's anecdote probably referred to Zachary Bayly, an enormously wealthy merchant and St. Andrew planter, who left behind an estate valued at £114,743 when he died in 1770. Bayly was also the uncle and patron of the historian and proslavery politician Bryan Edwards, author of one of the period's most influential books about the British West Indies.[11]

In *The History, Civil and Commercial, of the British Colonies in the West Indies,* first published in 1793, Edwards commented at length on Jamaica's unfamiliar racial classes and sexual culture for a metropolitan audience. He highlighted the central role played by "colored women," who, "such as are young, and have tolerable persons, are universally maintained by white men of all ranks and conditions, as kept mistresses." Edwards explained that the blame for such an immoral system should not fall on the women, whose sole duty was to serve white men: "These unhappy females, however, are much less deserving reproach than their keepers, as from the condition of their birth they are so unfortunately circumstanced, that not one in fifty of them is taught how to write or read. They are debarred therefore from necessary instruction; and the young men of their own complexion are in a state of too much degradation to think of entering into a matrimonial connection. On the other hand, no white man of a tolerable appearance will stoop to marry a mulatto." Such women had no other role than that of concubine. "How then can these ill-fated women be expected to act otherwise than they do," he stressed, "when they are prevented from arriving at the honour and felicity of wedlock; are insensible of its charms; ignorant of all moral and religious obligations; terrified by poverty, stimulated by their passions, and rendered bold by example?" As a slave-owning planter and long-serving member of the assembly, Edwards wrote from many years of personal experience. In 1759 he had gone out to Jamaica at age sixteen to live with his rich uncle Zachary Bayly, and Bayly later bequeathed to Edwards substantial sugar estates and slaves. But the desperate, unhappy state of women of African descent in a slave society, as described by Edwards and others, did not prevent men like Simon Taylor and his cousin John Tailyour from taking such women as their long-term sexual partners.[12]

By the time Tailyour arrived in Kingston to make a fresh start, Taylor had cohabitated with his housekeeper, Grace Donne, whom he described as "a free Quadroon woman," for a number of years and made provision for her in various iterations of his will. He mentioned Donne in a copy of his will and accompanying explanatory letter sent to his younger brother, Sir John Taylor, in England on January 27, 1783, shortly before his cousin Tailyour's arrival in Jamaica. "You will say I have made so great provision for the Woman who lives with me." "I own it," he admitted, "but she has been a faithful servant to me and I never had occasion to call her twice for anything or awake her in any of my very severe fits of sickness." By expressing his obligation to Donne in terms of "faithful services" rendered, specifically nursing, Taylor may have tried to present their illicit relationship with greater propriety to his relations in England, who were wholly unaccustomed to Jamaica's sexual culture. Taylor bequeathed Donne a fifty-pound annual annuity, several slaves, furniture, and the lifetime use of a house in Kingston, although she would ultimately predecease him in 1804. Taylor also made provision for two "natural quadroon" children named Sally Taylor and Jack Taylor, who may not have been Donne's offspring (or Taylor would most likely have classified them both as "mestee"—one step away from legal whiteness—since he referred to Donne as a "quadroon"). Having spent much of his life serving in the assembly and shaping Jamaican law, Taylor possessed a distinct knowledge of local racial classifications.[13]

Simon Taylor, perhaps the most influential slaveholding planter in Jamaica, exerted a great deal of mental energy considering how to resolve the colony's long-standing demographic crisis and dwindling white settler population. By the final decade of his life, aware of the pending abolition of the British slave trade, he appeared to have resigned himself to Jamaica's fate. His thoughts on the subject of white settlement began to circle back to the assembly's whitening approach of the more experimental pre-1760 era, when the 1733 elections act had, by delineating "mulatto" status, defined whiteness and its privileges as an attainable socio-legal identity for the mixed descendants of slaves. In 1804, in a letter to his London agent, George Hibbert, Taylor wrote of the impending birth of a "new Generation" in Jamaica. He predicted that "there will be [a] white population, but that will proceed from washing the Blackamoor white," rather than from natural increase among the white settlers or new arrivals from Europe or the United States. Taylor envisioned the complete whitening of the colony through racial mixture as inevitable, "for the law says that the four descent from the Negro shall be deemed white. I have a hundred and hundred times reflected on the means of Establishing a White Population here but the experience of forty three years shows me it is impossible to be done except in this manner." Taylor surely contributed to this process through his own relationships with women of African and mixed lineage over the decades. By the early nineteenth century, at an advanced stage of his life, Taylor had cemented his reputation as "an old bachelor" who "detests the society of [white] women" and held unofficial paternal blood ties to countless enslaved children, "some almost on every one of his estates."[14]

Simon Taylor's final will, written in 1808 and amended with a codicil shortly before his death on April 14, 1813, at age seventy-three, confirms that although Taylor held intimate connections with a number of women of mixed descent, both prior to and after Grace Donne's death, he fathered only a handful of "natural" children or grandchildren for whom he held special regard. Taylor made bequests of £500 Jamaican currency to Donne's niece, Grace Harris; to Sally Taylor; and to his most recent "free mulatto" housekeeper, Sarah Blacktree Hunter, to whom he also left several items of furniture. To Sarah Taylor, his illegitimate daughter with Hunter, he left £1,500 and a £30 annuity, and to her daughter, Sarah Hunter Taylor Cathcart, he bequeathed a £500 legacy, a £50 annuity, and a slave. Finally, Taylor left £700 in trust for a "quadroon" woman named Charlotte Taylor, born into slavery in 1795 and christened, along with a number of other slaves, in March 1798 at Golden Grove estate, to purchase her freedom and provide for her maintenance. These were abnormally large bequests for housekeepers and natural children or grandchildren but miniscule in comparison to what Taylor, one of the wealthiest men in the British Empire, bequeathed to his lawful blood relations. His two nieces Margaret Graham and Martha Harriet Spiers received £10,000 sterling each, his niece Eliza Mayne received £5,000 sterling, and £3,000 sterling went to his nephew Nicholas Graham. Finally, lacking a legal heir of his own, Taylor left the bulk of his personal estate—inventoried at £806,337, including all land, houses, sugar works, pens, and slaves—to his disappointment of a nephew, Sir Simon Richard Brissett Taylor.[15]

Eight months after Simon Taylor's death, the Jamaica assembly, in a concession to Jamaica's increasingly vocal free community, abolished the inheritance cap set in place since the controversial Devises Act of 1761, once again allowing white men and women to bequeath sizeable estates to "negroes and the issue of negroes." It is doubtful, however, that the repeal of this act would have altered Taylor's will to any significant extent. A leading member of the assembly for several decades, Taylor helped to fashion legislation geared toward the repression of enslaved and free people of African and mixed ancestry. As Alexander Lindsay, sixth Earl of Balcarres and a former governor of Jamaica, advised future governor Sir Eyre Coote in May 1805, "Be assured that you can carry no question in the house of assembly against the weight of Simon Taylor." Although Taylor engaged in long-term relationships with women of mixed lineage, and ruminated on the inevitable whitening of Jamaica through racial mixture, he firmly supported the legal, economic, and political subordination of nonwhites in the interest of society as a whole. Moreover, a man of his wealth and stature could have petitioned for and received an exemption in order to devise his estate as he wished; yet Taylor chose not to do so. "Mr T has all his life paid uncommon application to business," his cousin Tailyour observed thirty years earlier; "he is still desirous of increasing his fortune and expects every one about him to pay very great attention to Business." After half a century dedicated to building a vast colonial fortune and championing the rights of slaveholders, Taylor exited the world in a manner befitting a man of his station and racial ideologies.[16]

If John Tailyour aimed to conduct himself in Jamaica according to the example set by his cousin Simon, then it is unsurprising that he too took a mixed-race housekeeper to nurse him and tend to his various domestic and sexual needs not long after his entry into the Kingston commission business. Tailyour, a man without property or influence, had not yet achieved a stature sufficient to attract a free woman to live with him. He thus chose Polly Graham from among the slaves on Taylor's Lyssons estate. Tailyour hoped that by following his cousin's advice and becoming a partner in a commission house with two other town factors in Kingston, men who also looked to Taylor as their "patron," his fortunes would increase rapidly. "The business he proposes for me is the most desirable in the island, it's both the most creditable and the most profitable," he wrote to his brother Hercules in June 1783. In May 1784, after several periods of fever-induced incapacity, Tailyour confirmed that his predictions had borne fruit: "The partnership I went into the 1st Jan was advantageous to me, as it introduced me at once into a very respectable and considerable line of business—being almost wholly on commission it is not attended with any risk and the profits are considerable." By the following summer Tailyour was dealing almost entirely in African captives as a Guinea factor—he noted that Gold Coast and Ebo cargos "sell best"—and offering advice to prospective slavers in Kingston. In time, and over the course of a twelve-year career, Tailyour would become Kingston's second-largest slave trader.[17]

On August 28, 1786, Polly Graham gave birth to a son, James, the first of four illegitimate children she bore John Tailyour in Jamaica. The child was christened as "James, the son of Mary Graham, a free mulatto woman, by John Taylor" three months later in Kingston. However, Graham was not a free woman but the property of Tailyour's cousin, Simon Taylor. In Scotland, Tailyour's mother, Jean Tailyour, heard news of the birth of her illegitimate mixed-race grandson, James, and promised to receive him with every kindness if Tailyour sent him to Scotland. As her surviving letters attest, Tailyour's mother wanted her son to return home and recover his health, which had declined precipitously since his arrival on the island. Hence she assured Tailyour that his natural Jamaican son would not be unwelcome in Scotland. Two more sons followed in rapid succession and were christened in Kingston simultaneously on February 24, 1791: Simon, born on October 11, 1788, and John, born twelve months later on October 31, 1790. Upon learning of the new additions to Tailyour's informal Jamaican household, his mother expressed concern for her son's future marriage prospects. "I would wish you to have no more [children] till you have a wife," she emphasized. Tailyour, busy dealing in enslaved Africans and amassing a colonial fortune appropriate for retirement in Britain, may have agreed. Letters received from his brother, Robert Tailyour, in London indicate that, not long after the birth of his first illegitimate mixed son, James, Tailyour contemplated returning to Scotland and marrying, ideally before the age of thirty-six. "I am very glad to find you are so much bent on matrimony," wrote Robert, "as I think it will, in all probability, be the means of making you think seriously of leaving Jamaica sooner than you otherwise would." A prudent matrimonial choice, both men knew, offered the surest path toward respectability for a colonial merchant aspiring to live as a gentleman in Britain and convey to his legitimate blood heirs a worthy inheritance.[18]

The political turmoil fueled by the growing abolitionist movement in Britain in the early 1790s delayed Tailyour's plans, however. The attitude of the abolitionists and their sway over the British public troubled Simon Taylor exceedingly, but the responsiveness of the House of Commons and even the House of Lords to abolitionists' "tyrannical" attempts to halt the slave trade disgusted him utterly. Abolition, he wrote to Chaloner Arcedeckne in January 1790, is "a wicked scheme founded in malice and carried on by villainy." Leaving his cousin to manage his affairs in Jamaica, Simon Taylor set off for London to join forces with the Society of West India Planters and Merchants and lobby Parliament against the abolition of the African slave trade. After years of watching from the sidelines as the abolitionist movement gained force, the West India interest had finally come to terms with the gravity of the situation and begun to gather its forces. "The West Indian planters have hitherto appeared totally supine and inactive," Robert Tailyour wrote to his brother in Kingston on November 2, 1791, "but they now begin to see that their utmost exertions (and that by creating a parliamentary influence) will be necessary to encounter such a gang of enthusiastic fanatics as Mr Wilberforce has rais'd up in the nation." It would be Taylor's first and only trip to the metropole after his return to the island in 1760. Although Taylor initially expressed some interest in buying an estate in Britain, the public "frenzy for the abolition of the slave trade and the general prejudices against the West Indian colonies are carried so far as to disgust him altogether with England."[19]

In January 1790, in anticipation of his long-sought-after departure from Jamaica, Tailyour wrote to his cousin Simon to ask for the release of Polly Graham and her three children from slavery. Tailyour tread carefully, not wanting his Creole cousin to reject his appeal or deem it "improper." Taylor, as his cousin undoubtedly knew, did not universally free his own enslaved sexual partners or offspring from bondage, only those few for whom he had particular regard. Moreover, Taylor's approach to manumission was not atypical in a colony in which white men of all ranks indulged their sexual license without censure, and most lacked the financial wherewithal or desire to free their illegitimate mixed offspring from bondage. As Edward Long noted, "the issue of casual fruition" between enslaved black women and white men of the lower ranks, "for the most part, remain in the same slavish condition as their mother." "*Women* are the common vice of the country you are going to,"

Benjamin Vaughan warned his younger brother Charles on the eve of his trip to visit the family's Jamaican property in October 1777. Every estate bore evidence, he asserted, of "the distracted state of those who have mulattoes as their offspring, yet can neither patronize *educate* nor enrich them; and must see their own blood and substance groveling in low insensibility or shame." Residents and casual observers noted that plantation staff routinely relegated their own blood kin to slavery. "The overseers of estates have as many sable wives as they please, and change them as often as they please, and there are few properties, in the West Indies, on which families of mulattoes have not been left by each succeeding overseer, and also by the bookkeepers," observed Robert Charles Dallas in 1790. "A father parts for life from his child, whom in its very birth he consigns to slavery, with as much indifference as with his old shoe."[20]

Lacking the protection of the law or kin, enslaved women regularly faced the unwanted sexual attentions of white men. Thomas Thistlewood, an overseer in Clarendon parish who recorded "3,852 acts of sexual intercourse with 138 women in his thirty-seven years in Jamaica," regarded only one of these women and her child—Phibbah and her son "mulatto John"—as worthy of special consideration. Her owners, Mr. and Mrs. Cope, rented Phibbah out to Thistlewood during his lifetime and she cohabitated with him for a number of years and bore him a son, whom Thistlewood paid to manumit as a child but who drowned at age twenty. Although Thistlewood died in 1786 and left provision for Phibbah's manumission in his will, her owners delayed her release from bondage until 1792, when she had reached an advanced age and proved of no further use to the estate. Labor demands set limits on manumissions, and managers of Jamaican plantations regarded seasoned slaves as valuable commodities. Plantation owners, though open to requests to free enslaved children of mixed ancestry due to assumptions about their reduced utility as field laborers, did not always follow through. In 1771, Taylor wrote to Chaloner Arcedeckne in his capacity as agent to inform him that Dr. Collins, a former physician on Golden Grove estate, had left money for the manumission of "a Wench belonging to you named Catherine" as well as three of her mixed sons. Dr. Collins, Taylor pointed out, "gave himself no trouble about it in his life time but by his Will he mentioned it, and desires they may be bought." Taylor did not directly oppose their manumission, which Dr. Collins may have seen as an act of Christian charity, but it is doubtful that either Catherine or her children ever received their freedom.[21]

In some cases, white men in Jamaica offered to purchase their enslaved lovers or offspring from their owners rather than secure their manumission.

In February 1771, Roger Hope Elletson, absentee owner of Hope estate in St. Andrew, acknowledged that he had received a special request from Daniel Coe, the distiller at Hope. Coe wrote "begging most heartily that he might be permitted to purchase Maria and her Mulatto Daughter Mary, and that he would give two able field Negroe men for them." Elletson left the decision in the hands of his agent, Mr. Poole. After Elletson died in late 1775, his widow, Anna Elizabeth Elletson, took over the administration of Hope from afar as an absentee owner. On January 17, 1776, she wrote to her agents in Jamaica noting that "among Mr. Elletson's papers I found one which by the subject, I believe was intended to convey all the rights and title to a Negroe slave, named Maria, and her Mulatto daughter, to the said Mr Coe." Presuming her husband had meant to "execute the title," she instructed her agents to look into the matter. Yet Anna Elletson also expressed her misgivings, noting that "at the same time, I hope that black lady will not engross too much of his attention from his business." Even though five years had passed since Coe's initial request, Elletson did not want a member of her plantation staff side-tracked by daily access to his own personal slave woman.[22]

Thus the sensitivity with which John Tailyour approached the release of his enslaved housekeeper and her children from his cousin in 1790 conformed to island custom and the difficulties surrounding manumitting or purchasing enslaved women and children in a plantation society dependent upon slave labor. In his application to Simon Taylor, Tailyour inquired if his cousin "would grant Polly her Freedom and that of her children and allow me to put Negroes on Lyssons in their place." Tailyour couched his request in language calculated to win Taylor's favor. "Having now for several years experienced her care and attention both while I have been in sickness and health I confess myself much attached to her and I find myself very much so for her children; which makes me very desirous of putting them in a more respectable situation." Graham, like Taylor's long-term housekeeper Grace Donne, had nursed Tailyour and ministered to his various needs over multiple years. To emphasize the duty he felt he owed to Graham and her children, Tailyour concluded by stating, "I feel myself more anxious to obtain this favour than I can describe." Taylor granted his cousin's request, and eight months later Tailyour sent the manumission papers for Polly Graham and her children for Taylor to sign. Their manumission, resulting from an agreement struck between men in the same family, would not undergo an indefinite delay.[23]

As Tailyour prepared to leave Jamaica for good, he calculated how best to ensure that his newly freed, natural children would secure employment upon coming of age and provide for themselves without his assistance. Tailyour did not manumit and then abandon his offspring in Jamaica; he took pains to find a suitable place for his children in Britain and consulted his brother Robert for advice. For colonial British fathers of natural offspring born to non-European women, sending children to Britain offered a means by which, as Durba Ghosh argues, "mixed-race children were reeducated and resocialized to 'improve' themselves and undo the perceived effects of miscegenation." Robert sympathized with Tailyour's desire to educate his Jamaican children, writing that it "is surely incumbent upon us to provide for our offspring, whether Black or White," or "born in wedlock" or not. Yet he also advised Tailyour to send his eldest son, James, to a distant boarding school and keep him separate from his relations, especially his grandmother. "I think there is the greater chance of concealing from him his inferiority and preventing the mortification of being slighted by relations who from early habits he might consider himself perfectly upon a footing with," he advised. Besides, as a manumitted slave with African blood and hence limited social and professional prospects, "I really conceive it is of the utmost importance to his future happiness, that he is brought up with ideas suitable to the line of life you intend him for." If Tailyour anticipated returning to Scotland, marrying well, and elevating his own and his family's position with money earned from the transatlantic slave trade, propriety dictated that he keep his mixed-race children screened from polite society.[24]

In July 1792, John Tailyour sailed for Britain, where his son, James, was already ensconced at John Bowman's school in Yorkshire, a region of the country renowned for its many midrate boarding schools. Robert Tailyour regarded Bowman's school as fitting for a boy of his nephew's background, having encountered another West Indian absentee who boarded his own illegitimate mixed-race son there. "It is only 12 Guineas a year," Robert admitted, "which I confess is rather too cheap but it would answer no purpose to pay more." Indeed, "I have mention'd the plan to Mr Taylor who approves of it very much." In Jamaica, Tailyour left behind Polly Graham, heavily pregnant with their fourth child, Catherine, who would be born free on September 22, 1792, and baptized two months later in Kingston. Although Tailyour never returned to the island, he paid for John and Catherine to join their elder brother in Britain in 1796 and left Graham an allowance, several slaves, and use of a house in Kingston for life. Two clerks from Tailyour's Kingston firm, David Dick and John McCall, looked after Graham's affairs once Tailyour left Jamaica. Dick and McCall provided periodic updates concerning Graham and the remaining children and conveyed her requests to Tailyour. In May 1793, when Catherine (known as Kate) was still an infant, Graham requested that she be sent to Britain along with the boys, "as the girls *these times* are under no controal of their mother and also that she is not capable of bringing her up as she would wish." Graham underscored her desire that "when Kate is old enough to order her home." McCall and Dick helped Graham and the children to find more appropriate housing in Kingston after Tailyour's house was sold for £1,400 in 1793 and hired out Graham's slaves for fifteen pounds per annum, "which will enable her to live comfortably hereafter," if she exercised "prudence."[25]

Once Tailyour had transplanted all of his natural Jamaican children to Britain, he had neither time nor sympathy for Polly Graham. Built on the sale of thousands of bound African captives, Tailyour's colonial fortune had enabled him to marry and repurchase his family's lost fourteen-hundred-acre estate at Kirktonhill. In addition to updating the estate with "a remarkably elegant and capacious mansion" and extensive pleasure grounds and gardens, he purchased two additional estates in the area: a fifteen-hundred-acre estate called Garvock Proper and an eleven-hundred-acre estate known as Bradieston. Tailyour and his Scottish wife also had ten children, and he found himself stretched quite thin financially. Thus when McCall wrote to Tailyour with news that Polly Graham wanted additional financial support from him, he emphatically refused. "I think what I left her for life was sufficient," Tailyour said, and "I do not mean to give any more. I have expended a larger sum on the children already and they will still require a good deal more and I think what I did for the mother was fully as much as I ought to do." When Graham continued to press him, Tailyour lost his patience: "The duty I owe a very large family will not admit of my adding further to what I have already done for that woman." Graham, the formerly enslaved mixed-race Jamaican housekeeper, had reached the limits of Tailyour's gratitude for her services, which were no longer required. Although Graham had benefited materially from Tailyour's financial patronage over the years, the informality of their conjugal alliance and her inferior position meant that it was for Tailyour to determine whether or not he had met or surpassed his obligations to her.[26]

Contemporary commentators looked upon a woman of Polly Graham's lineage and situation—born to an enslaved black mother and later manumitted and enriched as a result of an illicit connection with a white male—with contempt and even pity. Britons considered women descended from heathen, enslaved ancestors innately inferior, both intellectually and morally, to white women and naturally and openly debauched. Dr. Jonathan Troup, a Scottish physician who recorded his experiences in the British Caribbean in the late 1780s, described "mulattoe women" as "slaves too most of them—taken as housekeepers" with "quite immodest discourse all of them whores and they throw themselves into a number of tempting positions—sometimes almost quite naked." White colonists defended their repressive treatment of free people of mixed blood by arguing that "the most idle, debauched, distemper'd, profligate wretches upon earth" sprung from the wombs of women descended from slave ancestors. Writing in 1788, the Reverend John Lindsay, rector in St. Catherine parish, argued that a "swarm of Free Women has been let loose upon the Public without the smallest tincture of Virtue or Good Behaviour, and from whom is sprung a Race of Idle Vagabonds." Rather than recklessly setting such women and their mixed offspring "loose upon the Public," rewarding them not for "*Merit* or *Good Deservance*" but for licentiousness, he argued, masters should be required by law to manumit only slaves who "have first passed an *Examination of Desert.*"[27]

The British and American wives of government officials and other visitors who spent time in Jamaica derided what they saw as the "pride, extravagance, and laziness" characterizing the island's many mixed-race females. Such women, they alleged, preferred to live in sin as the mistresses of white men so long as their paramours lavished them with material incentives. Because of the fondness of white men for "mulattoes," wrote Ann Storrow, the wife of a British army officer who lived in Kingston in the early 1790s, free women of mixed ancestry "look down upon the white ones with contempt. They possess the best houses, the finest furniture in town, their clothes if possible are finer and better than the white Ladies, their children are attended and dress'd in the first stile." Storrow, an Englishwoman of humble background, little wealth, and marginal social status, found the garish opulence of Kingston's community of free women unseemly. It frustrated her immensely that white men in Jamaica should fail to understand that

> these women are more expensive than wives, and the only difference, that theres no legal tye and a man may disengage himself whenever he thinks proper, but then the poor children are the sufferers, they cannot be introduced into company or be taken any notice of but by their own colour. If they are not sent home to England, which is often the case, their mothers have the care of them, the boys are sometimes put to trades—at other times turn vagabonds. The girls by the time

they are 15 commence prostitutes, or in the genteel phrase form connections. They live with a man till he is tired of them, or gets married,
then they go to another, and so on.

From Storrow's perspective and that of other white commentators, the attention white Creole men lavished on women of servile African ancestry served
as stark evidence of the absence of Christian morality in Jamaica as well as
the degradation of British male codes of honor. Metropolitan Britain might
have been awash in prostitution, but the women who engaged in such "infamous commerce" were relegated to the margins, degraded as public sexual
commodities. In Jamaica, men formed "temporary connections with females,
whom they both estimate and treat as creatures of an inferior species; they
procreate beings whom they also hold inferior to themselves, but superior
to their mothers." Yet these illegitimate African-descended women, critics
pointed out, nevertheless carried themselves as though they were equal or
superior to white women born in lawful wedlock.[28]

John Stewart, author of the popular *An Account of Jamaica, and Its Inhabitants* (1808), commented that women with any degree of white blood "feel a
kind of pride in being removed some degree from the negro race; and affect
as much as possible the manners, &c. of the whites." This stemmed in no
small part from the local practice that "those who are thus far removed from
the original negro stock, are considered by the law as whites, and competent,
in course, to enjoy all the privileges of a white." Accordingly, he observed,
women of mixed lineage considered it more "genteel and reputable to be
the kept mistress of a white man, if he is in opulent circumstances, and can
indulge her taste for finery and parade, than to be united in wedlock with a
respectable individual of her own class." For both enslaved and free women
seeking to improve their prospects and those of their future descendants
through legal whitening, submitting to or seeking out the attentions of white
men provided the only feasible path. But even their whitened offspring would
be "excluded [from] the society of the whites, and exposed to other mortifica-
tions, in consequence of the line of distinction which custom and the laws
draw between the whites and browns." That white Creole men relentlessly
pursued women descended from slaves, in spite of the outward signs of their
African origins, puzzled Stewart. "Many of the Quadroon and Mestee females are comely, if not beautiful, as they partake chiefly of the European feature," he admitted, "but the Mulattos and Sambos, as less removed from the
negro Stock, retain something of their thick lips and flat noses." The closer a

woman was to African ancestors along a line of descent, the more she repulsed Stewart's aesthetic—hence his assumption that white men of all ranks coveted women with the least amount of African blood.[29]

In a diary written during her stay in Jamaica in the early nineteenth century, Lady Maria Nugent, wife of Governor Nugent, highlighted the scandalous nature of Jamaica's sexual culture and the debauched behavior of upper-class white Creole males whose only pursuits were profit and corporeal pleasure. Applying the same climatic logic as Simon Taylor, she expressed amazement at witnessing "the immediate effect that the climate and habits of living in this country have upon the minds and manners of Europeans." "In this country it appears as if every thing were bought and sold," Nugent observed glumly, and sexual liaisons above all. "In the upper ranks, they become insolent and inactive, regardless of every thing but eating, drinking, and indulging themselves, and are almost entirely under the dominion of their mulatto favorites." On one occasion, after several "mulatto" women paid a visit to Nugent and shared their personal histories with her, she noted how "they are all daughters of Members of the Assembly, officers, &c. &c." But socializing with the island's white Creole women only confirmed in Nugent's mind the degenerative influence of African slavery on British colonists. "The Creole language is not confined to the Negroes. Many of the ladies, who have not been educated in England, speak a sort of broken English, with an indolent drawling out of their words, that is very tiresome if not disgusting." She recounted standing with a white Creole woman near a window and remarking on the cool breeze, "to which she answered, 'Yes, ma-am, *him rail-ly too fra-ish*.'" The prospect of Creole females providing cultivated and genteel companionship for white men, and thereby promoting the overall refinement of Jamaican Creole society, appeared highly unlikely.[30]

One of the many perceived benefits of informal cohabitation with a woman of African descent came to fruition for John Tailyour following his departure from Jamaica, as he unequivocally broke off his association with Polly Graham without any legal or social repercussions. Tailyour limited his attention to the fulfillment of what he saw as his paternal duty by assisting his natural Jamaican offspring to secure respectable employment somewhere well away from their relations in Scotland, preferably in the capital or wider empire. Therefore, when James and John completed their educations, Tailyour turned again to his brother Robert in London for assistance finding suitable professional positions for the boys. Although the ultimate fate of Tailyour's other two children remains unknown, surviving letters indicate that Simon sailed with his brother John to England and attended John Bowman's school with his brothers until at least 1803, after which point references to him disappear. Simon may have sickened and died before finishing his education, while Catherine remained with Tailyour's sister in Montrose. James and John both pursued professional paths that took them to the distant reaches of the British Empire: James as an East India Company cadet stationed in Madras and Mauritius and John as a captain's clerk on a merchant vessel headed to the East Indies.[31]

Owing to the boys' illegitimacy and mixed, servile lineage, the routes to these positions were neither smooth nor assured. With his uncle Robert's assistance, James passed his cadet examination before the Shipping Board at the India House on April 3, 1805, but not without enormous trepidation on his own and his uncle's part as a result of his swarthy appearance and suspect bloodline. To obscure his son's ancestry, Tailyour signed an affidavit attesting to James's birth and baptism in Kingston and swearing that "no copy or certificate of the registry of the said baptism" existed in Britain; James swore an additional oath confirming the truth of his father's statement. Robert had determined that his brother should enlist James as an East India Company cadet after consulting with others in the West Indian absentee community who had likewise sent their sons to India as cadets "under similar circumstances to yours." "I will do every thing in my power to get over any difficulty there may be as to his colour," he wrote to Tailyour in March 1805, prior to seeing James in the flesh.[32]

When James arrived in London a few weeks later and met his uncle Robert in person, Robert professed himself overcome with anxiety. His nephew's skin color betrayed a mixed heritage, Robert fretted, and he "really could not sleep the first night after he [James] came." As Robert later explained in a letter to Tailyour, James's complexion was not too dark—but dark enough to provoke questions. Moreover, "coupled with his being born in the West Indies gave rise to numberless objections and they are particularly strict in not allowing any natives of the East or West Indies who can be supposed to have any Black blood in them to go out in the company's service, and even require proof of being born from European parents." This policy originated with the military and civil reforms instituted under Governor-General Lord Cornwallis (1786–93). Cornwallis strove to purge the East India Company of corruption and immorality by adopting a stricter stance toward racial mixture, which, in his view, would improve "the Discipline and Reputation of H.M.'s troops employed in India." After 1790, the Company barred persons "born of Black women" from employment as officers or soldiers. Consequently, both

James and his uncle Robert worried that the Shipping Board would turn James away, for "illegitimacy is an objection—as well as colour," and the social repercussions of a potentially disgraceful public unveiling mortified Robert. Owing to immense feelings of "anxiety and fatigue" suffered on the day of the exam, Robert claimed, "I was really very ill the next day." But fortunately for Robert Tailyour, his worst fears for James were not realized. "I try'd him in Powder and various Colour'd dresses—Powder made him much worse—I got him a blue coat, and had his hair cut and in that way he pass'd the committee of shipping." James had successfully overcome his tainted background and would go out to India after all.[33]

James Taylor left England and took ship for Madras on April 10, 1805, to the immense relief of his British relations. "He was uncommonly lucky in passing," Robert admitted frankly to his brother a month after James's departure. "Some of the directors have said since—as they still think he must have some black blood, and there is nothing they are so particular about." Once in India, James experienced immediate culture shock; he found himself alone in an alien land, confined to a lowly position, and surrounded by "thousands of blacks." He lamented in letters to his father and uncle that he could "neither enjoy health nor happiness in this detested country." James begged repeatedly to return home to pursue another line of work. But his father refused, and his uncle urged him to be satisfied with his situation. As Robert stressed, James "never could be provided for one tenth part so well in this country" and "cannot be too soon recalled to a sense of his real situation and prospects." The Tailyours would not try the East India Company cadet experiment again with James's younger brother, John, however. James had barely made the cut and Robert fretted about John's color and deemed him "extremely slow" and "meek," "but at the same time inclined to be more expensive than he ought, which ought to be check'd as much as possible." John would have to make his way at the docks or on a merchant vessel rather than under the auspices of the East India Company and learn to live on his own earnings whatever path he followed. His natural father, John Tailyour, had, both in his own mind and in his brother Robert's, more than satisfied his paternal duty to his natural Jamaican sons.[34]

THE JOHNSTONS

When John Tailyour arrived in Kingston to seek his fortune with his cousin's assistance in 1783, Dr. Alexander Johnston—another member of "colonial society's professional 'classes'"—had finally attained the property and social status that had compelled him to leave Aberdeen, Scotland, for Jamaica twenty years earlier, never to return. But for Johnston, a man of middling background, navigating the channel to wealth in eighteenth-century Jamaica proved a long and arduous struggle. Success in the colony demanded constant striving, both to move up the ranks and to maintain equilibrium. "I have a valuable property now, in Lands, Slaves, and Cattle," he wrote to his brother James in Scotland in June 1783. Nevertheless, "this is the devil of a country, to be sure, for vexation and disquietude. Properties here are dearly earned and dearly kept up. But when a man once begins a plan, he must go thro with it the best way he can."[35]

Johnston's Jamaican plan had begun at the age of twenty-four when he set his sights on making quick money in the Caribbean, ostensibly by practicing medicine, although he lied about having earned a medical degree at the University of Aberdeen. Johnston, as Alan Karras notes, held great ambitions and willingly took shortcuts and fudged the truth a bit if he believed it would improve his chances of colonial success. He lacked the critical familial network and connections to prominent planters and merchants that would soon facilitate Tailyour's rapid upward rise as a thriving town factor and slave trader in Kingston. Johnston's lack of contacts did not stop him or a number of ambitious young men in his circle of acquaintances in Aberdeen from trying their luck in the sugar islands. Johnston knew he would have to hit the ground running and work extraordinarily hard to make his own wealth and forge ties with members of Jamaica's tight-knit Creole community. There were already plenty of so-called physicians peddling their services in Jamaica, and up to two-thirds of them were Scotsmen; thus Johnston's modest professional skills were not in great demand. But Jamaica, with its majority slave population and reputation for killing unseasoned European migrants soon after their arrival, desperately needed skilled white men in any capacity. Johnston, a young man eager to escape the backwardness of Aberdeenshire and dramatically improve his financial and social prospects, was willing to take the risk.[36]

Like Simon Taylor, Alexander Johnston was a man focused on business. Attention to business, he believed, would assure rapid upward mobility in a colonial society full of dissipated and indolent white men. The drawbacks of his upbringing in northeastern Scotland also weighed on him, particularly "that wicked, barbarous pronunciation that the people in Ab[erdeen] have— the wrong accent, the wrong emphasis, the shrill tone." Whenever possible, well-educated migrants from Scotland tapped into preexisting networks in the colonies, and Jamaica had a large concentration of Scots. Not Johnston. He wanted to go his own way and disassociate himself from his Scottish past, which he saw as a liability. Johnston thus did not let the grass grow under his feet and immediately after arriving in Jamaica signed a contract to work for wages for one year under and then partner with Dr. Alexander Fullerton, a respected physician of social and political importance in St. Ann. Johnston certainly had his work cut out for him. Newly arrived, fresh-faced doctors often faced stiff local prejudice. Jamaican colonists assumed these young doctors rarely knew what they were doing and, in any case, would not long survive the island's deadly climate. When the attending physician on Joseph Foster Barham's Mesopotamia estate died suddenly of the yellow fever on April 20, 1775, for instance, Barham's attorney urged him to take care choosing another doctor. He advised Barham not to send out "any young man in that capacity, particularly not single, it is unbecoming, besides I for my part would not choose to imploy any Dr who has not been here at least 3 years, the distempers and practice differ greatly from Europe and I would not think of trusting any stranger." "Besides," he concluded, "we have men of experience enough here."[37]

Johnston survived his first year of medical wage-labor in Jamaica and, as his record book indicates, built up a client list that consisted of a complete cross-section of colonial plantation society. In addition to numerous slaves, Johnston treated and inoculated wealthy white planters, merchants, and widows; white professionals including blacksmiths, masons, carpenters, coopers, attorneys, and surveyors; free people of mixed ancestry; members of Kingston's Jewish community; and sailors and soldiers. Out of the 330 clients listed in his medical ledger spanning the years 1768 to 1773, twenty-four were white women, most of whom saw him repeatedly. The client who demanded the largest share of his attention during this period was Ann Tucker, a wealthy widow and owner of one of the largest enslaved labor forces in St. Ann parish. Johnston tended to Tucker's slaves but primarily made visits "by desire to self" to her estate (277 in total) in response to Tucker's requests for blisters, opiate pills, laudanum, arsenic seeds, and purges. Repeated in-home visitations to prominent, well-heeled clients such as Tucker made for good business. More importantly, Tucker's home provided the opportunities for social intercourse with elite Creoles whom Johnston badly needed to establish his reputation.[38]

At the same time that he purged widows and treated a number of white men for venereal diseases, Johnston used his less-lucrative visitations to the slave plantations to his utmost personal advantage. In the early 1770s, he began having regular sexual encounters with a "mulatto woman" slave named Nelly at Richmond estate in St. Ann, owned by Philip Pinnock, an eminent sugar planter and political figure and one of Johnston's patrons. Pinnock, a former member of the island council and speaker of the assembly, owned a total of over four thousand acres in the parishes of St. Ann, St. Andrew, St. Thomas in the East, and St. George, as well as a large number of slaves—including Nelly. On January 2, 1772, Johnston noted the following in his daybook: "Today died my little boy, named John, upon the 9th day from the birth—the mother Mulatto Nelly." Nelly would remain a presence in Johnston's life over several years and give birth to two surviving children fathered by Johnston. In his daybook, Johnston noted repeated payments to Nelly, in the form of pistols and cash, both before and directly following (even the day after) his marriage to a respectable white Creole woman.[39]

Johnston, in accordance with his business plan, insinuated himself into polite society in St. Ann and beyond rather quickly. On February 7, 1773, Johnston married Elizabeth Gilbert of Kingston. While relatively few white men chose the route of matrimony, for a professional outsider such as Johnston it proved a wise strategy. As a Jamaican-born woman whose guardians operated a profitable merchant house in Kingston, Gilbert had strong ties to the mercantile community as well as business acumen. Marriage to a local woman also established Johnston's credentials as a man willing to put down roots and take his obligations seriously; marriage to a Creole confirmed he was no mere sojourner. In the mid-1770s, Johnston's patron, Philip Pinnock, fell on hard times, succumbed to ill health, and sold his property and slaves—including Nelly—at Richmond to William Gray, a planter in St. Andrew. Johnston remained the estate's attending physician, enabling him to continue his periodic visits to Nelly. Johnston had already benefited from Pinnock's slow decline, purchasing a number of acres and a house at Lewis's on the Richmond estate from Pinnock in late 1770, and he continued to try to build wealth by acquiring more property.[40]

Throughout the 1770s, Alexander Johnston purchased hundreds of acres of land and parcels of slaves, sometimes up to twenty at once, to add to his property holdings. He felt particularly motivated because he now had a growing family to support. Johnston's wife, Elizabeth, gave birth to five children—John, Alexander, Janette, James, and Robert—between 1774 and 1783. During this period, Johnston also fathered two "natural" enslaved children with Nelly at Richmond, named Jenny and Jemmy, whom he visited from time to time and brought small gifts. On October 29, 1774, for example, he gave "little mulatto Jenny" a yellow coat. In August 1782 Johnston gave Jenny and Jemmy a much more valuable gift: their freedom. William Gray agreed to manumit both children for £100 each but did not offer to do the same for their mother, Nelly, who remained enslaved. It is not exactly clear what happened to Jenny and Jemmy after their manumission, although evidence suggests they stayed with their enslaved mother at Richmond. As late as August 1786, Johnston noted he gave Nelly a dollar, probably for the children. In October 1786, three months before his death, he noted that "Nelly is meager, with child" but gave no indication of the identity of the child's father, nor did he include the unborn child in his will.[41]

By July 1784, Johnston had acquired three thousand acres, including two livestock pens, or grass farms, called Murphy's Penn and Annandale, and a lot of land near Richmond estate, as well as two hundred horned cattle, forty-seven horses, two jacks, and eighty slaves. A survey of Johnston's estate, which he commissioned, estimated its value at £19,300. However, when Johnston died two and half years later, on January 30, 1787, after a lingering illness involving diarrhea, coughing, weakness, and a "shiny and swelled" scrotum, which his friend William Robertson would later label "consumption," his estate inventoried for far less: around £10,000.[42] In his will, Johnston divided his estate equally among his four sons, John, Alexander, James, and Robert, and bequeathed £1,000 to his daughter, Janette. All of his relations in Scotland received ten guineas each and not a cent more. Johnston also specified "that a new negro be given to each of two people of colour, the children of a mulatto woman slave, at Richmond, named Nelly—their names are Jenny and James, and their freedom has been purchased." From beyond the grave, Johnston sought to elevate two freed slaves of his own blood to the status of slaveholders.[43]

Soon after Alexander Johnston's death, his executor, William Robertson, wrote to Johnston's brother James in Scotland that his "large purchases of land and negroes brought heavy demands against him, which will take many years to pay." In Robertson's opinion, Johnston should have long since sent his children to Scotland for their educations, and he assumed their father had not had enough liquid capital on hand for that purpose. Within six months of Johnston's death, his widow, Elizabeth, sent her eldest son, John, to Scotland to live with his uncle James and begin his education. She appointed William Robertson and Robert Grant guardians for the children's estate and then two months later, to the surprise of many, married Dr. Alexander Weir, a physician competitor whom Johnston had apparently "detested." By the summer of 1788, Johnston's widow—now Mrs. Elizabeth Weir—had shipped off all of her children to their uncle in Scotland, save the youngest, Robert, who remained with his mother and stepfather in Jamaica, where, Robertson feared, his education was sorely neglected.[44]

Robertson had little positive to say about Alexander Weir or his influence on the children's mother, Elizabeth. In his view, the Weirs took advantage of the situation by "using the children's negroes on their own property rather than at the children's plantation." Robertson urged James to send his nephew John back to Jamaica "as soon as he has a tolerable education that I may make him well acquainted with all the different accounts and transactions of his late father." As far as John's education, "buying and selling cattle is no great art here, the care and management of them and of slaves and the cultivation of the lands are mostly to be studied and what every overseer is expected to know well and what your nephew will soon be acquainted with." Traditional book study of arithmetic, planting, and slave management would help John to acquire the necessary skills to administer his colonial property but would never supersede on-the-spot experience in Jamaica. By September 1794, both Dr. Weir and Elizabeth Weir had died, leaving behind two small children, neither of whom could "make any claims on the estate." Although John Johnston had by this point come of age, Robertson and Grant urged him to remain in Britain due to two potential threats to his safety: war with the Trelawny Maroons in 1795 followed by a lethal yellow fever epidemic. Grant emphasized that "this is a very bad country for an idle young man" and advised John to find a productive line of work soon after arriving to "prevent you being idle, and in the same time instruct you in the nature of the business of this country, and how to manage your own property to the best advantage when you get it."[45]

In the spring of 1798 John Johnston, a headstrong twenty-four-year-old, determined to set out for Jamaica and claim his delayed paternal inheritance. After his arrival the following year, he wrote to his uncle in Aberdeen on September 30, 1799, expressing his disappointment regarding the mismanagement of their Jamaican property and his intention of enlarging and improving it. "I have had very good health since I arrived. I may probably send you some of my sugars—put no dependence on it for you may never finger an ounce of it." This latter statement was entirely apropos, for less than two months later, on November 16, 1799, John Johnston fell violently ill and died of yellow fever—one of the many "blessings of Jamaica" awaiting new arrivals (figure 6). As Robertson wrote, the poor young man "left this miserable world where he never seemed to have much enjoyment."[46]

6. *The Torrid Zone; or, Blessings of Jamaica* (London, 1803).
Courtesy of The Lewis Walpole Library, Yale University.

News of John's precipitous demise in Jamaica did not discourage his younger brother, James, from determining to set out for the island as soon as possible to stake a claim to his share of the Johnstons' Jamaican inheritance. "I mean to take in hand the management of my own affairs," he wrote to his uncle from London in June 1802, and "my presence there is much needed." On December 9, 1802, James wrote to both his uncle James and his younger brother Robert announcing his "safe arrival in my native Isle in perfect health and spirits." He was pleased to report that after six weeks on the island "am very fond of the manners and climate of Jamaica" and "very much respected here by the principal inhabitants especially by those mothers who has daughters to dispose of." James Johnston had no intention of seeking a Creole wife, however. He had traveled to Jamaica to assume control of Murphy's Hill and Annandale and to divest Grant, the remaining guardian, of his 6 percent commission. "When I am of age I mean to have a writ of division made of the property then I shall be my own master." For James, the promise of independence in Jamaica overcame the ghastly prospect of an early death.[47]

Two years later, James wrote to assure his younger brother Robert, with whom he shared an equal claim to the property in St. Ann, that he had made a number of profitable improvements to Murphy's Hill of his own volition. "I think the property has been long enough under Guardianship already," he stressed. "I can assure you there has been more done on the penn since my arrival than has been done for many years before." He had planted sixty acres of coffee at Murphy's and expected it to "net me £3,000 per annum independent of the penn." Additionally, James claimed that he had cultivated about twelve hundred acres of the twenty-seven-hundred-acre property with Guinea grass for cattle, fenced off in regular pastures of sixty acres each, and owned four hundred horned cattle and ninety-six slaves. By mustering financial figures and improvements to the pen for his brother's perusal, James hoped to convince Robert to either entrust his portion of the estate to James as his acting attorney or to let him purchase it from him outright. In the meantime, James reminded his brother that "although you are now of age and entitled to a handsome competency, you have by no means a fortune to support you in extravagance and dissipation." An enjoyable life of that nature would require marriage to a moneyed Creole heiress—a course James repeatedly urged his brother to pursue. On August 26, 1805, after three years hard at work on the island, Jamaica had lost its initial appeal for James. Jamaica "is a sad dull place, no amusements whatsoever, especially to a Bachelor," he wrote. "If any of your acquaintances in London (female I mean) wishes for a husband who can do their business properly if they have 20,000 pounds you may advise them to wait until I come but remember they must have no Negroe blood or else I am off." James Johnson understood the social disgrace that would befall a white man in Jamaica who married a woman tainted in any degree with "black blood."[48]

James Johnston never found a woman free of African blood to marry—wealthy or otherwise. He described his life at Murphy's as "very solitary and retired sometimes for days don't see a white soul except Mr. Hay (the overseer)," indicating limited opportunities for socialization with white Creoles, especially white women. Yet, like many of his fellow white male colonists in Jamaica, Johnston probably never set his sights on "fixing himself in the matrimonial noose," as one contemporary put it. In stark contrast to John Tailyour, who aimed to generate wealth, marry a respectable woman of impeccable British ancestry, and retire to Scotland post haste, James Johnston

favored staying in Jamaica and looking after his own affairs. He did not inherit the burning ambition of his father, Alexander Johnston, to elevate himself socially and work his way into Jamaica's white upper echelon. Indeed,
James Johnston's surviving legal and financial records and private correspondence with his brother Robert reveal that he remained a bachelor for life and
that he fathered at least two natural mixed-race sons named James and Robert
in Jamaica and later sent them to school in Britain.[49]

James Johnston kept a receipt, dated April 25, 1813, for his payment of fifty
pounds for the passage of two children to England. Beginning in 1814, James
spoke of them regularly in letters to his younger brother Robert as "the boys"
and expressed particular concern about the mounting expenses associated
with their British educations. Yet he rarely mentioned them by name, nor did
he ever name or make reference to their mother in his personal accounts or
family correspondence. There are also no manumission records for the boys
among James Johnston's legal papers, indicating their mother's possible status
as a free woman of mixed lineage. Included among a collection of Robert
Johnston's drawings is a charcoal sketch of his brother James in Jamaica with
his unnamed "sable princess," but this drawing is the only reference to her
that survives. Robert, however, directly mentioned one of the boys by name in
a letter to his brother dated October 1816: "Your son James is a sound scholar
and a fine disposed lad." Confirmation of the illegitimacy of James's sons and
their ineligibility to inherit the family estate is in a statement James made to
Robert in 1814: "I shall never marry, and for who am I toiling for, but your
eldest son, and [h]is name must be James, and I will make a man of him." He
followed this statement with a brief postscript: "Remember me to the Boys."[50]

After James Johnston sent his natural mixed-race sons to Britain in 1813,
he expressed ongoing concern that the English school his Scottish relations
had chosen for his boys, under the direction of one Mr. Hall, was too dear
and filling their heads with notions inappropriate to their situation in life. He
repeatedly wrote to his brother stating, "I wish them to be removed as soon
as possible to a cheaper place, as I do not wish them to be brought up with
any extravagant ideas, as I mean to bring them up as industrious tradesmen."
A school that instilled thoughts of extravagance in his sons' minds would
prove detrimental "for their future prospects in life, and putting me at the
same time to a heavy expence in paying for them." Worse still, he found the
education they had received under Mr. Hall at such a heavy cost disappoint-
ing in the extreme. "I trust in God, their education will be more attended to
especially their writing, their last letters from them to me was a shame to be

seen, in fact they wrote much better when here," James exclaimed in disgust to his brother in a letter dated October 6, 1815.[51]

By December 1815, James Johnston had grown apprehensive that his brother's disregard for his illegitimate, mixed-race nephews had led him to neglect their upbringing. "I have wrote so often and so fully about the boys that I am almost ashamed to say anything further," he complained to Robert two days after Christmas. James nonetheless had a great deal more to say on the subject of his boys. "I am very much displeased with their present situation, and the progress they have made in their education, and if you, as an only brother do not wish to trouble yourself about them, I pledge my sacred word if you will only intimate the same to me that their names shall never be again mentioned to you in any letter of mine." He proposed several options for their education and then returned to the principal matter at hand: whether or not his brother cared for his nephews and their future. "I humbly request that you will write me your candid sentiments about the boys as I am determined, poor fellows as they have no fortune to expect from me, that they shall have a liberal education to enable them to be plain and industrious trader men which I intend them to be. I hope this letter will have some effect, and that your answer will be as candid in your sentiments to me as I have been to you." The response to this letter does not survive, but it is probable that Robert reassured James that he bore no ill will toward his natural Jamaican nephews. It is equally probable that Robert held no real affection for them either. Two years later, in a letter James wrote congratulating his brother on his engagement to Catherine Cole Taylor, a Creole heiress with a substantial Jamaican fortune, whom James had long schemed for Robert to marry, he added, "You never mention the boys, do write me about them."[52]

The following year, on June 25, 1818, Robert Johnston, now a university-educated physician in his midthirties, disembarked in Kingston with Catherine Cole, his pregnant wife of five months, after a long voyage from England. Robert and his new wife had arrived to claim his share of the Johnston family inheritance, including Murphy's Penn and Retirement, and to assume control of his deceased father-in-law's significant slave estates, Harmony Hill and Running Gut in St. Ann. Robert Johnston was therefore fully intent on immersing himself in and profiting from Jamaican plantation society and raising a family on the island. Yet he did so with some trepidation. Robert had visited the island only once before, in 1808, after receiving a medical degree from the University of Aberdeen. He then spent several years traveling extensively throughout continental Europe and Russia on a young gentleman's grand tour. Robert Johnston regarded himself as a cultivated, learned man but feared his body and mind would deteriorate under the influence of Jamaica's torrid climate. "Here man toils under an oppressive heat," he wrote in his journal soon after arriving in Jamaica, "and the *moral* constitution soon partakes of that lassitude, which pervades the *physical.*" "In a small and remote colony like this," Johnston envisaged, "the object of immediate gain supersedes every other feeling and day succeeds to day in endless succession with the same temperature of heat and inaction and beholds the toiling colonist grasping at the visionary fabric [of] fortune."[53]

Robert Johnston's journals and miscellaneous documents indicate that his exposure to the scientific racial theories of the era and proslavery lobbying impressed a notion of innate African inferiority on him long before his arrival in Jamaica in 1818. That his elder brother, James, had had intimate relations with a "sable princess" and fathered two mixed-race children had far less of an impact on his racial ideologies than his education in Britain and European travels. In a commonplace book dated 1811, he jotted notes "on species of men" and pondered the accuracy of the theory of monogenesis. While reading Lord Kaims's four-volume *Sketches of the History of Man* (first published in 1774), Robert found of particular interest a passage concluding that black-white intermixture resulted in the degradation of both races. As he recorded, "If a white mix with a black in whatever climate, or a Hottentot with a Samoide, the result will not be either an improvement of the kind or the contrary but a mongrel breed differing from both parents." Whether or not he considered his mixed-race nephews, James and Robert, in his racial calculations is impossible to ascertain.[54]

Settling in Jamaica seven years later inspired Robert Johnston to return to his earlier musings on racial difference. By this point, the ideas recorded in his journal, while bearing the stamp of Kaims and other racial theorists, were his own rather than copied verbatim from a published text. He wrote the following passage, for instance, the day his ship first docked in Kingston on June 25, 1818, after a brief commentary on the fashions of the "coloured people," particularly their fascination with hats:

> The African has a peculiar shaped head and profile. The back part of the head rises almost straight up and outwards. The top cone shaped and round. The forehead is strikingly depressed, the nose flat, and the lower lips large. Here is a form of skull that can never produce genius—all the marks of the animal are implanted in the quantity of

Brain lodged in the back part of the skull. The forehead, the seat of
our moral faculties and properties, are defective. It contains too small
a quantity of brain, as bespeaks the inferior scale in the rank of the
human species in which Africans will never move. Africa *may* be come
a civilized nation, but never a great one. She may acquire *talents* but
genius will never be found in her extended surface. The angle of the
forehead becomes so acute, as to rank near to that of the monkey tribe,
and shews that animal properties are more inherent in the African.

Living in Britain's most profitable and brutal Caribbean slave society during
the era of amelioration did not improve Robert Johnston's opinion of Africans. He continued to lobby on behalf of the slave interest and wrote letters
to British newspapers under the pseudonym "A Patriot," encouraging poor
whites to emigrate to Jamaica and save the shrinking white settler population
from destruction.[55]

After the Christmas Rebellion of 1831, the largest slave uprising in the
British West Indies, which resulted in the destruction of the entire sugar har-
vest and over £1 million in property losses, Robert Johnston wrote a scathing
letter to William Wilberforce. Dated October 16, 1832, Robert's letter laid
the carnage in Jamaica at Wilberforce's feet. "The talent and energy you have
displayed during the course of a long life in the cause of the Negro will ever
entitle you to the applause and admiration of posterity," wrote Johnston in
an acerbic tone; "but it is to be regretted that men not animated by the same
noble motives as yourself have attempted to emulate your endeavours by conduct entirely opposed to the well being of the negro. The consequences of
which have been an insurrection in Jamaica of unparalleled extent, characterized by the most cruel barbarities particularly towards the innocent female,
and attended with lamentable destruction of life and property." In 1832, in
anticipation of the British Parliament's passage of an emancipation bill, Robert Johnston hastily sold the bulk of his possessions and uprooted his wife and
four children, Catherine, Mary, Robert, and Annie, to Rhode Island. With
the impending collapse of the British Atlantic slave system, Jamaica had forever lost its appeal for Johnston.[56]

One or two clues remain as to the possible fates of James and Robert, the
mixed-race sons of James Johnston. On October 17, 1824, James wrote to his
brother that he was considering taking a trip to England, "as I am most anxious to do something with my poor sons." "I now repent I did not do so four
years ago," he continued. "I am afraid James is delicate and will not answer

the trade of a coach maker, and as to poor Robert, I do not know what to do with him, and his expence come very high and expensive." One of the boys later returned to Jamaica, probably James. In 1830, a case relating to the legal definition of whiteness and the militia law was presented to Fitzherbert Batty, Jamaica's attorney general, for his opinion. "Mr _____ Johnston," the brief detailed, "a young Man liberally educated in Great Britain and lately returned to the Parish of St Ann, in compliance with the Militia Law offered himself as a recruit to the Colonel commanding the St Ann's Eastern regiment of Militia who declined to appoint him to a *White* Company, alledging that being a Man of Colour he should do duty in a *Brown* Company." Johnston vehemently contested his status as a "coloured man," arguing that he was "entitled to *all* the privileges and immunities of His Majesty's white subjects of this island, being *three* degrees removed in a lineal descent from negro Ancestor *exclusive,* and brought up in the Christian Religion." The colonel did not agree, and Johnston was threatened with a court-martial for "declining to serve in a Brown Company, notwithstanding he has offered and is ready to serve in a White Company, and is ready to prove by the most respectable Evidence that he is removed from a Negro Ancestor so as to entitle him to *all* the privileges of a White Subject according to Law."[57]

The question put to Batty was the following: could a commanding officer "legally compel [Johnston] to do Militia Duty in a Brown Company or Not"? In Batty's professional opinion, dated February 14, 1830, Johnston probably had a faulty understanding of his racial status under Jamaican law. Legally speaking, a mixed bloodline conferred nonwhite status, and Johnston was "*only three* degrees removed from the Negro Ancestor, i.e. a *Mustee,*" whereas automatic conferral of legal whiteness in Jamaica was reserved solely for "the *issue* of a *mustee* woman." Batty also weighed in on the issue of white racial identity more broadly, including the extent of a parish militia colonel's authority "to compel a White Man to join a Black Company." If a man regarded himself as white and fell within the legal definition of whiteness, it behooved the colonial government not to force him to serve alongside men he regarded as his racial inferiors. "Tho' per the general feeling that pervades society here," Batty concluded, "I have no doubt that if a white person or one white by law were under such circumstances to refuse to join a Black or Brown Company, that the sentence of any court martial against him would be so lenient as to be no punishment at all." Johnston, however, did not meet the legal requirements of whiteness. Returning to the island of his birth after a youth spent in England, the illegitimate mixed-race son of James Johnston discovered that

Jamaican law and custom pronounced him incapable of exercising the full rights of a British subject or determining his own racial identity. Although blood inherited from both British and African ancestors ran in his veins, the supposed taint of black heredity overrode all other factors, including physical appearance, comportment, and education, to determine James Johnston's destiny in colonial Jamaica.[58]

As the cases of John Tailyour and Alexander Johnston and their illegitimate Anglo-Jamaican descendants demonstrate, free individuals of mixed heritage experienced varying degrees of difficulty in proving their racial purity and authenticity as a means of securing the rights and opportunities available to white subjects. Their personal stories were intimately bound up with the sexual relations of slavery and a racialized and gendered colonial system that empowered white men not only to sexually exploit and then dispose of women of African descent but also to determine the nature and extent of their filial responsibility toward their own illegitimate mixed-race offspring. Whether white men took enslaved and free women as short- or long-term sexual partners, or rewarded them materially for their loyalty and faithful service, slavery's sexual economy rather than the bonds of matrimony governed the nature of their intimate relations with and familial connections to women and children descended from slaves. Moreover, the exploitation of black female bodies and the ambivalent racial status of persons of mixed blood did not remain confined to the colonial Caribbean but also informed the treatment of enslaved women and their mixed descendants in the British metropolitan imagination. As British graphic artists, playwrights, novelists, and songwriters contemplated the subversive and comic possibilities of interracial sex amid a rising tide of abolitionist fervor, they collapsed the distinctions between colony and home and in turn revealed that the commodification of the enslaved female body had already reshaped metropolitan tastes and racial sensibilities.

CHAPTER 5

Enslaved Women and British Comic Culture

In February 1798, at the height of the British slave trade and two months prior to the defeat of William Wilberforce's annual motion for its immediate abolition, William Holland's Oxford Street print shop issued *Tit Bits in the West Indies,* a hand-colored etching and aquatint triptych, possibly designed by Holland himself or Richard Newton (figure 7). This large, crudely etched graphic print shows three distinctive white colonial male types debauching enslaved women, grotesquely caricatured, in a Caribbean setting. In the panel to the right, an oafish man garbed in characteristic planter fashion—blue waistcoat, wide-brimmed hat, tan breeches, and leather boots—stands outside a crude hut embracing a fat, leering black female, naked except for a straw hat perched on top of an African-style head wrap, an imitation of a style favored by white West Indian women. The left panel shows two dissolute sailors fighting over a nude, corpulent charcoal-colored woman with large breasts, thick lips, ape-like arms and legs, frizzy hair, and a mouth down-turned in reluctant submission. Marked by his clerical dress, a tongue-lolling parson lusts after a well-proportioned woman of probable mixed ancestry in the center panel. Her body half draped and adorned in gold jewelry and a headdress, she fans herself with a straw hat while reclining on a mound of grass, eyes closed and lips parted, legs suggestively splayed, and breasts bared to the viewer.[1]

TIT BITS in the WEST INDIES.

7. *Tit Bits in the West Indies* (London, 1798). Original in the
John Carter Brown Library, Brown University.

Tit Bits in the West Indies lacks accompanying text and at first glance offers
a simplistic caricature of white West Indian men of all ranks' purported sexual
enthusiasm for women of African ancestry. But the pun underpinning the
title phrase offers a clue to the print's deeper cultural meanings, inviting viewers to take a stab, as Robert Darnton urges, at "getting the joke." Eighteenth-
century British authors commonly used the phrase "tit bit"—a variant of "tid
bit," a small, delicate morsel or an interesting piece of news—to characterize
one or more of the following: poached "meat" (meaning game and/or a prohibited female), a woman of loose character, an adolescent prostitute, and
female genitalia. The punning title thus not only carries a sharp judgment of
white Creole males' aberrant sense of taste, it also serves to commodify and
fetishize the black female body. By granting viewers access to geographically
distant enslaved women through the prism of colonial white male desire,
which itself is rendered as depraved and repugnant, Holland's satire reduces
all women of African descent to grotesque sexual objects of the degenerate
male gaze. This particular print proved sufficiently germane to prompt a re-
issue in 1803, when Holland published a series of West India–themed prints,
including five scathing caricatures of colonial Jamaica drawn by Abraham
James, an ensign stationed on the island from 1798 to 1801 with the Sixty-
Seventh South Hampshire Regiment of Foot. Altering the title of the second

edition to *Black Beauties; or, Tit Bits in the West Indies*, Holland omitted the middle panel and focused exclusively on the coarsest elements of the original version: debauched white men lusting after corpulent, aesthetically repulsive black women. With prescient timing, Holland capitalized on Britain's resumed conflict with France and Napoleon's attempt to reinstate slavery into the French Empire, both of which made the cause of abolition and the denigration of West Indian slaveholders increasingly palatable in Britain.[2]

Print sellers based in London's West End, including William Holland, Hannah Humphrey, Samuel W. Fores, and Thomas Tegg, produced many such humorous and derisive caricatures skewering those on both sides of the abolition question during the 1790s and early 1800s. These decades encapsulated the legislative battle to abolish the African slave trade and the golden age of graphic satire, when London print sellers sold thousands of mass-produced single-sheet etchings to elite and middling purchasers for a standard price of one shilling plain and two shillings colored and drew crowds of viewers to their display windows and showrooms. With their fingers on the pulse of the nation, enterprising artists and commercial printmakers produced timely pictorial satires that "made few concessions in the way of broad contextual explanations, and presupposed an up-to-date knowledge of affairs," ranging from current parliamentary debates and political issues to social trends and passing scandals. While higher-end caricatures may have been "Westminster-oriented, licensed satire," designed primarily for the amusement of fashionable, politically aware London elites, as Eirwen Nicholson and Sheila O'Connell contend, cheaper versions had the potential to reach a large audience. Diana Donald argues persuasively that satirical prints could speak to all social classes; hung on the walls of coffeehouses and taverns, or viewed through showroom windows, graphic prints invited the British public to decipher their coded visual and verbal commentary on current events.[3]

The slavery debate proved one of the most newsworthy topics of the day. Beginning in 1787, abolitionist propaganda mobilized a nationwide anti-slave-trade petitioning campaign, instigating a Privy Council investigation and ongoing parliamentary proceedings that received extensive coverage in British newspapers. Millions signed abolition petitions, and a number of leading politicians championed their cause. British slavers and West Indian planters and merchants, though regularly lampooned in the public sphere, found allies in imperial officials and members of the aristocracy who stressed the importance of the slave trade to national commerce and prosperity. Vocal opponents of abolition cast the transatlantic trade as a means of "improving"

Africans or as a regrettable but necessary evil, the closure of which would ruin the Caribbean colonies and threaten Britain's wealth and power. The marked duality in British attitudes toward the slave trade—the divisive notion, held by some and fiercely contested by others, that economic activities need not be morally right so long as they served the national interest—inflamed passions on both sides of the issue for well over two decades.[4]

It also made for excellent satire. Indeed, single-sheet graphic prints emerged as a highly sought after consumer product conterminously with the abolitionists' campaign of mass distribution. Dozens of prints accompanied the progression, backlash against, and ultimate triumph of Britain's abolitionist movement, infusing the slavery debate with iconography familiar to the learned elite and, potentially, to a much broader audience about whom we know very little. Yet scholars have largely neglected the racially vulgar and sexually crude aspects of abolition-era culture, leaving uninterrogated the golden-age origination of the gendered racial stereotype of the huge, voracious black woman, her grotesque body a blatant perversion of neoclassical aesthetic ideals of "pure, austere, almost absolute beauty." Inattention to Georgian racial depictions designed to titillate and amuse white male viewers is perhaps due to the difficulties posed by "the elements of exploitative salaciousness and invitations to voyeurism that reside in some of this imagery," which Geoffrey Cubitt terms "atrocity imagery."[5]

This chapter builds on the critical insights of Marcus Wood, Kay Dian Kriz, and Catherine Molineux concerning the transformation of black iconography in eighteenth-century Britain, specifically the emergence of the black female body as a visual reference point against which to evaluate the aesthetic judgments guiding presumably divergent sexual tastes in the metropolitan center and Caribbean periphery. It shows how graphic prints worked in conjunction with British comic texts to forge an erotically charged, fetishizing racial trope: that of the frighteningly corporeal, hypersexual black woman whose combination of baseness, insatiability, and accessibility proved irresistible to white males with gross appetites and unrestrained sexual access to the enslaved female body. Highlighting the status of the black slave woman as both capital and sexualized consumer product, metropolitan mass media projected the most repellant aspects of slave culture onto the female body, casting white male lust for the grotesque black female as a perverse byproduct of West Indian slavery. The same dehumanized female body denigrated as an unruly distortion of the Eurocentric, and implicitly white, neoclassical ideal not only generated products of economic and material value to slaveholders and the British public—sugar, slaves, and the breast milk that sustained the next generation in bondage—but also spurred the basest lust in the men who exercised their "property rights in pleasure."[6]

Sexualized depictions of women of African ancestry did not emerge out of whole cloth in the late eighteenth century, however. Abolition-era textual and visual imagery represented a potent reiteration of a long-standing English cultural trope, dating to at least the Jacobean era, associating darkness and the black female body with sin and rampant carnality. Through graphic depictions of the black female grotesque in contemporary metropolitan and Caribbean settings, British cultural productions transformed distant enslaved women into digestible "tit bits" for public consumption and clinched the association of West Indian colonists with racial immorality. Abolition-era comic culture, by depicting white men of all ranks quenching their irrepressible lust with the bodies of black slave women, significantly weakened popular support for the proslavery cause. Yet it also raised the alarming prospect that Creole male sexual appetites had in fact already contaminated Britain, leading to the incursion of monstrous black women into metropolitan bedchambers and, worse still, the proliferation of their racially tainted mixed offspring.

TAKING BLACK FOR WHITE

On August 4, 1787, more than a century after Richard Ligon introduced the tragic tale of Inkle and Yarico in his *True and Exact History of Barbados* (1657), later revived by Richard Steele's popular periodical *The Spectator* (1711), which spawned numerous reprints, translations, and spin-offs across Europe, George Colman's ballad opera *Inkle and Yarico* debuted at London's Haymarket Theatre. By far the most popular opera of the 1787 theater season, Colman's *Inkle and Yarico,* with music by Samuel Arnold, became one of the most frequently performed plays of the late eighteenth century, staged in London a total of 164 times between 1787 and 1800. Performed widely throughout the British Isles, *Inkle and Yarico* also enthralled audiences in Kingston, New York, Philadelphia, Calcutta, and Boston, with regular revivals at home and abroad until the mid-nineteenth century. Praised by the *Monthly Review* for his skillful addition of multiple new characters, "almost as important and interesting as the two principal characters," Colman complicated the familiar story of Yarico, an Indian woman who rescues and falls in love with a stranded English merchant, Inkle, protecting him until the arrival of a vessel bound for the Caribbean. Although she abandons her way of life to accompany Inkle to Barbados, he promptly sells Yarico (who in Steele's retelling claims she is with child by him, inducing Inkle to raise her price) into slavery for monetary gain. "And so poor Yarico, for her love, lost her liberty," Richard Ligon concluded. By contrasting a compassionate female "savage" with a callous European male, Ligon's and Steele's earlier versions captured the tension between self-interest and moral principle at the core of overseas colonial and commercial expansion.[7]

A critical feature of the tale of Inkle and Yarico, and the key to its longevity, is that it lends itself to alterations and embellishments suited to shifting historical and cultural contexts. Colman's late eighteenth-century adaptation linked the tale's earlier focus on the corruptive greed of the colonial enterprise to issues related to the burgeoning anti-slave-trade movement and the interracial sexual contact underpinning the slave-based colonial order. In Colman's updated version, the shipwrecked Inkle and his cockney servant Trudge take shelter in a cave and stumble, according to the stage direction, upon "*a rude kind of curtain, by way of door to an inner apartment,*" in which they discover the sleeping Indian maiden Yarico, "beautiful as an angel," and her darker-skinned maid Wowski. While Inkle waxes poetic about Yarico's wild beauty, Trudge focuses his attentions on her sable attendant Wowski, "a nice, little plump bit in the corner; only she's an angel of rather a darker sort." When Wowski declares Trudge her "chum-chum," he concedes, noting, "As my master seems king of this palace, and has taken his Indian Queen already, I'll e'en be usher of the black rod here." The subplot of their interracial romance at once offers comic relief and subverts gender, racial, and aesthetic norms. The dark-skinned, fleshy Wowski speaks in a crude pidgin dialect, admits having had a "great many" black lovers, and boasts manly fighting skills. Still, Trudge declares, "she'll be worth a hundred of your English wives."[8]

Once in Barbados, removed from the obscurity of the cave, the paths of Colman's two pairs of unlikely lovers diverge. Inkle, determined to turn a profit in a materialistic slave society, sells Yarico to the governor of Barbados. "Here, tis money which brings us ease, plenty, command, power, every thing," he explains to the devastated Yarico. "You are the bar to my attaining this; therefore 'tis necessary for my good." In Colman's colonial Caribbean, interracial sexual cohabitation is deeply frowned upon, and the terms "black" and "black-a-moor" are applied indiscriminately to describe anyone of non-European ancestry. When Patty, a chambermaid, learns of Inkle's relationship with the "tawny" Yarico, she exclaims, "Oh! the monster! the filthy fellow! Live with a black-a-moor!" Trudge opts to remain faithful to his "poor, dear, dingy" Wowski, refusing a planter's proposition to purchase her. But Trudge's steadfast affection for the unappealing Wowski is the play's comic foil, plausible only for an ill-bred man of risibly low social standing lacking good taste and refinement. Trudge clarifies his motivation when he compares his inverted interracial romantic situation favorably to that of Othello and Desdemona, singing,

> *With jealousy I ne'er shall burst*
> *Who'd steal my bone of bone-a?*
> *A white Othello, I can trust*
> *A dingy Desdemona.*

The liaison between Trudge and Wowski exemplifies how Coleman and other Britons interpreted interracial sex between white men and black women in the colonial Caribbean through the lens of lower-class debasement.[9]

Writing in the midst of antislavery agitation and mounting criticisms directed at returning East and West Indian "Nabobs" flaunting their obscene fortunes in the streets of the capital, Colman chose to release Yarico from bondage and reunite her with a remorseful Inkle, who marries her. In contrast to Trudge's selection of an undesirable woman of inferior racial, aesthetic, and social standing, the repentant Inkle chooses Yarico as his wife because of her virtue and integrity, confirming the importance of moral rather than material capital. The opera concludes on a light note with arias by Trudge ("*Shobs! now I'm fix'd for love, /My fortune's fair, though black's my wife*") and Inkle (*Love's convert here behold, /Banish'd now my thirst of gold*), affirming the parallel interracial marriages of both couples and the triumph of love over monetary concerns. But it is Patty, the disgusted chambermaid, who refocuses the audience's attention on the farcical nature of interracial marital bliss, singing,

> *Sure men are grown absurd,*
> *Thus taking black for white!*
> *To hug and kiss a dingy miss,*
> *Will hardly suit an age like this—*
> *Unless here, some friends appear,*
> *Who like this wedding night.*

In Colman's hands, the tragic tale of Inkle and Yarico is rewritten as a sentimental farce, critical toward and yet forgiving of colonial commercialism and masculine heartlessness. Underlying it all is a sense of the absurdity of interracial love and marriage anywhere but the playhouse, among the lowest classes of colonial society, or far removed from the light of day.[10]

A comedic interracial romance set in the cruel and dehumanizing world of Atlantic slavery, the wildly popular play benefited from and helped focus attention on the burgeoning abolitionist movement, which rapidly mobilized the masses throughout Britain, gaining parliamentary supporters and generating a public debate over slavery and the slave trade. An elusive noble savage, Yarico played a pivotal role in the early stages of British abolitionism; her ambiguity as a heroine of distinctly non-European yet malleable lineage allowed for creative interpretation on the part of theater management, actresses, audiences, and the broader public. Although Colman retained Yarico's Indian identity, he altered her complexion, originally described by Ligon as simply "bright bay" or reddish brown, into "good comely copper" that is also "quite dark; but very elegant; like a Wedgwood tea-pot." As the abolitionist potential of Colman's opera became apparent throughout the 1787 and 1788 theater seasons, Yarico became the subject of antislavery poems, Wowski appeared in overtly sexual situations in graphic prints and as a recognizable black-faced character at masked balls, and playhouse managers encouraged actresses to darken their complexion and play Yarico as a sympathetic African woman. Yarico commanded the British public's fascination due to her character's ability to combine feminine virtue and delicacy, in accordance with metropolitan gender ideals, with aesthetically appealing yet decidedly non-European ancestry and physical features. "She's of no common stamp," Inkle insists to the governor of Barbados. Rather, Yarico is ideally suited to satisfy his fancy for "a delicate girl, above the common run, and none of your thick-lip'd, flat-nos'd, squabby, dumpling dowdies." Colman, and those who sought to build upon his play's success, set the well-spoken and well-proportioned Yarico apart from the comic iconography of the primitive, voluptuous black female. She did not boast the massive exposed breasts, gaping mouth, thick, unruly limbs, and bare and pungent genital organs associated with the early modern female grotesque.[11]

Nor did Yarico exhibit the thick, insensitive skin that Europeans, Mark M. Smith argues, so often attributed to African slaves and cited as evidence of their suitability for manual labor and violent reprimands. Like the African character Imoinda, described as a "beautiful *Black Venus*" with "charming" features and "delicate Vertues" in Aphra Behn's 1688 novella *Oroonoko; or, The Royal Slave,* Yarico melded the beauty of a classical heroine with the innocence of the idealized noble savage. Her dramatic efficacy lay in her transmutability as a character, capable of shifting from Amerindian to African while still retaining audience sympathy, in much the same way that playwrights such as Thomas Southerne transformed Behn's Roman-featured, ebony Imoinda into a white woman in subsequent retellings of the novella. In stark contrast, Colman described Yarico's attendant Wowski as "black," a "plump bit," and, most frequently, "dingy," marking her as racially inferior and aesthetically unappetizing, a conduit for sexual and reproductive contamination.[12]

Such visual and verbal cues granted the opera's audience the keys necessary to decode Yarico's and Wowski's place within a racial taxonomic system whereby lineage, physical appearance, and social status overlapped and were conflated with one another. For example, in its review of Colman's opera, the *New London Magazine* extolled and eroticized Yarico as a "sable nymph" but dismissed Wowski as "a girl of darker complexion and meaner habiliments." Descriptions of this nature emphasized the foreign bodies and backgrounds of the two primary female protagonists as well as their potential enslaveability as bearers of dark skin. They also clarified the central distinction between the two female characters: Yarico, like other rare "Afric nymphs," who "in form and feature would bear a comparison with the average of European beauties," warranted elite and middling white male attention; the dumpy, dowdy Wowski, more representative of a typical enslaved woman in the metropolitan imagination, offered, at best, lower-class satisfactions. Thus Yarico, like a Wedgwood teapot, became a unique, highly prized commodity, worthy of the esteem of refined white audiences, while the grotesque and comical Wowski merited laughter and disdain. Indeed, the more unappealing and base Wowski appeared, the more bluntly her black female body conveyed its sexual availability (if not its desirability) to white men of all ranks, including those of wealth and breeding.[13]

The ready availability of the black female body for sexual service is well captured in James Gillray's humorous etching *Wouski* (figure 8), published by Hannah Humphrey in January 1788. The print depicts Prince William Henry, third son of George III, embracing a voluptuous dark-skinned woman while lying suspended in a sailor's hammock in a room imitative of a ship's cabin. The pair stare longingly into each other's eyes, Prince William's left leg draped provocatively over the woman's body, a puncheon of Jamaican rum and a chest marked with the initials P. W. H. sitting directly beneath them. Prince William began a career in the Royal Navy at age fourteen and, after his promotion to captain of the *Pegasus* in the late 1780s, was posted to

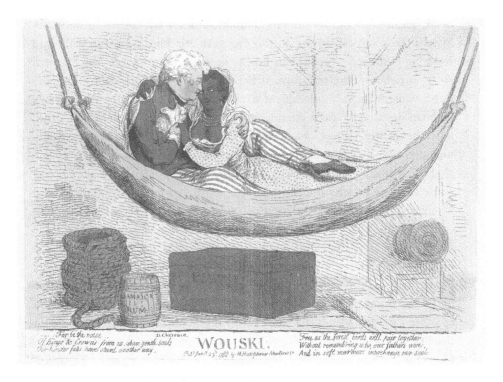

For be the noise
Of kings & Crowns from us whose gentle souls
Our kinder fate have steer'd another way.

D. Clarence.

WOUSKI.
Pub'd Jan'y 23'd 1788 by H. Humphrey New Bond S.t

Free as the forest birds well pair together,
Without remembring who our fathers were,
And in soft murmurs interchange our souls.

8. James Gillray, *Wouski* (London, 1788). © The Trustees of the British Museum.

the British West Indies. Once stationed in the Caribbean slave islands, the prince indulged often and freely in all of the dissipations on offer, including drinking, feasting, and fornication, and became friendly with members of the Jamaica assembly. In May 1787, he took a mercury cure, as he explained to his older brother George, Prince of Wales, for "a sore I had contracted in a most extraordinary manner in my pursuit of the *Dames de Couleurs*." The following year, his physician, Dr. Fidge, confirmed that Prince William had contracted gonorrhea and suffered from periodic reoccurrences of the venereal disease. The prince's venereal affliction, characterized by intermittent manifestations of painful genital sores, did not curtail his enjoyment of the West Indian sexual economy. "I am sorry to say that I have been living a terrible debauched life, of which I am heartily ashamed and tired. I must in the West Indies turn over a new leaf," he swore on October 26, 1788, "or else I shall be irrevocably ruined." Colonists in the British Caribbean, such as Dr. Jonathan Troup, a Scottish physician who practiced medicine in Dominica and kept a daily journal, made note of the prince's ready participation in the sexually exploitative practices of a white, heterosexual, and masculine Creole culture. "Introduced to the mollatoe girl who was kept by Prince Wm Henry—a very nice and well dress'd girl and handsome," Troup noted on May 15, 1789.[14]

Gillray counted on the metropolitan public's familiarity with the theatrical character of the lowly, sexually servile Wowski to deride the prince for his interracial sexual escapades and known sympathy toward West Indian slaveholders, whose degraded tastes he apparently shared. That even a well-bred young man of royal blood, third in line to inherit the British throne, had indulged his passions with enslaved and free women of mixed ancestry made Gillray's *Wouski* all the more laughable and grotesque. By engaging in lecherous, racially immoral behavior in the West Indies, the prince marked himself as a fair target of public reproof. That Britons saw news of Prince William's sexual exploits with mixed-race women in the Caribbean as scandalous is also substantiated by the publication of a second print, *The Royal Captain,* published in *Rambler's Magazine* in April 1788 and no doubt inspired by Gillray's *Wouski,* in which the prince fondles a black woman inside a ship's cabin. Whether serious or comical, contemporary textual and visual allusions to Colman's *Inkle and Yarico* yoked the opera to the pressing issues of African slavery and interracial sex in the British popular imagination. As Elizabeth Inchbald, the playwright and actress who penned the preface to the opera's later editions, noted, Colman should have set the opening scene in Africa. "As slaves are imported from Africa, and never from America," she wrote, "the audience, in the two last acts of this play, feel as if they had been in the wrong quarter of the globe during the first act."[15]

THE BLACK JOKE

In May 1788, just as Prime Minister William Pitt, responding to public fervor for abolition, persuaded the Commons to debate the slave trade in the next session, the first in a series of graphic prints showing a white man discovering a black woman in bed appeared. Deriving their commercial and symbolic power from a wide variety of themes, including the slavery debate and the popularity of *Inkle and Yarico* as well as a theatrical tradition of bed tricks involving the clandestine sexual substitution of one person for another, these sensational images drew attention to the black female body as a site of forbidden pleasure and racial pollution. Samuel Ireland's *The Discovery* (1788), for instance, after a William Hogarth engraving recounting a trick played in 1744 on John Highmore, the womanizing manager of Drury Lane Theatre,

Qui Color albus erat, nunc est contrarius albo.

Etch'd by Sam.ʳ Ireland, from a very scarce Print in his Collection engrav'd by HOGARTH. The gallant Hero who gave rise to this design was Mr. HIGHMORE formerly Manager of Drury lane Theatre, by purchase of Cibber's share in the Patent. Few impressions were taken from the Plate when it was destroy'd Mrs. HOGARTH recollected the Print by the title of the DISCOVERY. London, Publish'd 1ˢᵗ May 1788, by Molton & C.º 132 Pall Mall.

9. Samuel Ireland (after William Hogarth), *The Discovery* (London, 1788).
Etching and engraving; second state of three, sheet 7 13/16 × 8 7/16 in.
(19.8 × 21.5 cm). Harris Brisbane Dick Fund, 1932 (32.35(240)). Image copyright
© The Metropolitan Museum of Art. Image source: Art Resource, NY.

involving an assignation with an actress and the surprise substitution of a
black prostitute, shows three men barging into a darkened bedchamber (figure 9). They draw back the curtain on Highmore's concealed sexual partner,
illuminating her blackness. The woman, lying in a state of dishevel, her right
breast bare, reaches out to touch her lover's startled face, grinning coyly, while
two of his interloping friends point to the exposed skin of her chest. Underneath the scene is a Latin text from Ovid's *Metamorphoses:* "Qui Color albus
erat, nunc est contrarius albo" (He/she who was once white is now the oppo-

site), indicating Highmore's astonishment upon discovering the switch. Here, black-white sexual intimacy is evoked to poke fun at the sordid character of the white male partner, and, as David Dabydeen suggests of the presence of black prostitutes in Hogarth's prints, to amplify the atmosphere of obscenity. In eighteenth-century culture, indulging a taste for black women, long conceptualized by Englishmen as monstrous and sexually insatiable, was associated with "a desire for retrogression, for the dark animal sensations symbolised by the black woman."[16]

That the black woman herself grins amusedly in *The Discovery* hints that an "obscene pun is also involved for her laughter evokes the term 'black joke' which was slang for the female sexual organs." Sung in British taverns and evoked in poetry, plays, novels, and jest books, the "black joke" originated with an Irish ballad and derived its efficacy from the sexual imagination of the Stuart era, when authors deployed all manner of bawdy references to the color black—"black thing," black hole," "black legacy," and "black art," to name but a few—to allude to female genitalia or pubic hair. In one telling seventeenth-century poem, "On Black Hayre and Eyes," ascribed to several authors including John Donne, the narrator reassures his lover that her dark hair and eyes are deeply alluring:

> And as by heads of springs men often knowe
> The nature of the streames that run belowe,
> So your black haire and eyes do give direction
> To make me thinke the rest of like complexion.

"And if I might direct my shaft aright," the author concludes provocatively, "The black mark would I hitt and not the white."[17]

If sexual puns about black objects signified certain male fantasies in the seventeenth century, the "black joke" became a veritable cultural phenomenon during the following century. Firmly ensconced in the English cultural lexicon as a reference to "the female pudenda," Vic Gatrell explains, the black joke "was lewdly known to every tavern frequenter from the 1730s to the 1810s, and it featured in print culture as well." Included in a single-sheet edition of songs in the Bodleian Library, the earliest extant version of the tune entitled "The Original Black Joke, Sent from Dublin" (c.1720) describes men of various ages, nationalities, and professions lusting after a woman's "coal black joke, & belly so white," with the implication that "all degrees of Mankind do covet/A Coal black &c." The black joke tune exploded in popularity after an innocuous version appeared in Charles Coffey's ballad opera *The Beggar's*

Wedding, which premiered in London at the Little Haymarket Theatre on May 29, 1729. English authors raced to produce new songs to the air of the "Coal-Black Joak," with lyrics ranging from the suggestive to the very explicit, and the tune's inexorably bawdy undertone may help to explain its widespread popularity. "The Black Joak" appeared in a collection of popular songs published in 1730 and in John Gay's comic opera *Calista* (1731). The following year, the *Gentleman's Magazine* capitalized on the black joke's notoriety, musing about the adventures of "Honest *John Cole*," "who from his Antipathy to every Thing white" married a "Blackmore at *Blackwall*" and enjoyed intrigues "with several Cole-Black-Jokes, Brown Jokes, and Jokes as Sweet as Honey." William Hogarth certainly grasped its lewd connotations. In *A Rake's Progress,* plate 3 (1735), he depicted a pregnant singer holding "The Black Joke" song sheet amid an orgy of debauchery taking place inside the Rose Tavern.[18]

After 1730, multiple iterations of the black joke tune hit the tavern and theater circuit and made their way into British plays, operas, graphic prints, and collections of popular songs. Fashionable dictionaries such as *The Female Glossary* (c. 1732) connected the black joke to prostitution early on by claiming that, of all the "Jokes," including black, white, red, and brown, "The *Black Joke* . . . is the best for Service." The tune's emphasis on disembodied female genitalia fostered such connections. References alluded to the sexual misadventures of a comical whore who, like "Miss Kitty" in *The Musical Miscellany* (1760), looked "for some Cull for to draw in/To her black Joak and belly so white." An obscene version of the black joke tune, published in a 1769 songbook, caricatured female genitalia by contrasting its objectionable exterior appearance with the pleasure afforded by its interiority:

> O Maggy, O Maggy, your c_____t it is black!
> And d_____n you, you dog, and what of that?
> Tho' it's black without, it is velvet within,
> Then out with your whistle, and whip it in
> To my black joke and belly so white.

In a less explicit version, published nearly two decades later in *The Convivial Songster,* the author declared that all men

> Love a coal-black joke that will passion provoke;
> It is like a Scotch coal, it will burn without Smoke
> —A black joke and belly so white.[19]

The black joke's inseparable association with female genitalia secured its place in the enlarged second edition of Francis Grose's *Classical Dictionary of the Vulgar Tongue* (1788). Grose described it as "a popular tune to a song, having for the burden, 'Her black joke and belly so white'; figuratively the black joke signifies the monosyllable"—which Grose identified as "a woman's commodity." Grose also defined "Bottomless Pit" and "Brown Madam, or Miss Brown," among others, as euphemisms for "the monosyllable," capturing the prevailing cultural link between the dark perils of hell and female sexual power. As Lear, railing against female sexuality, exclaims in Shakespeare's *King Lear* (first performed 1606, first printed 1608),

> down from the waist they are centaurs, though women all above;
> but to the girdle do the God's inherit, beneath is all the fiends.
> There's hell, there's darkness,
> There is the sulphurous pit,
> burning, scalding, stench, consumption.

While Britons who reveled in ribald humor may have found sexual metaphors linking female genitalia to a hellish pit amusing, the inclusion of dark-skinned women in the iconography of the black joke conferred an additional element of incongruity.[20]

John Nichols, contemporary biographer of Hogarth, claimed that when Hogarth's wife recounted the bed-trick event upon which her husband based his original version of *The Discovery*, she deemed it "a very laughable circumstance here commemorated by her husband's pencil." Replacing a white prostitute with a black prostitute, and successfully duping her white lover, took the concept of the black joke to an entirely new and ironic level. The apparent success of this black joke, however, also belied its potentially troubling undercurrent: that with difference subsumed by darkness, the tactile experience of a black woman's body might mimic that of the white female body. Highmore's failure to identify his bedmate as a black woman lacking a "belly so white" implied, as Wendy Doniger elucidates with reference to classic tales of sexual masquerade, "that sex is an act in which the parties are interchangeable, that bodies can be changed without one's knowledge." Collapsing the distinction between white and black female bodies in a darkened bedchamber complicated contemporary ideas about the physical distinctiveness of race while simultaneously presenting all women's "commodities" as the exclusive preserve of white males. Unchecked sexual desire, these images and texts implied, held the power to collapse the supposedly inherent conceptual and physical distance separating black and white bloodlines.[21]

In addition to the private joke immortalized by Hogarth's print, *The Discovery* also seized on a well-circulated rumor, later recounted by Sir Walter Scott and others in the nineteenth century, that in 1773 Charles James Fox, a young, indebted Whig politician known for his swarthy features, had fallen victim to a swindler known as Mrs. Grieve. An expert in defrauding respectable men, Mrs. Grieve claimed she would arrange a match between Fox and a Miss Phipps, "a *hyaena,* that is an heiress—an immense Jamaica heiress," who had recently arrived from the West Indies with an absurdly large fortune of £80,000. Encumbered with gambling debts, Fox pursued the potential match in earnest, undeterred by Mrs. Grieve's repeated cancellation of their intended interview and declaration that the Creole heiress preferred fair men, "and as he was remarkably black, that he must powder his eyebrows." According to Scott's version of the tale, Mrs. Grieve, fearful of discovery, later attempted to dissuade Fox from the match by alleging that Miss Phipps had birthed an illegitimate child. When this failed to deter him, she finally convinced Fox to abandon his pursuit of the fictitious heiress by "doubl[ing] the disgusting dose." "'The poor child' she said, 'was unfortunately of a mixd colour somewhat tinged with the blood of Africa—no doubt Mr. Fox himself was very dark and the circumstance might not draw attention' etc. etc." In these retellings, Mrs. Grieve refers deliberately to racial mixture and African blood for maximum effect. A politically ambitious British gentleman with a tawny complexion would not dare to darken his reputation with the stain of racial impurity.[22]

The popular playwright Samuel Foote exploited Fox's supposed disgrace to great comical effect in *The Cozeners,* first performed on July 15, 1774, at the Haymarket in London, without referencing the politician directly. In the play, Toby Aircastle, a foolish and materialistic young man, casts aside Betsey Blossom, the woman he loves, in favor of a West Indian heiress promised to him by the charlatan Mrs. Fleecem. To authenticate the ruse, Mrs. Fleecem suggests that Aircastle "blacken" his eyebrows before meeting a Creole heiress accustomed to gentlemen of "rather a fallower hue." She orders her black maid Marianne to pose as the heiress, knowing that "her complexion will betray her at once" unless Marianne conceals herself within a curtained bed in a dimly lit room. The importance of both darkness and dialect to the success of the hoax is made clear by Mrs. Fleecem's instructions to Marianne: "Go in and throw yourself on the bed; and, do you hear, let the window be shut, and the curtains drawn exceedingly close. . . . You will only be asked a question or two . . . to which you need say nothing but Yes. . . . And, Marianne—no candle."[23]

When Aircastle enters the room "as dark as a dungeon" to inquire after the purported heiress's health, the concealed Marianne obediently responds "yes" to every question he asks of her. This outlandish scenario becomes increasingly humorous for the audience, as Aircastle approaches the curtained bed, sans candle, completely unaware that he is the butt of a cruel joke:

> TOBY. [M]ay I crave leave to kiss your lily white hand?
> MAR. Yes.
> TOBY. On my knees let me thank you, fairest creature—
> her skin is vast soft—they be wonderful pretty things I have
> brought you. . . . May I draw the curtain a bit, only just to
> give you a glimpse?
> MAR. Yes.
> TOBY. So I will—I should be glad to take a peep at her too;
> she is a mighty agreeable body; does not talk much, indeed,
> but is vast sensible.

Demanding audience complicity while ratcheting up the suspense, Foote allows Aircastle to part the curtains but delays Marianne's unveiling until the last possible moment. According to Scott, one female audience member later remembered, "The laugh was universal so soon as the black woman appeard [*sic*]." Marianne's black skin and servile speech patterns provoke amusement for the audience but pure horror for Aircastle:

> TOBY. hey! What is this? Lord have mercy on me, she is
> turned all of a sudden as black as a crow . . .
> MAR. Massa, won't you come here?
> TOBY. Not I.
> MAR. I come to you.
> TOBY. The devil you will; you must run pretty fast then—
> keep off me—holloa house; stop the black thing that is hard
> at my —. [exit]

This provocative "dark-chamber scene," one of Foote's biographers later admitted in his remarks on the play, "must be acknowledged a little *outré*, even for farce."[24]

THE CANDLE OF REASON

Foote was far from the first dramatist to rely upon the technique of a darkened bedchamber to bring together unusual or comic couplings. English playwrights capitalized on the popular bed-trick theatrical device to explore questions about sexuality, race, and identity long before Foote's *The Cozeners* entertained audiences with a black maid's near-successful duping of a white man. Bed tricks involving a "blackamoor" servant woman, lying in wait as a substitute bedmate in order to surprise and chastise a white mistress's sexually aggressive suitor, occurred regularly in seventeenth-century plays. Through the motifs of disguise and mistaken identity, early modern bed tricks facilitated an unsolicited interracial sexual union only to dissolve it before consummation. The duped male victim, after discovering the substitute bedmate, nearly always reacted with fear, horror, or violence, confirming not only the insufficiency of the dark-skinned female servant as a surrogate romantic partner or potential mate but the perceived repulsiveness of black femininity and the association of black skin with the devil. By drawing together incongruously paired bedmates, bed tricks worked to stage a carefully contained and therefore amusing transgressive sexual fantasy.[25]

A representative Jacobean example is John Fletcher's *Monsieur Thomas* (written c. 1610–16, first published in 1639). Thomas is tricked into getting into bed with Kate, a black maid. Kate's chaste white mistress, Mary, forewarned of Thomas's sexual intentions, has instructed her maid to lie in bed in her place. The stage direction for this scene anticipates the bed trick, specifying that the audience should see *"a bed discovered with a Black More in it."* After kissing his bedmate in the dark, Thomas discovers her true identity by candlelight and exclaims in horror,

> Holy saints, defend me.
> The devill, devill, devill, devill, O the devill!
> . . . I am abus'd most damnedly: most beastly,
> Yet if it be a She devill . . .

Simultaneously terrified and repulsed by her dark skin, Thomas assumes that Kate is a devil. Yet driven by a combination of lust and rage, he proclaims his determination to bed the "She devill" to spite her white mistress, who watches from the sidelines. "Woman, I here disclaime thee; and in vengeance/Ile marry with that devil," he tells Mary. Whether Thomas follows through on his threat or simply beats Kate and then flees is unclear, but the underlying tone of their final scripted exchange in bed is one of brutal sexual domination:

> THO.   Plague O your Spanish leather hide; ile waken ye:
>   Devill, good night: good night good devill.
> MOORE [KATE].   Oh!
> THO.   Rore againe, devill, rore againe. *Ex. Tho.*
> MOORE.   O, O, sir.

The ill-treated Kate responds to Thomas's physical and implied sexual abuse by chastising Mary: "Pray lye here your self, next Mistris/And entertaine your sweet heart." Although Mary, the desirable white heroine, devises the bed trick to preserve her own virtue, it is Kate, her lowly black maid, who suffers the brutal consequences of this "black joke."[26]

That the preservation of elite female chastity demands in exchange the defilement of a woman of lower status is a common theme in seventeenth-century plays. Dramatists utilized the bed-trick motif to enable heroines either to avoid copulation by sending a surrogate in their place or to impersonate someone else in order to engage in forbidden sexual behavior. However, not all staged encounters between white men and black women occurred as a result of a ruse instigated by a white heroine. English dramatists both harnessed and reinforced the traditional association between blackness and evil by linking dark-skinned characters with sin, violence, and the demonic. Take John Fletcher's tragic play *The Knight of Malta* (first staged in 1617). Mountferrat, a knight who has taken a vow of chastity, is spurned by the virgin noblewoman Oriana, whom he greatly desires. Incensed by Oriana's rejection, Mountferrat feigns love for her black servant, Zanthia, and persuades her to forge a letter declaring that her mistress intends to pursue a treasonous marriage with a Turk. Zanthia, recognizing a nefarious kindred spirit in Mountferrat, attempts to redirect the knight's passion away from his idealized fair lady. She assures him that her black body is as desirable as any white woman's:

> No bath, no blanching water, smoothing Oils
> Doth mend me up; and yet *Mountferrat,* know,
> I am as full of Pleasure in the Touch
> As e're a white-fac'd Puppt of 'em all
> Juicy, and firm.

Mountferrat later broadcasts his willingness to assuage his indiscriminate sexual appetite with a lowly black female.

> It is not Love but strong Libidinous Will
> That triumphs o'er me, and to satiate that,
> What Difference 'twixt this *Moor*, and her fair Dame?
> Night makes their Hues alike, their Use is so;
> Whose hand is so subtle, he can Colours name,
> If he do wink, and touch 'em? Lust being blind,
> Never in Women did Distinction find.

While proper, legitimate love demands fair skin, blind lust does not. Isaac Teale's "The Sable Venus: An Ode," first published in Kingston in 1765 for Bryan Edwards, captured this sentiment more than a century later: "Both just alike, except the white,/no difference, no—none at night."[27]

After lust and darkness dissipate, masculine reason and aesthetic sense return and black and white resume their assumed innate differences. The despoiled black woman is readily discarded in preference for the chaste white heroine. Zanthia underlines the disposability and sexual objectification of the black female body for the play's audiences and readers when she tells Mountferrat,

> like a Property, when I have serv'd
> Your Turns, you'll cast me off, or hang me up
> For a sign somewhere.

It is unsurprising, then, to learn that Mountferrat, as punishment for his villainy, is forced to degrade both his reputation and his bloodline by marrying the lowly black servant he reviles as a "night Hag" and "Hell itself confin'd in flesh." Dramatic representations of immoral dark-skinned female characters thus reinforced the status of black women as debased sexual objects, fit for public display, consumption, and scorn, long before the English came into contact with women of African ancestry or learned of West Indian debauchery. Some of the earliest images of men and women of African descent objectified and fetishized the black body, using the artifice of blackness to accentuate the power and supposed purity of whiteness. Paintings of the aristocracy and gentry accompanied by their black slaves signified the role of black servile figures as property and exotic objects of display. British cultural productions assigned social and moral meaning to the black female body, and the only way to "discover the meaning," Roxann Wheeler points out, "is to consider the context."[28]

Invented scenarios of mistaken identities and racial immorality, once so far removed from everyday life in Jacobean England, assumed greater significance against the backdrop of abolitionist and proslavery debate in the late eighteenth and early nineteenth centuries. The circulation of abolitionist texts and images, and well-publicized parliamentary debates on the slave trade and colonial slavery, enhanced public awareness of the harsh treatment of slaves—particularly enslaved women—in the West Indian colonies. Discussion of the plight of distant slaves, imprisoned in factories on the West African coast, trafficked across the Atlantic and beyond, or compelled to toil on Caribbean sugar plantations, coincided with the greater visibility of individuals of African and mixed ancestry in metropolitan Britain. Over the course of the eighteenth century, colonial merchants, planters, government officials, and naval officers returned home with scores of slaves in tow; some Britons also arrived accompanied by free women of African descent as well as their own or others' illegitimate mixed offspring. For the residents of major port cities such as London, Bristol, and Liverpool, encounters with black men and women were no longer reserved almost exclusively for the stage or printed page. Evidence of social, economic, and sexual intercourse between Britons who had lived or worked in the Atlantic empire and individuals born to enslaved mothers was now readily apparent, and the future prospect of free and unregulated interracial relations in Britain secured.[29]

Georgian caricaturists increasingly deployed the imagery of the black woman discovered in bed to envisage the disturbing aftermath of interracial sex from the perspective of the white male metropolitan gaze. By framing interracial sexual encounters as illicit yet distastefully nightmarish scenes, artists invited white male viewers in Britain to indulge their appetite for sexually accessible black women while simultaneously rendering such women too repulsive and monstrous for a legitimate attachment. Graphic satires laid bare the degraded position of enslaved women as fetishized commodities of public exchange, denied the benefits and privileges of privacy and Christian familial attachments because of their chattel status and servile heathen lineage. The sight of a dark-skinned woman in an intimate space also marked the dramatic absence of the scene's rightful subject: the desirable fair beauty. This substitution appeared more conspicuous and therefore humorous when caricaturists depicted the black woman discovered in bed as a grotesque erotic nightmare, as in Richard Newton's titillating 1796 graphic print *What a Nice Bit!* (figure 10). A geriatric white man stands shocked and quivering in nightgown and cap, his eyes round and terrified, his mouth twisted into a grimace, as he

10. Richard Newton, *What a Nice Bit!* (London, 1796).
Courtesy of The Lewis Walpole Library, Yale University.

illuminates by candlelight a somnolent black woman whose large, uncovered breasts are fully exposed to the viewer. Her dark skin, gaping too-large teeth, distorted, swinish nose, and beefy arms indicate her obvious misplacement in this elaborate four-poster bed, to amusing effect. The artists and printmakers who produced such prints, and the members of the British public who purchased them, well knew not to take literally colloquial proverbs such as "*A black plum is as sweet as a white*—And a black Woman as agreeable (at least to some, for what Fancy makes it) as a fair one." Newton's invitation to viewers to savor this "nice bit" is ironic in the extreme.[30]

Caricaturists understood that penetrating the privacy of a bedchamber only to uncover a grotesque black woman would provoke viewers to laughter, even as they reflected on the erotic possibilities of this unusual scenario. Similar circumstances had done so repeatedly for centuries. "Laugher depends on the sudden and surprised recognition of *incongruity* between two mutually exclusive codes or contexts, when these are unexpectedly yoked together in verbal play, images, or behaviour," notes Vic Gatrell. By replacing a sleeping white woman with her hypersexual racial counterpart, the print imagines the sexual conquest of the black female body as an appalling comic inversion.

For while the defenseless woman seems to discharge a masculine sexual fantasy, her black skin and distorted features indicate her status as a strange and unwelcome bedfellow, a perverse nightmare. This playful nighttime fright infused the familiar bed-trick motif with the sexual horror of Henry Fuseli's popular dreamscape engraving *The Night Mare* (1782), depicting a pale young woman swooning in her curtained bed under the erotic force of a dark, squatting incubus while a white-eyed horse watches. A mock sinister figure, the large slumbering black woman thus served a dual role as a sexualized object of ridicule and the embodiment of moral depravity.[31]

THE SEXUAL EXPLOITS OF BLACK MOLL

The effectiveness of such iconography in late eighteenth-century Britain stemmed from black women's historical association with sin and deviant sexuality, marginal social and economic status in the metropole, and presumed inferiority as members of a "servile" race. Employed in England as servants, slaves, entertainers, and prostitutes since the late sixteenth century, women of African descent held one of the most debased positions in British society. Their concentration in the capital, limited employment options, and lowly standing meant that they could be found among London's marginalized underclass, living in crowded, poverty-stricken communities composed primarily of poor whites. London's poorest slums, Gretchen Gerzina reminds us, "were also populated by those whose only recourse [from] starvation and death was frequently theft, prostitution and beggary."[32]

Theatrical productions such as John Gay's enormously influential *The Beggar's Opera* (1728), which referenced the trial of a "very active and industrious" cutpurse known as Black Moll, paved the way for the association of prostitutes with crime, and eventually both with black women, well before the abolition era. When Black Moll sends word to Peachum, the thief-taker, that she seeks legal assistance at her trial, he responds, "Why, she may plead her belly at worst [i.e., claim pregnancy to avoid execution], to my knowledge she has taken care of that security." That a woman named Black Moll would be both a common criminal and a common prostitute would not have surprised British audiences. In metropolitan culture, the name "Moll" was synonymous with "whore," based in large part on city comedies such as Thomas Dekker's *The Roaring Girl; or, Moll Cutpurse* (1611) and Daniel Defoe's infamous 1722 novel *Moll Flanders,* about a country girl imprisoned for prostitution and theft. William Hogarth drew on these cultural connections in his Harlot's Progress series, in which he detailed the experiences of Moll Hackabout, a country girl turned harlot corrupted by the commercialism of the city, in visual form.[33]

While Black Moll started her theatrical career as a compromised thief relegated to a minor, offstage role, during the abolition era she emerged as a stock character signifying a crooked/black prostitute. Literary and visual references to dark-skinned ladies of pleasure far outweighed black women's demographic presence in Britain, where the free black community was predominantly male and concentrated in shipping and domestic service. Peter Fryer and Felicity Nussbaum note the existence of several notorious black streetwalkers in late eighteenth-century London, including "Sarah," "Miss Wilson," and "Black Harriot" (a former Jamaican slave who operated a brothel) as well as an actual "Black Moll," but stress, as Nussbuam explains, that "their small numbers made their appearance an unusual occurrence." In the mid-1770s, the diarist Thomas Boswell reported hearing of a "black bawdy-house," staffed exclusively by black women and catering to an elite clientele, but apparently never visited the rumored establishment in person. Although lower-class white women dominated London's sex-for-hire market, the infrequency of black prostitutes did not prevent comedic authors such as William Winstanley from lumping together common "whores," including "Long Meg, Black Moll, [and] Dirty Paps, all in a tether." Black Moll also made regular appearances in bawdy tales, plays, and songs about London prostitution, such as "Song LII" of *The Bacchanalian Songster* (1783):

> My peepers, who've we here now! Why this is sure Black Moll:
> My ma'm, you're of the fair sex, so welcome to Mill Doll.
> The cull with you who'd venture into a snoozing ken,
> Like blackamoor Othello, should put out the light, and then—

This lighthearted colloquial song uses slang and cant terms—such as *Black Moll* (a crooked or black whore) *Mill Doll* (Bridewell), *cull* (a prostitute's client or target), and *ken* (alehouse)—to evoke the criminal lifestyle of prostitutes and the folly of the men who are their prey. It also alludes to Shakespeare's play *Othello* (first performed in 1604) and the moment at which the impassioned Moor, believing his fair-skinned wife, Desdemona, has betrayed him, enters their bedchamber and extinguishes her life by candlelight.[34]

Darkening the light of reason to indulge unruly passions, particularly with black women, is a recurrent theme in Georgian visual, literary, and dramatic imagery. Although the underlying implication is that all women's bodies are interchangeable and equally subject to white male desire and dominion, the promiscuous pleasure of a racially exotic "commodity" is more appropriately confined to darkened bedchambers, behind closed doors. Primitive, unthinking pleasures are permissible only in the dark. For example, in the poem "In Praise of a Negress" (1778), by the Irish poet Reverend James Delacourt, a black woman remarks on her white teeth, black eyes, unfamiliarity with "paint or patches, [or] perfum'd fraud," and soft, velvety skin. "Ah! who will on those alters sacrifice?" she implores.

> But if I please less in the sultry day,
> My colour with the candles dies away;
> Since to our hue the light is deem'd a foe
> Night will a THAIS in my charms bestow.[35]

Abolition-era prints featuring women of African ancestry engaged in sexual scenarios with white men in metropolitan settings reinforced the connection between blackness and pleasurable sites of contact on the female body, yet did so with tongue planted firmly in cheek. Carnal relations with hypersexual, compliant, disposable black women, caricaturists hinted, would maximize white male gratification—but at the expense of debasing their rational and moral faculties.

Caricaturists also pictured the horror of the next morning, as an evening of interracial licentiousness gave way to the brutal light of day. Isaac Cruikshank's *The Humours of Belvoir Castle; or, The Morning After,* published by S. W. Fores in 1799, presents confrontations between eight odd couples following a night of unbridled debauchery. In the second encounter on the top left panel (figure 11), a plump black woman in a flimsy low-cut nightgown, cap, and red slippers holds a candle up to her sexual partner, a rosy-cheeked, homely white man with wild hair, an unbuttoned shirt, and clenched fists. Seeing his sexual partner of the previous night clearly in the candlelight, he exclaims, "Oh Lord! Oh Lord! why I have not slept all night with you—you Black Devil have I?" "Ifs you did, and you be very pretty man," she confirms with a wry grin. This unlikely pair seems to validate the old adage, frequently mocked by eighteenth-century satirists and recast in explicit sexual terms, "But the Light of Reason will be very dark without the Candle of Virtue." The success of the "black joke" depended on some measure of public agreement that darkness/night/blackness aligned with sin and lust and brightness/day/ whiteness with reason and Christian virtue.[36]

11. Isaac Cruikshank, *The Humours of Belvoir Castle; or, The Morning After* (detail) (London, 1799). Library of Congress, British Cartoon Collection.

MALE PLEASURE AND THE GROTESQUE AESTHETIC

The growing conceptual gulf between Europeans and Africans, specifically the dehumanization and commodification of the enslaved black female, overlapped with comic imagery of interracial sexual permissiveness to provoke uneasy laughter. Plenty of caricaturists depicted white women from all social classes in degrading, overtly sexual situations. Yet the aesthetic judgment underlying satirical depictions of black women with corpulent, ill-proportioned bodies and exaggerated, bestial facial features, all of which their white male lovers turn a blind eye to in exchange for unrestricted sexual gratification, is that "taste, like common sense, resides between sense and intellect, facilitates the development of reason, and is innate but developed through cultivation." For eighteenth-century aesthetic theorists, taste therefore "serves both a private function and a social one, as it begins with personal experience, is refined through contact with others, and in the process ultimately strengthens the natural bonds that provide social stability." The personal revulsion occasioned by an encounter with outward deformity safeguarded social and gender norms. "Beauty is that form of an entire body, which pleases every one of our senses," noted the author of *The Art of Beauty* (1760). "The best limb'd and best featured body becomes deformed, without an exact and necessary proportion of fat," he cautioned. "In general, too much fatness spoils beauty; for it effaces all those fine features which Nature draws with such art and delicacy. It thickens the neck, which under its natural form, excites both love and affection; but by the huge bulk it acquires by fatness, disgust. It destroys the graceful stature, which promises the most sweet, and the most delicate pleasure." In its affront to communal aesthetic standards, the body of the grotesque black female signaled its destabilizing power as a fetishized object of degenerate white male desire.[37]

Drawing on a powerful Christian tradition of depicting black Africans as savages, European naturalists, travelers, and philosophers played a central role in shaping the intellectual and cultural discourse that categorized enslaved women as monstrous and deformed. The Comte de Buffon famously invested African women with the capacity for interbreeding with primates by claiming that orangutans "surprise negresses, whom they detain for the purpose of enjoying them, and entertain them plentifully." "I knew a negress at Loango who remained three years with these animals," he assured readers. That orangutans, long imagined as "a kind of mean Rank of Beings between Men and Baboons," lusted after African women—elevated only slightly above beasts in the Eurocentric great chain of being—struck many Enlightenment writers as plausible, including Thomas Jefferson. Whites of European ancestry, Jefferson argued, possessed "superior beauty," owing to their skin color, hair texture, and "more elegant symmetry of form." Consequently, members of other races naturally preferred whites as sexual partners, "as uniformly as is the preference of the Oranootan for the black women over those of his own species." Owing to widespread speculation about the hybrid lineage of the orangutan, "some Travellers have been silly enough to think it might be the Offspring of a Woman and a Monkey: a Chimera which the Negroes themselves laugh at," remarked Jean-Jacques Rousseau. Proslavery authors nevertheless paid close attention to fringe claims that primates and Africans shared a common bloodline. Edward Long pointed to imagined parallels between "Negroes" and orangutans as evidence of a natural racial gradation "from the first rudiments perceived in the monkey kind, to the more advanced stages of it in apes, in the *oran-outang,* that type of man, and the Guiney Negroe; and ascending from the varieties of this class to the lighter class, until we mark its utmost limit of perfection in the pure White."[38]

The white gaze that viewed Africans and their descendants as one step away from primates, and black skin and physiognomy as an outward manifestation of an inherited moral defect, also found the prospect of interracial sex profoundly troubling. If the white European, as Long hypothesized, represented the "utmost limit of perfection" and the black African marked the borderline between human and beast, the former had nothing to gain and everything to lose through mixture with the latter. "Their deep black hue, with Wool instead of Hair, the flatness of the Nose, the thickness of the lips, in general the large and wide mouths, with the disagreeable smell of a rank he goat," wrote Reverend Lindsay, rector of Jamaica's St. Catherine parish, in his characterization of African slaves' physical appearance. Saugnier, who in 1792 published details of his travels in West Africa in 1785, expressed his personal disgust at the prospect of intimacy with a black woman. "The negresses, especially, who have naturally an ill smell, exhale a scent sufficient to disgust a man of the least delicacy; insomuch that, notwithstanding my acquaintance with the country, I rather chose to sleep in the open air, than to remain in the same tent with a negress." The anticipated revulsion provoked by a physical encounter with the black female body is captured in Richard Newton's hand-colored etching *The Full Moon in Eclipse* (1797). The print depicts a man gazing through a telescope at the massive exposed buttocks of a squatting black woman while he and his dog wrinkle their noses in disgust. A little over a decade later, London print sellers sought to capitalize on the public fervor to view and touch the buttocks of Saartjie Baartman, known publicly as the "Hottentot Venus." The seminude body of Baartman, the first African woman exhibited in Britain as a "perfect Specimen of that race of people," was associated with black female hypersexuality and appropriated repeatedly to mark the extreme outer limits of both human femininity and white male desire (figure 12).[39]

Contemporary commentators insisted that women of African descent possessed an inexhaustible and indiscriminate sexual hunger as a result of their heathen origins and moral and physical deformities. They also assumed that monogamous Christian marriage encouraged natural reproduction, while haphazard sexual intercourse led to barrenness. Black women's innate sexual proclivities and incapacity for monogamy, some authors asserted, pre-

12. *Love and Beauty—Sartjee the Hottentot Venus* (London, 1811).
Library of Congress, British Cartoon Collection.

vented the increase of the West Indian slave population. "Were *one third* of
the Slaves who are fit for propagation, to be regularly joined in wedlock, and
were they to conform even tolerably to its institutions, the number of Negroes would be considerably increased," claimed Hector Macneil, a Scottish
poet who spent several years in Jamaica and St. Kitts. "But the Negro, and

particularly the Negress are by no means calculated for this state. The infidel-
ity of the ladies . . . must always raise a powerful barrier against prolification."
Reports of the immoral conduct of slaves displaced white men's responsibility
for their sexual exploitation of enslaved women onto the women themselves.
"The Negroe Women go many of them quite naked, they don't know what
Shame is; and are surprised at an *European's* Bashfulness, who perhaps turns
his Head aside at the Sight," noted Charles Leslie in *A New and Exact Account
of Jamaica* (1740). "Some of them go neat enough," he conceded, "but these
are the Favourites of young Squires, who keep them for a certain Use." Leslie's
observation, which jumbled together a presumed lack of Christian modesty
with black female lasciviousness, clarified what European males could expect
from the African women they held in bondage.[40]

Assumptions about African women's bestial nature, offensive bodies, and
uncontrollable lust informed the slavery debate, with negative implications
for the moral character and respectability of the white men whose passions
they incited. For a man to give license knowingly to interracial desire, to find
pleasure in the body of a degraded and brutish woman, would demonstrate
nothing more than the depth of his depravity. Only men of low status such as
"*Creoleans,*" "whose Tastes are so degenerated," to use Captain Charles Johnson's words, would prefer "Negroes to fine *English* Ladies." Observers considered Creole lust for black women and abuse of the enslaved as two sides of
the same degenerate coin. "I compared the Pomp to which some of the black
females were Exalted with ye miserable State to which the rest were reduced,"
noted J. Hector St. John de Crèvecoeur during a visit to Kingston in the
1760s; "the first derived from a perversion of appetites and the other from a
total disregard of humanity." In his withering account of the sexual culture
of Caribbean slavery, Robert Charles Dallas poked fun at a Jamaican colonist known as Franky, deemed "by the courtesy of the island, a gentleman."
Franky, he detailed, "continues a bachelor for a very odd reason, a paradox,
because he is much attached to one of the sex: but the mystery drops when you
learn that his mistress is a fat negro wench, who governs him with as absolute
a sway, as did ever the most fair and beautiful virago her Jerry Sneak. There
are prodigies here that want explanations." Why would an English bachelor
"with an affectation of superior breeding" tie himself to a domineering black
woman? The answer lay, Dallas argued, in Franky's taste for exotic pleasures:
"Benniba, this jetty dame, is the caterer to all his appetites: by her are his daily
luxurious repasts prepared, and in her arms are his happy evenings closed. . . .
Is not Franky a happy man?" George Pinckard, an army surgeon who toured

the Caribbean in the 1790s, interpreted white male lust for enslaved women as evidence of degraded Creole sexual standards. He described visiting a sugar plantation whose owner proclaimed that "all he had, his *Wowski* excepted, was at our command." To Pinckard's shock, the planter's prized "*Wowski*" was a "disgusting black woman," and the jealous planter refused to allow her "to share with others those joys he expects her to reserve for him alone."[41]

Once the abolition of the slave trade became imminent, British West Indian white males came under increased attack in Britain for their casual approach to interracial sex. Caricaturists implied that Caribbean slaveholders should avoid antagonizing enslaved women, whom they would now have to depend upon to birth the next generation of slaves. In Isaac Cruikshank's *A Morning Surprise* (figure 13), published to coincide with the passage of the Abolition Act in 1807, an appalled white man in nightcap and gown sits up, clutching the drawn curtains of his four-poster bed. With wide eyes and an open mouth, the horror-struck man gapes at a sinister, grinning black woman

A MORNING SURPRISE
"Why who the Devil have we got here."- It is only me Massa .

13. Isaac Cruikshank, *A Morning Surprise* (London, c. 1807).
Courtesy of The Lewis Walpole Library, Yale University.

who has infiltrated the privacy of his bedchamber. She is also attired in night-wear, with her breasts exposed, and her smile full of gleaming teeth indicates her pleasure at his shock and discomfort. As the man's hair rises through his nightcap, he exclaims, "'Why who the Devil have we got here!!" "It is only me Massa," she responds with relish. In this scene, the white slave master has become the frightened target of the rampant sexuality of his black female slave rather than the other way around. Instead of provoking British male view-ers' commiseration with a naïve white man hoodwinked by a lascivious black woman in the night, the duped slave owner elicits nothing but scorn. His response confirms his inability to control the monstrous black female that he and other depraved Creole males have unleashed upon white civilized society.

West Indian slaveholders were not the only British males indicted for their unnatural and destructive lust for slave women in Georgian visual and literary culture. Politicians, sailors, merchants, and slavers also shared the blame. In her popular novel *Desmond* (1792), Charlotte Smith, who ben-efited financially from her West Indian husband's plantations yet expressed distaste for Creole slave society, suggested that the highest levels of the British government shared culpability for the sins of interracial sex. In a conversa-tion between the eponymous hero and a Caribbean plantation-owning mem-ber of Parliament, Desmond rejects the M.P.'s assertion that "Negroes" are "a very distinct race from the European" and "not to be called men—they are monkies." Desmond counters by pointing out that the same British males who deem Africans an inferior species nonetheless "prefer the sable nymphs of Africa to the fairer dames of Europe." "I have formerly, in moments of unguarded conviviality, heard you say, that when you were a young man, and in the sea service, you had yourself indulged this partiality for these monkey ladies," he reminds the mortified M.P.[42]

Desmond's mention of the "sea service" is telling. The British Royal Navy commonly invited prostitutes on board ships of war after arrival in port. Many of the women remained carousing with officers and seamen on the lower deck until the ship put to sea again. Moralists and social reformers decried the admission of disease-infested prostitutes "of the vilest description" on board naval ships, citing the custom as a detriment to "the morals of our seamen." "The tendency of this practice is to render a ship of war, while in port, a continual scene of riot and disorder, of obscenity and blasphemy, of drunken-ness, lewdness, and debauchery," argued one critic. Moreover, seamen whose families came aboard were forced to mix with "these abandoned women, whose language and behavior are usually of the most polluting description."

Sea captains, sailors, officers, and seamen also solicited prostitutes on shore, particularly in port districts, such as Wapping, Portsmouth, Gravesend, and Chatham, notorious for their population of taverns and prostitutes ready to gratify all manner of appetites.[43]

Early nineteenth-century satirical prints excoriated British ports as unregulated metropolitan sites of interracial and intercultural miscegenation. Rowlandson's print *Black Brown and Fair,* a hand-colored etching published by Thomas Tegg in 1807, poked fun at the number of prostitutes of various descriptions servicing a multiethnic stew of clients in a Wapping bathhouse, ranging from black and white seamen and East Indians to Jews and drunkards. Below the elaborate etching, a poem in three verses offers a parody of a love letter, written by a patron of Wapping's multiracial prostitutes to his English sweetheart: "With Black, Brown, and Fair I have frolick'd 'tis true,/ But I never lov'd any, dear Mary, but you." Artists used the motif of the large, sexually insatiable black woman to highlight the corruptive nature of the sexfor-hire port culture. Thomas Rowlandson's *Sea Stores* (figure 14), published by Thomas Tegg in 1812, draws attention to the unsavory events occurring at the docks, as prostitutes fleece naval officers, ostensibly through sexual services but also by means of pilfering. Including a dark-skinned woman with thick, protruding lips in the joke demonstrates the perceived integration of black women into the subcultures of vice rife in Britain's port cities, where debauchery begets theft and "makes sin cheap."[44]

Rowlandson's *Land Stores* (figure 15), the companion print to *Sea Stores,* further elaborates the grotesquely comical vision of flagrant interracial sex between naval officers and black prostitutes. On the ramparts of a military fortification, a thin, elderly officer buries his face in a monstrously large black woman's exposed chest while attempting to cock his left leg over her thigh. Meanwhile, another officer walks away buttoning his trousers. The woman is a garish distortion, with enormous open lips, gaping teeth, vast fleshy arms, a protruding stomach, and massive breasts. Behind her head is a placard reading, "Voluntary Subscription for a Soldiers Widow the smallest donation will be gratefully received—By Rachel Ram Part." *Land Stores* and *Sea Stores* came into circulation in an era of increased British naval activity and economic and political uncertainty during the Revolutionary and Napoleonic Wars. By depicting officers as pitiable fools, losing their money to prostitutes and being sexually engulfed by vast black women on shore, engravers playfully mocked the nation's heralded naval strength. Vulnerable to the charms of the most unappealing females, lascivious naval men affronted the image of "loyal,

14. Thomas Rowlandson, *Sea Stores* (London, 1812). Courtesy
of The Lewis Walpole Library, Yale University.

masculine 'jack tars' enthusiastically defending her [Britain's] shores" that,
Cindy McCreery argues, helped distract the public from threats to national
security.[45]

Prostitution aboard ships, in military garrisons, at hotels, or in taverns
also occurred with great frequency when the Royal Navy docked in Caribbean port towns such as Kingston and Bridgetown. Unlike the women for
hire in British port cities, however, the vast majority of Caribbean prostitutes
were enslaved women of African descent forced by their owners to perform
sexual services for sailors, naval officers, common soldiers, and merchants
in exchange for payment. Local naval and military commanders licensed

certain slave women, whose owners rented them out expressly for this purpose, to sell their sexual services in military areas. Female hoteliers and slave
owners of European, African, and mixed ancestry found participation in the
sexual economy of bustling port cities a viable means of attaining financial
independence. Rachel Pringle-Polgreen, a free woman of color and one of
the most successful of these lodge keepers, owned the Royal Naval Hotel in
Bridgetown, famed for catering to the sexual needs of naval officers during
the 1770s and 1780s. Yet the open sexual exploitation of enslaved women,
and the brutalizing punishments to which their bodies were subjected, met

LAND STORES.

15. Thomas Rowlandson, *Land Stores* (London, 1812).
Courtesy of The Lewis Walpole Library, Yale University.

with growing public disapproval in Britain. White male abuse of slave women represented not only a gross misuse of power but also evidence of the corrupting influence of slavery and slave trading on British men.[46]

To abolitionists and their supporters, the molestation of female slaves by white men offered evidence that slavery dehumanized enslaved and enslaver alike. Tales of slave women stripped naked and flogged "cruelly in the back, belly, breasts, and thighs" by masters or overseers for trivial offenses filled the pages of the British press. The most sensational case involved William Wilberforce accusing John Kimber, captain of the *Recovery,* a Bristol slave ship, of flogging a young female slave to death in September 1791 for refusing to dance naked on the deck of his ship. The ship's surgeon told the story to Wilberforce, who brought it before the House of Commons, ensuring that Kimber's conduct would become public fodder in support of Wilberforce's campaign to end the slave trade. On the evidence of the ship's surgeon and mate, the High Court of Admiralty tried Kimber at the Old Bailey in June 1792, charging him with the murder of two enslaved girls on his ship. The jury concluded that disease, not cruelty, had caused the girls' deaths and acquitted Kimber of all charges. Kimber's subsequent demand for a public apology as well as £5,000 and a government post dealt a humiliating blow to the abolitionists' cause.[47]

In April 1792, the printing house of S. W. Fores capitalized on the public fervor surrounding Wilberforce's lurid account of Captain Kimber, publishing a graphic print by Isaac Cruikshank entitled *The Abolition of the Slave Trade* (figure 16). It shows the deck of a slave ship, on which a terrified, mostly naked African woman hangs suspended by her ankle from a rope held by a sailor. He leans back, muttering, "Dam[n] me if I like it I have a good mind to let go." In the background, three naked female slaves cower on the extreme left while, on the extreme right, two sailors walk away from the scene, saying, "My Eyes Jack our Girles at Wapping are never flogged for their modesty" and "By Gales that's too bad if he had taken her to Blackwell would be well enough, Split me I'm allmost sick of this Black Business." The captain, laughing gleefully, holds a whip in his right hand, poised to strike his cowering victim. Assorted scourges lie on the ship's deck beneath her exposed body. The caption underneath the print's title reads, "Or the Inhumanity of Dealers in human flesh exemplified in Captn Kimber's treatment of a Young Negro Girl of 15 for her Virjen [sic] Modesty." Although the print appears to expose the callousness of slave traders, its critique is ambiguous and could also serve the proslavery clause. Cruikshank's sensational embellishment of Kimber's alleged crime casts doubt on the validity of Wilberforce's accusation

16. Isaac Cruikshank, *The Abolition of the Slave Trade* (London,
1792). Library of Congress, British Cartoon Collection.

and on the reliability of other allegations made against British slavers. Satirists like Cruikshank, and the publishers with whom they worked, appealed
to stereotypes about the brutality and perverse sexuality of male enslavers to
profit from the ongoing controversy generated by antislavery sentiment. To
attract a predominantly male customer base, they also drew upon the late
eighteenth-century mania for flagellation imagery, which associated whipping with sexual arousal.[48]

Caricaturists attacked British males on both sides of the slavery debate,
linking white male involvement in the transatlantic slave trade, Caribbean
plantation management, or the abolition movement to an aberrant taste for
the enslaved black female. By replicating comic racial caricatures of lusty, un-
inhibited black women, satirical prints helped to fundamentally reshape contemporary identity politics in Britain. Artists derided Wilberforce and other
prominent supporters by suggesting, as Marcus Wood aptly observes, "that
their motives for supporting abolition were not entirely distinct from a desire

for the oversized sexual charms of black women." One of the most memo-
rable of these attacks, James Gillray's *Philanthropic Consolations after the Loss
of the Slave Bill* (1796), has Wilberforce and Bishop Horsley consoling themselves after their defeat by debauching with two voluptuous, bare-breasted
black women in an opulent room filled with symbols of bodily excess, sexual
immorality, and miscegenation (figure 17).[49]

Wilberforce sits cross-legged on a settee, smoking hookah with a black
woman in a head wrap and straw hat wearing a polka-dot gown and gold
jewelry. On the right, Bishop Horsley embraces an outsized black concubine,
who sits on his lap, her legs splayed and wine glass held aloft, as he kisses
her. While the two men indulge their perverse appetites, an exotically garbed
black serving boy stands ready with a goblet-filled tray. On the wall above
Wilberforce's head is a framed portrait of Inkle and Yarico, with Yarico posed
suggestively on the ground, topless. To the upper left, above the open door, is
the lower portion of a portrait entitled *Captn. Kimber in the Cells of Newgate*.

17. James Gillray, *Philanthropic Consolations after the Loss of the Slave Bill*
(London, 1796). Library of Congress, British Cartoon Collection.

Lying on the floor directly beneath Wilberforce's feet is a pamphlet, "Tryal of . . . & . . . convicted of Perjury in the case of Captn Kimber," drawing attention to Wilberforce's failed accusation against Kimber. On the table to the right sits *Rochester's Jests,* a fashionable collection of raunchy jokes and puns, including the following riddle:

> I have not to boast of much Humour or Wit;
> The Thing that I'm priz'd for, is mostly a *Slit.*
> I'm black at the Bottom; but if you look higher,
> I'm as *white* and as *smooth* as a *Man* can desire.
> To the Lover's soft Passions I often give Ease,
> Who wriggle me up and down just as they please.

Wilberforce and Bishop Horsley are depicted in a state of wanton and indecent luxury, reveling in smoke, drink, and "black jokes" behind closed doors. A scene like this relies upon a cultural connection between sexual vulgarity and the corpulent black female and suggests that abolitionists secretly envisioned a future in which men in Britain could partake freely of the interracial pleasures enjoyed openly in the slave colonies.[50]

The trope of the superficially genteel white male with an insatiable and degenerate appetite offers insight into the close positioning of sex and food on the early modern spectrum of sensory experience. The sins of lust and gluttony owed their birth to incontinence, and the Creole male, as a distinct character in British novels and plays, was associated with uncontrolled passions imbibed from his natural surroundings. "Hot as the Soil, the clime, which gave him birth," the West Indian in Britain, imagined the playwright Richard Cumberland, was a man set apart; "his manners, passions and opinion are not as yet assimilated to this climate; he comes amongst you a new character, an inhabitant of a new world." Exposed to a hot, alien climate and unfamiliar food such as peppery hot pot, surrounded by sexually accessible enslaved women, and debarred the privilege of civilized Christian society, Creole males had no opportunity of refining their taste. Rather, living in Caribbean slave society had dulled their senses entirely. Robert Charles Dallas encapsulated such assumptions when he portrayed a West Indian colonist's life like this: "An Englishman, in the torrid zone, loving a greasy old black woman, indulging his gross appetites, a gentleman, a companion in request, self-approving, eating, drinking, sleeping away his life in solid and substantial happiness."[51]

Contemporary observers mocked the lasciviousness of Creole males as not only excessive but deeply repugnant, arguing that their frequent enjoyment of "negro" dishes had transformed the most objectionable commodities of slave society into savory "tit-bits." J. B. Moreton recounted, "It is quite usual for a Creole gentleman after dinner to send to the field for one of his favourite wenches, who is instantly hurried home and conveyed to his chamber, (or if he has a wife, to some other apartment) piping hot and drowned with perspiration, in which condition he enjoys the savoury object." "After which," Moreton concluded dryly, "he takes a nap for an hour or so, and she returns to labour till night." While metropolitan norms dictated that an honorable man hide his passion for black women from polite society in Britain, there was no need for concealment in the colonial Caribbean. Rather than engaging in interracial sex under the cover of darkness, or as a result of misplaced identities in a darkened bedchamber, Creole males sent for perspiring female slaves straight from the field, cognizant of their tainted racial status and supposedly distasteful physical appearance.[52]

In Georgian Britain the vernacular association of tasty morsels with women's bodies played a central role in the world of prostitution lingo. In pamphlets intended to curb the spread of prostitution and guidebooks aimed at helping male customers locate a sexual partner for hire, authors characterized London's younger prostitutes as "tit bits." "How ridiculous to limit the age in which the female is ripe for matrimony to eighteen," wrote Charles Horne disapprovingly in *Serious Thoughts on the Miseries of Seduction and Prostitution* (1783), "when she is thought very fit for prostitution any age after twelve, and termed a tit bit." *Harris's List of Covent-Garden Ladies,* a bestselling guidebook to the capital's prostitutes, updated annually between 1757 and 1795, frequently labeled adolescent girls as "tit bits." *Harris's List* for 1788, for example, describes "Miss T——f——n, No. 2, *Glanville-Street*" in the following manner: "This tit bit is not above fourteen, rather short, but pretty, having an excellent complexion, with fine blue eyes, light hair, and a very white, and regular set of teeth." Like other girls and women for hire included in the guidebook, Miss T——f——n is presented as both willing and sexually voracious, "inclined to give delight in every possible attitude, and has no kind of objection to yield."[53]

Satirical references to corpulent dark-skinned female characters as "tit bits" positioned enslaved women as public sexual commodities, rendered intelligible in Britain by association with London prostitution. The phrase "tit bit" also carried connotations of a choice bit of meat (e.g., a desirable young girl), thereby adding an ironic comical edge when applied to the caricatured body of a grotesque black female. This is evident in Isaac Cruikshank's *A*

Meeting of Creditors (figure 18), published by S. W. Fores in April 1795, lampooning the scandalous behavior of the Prince of Wales and future George IV. He stands frowning, his thumbs twirling, surrounded by a group of bawds and prostitutes, who demand payment for sexual services rendered. On the far right, an elderly bawd holds a jelly glass in her right hand and with her left clutches a long scroll at the top of which is inscribed, "First slice of a nice tit bit only 12 years and 6 hours—1000." She comments, "How he stares he seems to be struck Comical." A young girl to the extreme right holds a paper reading "Maidenhead." Other female characters of various ages clamor to present their bills, and the most visually arresting is a hideous, plump black woman. Seated in a chair on the extreme left, she says, "Come Massa come and settle my count de affair you know has been long standing." Headed "Black Joke 300," her account of payments owed by the prince is one of the lengthiest, listing itemized services including "Black Dance 330" and "Tipping the Velvet 500" and signed "Black Moll, Hedge Lane."

Gendered sexual imagery amused the male, urban clientele who purchased graphic prints, and raunchy jokes outside the respectable norm made for better satire. When an unknown, hideous black woman appeared in these images,

18. Isaac Cruikshank, *A Meeting of Creditors* (London, 1795).
Yale Center for British Art, Paul Mellon Collection.

her presence accentuated and amplified rumors of lurid behavior and also signaled connections between prominent individuals and the slavery debate. Prince William, now Duke of Clarence and a vocal proslavery supporter, gave speeches in the House of Lords against two measures supported by William Pitt, the 1799 slave trade bill and a divorce bill granting wives the ability to separate from unfaithful husbands in 1800, both of which were printed and widely disseminated. His characterization of abolitionists as "fanatics or hypocrits" akin to French revolutionaries greatly impressed his brother George, Prince of Wales, who boasted privately that "William made a *most incomparable speech* on the slave trade . . . wishing to convince the House how near the principles of the abolition of the slave trade were synonymous & congenial to the general tenants of the National Convention." However, the Duke of Clarence's opposition met with public ridicule. Contemporaries and later biographers noted with scorn that his personal hostility to the divorce bill, and that of the other Royal Highnesses, the Prince of Wales and the Duke of York, stemmed from "each of them at the time living in a state of adultery and fornication."[54]

In June 1800, the caricaturist George Woodward mocked the Duke of Clarence's determined opposition to both the regulation of the slave trade and the divorce bill in *Unexpected Visitors on the Subject of the Divorce Bill* (figure 19). Standing meekly in the middle of the composition surrounded by a chorus of outraged women from the middling and lower classes, the duke pleads his innocence. "Indeed Ladies it is no fault of mine—I would not do you any harm for the World!—notwithstanding what some people say—I am remarkably fond of the Ladies I am indeed—got two or three Tit-Bits in a corner I have I assure you," he pleads. A leering black woman with monstrous facial features stands directly to his left, grasping his arm, saying accusingly, "You might have some regard for the fairer part of the Creation." As they lampooned the behavior and political stances of a wide range of British males, including members of the royal family, caricaturists fashioned a deeply distorted and increasingly recognizable iconography of black femininity. These rough-and-ready depictions overlapped with historical, philosophical, literary, and dramatic works, shaping metropolitan conceptions of women of African descent and the supposedly tainted racial inheritance they transmitted to their offspring.

BLACKENING BRITONS ON THE PERIPHERY

That the majority of British verbal and visual depictions emphasized the repulsive, amusing, titillating, and brutish aspects of black womanhood in-

19. G. M. Woodward, *Unexpected Visitors on the Subject of the Divorce Bill* (detail) (London, 1800). Courtesy of The Lewis Walpole Library, Yale University.

dicates the extent to which debates over the slave trade and colonial slavery overlapped with concerns about interracial mixture and hereditary racial inferiority, further degrading the black female image in Britain. Satirical prints were part of a broader metropolitan cultural trend toward exaggerated consideration of the potential integration of African slaves and their descendants into the British polity as free subjects. Artists and authors displaced the nationwide anxiety regarding Caribbean slave emancipation and black-white social and sexual intermingling onto the bodies of black female characters. With their cavernous mouths full of white teeth, protruding lips, fleshy bodies, and enormous breasts, these grotesque black women were not vulnerable objects of pity in need of white mercy but coarse, carnal figures responsible for their own abuse (figure 20). If abolition-era images and texts relegated black women in Britain to the category of sexually-depraved femininity, depictions of slave women in colonial Caribbean contexts deepened this criticism and sharply magnified the repercussions of their sexual unions with white men.

Satirical prints of Caribbean life highlighted the extent to which Creole male debauchery and widespread concubinage with female slaves represented a potential imperilment not only of the stability of slave society but, more troubling for metropolitan audiences, the integrity of British lineages. For not only did British West Indian white males engage in interracial liaisons with black women, both enslaved and free, they also frequently sired progeny of mixed ancestry. Worse still, some colonial fathers manumitted their illegitimate mixed-race offspring and, if the children were educated and fair enough, even left them their fortunes or sought to pass them off as white in Britain. Emphasizing such a presumably horrific outcome of the sexual practices of Caribbean slave society takes the bed tricks and racial role reversals so popular in the Stuart era to their logical and deeply troubling conclusion. The consummation of interracial sexual desire, and the successive whitening of generations of mixed-race children, drew racial boundaries into question in a way never before contemplated by seventeenth-and early eighteenth-century authors and artists. White and black bodies, male as well as female, had become potentially interchangeable in the light of day. This unwelcome scenario turned the identity reversal motif, with its comical, hideously promiscuous black woman as the centerpiece, on its head by implicating Creole males in deliberately mixing the bloodlines of distinct races, blackening and corrupting the British racial stock in the process.

Satiric images of West Indian society explored the morally and sexually corrupting influence of slaveholding on British men, underscoring how control over the black female body led to inappropriate and degrading expressions of white male desire—with dangerous consequences. A striking example is *Johnny Newcome in Love in the West Indies* (figure 21), a six-paneled etching with aquatint published by William Holland in April 1808, shortly after the abolition of the slave trade. In the first vignette, a voluptuous, garish black woman with enormous sagging breasts and a leering smile enraptures Johnny, a West Indian planter, "smitten with the charms of Mimbo Wampo,

THAT WAS A MONSTROUS DROLL STORY, *now Was'nt It.*

20. Charles Williams, *That Was a Monstrous Droll Story, Now Was'nt
It* (London, 1810). © The Trustees of the British Museum.

21. *Johnny Newcome in Love in the West Indies* (London, 1808).
Courtesy of The Lewis Walpole Library, Yale University.

a sable Venus." When Johnny declares his passion for the grotesque Mimbo
Wampo in the second panel as she picks chiggers off his leg, she replies, "'You
lib me Masa' eh eh?" Johnny then consults an obeah man named Old Mimbo
Jumbo in the third scene, asking him "how to get possession of the charming
Mimbo Wampo." By the fourth panel, Mimbo Wampo has become "queen of
the harem" and has made "Mr Newcome happy," to the chagrin of four other
women of more delicate physique and coloring who stand nearby watching
dejectedly.

This print moves beyond interracial desire itself to capture the disquieting
and potentially perilous aftermath of its consummation in a slave society. In
scene five, Johnny and Mimbo Wampo embrace while a naked child with
fair skin and dark, coiled hair pulls on her dress. Two other black women
in the room, presumably nursemaids, tend the couple's other young mixed-
race children, most of whom are naked. The text indicates that Johnny, after

satisfying his base lusts with Mimbo Wampo, is "taking leave of his Ladies & Pickaneenees, previous to his departure from Frying Pan Island, to graze a little in his Native Land." The final scene, titled "A few of the Hopeful young Newcomes," shows portraits of the nine mixed-race offspring born of Johnny's unrestrained, depraved sexual appetites. These include, #1, "Lucretia Diana Newcome, a delicate Girl very much like her Mother; only that she has a great antipathy to a pipe, and cannot bear the smell of Rum"; #3, "Quaco Dash Newcome prodigiously like his father"; and #8, "Hector Sammy New-come, a child of great spirit, can already Damnme Liberty and Equality and promises fair to be the Tousaint of his Country."

For all its intended humor, this visual parody of the sexual excesses and crude social conventions of West Indian colonial life also confirmed and re-inforced the unsettling outcome of interracial sexual unions between white men and enslaved women of African ancestry. Its efficacy as satire stemmed from the recognizable iconography of the grotesque black woman, a sardonic embodiment of the black joke, as well as the ubiquity of racial mixture on the Caribbean periphery. But rather than depicting the racially transgressive fantasy explored in images of interracial intimacy set in metropolitan Britain, this print captured one of the most contentious issues of the abolition debate: that white male control over and degenerate desire for black female sexuality threatened to imperil the colonial slave system and British identity. Although Johnny's desire for Mimbo Wampo has bolstered the slave population by pro-ducing nine illegitimate, mixed-race children, one of them (Hector Sammy Newcome) appears poised, like the Haitian revolutionary Toussaint Louver-ture, to subvert and topple the slave order. In the wake of the Abolition Act, such caricatures sought to discredit West Indian claims that the end of the slave trade rather than their own perverse appetites heralded the collapse of Britain's lucrative colonial slave system.

Graphic images underscoring the racially deviant products of the sexual economy of the colonial Caribbean also shared features with popular texts exploring the uneasy status of mixed-race individuals in metropolitan Brit-ain. Edward Long detailed how wealthy white fathers in Jamaica often sent illegitimate children born to enslaved and free women of African descent to Britain for their education, while contemporary novels such as Mrs. Charles Matthews's *Memoirs of a Scots Heiress* (1791), Amelia Opie's *Adeline Mowbray* (1805), and *The Woman of Colour* (1808) used the specter of African blood to revoke the liberty, or destroy the lives and marriage prospects, of young women of mixed racial lineage. In *Memoirs of a Scots Heiress,* a mulatto woman named Miranda is engaged to Cyril, the white male protagonist, who finds the thought of such a wife repugnant to his "optic faculties" but still agrees to wed her. However, Miranda, sick with anticipation of her future husband's revulsion at her "jetty skin," collapses and dies during the ceremony, dissolving the dreaded interracial conjugal union before it takes place.[55]

In *Adeline Mowbray* a mixed race ex-slave from Jamaica named Savanna, referred to as "the mulatto," endures racial slurs from English males who call her "ugly black b_____h" and must devote herself entirely to her white mistress, Adeline, for releasing her husband from debtor's prison in lieu of purchasing a pineapple. As Cora Kaplan observes, Savanna's virtual re-enslavement in Britain through a debt of gratitude to a white woman offers an "account of the human and economic traffic between home and empire centere[d] on the presence in England of nominally free persons of colour." Olivia Fairfield, the illegitimate mixed-race heroine of the epistolary novel *The Woman of Colour,* also struggles to come to terms with her tainted racial past, ultimately returning to Jamaica disillusioned and unwed. Even with wealth, beauty, and education, female characters of mixed blood remained in bondage to their servile African origins. Freedom from this dark inheritance, these texts suggest, cannot be accomplished by means of passing or further blanching of corrupt bloodlines but only through the truth of discovery and the women's disassociation with whiteness.[56]

The themes of mistaken identity and tainted racial lineages revealed are evident in a humorous British engraving entitled *A Disappointment* (figure 22), dating from the early nineteenth century. In it a well-dressed British gentleman removes a white veil covering the face of a woman asleep in a chair under a tree on the grounds of an estate. Her fine, high-collared gown, shapely bosom, white gloves, and dainty shoes hint at wealth and refinement, and perhaps he lifts the veil in an effort to confirm that the beauty of her face matches her polished outer appearance. Instead, with eyes raised in shock and his mouth twisted in a grimace of disgust, he notes her dark complexion and exclaims, "Da_____n me, she's a Black one." The man's reaction is striking, both for the revulsion it captures at his discovery of her "true" racial identity and for the subtle indication that there may be more ("she's a Black *one*") such alluring, racially ambiguous women in Britain.

The moment of horrified discovery depicted in *A Disappointment* is also significant for another reason. It captures the culmination of the racially transgressive yet mostly contained metropolitan fantasy of white-black sexual intimacy, stretching over two hundred years and documented throughout

22. *A Disappointment* (London, c. 1815). Courtesy of
The Lewis Walpole Library, Yale University.

this chapter. As the white British male in the image uncovers a dark-skinned woman hidden beneath a veil, it is apparent that the sexual interchange of black and white bodies—ever popular on the British stage, in novels, songs, jokes, and graphic prints—has indeed been actualized, with disconcerting results. The shocking unveiling of this particular well-dressed woman's delicate dark-skinned body precipitates larger questions about the perceived social consequences of interracial intimacy in the British Atlantic. More importantly, it underscores the metropolitan tendency to evaluate racial mixture between white men and black women in terms of degenerative blackening rather than redemptive whitening.

Viewed in this light, interracial sexual unions on the periphery, by mixing the previously distinct bloodlines of free Britons with those of African slaves and their descendants, portended the contamination of whiteness and the degradation of the British racial inheritance. The prospect of black-white intimacy nevertheless retained its titillating appeal for segments of the metropolitan public at once amused and horrified by incongruous couplings. If abolition-era comic culture is any indication of British racial attitudes, the notion that "blood will tell" may have offered some consolation to Britons concerned about the future racial complexion of the nation in a world of unchecked interracial mixture. Efforts to ameliorate West Indian slavery focused renewed attention on the need to reform the alleged moral corruption of black women as a means of securing the continued viability of the British Atlantic slave system and preventing further unwanted sexual contact between Britons and Africans.

CHAPTER 6

*Inheritable Blood and
the Imperial Body Politic*

On January 30, 1788, Stephen Fuller, Jamaica's London agent and a leading member of the West India lobby, wrote to apprise the Jamaica assembly of the political impact of the pamphleteering campaign unleashed by the Society for Effecting the Abolition of the Slave Trade, founded eight months earlier by a combined force of Quakers and Anglicans. "The Press teems with pamphlets upon this subject," he noted, "and my table is cover'd with them." Although Fuller admitted that the society's agitation had stirred up popular enthusiasm for the abolitionist cause, he expressed his opinion that the pamphlets and their authors had no real teeth. "The West India Gentlemen have shewn a singular instance of their Patience, as well as their good sense, in taking no manner of notice of them," Fuller noted; "indeed we have nothing as yet but a Phantom to combat with; when it puts on a bodily form we are ready to encounter it."[1]

As Fuller's observation suggests, the West India lobby in London, also known as the West India interest, comprising island agents, merchants trading with the Caribbean colonies, absentee plantation owners, and members of Parliament with interests in the West Indies, initially exhibited little outward concern at the prospect of abolition. The transatlantic slave trade was at its peak, generating robust profits and transporting, on average, seventy-eight thousand African captives per year to the Americas, half of them carried in

British ships. West Indian sugar exports to Britain, after a temporary dip as a result of the disturbances of the American Revolution and a series of devastating hurricanes that swept across the region in the early 1780s, had increased to rates higher than those of the 1760s and 1770s. French and British colonies, led by Saint-Domingue and Jamaica, dominated the international sugar market, and vast fortunes remained to be made from slave-based agricultural production in the West Indies.[2]

The West India interest in Britain thus regarded this latest attack on the slave trade as nothing more than a fringe phenomenon instigated by a handful of misguided humanitarian radicals. "The stream of popularity runs against us," concluded Fuller; "but I trust nevertheless that common sense is with us, and that wicked as we are, when compared with the Abolishers, the Wisdom and Policy of this country will protect us." Fuller, quietly confident that British business acumen and financial prescience would carry the day, worried nonetheless that abolitionist rhetoric would incite the slaves to rebel and imperil the lives and properties of his constituents. He appealed to Lord Sydney, the minister of colonial affairs, to consider the precarious state of Jamaica, where approximately "255,700 Negroes at £40 per head" worth an estimated £10 million dwarfed a white population of at most 13,000, or so Fuller approximated. Jamaica, he insisted, with the largest demographic imbalance between free and enslaved and the highest rate of slave revolts in the British Caribbean, was ripe for another rebellion. "Your Lordship may depend upon it, that during the time this business is agitated in Parliament, the Slaves will be minutely acquainted with all the proceedings," Fuller underlined. When the news inevitably reached Jamaica that members of the Commons aimed "to abolish the Slave Trade intirely, and in the end to set all the Slaves in the Sugar Colonies free," he warned, "I submit it to your Lordship whether it is most probable that they will wait with patience for a tardy event, or whether they will not strike whilst the iron is hot, and by a sudden blow finish the business themselves in the most expeditious and effectual manner, without giving their zealous friends here any further trouble."[3]

For William Pitt's government, however, mounting public pressure trumped concerns for the safety of British West Indian colonists. Beginning in 1787, the distribution of abolitionists' tracts, pamphlets, and images mobilized an unprecedented number of men and women of all social classes to form abolition committees and sign hundreds of petitions against the African slave trade. In December 1787, over ten thousand inhabitants in Manchester, a northern city with strong economic ties to the trade, signed a petition in support of abolition and sent it off to Parliament. Two months later, as anti-slave-trade petitions continued to pour in, William Wilberforce persuaded Pitt to support his plan to take up the abolitionist cause in the House of Commons. Pitt also requested the trade committee of the Privy Council to conduct an investigation into the present state of the African trade and, after gathering evidence respecting the trade in Africa, the conditions on the vessels, and the treatment of slaves in the Caribbean plantations, to prepare an official report. By the Easter recess of 1788, seventy-four petitions lay upon the table of the Commons and more arrived daily from all corners of the nation. Abolition-ist fervor had fanned out across the country, producing, as Thomas Clarkson later described, "a kind of holy flame, or enthusiasm, and this to a degree and to an extent never before witnessed."[4]

In this highly charged environment, mobilizing public opinion in favor of the slave trade and West Indian slaveholders would not be easy. "It is dif-ficult to say what should be done," Fuller admitted to the Jamaica assembly on May 6, 1788, following four months of frenzied activity on behalf of the West India interest. "We that are the defenders, cannot make the attack," but "the sooner it is discussed the better; because I think now as I did at first, that our danger is not so much in the determination as the agitation of it." In his letter, Fuller included a list of assertions emerging from the Privy Council in-vestigation that he urged the assembly to address immediately. Chief among these were claims that masters compelled slaves to labor incessantly without sufficient rest, that Europeans or white persons were very capable of perform-ing agricultural labor, and that immoderate labor and ill usage by plantation staff prevented the natural increase of the slaves. Convincing the British gov-ernment of the impossibility of Caribbean agricultural cultivation by white laborers, due to the inherited nature of the European, formed a central plank of Fuller's strategy to combat abolitionism, as would the passage and dissemi-nation of ameliorative measures intended to enhance slave reproduction and survival rates.[5]

In his endeavors to assemble a list of Jamaican slave laws in the interests of furthering the Privy Council inquiry, Fuller seized on a clause in the Con-solidated Slave Act, revised and renewed in response to abolitionist agitation in December 1787, that pronounced it a felony without benefit of clergy to murder a slave. Additional measures acknowledging the basic rights of slaves as British imperial subjects, indeed any movement away from "penal clauses respecting the Slaves, as have given rise to many severe imputations on this side the Atlantic," he insisted, "would be of singular use to the Cause." Fuller strongly advised his constituents to engage in a proactive legislative offensive: to use the rule of law to combat what the slave interest in Britain considered unmerited and overblown accusations of West Indian inhumanity. Countering metropolitan charges of planter brutality with counternarratives, Fuller believed, would only quell the abolitionist cause up to a point. The Jamaican legislature would achieve a great deal more in their opposition to the abolitionists if the gentlemen of the assembly took material steps to "promote such further Regulations, as they think will conduce to the melioration of the condition of the Slaves," particularly enslaved women and children.[6]

By the 1780s, the conception of white Europeans as inherently incapable of or less fit for hard physical labor in tropical climates had long infused British colonial histories, travel narratives, and medical tracts. Prevailing theories about inherited racial and national characteristics emerged as a central bone of contention over the course of the abolition debate. In colonial Jamaica, the survival and increase of the white settler population had remained a topic of perennial concern for nearly a century. The Jamaican legislature had tried and failed to augment white numbers through emigration, with the exception of the arrival of American loyalists, and the encouragement of marriage. Moreover, mixture with the descendants of African slaves for whitening purposes appeared to harbor as many risks as potential rewards. The charges of British abolitionists and their supporters in Parliament focused renewed attention on racialized bodies and hereditary blood status. The extent to which bloodline determined behavior, intelligence, morality and emotional expression, suitability for labor, sexual behavior, and a people's capacity for exercising common law liberties infused critiques and defenses of the West Indian slave system. Both sides of the slavery debate deployed the cultural meanings and ambiguities surrounding blood inheritance as a metaphorical weapon to further their own agenda.

West Indians countered abolitionist doctrine by elaborating and circulating an exclusive understanding of British racial and national identity rooted in the inherent rights, inner qualities, and physical characteristics that inhered in the blood of white Britons. According to this line of thinking, West Indian settlers, as the pure descendants of freeborn British subjects, held an inherited constitutional right to profit from the slave trade and the labor of enslaved Africans unimpeded by metropolitan intervention. Furthermore, the indefinite continuance of a colonial racial order based on hereditary black slavery and white hegemony offered the surest means of preserving British racial purity and the birthright liberties of the subject. By articulating an argument in defense of the innate superiority and distinctness of British bloodlines, West Indian slave owners and their supporters hoped to reconfigure racial constructs and concepts of subjecthood in metropolitan Britain. In contrast to African slaves and their descendants, who allegedly inherited inferior physical, intellectual, and moral traits associated with servile, heathen ancestry, freeborn British subjects enjoyed English liberties, privileges, and franchises and the Protestant religion by virtue of descent. The visible manifestations of Britons' supposedly civilized racial inheritance also determined the fate of their white bodies in hot climates and their failure to establish naturally reproducing white settler populations in the West Indies.[7]

As the prospect of ending British involvement in the transatlantic slave trade loomed large and then became certain with Parliament's passage of the Slave Trade Abolition Act in March 1807, abolitionists as well as West Indian writers, lobbyists, and planters proposed a variety of pronatal plans seeking to expand the slave population by naturally regenerating laborers. Calls for the amelioration of slave conditions in the West Indies and the encouragement of natural increase brought the enslaved female body and its reproductive capacities to the fore of public and parliamentary debate. The sexual behaviors, maternal practices, and spiritual beliefs of Caribbean slave women emerged as a central issue in discussions about slavery and the abolition of the slave trade and in the ameliorative policies developed to encourage slave breeding and long-term survival on the plantations. At the same time, the proslavery emphasis on white men's presumed inability to toil in hot climates led to disputes with the British imperial government over the use of black and "colored" troops in the West Indies at the turn of the century. If, as West Indian colonists asserted, inherited characteristics had inured African-descended peoples to the Caribbean's tropical climate and toxic disease environment, then employing them regularly for defensive purposes promised to save the lives of thousands of white settlers and British soldiers in the process. After a slave rebellion erupted in Saint-Domingue in August 1791, marking the beginning of a bloody revolution that would last until 1804 and establish Haiti as the first black republic in the Western Hemisphere, the prospect of relying upon slaves or nonwhites for military defense struck Jamaican colonists as too dangerous to contemplate. The rebellion of the Trelawny Maroons in 1795 further stoked fears in Jamaica that the radical ideologies underlying the French and Saint-Domingue revolutions, and fomented by British abolitionists, would exacerbate local grievances among the island's racial classes and destabilize the colony. The survival of the British constitutional and racial inheritance, Jamaicans and the West India interest in London increasingly argued, depended upon the differential treatment of the empire's white, brown, and black subjects.

THE BIRTHRIGHT OF ALL MANKIND

Well before the public assault on the African trade and West Indian slaveholders that followed on the heels of the foundation of the Society for the Abolition of the Slave Trade in 1787, Britain's new territorial acquisitions at the conclusion of the Seven Years' War underscored the pervasiveness of colonial slavery and the apparent lack of viable alternatives for the future development of the Atlantic empire. Further imperial expansion into tropical zones, British writers and theorists assumed, required the participation of African-descended peoples due to the supposed physical limitations inherent to European bloodlines. "It is certain," claimed John Huddlestone Wynne, author of *A General History of the British Empire in America* (1770), "that Africans, or their descendants, are better able to support severe labour in hot countries than any of European blood." Wynne considered the intrinsic hardiness of African blood unfortunate because it encouraged black slavery, and "no institution is so apt as slavery to extirpate the milder and more amiable virtues of compassion and humanity, and to render men cruel, hard-hearted, and remorseless." However, for colonial promoters, land developers, slave traders, and investors intent on exploiting the agricultural potential of Britain's newly acquired Caribbean colonies—Dominica, Grenada, St. Vincent, and Tobago—the expansion of Britain's Atlantic empire reinforced rather than diminished the value of slave labor.[8]

The territorial gains of the Seven Years' War left Britain as the dominant imperial power in the Atlantic world and intensified government discussions focused on the legal and administrative consolidation of the British Empire. Following the Treaty of Paris in 1763, advisors on colonial administration in Britain, including the absentee Georgia slaveholder William Knox; John Pownall, the Board of Trade secretary; and Maurice Morgann, an advisor on colonial policy to Lord Shelburne, set to work formulating imperial doctrines to centralize control over an empire characterized by a patchwork of legal jurisdictions. In addition to calling for widespread slave conversion and urging Parliament to halt the slave trade and, in Knox's words, to "[declare] the offspring of Negroes already imported to be free," one of their proposed ambitions included the integration of former African slaves and their descendants into the imperial polity as free subjects in exchange for military service. Morgann in particular envisioned an empire, as Christopher Brown details, based on "nothing more than allegiance," in which hardy men of African descent would form "the 'sable arm' of British authority" and, with their bodies adapted to hot climates, help to "secure British supremacy in the Americas." These unconventional theories of empire, though essentially thought experiments that remained in draft form, set forth a bold and expansive concept of subjecthood that incorporated all of the inhabitants of the British-controlled territories under the imperial Crown's jurisdiction, notwithstanding their legal statuses or racial classifications at the provincial level.[9]

Although the British government never implemented such proposals during this period, tensions surrounding the potential blurring of boundaries between colonial and metropolitan legal jurisdictions gave rise to arguments casting colonial slave systems as repugnant to English laws and the ancient constitution. In *A Representation of the Injustice and Dangerous Tendency of Tolerating Slavery; or, Of Admitting the Least Claim of Private Property in the Persons of Men, in England* (1769), Granville Sharp, a young lawyer deeply critical of slavery, promulgated his vision of British settlers in the slave colonies as wholly unchristian, un-English, and inhumane. Pointing to a wide range of repressive statutory innovations designed to extract maximum profit from bound laborers, including white servants and slaves of African, Indian, and mixed lineage across the Caribbean and Chesapeake colonies, Sharp argued that colonial slavery contravened natural law, the universal rights of man, and the established liberties that formed the cornerstone of the British constitution. "Now, as freedom is unquestionably the birthright of all mankind, *Africans* as well as *Europeans*," he suggested, "to keep the former in a state of slavery, is a constant violation of that right, and therefore of justice." Sharp unequivocally opposed the creep of the "uncivilized customs which disgrace our own colonies" into the metropolis, where they would in short order contaminate the populace, leading Britons to "insensibly degenerate to the same degree of baseness with those from whom such bad customs were derived."[10]

While Sharp's impassioned intervention against colonial slavery gained little traction upon its initial publication, the case of *Somerset v. Stewart* in the Court of King's Bench enabled Francis Hargrave, Sharp's friend and Somerset's legal counsel, to present the institution of slavery as repugnant to the British constitution before an esteemed judicial tribunal. Hargrave argued that colonial slavery was governed by "arbitrary maxims and practices" at the local level that diverged dramatically from English law and, moreover, held no legal weight in Britain. He requested a writ of habeas corpus to prevent the forcible removal of his client, James Somerset, a recaptured slave who had escaped his master in London in 1771, from Britain. Lord Mansfield's ruling in Somerset's favor on May 14, 1772, exposed underlying tensions between the legality of slavery in the Atlantic colonies and the principles of English law. As Mansfield saw it, the central issue of contention in the Somerset case focused on whether or not Charles Stewart, Somerset's owner, "had a right to detain the slave, for the sending of him over to be sold in Jamaica . . . contrary to the municipal law of *England*." After "weighty consideration," Mansfield rendered a narrow decision in Somerset's favor, arguing that, as English law reigned supreme in the metropole, the absence of a positive law on slavery in England meant that a slave could not be taken from the country against his will—"let justice be done whatever the consequences." Confusion over the legal implications of the well-publicized outcome of the Somerset trial led to a wide variety of interpretations of Mansfield's ruling and its implications. While the ruling did not prohibit slavery in England, and the enslaved retained their subjugated property status while in the metropole, it granted the legal right of habeas corpus—long celebrated as the "palladium of Liberty" safeguarding the rights and physical security of the subject—to an enslaved African. The outcome of the Somerset trial of 1772 thus called into question the colonial statutory definitions of slave status upon which millions of pounds of property claims and racial distinctions in the British Atlantic colonies rested. Could African slaves in England be at once the inheritable property of subjects and rights-bearing subjects?[11]

West Indians, including Edward Long, busy at work on his soon-to-be-published three-volume *History of Jamaica,* and the Barbadian planter Samuel Estwick, promptly issued scathing rebuttals of Lord Mansfield's decision. Long pronounced it inexplicable that "Negroes, who are by statutes declared *merchandize,* should, by a strained construction and refinement of other statutes by the courts of law, be proclaimed *subjects of the realm,* and held entitled to all the rights, liberties, and privileges of natural, or free-born subjects." Estwick pointed to the joint opinion given by Attorney General Philip Yorke and Solicitor General Talbot to a deputation loosely connected to the Anglican Society for the Propagation of the Gospel in Foreign Parts in 1729, "by which they pledged themselves to the British Planters for the legal consequences of bringing Negroe-slaves into this kingdom," stating that "*upon their best consideration they were both clearly of opinion,* that a slave did not in the least alter his situation or state towards his Master or *Owner*, either by being christened, or coming to England." The Yorke-Talbot decision, by interpreting existing English law as compatible with the rights of colonial slaveholders, held important implications for the legal development of slavery in the British Empire. While those who lobbied for and publicized the Yorke-Talbot decision sought to overcome slaveholders' objections to the conversion of their slaves to Christianity, the decision established a precedent for the rights of colonial masters until Lord Mansfield's ruling shook its ideological underpinnings in 1772.[12]

In both his private musings on slavery and his published rebuttal of the Somerset ruling, Edward Long held that the Magna Carta had guaranteed the liberties of the subject solely to freemen of England and their heirs forever, to the exclusion of all those of unfree status. "No freeman shall be deprived of life, limb, or goods except by judgement of his peers. The term free is here in contradistinction to villeins or slaves, who remained almost unprotected in body or goods, held both at arbitrary pleasure of their lords, and were not entitled to benefit of trial by jury," he noted. Even with the passage of positive laws, such as the Habeas Corpus Act of 1679, confirming subjects' rights, "there is no reason to believe, that Negroe-slaves belonging to our Plantations, were then considered as *subjects of the realm of England.*" Therefore, Long concluded, it is correct to assume, as Justice Powell stated in the case of *Smith v. Brown and Cooper* (1702), "'that the law takes no notice of a *Negro*'; that is to say, this class of people were neither meant, nor intended, in any of the general laws of the realm, made for the benefit of its genuine and natural-born subjects." Yet Long misappropriated the meaning of Justice Powell's declaration, which followed Chief Justice Holt's reasoning that, in England, "the common law takes no notice of negroes being different from other men." As a result, "no man can have a property interest in another." In Britain, it was the institution of slavery that was outside the common law, not "Negroes."[13]

Estwick joined Long and other proslavery supporters in challenging the claim that the status of African slaves as property did not exist as positive law in England. He laid out an elaborate case respecting the parliamentary foundations for "the *legal nature* of Negroes," arguing that the charter granted to the Royal African Company during the reign of King Charles II declared "Negroes" property, "in like manner as personal estate, to be disposed of, for the payment of debts due to the King and his subjects." Estwick then turned to the repugnancy principle outlined in 7&8 William 3, c. 22 (1696): "that no law, usage, or custom, shall be made or received in the plantations, repugnant to the laws of England." "If property, therefore, in Negroes, was repugnant to the law of England, it could not be the law of America," he wrote; otherwise the Board of Trade's legal counsel, "whose especial business it is, to examine all the colony acts, and thereupon to make his report, if necessary, antecedent to the royal confirmation of them," would have called for its immediate repeal. Instead, the Crown had confirmed colonists' right to slave property time and again. In sum, Estwick pronounced, "the right and property, not only of Mr. Steuart in his Negroe Somerset, but of every subject of Great Britain in his Negroe or Negroes, either in the colonies or elsewhere, is a right and property founded in him by the law of this land; that the royal grants, letters patent, and charters, for and of the African trade and company, confirmed and established by acts of Parliament, are the foundation whereupon all the laws of the colonies, respecting their Negroes, are built; and that, without such sanction, those laws could never have been made." The British Parliament, not colonial legislatures, had established slaveholding as the constitutional right of all free subjects.[14]

The central message that Long and Estwick sought to convey combined legal and racial arguments to prove that the foundation for hereditary racial slavery (rather than universal rights) lay in natural as well as positive law. Writers on the subject generally agreed, Estwick elucidated, that African customs, values, spiritual practices, familial relations, and physical features demonstrated "that they were an inferior race of people." The English legislature, then, "perceiving the *corporeal* as well as *intellectual* differences of Negroes from other people, knowing the irreclaimable savageness of their manners," determined to "follow the commercial genius of this country, in enacting that they should be considered and distinguished (as they are) as articles of its trade and commerce only." In Estwick's view, those who argued for a "universal sameness in human nature" and denied "Negro inferiority" suggested that whites and blacks shared the same inherited nature; they "say, in fact, that Englishmen are Negroes, and Negroes are Englishmen, to all *natural* intents and purposes." He drew a direct connection between natural arguments in support of African slavery and the wisdom of the English legislature in recognizing these causes and legislating black slaves to the level of property. "The writ of Habeas Corpus is a writ of right given to the subjects of the Crown of England, for the security of their liberties. If Somerset can fall under this predicament and description, he is open to the benefits that may arise therefrom; but if the law has already fixed the *fiat* of property on him, I apprehend it a legal exception to the writ, and his right is foreclosed thereby." Estwick posited the existence of two distinct racial classes whose lineage determined their legal status: Africans, subject to the law of property; and Britons, protected by the law of freeborn subjects. Preventing British and African bloodlines from intermingling, he maintained, would protect the integrity of the more elevated British race and ensure that blacks remained relegated to their rightful position as property. Estwick thus concluded his tract with a proposal to prohibit the importation of black slaves into Britain, which would "preserve the race of Britons from stain and contamination; and you will rightly confine a property to those colonies, upon whose prosperity and welfare the independent being of this country rests."[15]

Other proslavery authors echoed Estwick's warnings that the mixture of Britons and former African slaves in the metropole portended the contamination of British bloodlines and the degeneration of whiteness. Long argued that the contaminating influence of black blood would first infiltrate the lowest levels of society through the sexual indiscretions of lower-class Englishwomen, who "are remarkably fond of the blacks, for reasons too brutal to mention; they would connect themselves with horses and asses if the law permitted them." Owing to their alleged proclivity for black men, such women, he predicted, would bear "a numerous brood" of children of mixed blood. "Thus, in the course of a few generations more, the English blood will become so contaminated with this mixture, and from the chances, the ups and downs of life, this alloy may spread extensively, as even to reach the middle, and then the higher orders of the people, till the whole nation resembles the Portuguese and Moriscos in complexion of skin and baseness of mind." Writing in 1778, the British author and former resident of Jamaica Philip Thicknesse cautioned that in a few centuries "very unnatural (for unnatural they are) alliances" between black men and white women would produce "a succession of black, brown, and *whity* brown people." "London abounds with an incredible number of these black men," he asserted, "and every country town, nay in almost every village are to be seen a little race of mulattoes, mischievous as monkeys and infinitely more dangerous." Racial mixing might begin with the lower orders, argued these authors, but the contagion it produced would infect the entire nation: "A mixture of negro blood with the natives of this country is big with great and mighty mischief, and that if they are to live among us, they ought by some very severe law to be compelled to marry only among themselves, and to have no criminal intercourse whatever with people of other complexions." Others, such as the merchant John Scattergood, held that if the British government welcomed Africans, "Negroes from all parts of the world will flock hither, mix with the natives, spoil the breed of our common people, increase the number of crimes and criminals and make Britain the sink of all the earth, for mongrels, vagrants, and vagabonds." Although satirical prints focused on racial indiscretions across the social spectrum, these writers envisioned racial contamination spreading from the bottom up.[16]

CREOLE PROFLIGACY AND ABOLITIONIST AGITATION

In the colonial Caribbean, the tainted "property" of which Estwick, Long, and Thicknesse spoke had long since mingled with British settlers to produce a growing class of people of varying degrees of European and African ancestry, most of whom never escaped bondage. In the period preceding the American Revolution, the influential voice of West Indians in Parliament prompted some North American colonists to distinguish themselves as superior by drawing attention to the widespread race mixing in the British West Indian islands. James Otis of Massachusetts, a lawyer, politician, and author of a foundational prerevolutionary tract, *The Rights of the British Colonies Asserted and Proved* (1764), expressed his displeasure that colonial histories, guidebooks, and legal texts regarded the Atlantic empire as merely a "parcel of *little insignificant conquered islands,* than as a very extensive settlement on the continent." To "speak of the *British* plantations abroad as consisting chiefly of islands," Otis emphasized, was a grave mistake. Undue focus on the West Indies detracted from the most valuable segment of the British Atlantic empire: the well-settled, Anglicized northern colonies. Yet writers typically listed the British settlements

> in this order—*Jamaica, Barbados, Virginia, Maryland, New-England, New-York, Carolina, Bermudas.* At the head of these islands stands Jamaica, in truth a *conquered* island; and as such, this and all other little West-India islands deserve to be treated for the conduct of their inhabitants and proprietors with regard to the Northern Colonies: divers of these colonies are larger than all of those islands together; and are well settled, not as the common people of *England* foolishly imagine, with a compound mongrel mixture of *English, Indian* and *Negro,* but with freeborn *British white* subjects.

As Otis saw it, for metropolitan observers to paint the inhabitants of North America and the West Indians with the same brush, assuming they had equally degenerated into "mongrels," undermined American colonists' claim to an equal inheritance with British subjects.[17]

In the British West Indies, the absence of antimiscegenation laws everywhere except for Antigua, Bermuda, and Montserrat influenced the ubiquity of sexual relationships between white men and women of African descent, but colonial demography also played a dominant role. In Jamaica, where unmarried or widowed men constituted the vast majority of the largely immigrant white community, pervasive interracial liaisons transformed the complexion of the free population. The Jamaican census of 1788 provided an estimate of 9,405 "free people of colour," constituting 3.7 percent of the colony's overall population, including slaves, but 34 percent, or more than one-third, of the total free population. This figure takes into account the influx of around 3,000 white American loyalists who dramatically increased the numbers of white settlers after 1785. Prior to the arrival of the loyalists, free people composed an even higher share of the island's total free population. By comparison, in the British Leeward Islands in 1788 free people of African and mixed ancestry accounted for 1.6 percent of the total population, or roughly 1,450 of the islands' 91,000 residents. In Barbados, a reported 528 free people made up 0.6 percent of the island's nearly 88,000 inhabitants during the 1770s, though the Afro-Barbadian segment of the free population increased rapidly beginning in the 1780s.[18]

Although white West Indian men seeking to indulge their lusts or find companionship with African-descended women faced few obstacles, commentators on both sides of the abolition debate decried the "spurious issue" born of such unions as a detriment to the increase of the two most important classes of the colonial population: slaves and white settlers. The first and largest class generated agricultural output and financed the project of colonialism and the second, much smaller, class exercised British dominium, but the third, intermediate, class contributed to neither of these goals. Plantation management staff routinely pronounced enslaved children descended from white fathers and black mothers of little worth in the fields. William Smalling, overseer of Joseph Foster Barham's Mesopotamia estate, summed up these assumptions in 1773, saying, "I think children of that kind are a very indifferent commodity on estates." Anna Eliza Elletson, who assumed control of Hope estate after the death of her husband, Roger Hope Elletson, granted white male workers titles to their mulatto children in exchange for "able Negroes" and encouraged her attorney "to do the like with all other mulattoes that are upon the Estate." But for critics of the colonial slave system, especially after the humiliating loss of the American colonies, the crux of the matter lay not in the presumed insufficiencies of mulattoes as field laborers but in their status as the spurious fruits of racial licentiousness.[19]

In his 1784 *Essay on the Treatment and Conversion of African Slaves in the British Sugar Colonies,* the Reverend James Ramsey, an Anglican minister who spent twenty years on the island of St. Kitts, portrayed white men's free enjoyment of enslaved women's bodies as conducive to an overall plantation culture of sexual profligacy. He began his discussion by charging plantation owners with creating conditions on their estates that allowed unabashed debauchery to flourish. When selecting a new estate manager, Ramsay claimed, owners frequently passed over a married man in favor of a dissipated youth or a "groveling, lascivious, old batchelor (each with his half score of black or mulattoe pilfering harlots, who, at their will, select for him from among the slaves, the objects of his favour or hatred) rather than allow a married woman to be entertained on the plantation." That depraved overseers forced themselves on unripe slave girls incapable of repudiating inappropriate, base white male attention disgusted Ramsay. As a result of the unchecked sexual license granted to overseers, on the majority of slave estates "shameless profligacy usurps the place of decency, sympathy, morality, and religion; and headlong unthinking lust alone produces all the wasting effects of dishonesty, cruelty and oppression." Unchecked individual passions had led to a broader pattern of immorality that degraded the collective culture of the British Caribbean and its free and enslaved inhabitants.[20]

Ramsay's condemnation of the exploitation of female slaves in the British West Indies did not provide the final word on the matter of interracial sex—far from it. His text intensified controversy between the two sides in the public debate over colonial slavery and the slave trade. While neither camp disputed the existence of racial intermixture in the Caribbean colonies, the meanings individual commentators attached to the sexual economy of slavery could vary significantly. James Tobin, in a rebuttal to Ramsay's statements the following year, accused the minister of gross exaggeration; he took particular exception to Ramsey's praise for the French practice of encouraging marriage among the slaves. Citing what he characterized as rampant racial immorality in the French islands, Tobin argued that among French slaveholders "promiscuous commerce with coloured women is carried to such an indecent height, that in a planter's house, the *white* wife is frequently the person of least consequence in the family." He charged French planters with producing hordes of "Mulattoes, Meztizes, and other shades," so many, in fact, that owners of estates turned their own "mixed breed" out to labor in the "common fields," where "I have frequently seen, the whip of a French overseer laid over a pair of naked shoulders much whiter than his own." Tobin did not deny the charge that white men in the British Caribbean engaged in promiscuous intercourse with slave women. Rather, he contrasted supposed English propriety with French depravity, declaring that in the British islands "a Mulatto is seldom or ever found in the field, or at other common hard labour. If there is no merit, there is most certainly a decency, in preserving this distinction. I have actually had a rich French planter pointed out to me, who took a pride in boasting, that at least one third of his field-gang were the produce of his own loins." The wording of Tobin's critique highlights in distinct terms the perceived connection between bloodline and inherited physical characteristics and aptitudes—a correlation recognized by all "decent," civilized nations—that featured in British proslavery writings of the abolition era.[21]

The capacity of people of mixed blood, whether bound or free, to perform arduous physical tasks in a hot climate emerged as a critical point of interest against the backdrop of abolitionist campaigning. If individuals born of mingled European and African stock could perform the labor required of slaves, even for wages, cutting off the labor supply from Africa would prove inconsequential to plantation output over the long term. The assumed biological fitness of "mulattoes" for fieldwork, however, was a point on which the slave interest refused to find common ground with abolitionists. Tobin argued that people of color, especially among the free community, refused to work in the fields, viewing such physical labor alongside black slaves as degrading and unsuitable to their condition. Free people, confirmed Rev. John Lindsay, "*do not*—nay they *will not*—*work*" and "white people in the torid zone *cannot*." Neither whites nor free people of mixed blood possessed the requisite physical or intellectual qualities to cultivate sugarcane, William Beckford concurred. That the continued intermingling of British and African bloodlines could produce a new generation capable of replacing the slave population in the fields, he wrote, "is absurd in the extreme"; "the colour of the mulatto, his birth, and education, naturally exclude him from the possible severity of toil." To relegate to hard labor persons of mixed blood intent on "advancing towards being Whites," in the words of Bryan Edwards, would be to "throw them back," as though "they have gone backwards towards the negro race." To extend a greater degree of liberty to mixed-race people, Long surmised, would serve the British West Indies far more than confining individuals with some portion of white blood in their veins to a life of drudgery among their racial inferiors.[22]

If the West India interest reasoned that persons of mixed lineage lacked the innate capacity to undertake intensive agricultural labor due to their divided racial inheritance, they insisted that whites of "pure" ancestry held no chance of success. Under the heading "The Impossibility of cultivating with Whites," included among Edward Long's miscellaneous papers, the proslavery historian observed that the "nature of the W. Indian climate, and of Northern People, [prove] the impossibility of cultivating the Soil of the torrid zone by any other than Negroe Labourers as it was first the occasion of employing them, so it must ever remain as long as our Colonies exist, because this natural necessity admits of no alternative." Authors who argued otherwise "deal in reveries, and seem entirely ignorant both of the subject and climate they treat upon." Continual examples of white decrease "are sufficient to prove incontestably how ill adapted the strongest European Constitutions are to endure the effects of the Tropical Climate." Consequently, Long avowed, "we must continue as we have hitherto successfully done by the labour of Negroes, whose constitutions being by nature and the divine will appropriated to these climates, they are evidently the fittest for such employments thence." To explain the fitness of Africans alone for hard labor in the Caribbean, Long invoked a global natural and divine order that assigned certain characteristics to distinct races. Only fools, he insinuated, would attempt to rail against both the laws of nature and God's will.[23]

In their defense of African slavery, West Indian authors articulated an ideology of fixed racial inheritance in which the natural order of things, rather than man-made hierarchies, established an original, permanent distinction between whites and blacks. William Beckford put the matter bluntly: "If the colonies were to be attempted to be cultivated by white people the whole population of Great-Britain would be unequal to the object, and would in the course of a century be melted down and become extinct." For defenders of the colonial slave system, neither drink nor loose living precipitated the deaths of white settlers in the Caribbean, as British satirical prints detailing the exploits of Johnny New-come suggested (figure 23), but rather an inherited nature unequal to the task of settlement. The hereditary racial traits of "Negroes," in contrast, suited them for heavy toil. Ramsay offered a ready answer as to why this was the case: "They are not really *the same brethren with us;* but that God himself, having design'd them from the Creation, for that

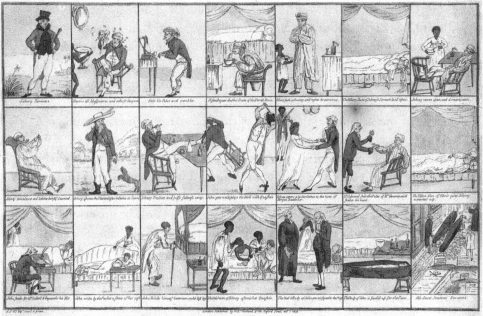

JOHNNY NEW-COME in the ISLAND of JAMAICA.

23. Abraham James, *Johnny New-come in the Island of Jamaica* (London,
c. 1800). Original in the John Carter Brown Library, Brown University.

very hard labour necessary thro all his Torrid Zone has therefore been pleased
to form them of *coarser stuff* and more *stubborn Nature,* the better to endure
this sort of Labour—and with *less feelings,* the better to bear those Punishments, which the incorrigible, the thieving, and the lazy will indoubtably
bring upon themselves." In sum, Africans transmitted to their descendants a
coarse, insensitive nature that, unless reined in and productively harnessed by
Europeans, tended toward violent criminal behavior. For this reason, Britons
should extend to neither slaves nor their free descendants the common law
rights reserved for subjects.[24]

Abolitionists dismissed proslavery defenses rooted in fixed racial essences
as self-serving. They not only invoked free-labor ideology, insisting that freemen, whatever their racial lineage, made far better workers than slaves, they
also argued that planters' insistence on the intrinsic suitability of Africans for
hard tropical labor lacked basis in reality. William Belsham's *An Essay on the
African Slave Trade* (1790) reiterated the arguments made by slaveholders relating to inherited racial differences and then proceeded to break them apart.

"The plantations in the West Indies can be cultivated only by Negroes; the climate is fatal to all but African constitutions, and the labour such as that hardy race of men only can support," he wrote, outlining a common line of reasoning proposed against abolition. Yet demographic evidence suggested to Belsham that slaves succumbed to tropical disease, poor treatment, and the fatigues of ceaseless toil. While West Indian planters argued passionately in defense of the slave trade, the dearth of colonial statutory measures designed to ameliorate conditions on the plantations in the interest of curbing slave morbidity confirmed white Creoles as a class of people "who wish much to be virtuous, but more to be rich." "Numerous and well-authenticated facts incontestably demonstrate that, with mild and indulgent treatment, the present number of slaves in the West Indian islands might not only be preserved from diminution, but would admit of considerable increase," Belsham concluded. Ramsay agreed, arguing that neither "white nor black can support unremitting labour, without food or rest. But white men kept from new rum, may, in the morning and evening, perform double the present task of slaves, without suffering from the climate." Most decisively, "Barbados, St Kitts, and Nevis were originally settled by white men," Ramsay pointed out, presenting a line of argument Stephen Fuller considered as damning to the slave cause unless disproved. "It was only on the introduction of negroes, that they began to decrease in numbers." For the slave interest, trumpeting the supposedly divergent racial inheritance of whites and "negroes" offered the surest and indeed only path forward for undercutting their opponents' focus on the universal characteristics shared by the human race.[25]

MISREPRESENTED IMPERIAL SUBJECTS

On October 16, 1788, in response to letters received from its agent in London, the Jamaica assembly attempted to formulate its first official counterresponse to the groundswell of popular support for abolition in metropolitan Britain. For months, colonists had expressed their anxieties concerning the mass petitioning campaign in Britain and the possibility that Parliament might take action destructive to their properties, reputations, and lives. As Lieutenant Governor Clarke explained to Lord Sydney in a letter dated April 22, 1788, "the petitions which have been presented to the House of Commons, relative to the Slave Trade, have already occasioned great alarm in all ranks of people here, not only for their Credit at home, but for their immediate safety." West Indians and their contacts in Britain exchanged a flurry of letters across the Atlantic, appalled by the sudden "phrenzy relative to the Slave Trade" in the mother country, which had morphed into a general attack on colonial practices and slaveholders. Many assumed that "the wild idea will come to nothing" and pronounced the abolition movement the product of a combination of "enthusiasm" and "wickedness." Clarke trusted that sending the British government Jamaica's newly revised Consolidated Slave Act, with its liberal provisions for the "government and management of slaves at present in force here," would put the matter to rest.[26]

The assembly's defensive strategy aligned with Fuller's proposed method of attack, but island legislators also strove to correct what they saw as "unqualified allegations" circulating in Britain. While they conceded that Parliament, in the due course of time, might exert its authority to regulate African commerce in a manner beneficial to the sugar colonies, they did not believe West Indian colonists should bear the brunt of public rancor for the abuses of "a British trade, carried on by British subjects, residing in Great Britain, on capitals of their own." Furthermore, they stressed, "the connection and intercourse between the planters of this island, and the merchants of Great Britain trading to Africa, extend no further than the mere purchase of what British acts of parliament have declared to be legal objects of purchase." Shifting focus away from public misgivings regarding the morality of the African trade—the focal point of the petitions, to which they denied all connection—the assembly thus concentrated on repairing the damaged reputation of West Indian slaveholders. As Fuller had informed the assembly in May 1788, "the West India planters were stigmatized all over the Kingdom as brutes," and the absentee proprietors in Britain "wished for the earliest opportunity to vindicate their characters." Unless the West India interest reestablished the basic humanity of colonial slaveholders in the public mind, the abolitionists would continue, as Simon Taylor remarked bitterly, "to poison the minds of the people."[27]

To combat the primary accusations leveled at West Indian planters, the assemblymen proposed a four-pronged counterargument centered on the divergent treatment of slaves permitted as a result of the constitutional relationship between the Crown and the colonies. First they drew up a statement claiming that slaves were both "legal objects of purchase" and "under the protection of the common law, with the rest of His Majesty's subjects residing on this island, except in cases where it has been found necessary to enact limitations." However, after some debate, members agreed on a revised version of this first statement to more accurately capture the separation between the common law rights of freeborn white British subjects and slave law:

1st. That negroes in this island are under the protection of lenient and salutary laws, suitable to their situation and circumstances.

2nd. That the slave laws are executed with humanity, mildness, and mercy.

3rd. That the laws have made provisions to grant slaves days of rest, and to prevent their being in want of the necessaries of life.

4th. That the decrease of our slaves does not arise from the causes alleged in the petitions presented to the House of Commons, but from various other causes, not imputable to us, and which the people in Great Britain do not seem to comprehend.

The following month, colonial officials in Jamaica returned to the subject of abolition, seeking to demonstrate through the weight of statutory evidence that white settlers neither mistreated African slaves nor regarded them as expendable commodities. To appease a distant public, they would offer up prescriptive measures as singular "proof" of their leniency toward the enslaved population. English common law protections, they maintained, did not suit the master-slave relationship, which, though private in nature, benefited the collective good by holding the savage, refractory nature of Africans in check. Consequently, colonial slave law served as the ultimate arbitrator, for it ensured that the governance of enslaved Africans accorded with their inherited nature.[28]

In methodical detail, the assembly spelled out in precise terms what it saw as the humane and protective measures confirmed by Jamaica's Consolidated Slave Act (first passed in 1781, revived with amendments in 1787, modified again in 1788). Provisions included limitations on the number of lashes overseers or others could inflict on slaves (no more than ten at a time) without the owner's supervision (in which case, no more than thirty-nine); plans to encourage planters to facilitate the "instruction of their slaves in the principles of the Christian religion"; and regulations to punish whites for excessive slave mutilation or other forms of cruelty. Fuller had already published copies of the act in London, hoping to sway the British public to view the slave cause as, if not just, at the very least benevolent but firm. Since its publication, he wrote to the assembly, "I have seen no strictures upon it in the publick papers, but I expect some in the Reviews; which will be but very little hard, as I learn from everybody that it has been well received by the Publick." Three months later, on December 3, 1788, Fuller wrote to express his satisfaction that the Consolidated Slave Act "has done more towards the opening of the Eyes of this country, then everything that has been hitherto written or said upon the subject of Slavery, and it will convince the whole world that you neither stand in need of the instruction of the mother country, nor the stimulation of an impertinent set of Fanaticks to do, what your own humanity and feeling has prompted you to do already." Humane legislative policies confirmed for the metropolitan public what slaveholders already believed to be true: that slavery was not repugnant to the British constitution. Fuller thus encouraged the gentlemen of the assembly to add any new ameliorative clauses they could devise to update the act—and quickly.[29]

ENSLAVED WOMEN AND NATURAL INCREASE

Taking a similar approach as the Commons to address high slave mortality rates, members of the Jamaica assembly canvassed the opinions of planters and physicians regarding the failure of the slave population to reproduce itself through natural increase. The general consensus held that "the negro women whether slaves or free, do not breed so frequently as the women amongst the labouring poor in Great Britain." Explanations for black women's supposed disinclination to breed centered chiefly on "the promiscuous intercourse which the greater number of negro women indulge themselves in with the other sex," coupled with frequent abortions to rid themselves of burdensome offspring. The children they did manage to produce, witnesses claimed, often perished for "want of maternal affection." "The infertility of Negroes," speculated Reverend Lindsay, likely arose from the "state of uncurb'd Nature among them. Both men and women changing mates as often as Humours and Conveniency shall suit them." "The fact is, that it is the *libidinous practices* of negroes which want *reform*," opined Jesse Foot. "They are so amply provided for, and their toil is so light—they have so little concern for the provision of the day—are so free from the incumbrance of providing for a family . . . that their burthen of life is ever light, and their anxiety for their *children* is as short as that of a bird whilst its young are fledgling." The supposed natural inclinations of African women, not poor treatment by overseers, led to slave decrease.[30]

These theories differed substantially from those later proffered by white male witnesses who testified on the mistreatment of slaves, including pregnant women, in the House of Commons and sought to distance themselves and the British nation from the horrors of Caribbean slavery. One witness, for example, claimed that plantation staff dug a hole in the ground, "in which they put the bellies of pregnant women, while they whip them," as a means of physically punishing pregnant slaves without damaging their wombs. Another reported seeing female slaves heavy with child working in the fields until the moment of their delivery. Whether enslaved women were the instigators or the victims of ill treatment and slave morbidity depended on the perspective of the author or eyewitness relating a narrative. In Jamaica, officials wedded arguments underscoring the excessive profligacy of black women to a declaration to which the slave interest would return repeatedly throughout the debate: "That it is absolutely impossible to cultivate the West Indian islands, so as to produce any commodities that would enrich the mother-country, by white labourers: Fatal experience demonstrates the fallacy of such an expectation." To stimulate slave increase in the West Indies, enslaved women needed reforming, not planters.[31]

Joseph Foster Barham II, an absentee plantation owner who inherited his father, Joseph Foster Barham's Jamaican estate, Mesopotamia, after the latter's death in August 1789, came into his tenure as an absentee planter in the midst of abolition debates about slave management, natural increase, and the treatment of enslaved women. He instructed the managers of his estate to treat his slaves humanely and "ease the labor of my slaves and make their task light and to enable them to enjoy that state of comfort and ease which will be more satisfactory to me than any augmentation of my income." Plantation staff were to allow Moravian missionaries on the estate, allot time for the slaves to receive regular religious instruction, exhibit every manner of care and attention to the "breeding women," and encourage monogamous Christian marriages. By 1800, the Jamaican legislature actively promoted such ameliorative strategies, anticipating that exposure to Christian precepts would improve the "immorality of the Negroe Mothers," effectively "removing and wearing out their barbarous and heathenish persuasions many of which tend to the prejudice of natural population." Barham's directives capture his aspiration to embody the example of the benevolent Protestant master idealized in Georgian culture as well as his embrace of proslavery and abolitionist arguments focused on improving slave women's morality to the benefit of their reproductive capacity. In anticipation of the demise of the African trade, he urged his staff to purchase as many young females as possible and reward them for reproducing and caring for their offspring.[32]

Nonetheless, Barham's superficially magnanimous methods did not produce the anticipated outcome, and the slave population on his estate declined precipitously. "Is there no inducement by which they [slave women] may be led into habits more favourable to breeding?" he wrote to his agent in exasperation. "As we are now absolutely precluded from importation it is become a matter of the highest moment." In a letter to the abolitionist William Smith in 1806, Barham professed his support for ending the slave trade and addressed what he saw as enslaved women's failure to breed: "It is their dissolute manners which prevents their breeding and causes this neglect of the few children they bear, to which the decrease of population must chiefly be ascribed, and to this unfortunate cause we know not what remedy now to apply." Still, Barham continued his experiments. He ordered his agent to release pregnant women from manual labor and offer them a "pecuniary reward" after a child's birth, to reward mothers of multiple children with gifts of clothing and livestock, and to indulge slave couples who lived "in Christian marriage" and reared seven surviving children by permanently exempting the mother from work on her master's behalf and allowing the father to keep a beast. By 1813, Barham expressed his willingness to reward couples "who live in anything like a state of regular family connexion for on the want of this I apprehend the chances of natural increase must chiefly depend." As these plans failed, Barham's frustration mounted; he insisted that "vigorous stakes should be tried to put an end to the practice of procuring abortion or even neglect." It exasperated him that his managers could compel only seven out of the sixty women of childbearing age on the estate to "breed." If the "young women will persevere in malpractices to avoid childbearing at Mesopotamia," Barham preferred that they be sent away, sold, or hired out as punishment; "for at Mesopotamia they shall not stay." Barham feared that with the supply of fresh slaves from Africa permanently cut off, no future remained for a Caribbean estate stocked with women who refused to engage in the reproductive labor required to produce the next generation in bondage.[33]

A CONSTITUTIONAL RIGHT TO RACIAL SLAVERY

Beginning in 1789, as the abolitionist campaign generated vigorous popular support, agent Stephen Fuller privately emphasized to his Jamaican constituents that the West India planters must come forward "united in one common cause." The time for inactivity and complacency had passed. He published twelve hundred copies of the most recent version of the Consolidated Slave Act, which Fuller described to the British public as "the Present Code Noir of that Island," implying that it bore the stamp of royal sovereignty. He sought to demonstrate links between the French islands, where a central policy guided the actions of colonial administrators, and the British islands, where legislators held near-total discretionary authority over local matters. To persuade Parliament of the absolute necessity of the African trade, Fuller proposed a straightforward approach underscoring Jamaica's prominence as the leading sugar producer in the British Empire. Jamaica, as the most valuable British Caribbean colony, he maintained, must lead the way in the struggle against abolitionist fervor. According to Fuller's calculations, for the twelve-month period between March 25, 1787, and March 25, 1788, Jamaica had supplied 40 percent of the sugar and 85 percent of the rum imported to Britain from the West Indies. By comparison, Antigua, the second-largest producer, supplied 14 percent of the sugar and 3 percent of the rum imported during the same period. "We have very little more to do, than to make it appear to the House that Europeans cannot bear field labour in our Island," Fuller outlined to the assembly, "and that we cannot extend nor even keep up our present cultivation, without an annual importation of Negroes." While eradicating the African trade might "save the lives of a few Negroes," Fuller deemed that too heavy of a price to pay if it meant "the destruction of all the Whites in Jamaica."[34]

Fuller's Jamaica-focused strategy influenced the overall defensive approach of the Society of West India Planters and Merchants. He attended a number of society meetings during which members expressed concern that as a consequence of abolitionist agitation "a Spirit of Mutiny will break forth amongst the Negroes, especially in the Island of Jamaica." Society members claimed that they, unlike abolitionists, the British public, or government administrators, knew all too well "the disposition and temper of mind of the Negroe Slaves," particularly their innate propensity to draw "erroneous conclusions." Unless the abolitionists abandoned their fanatical crusade, bloodshed would inevitably ensue in the West Indies due to "the great disproportion of Blacks to Whites in these Colonies." Racial assumptions rooted in notions of blood inheritance also influenced the society's defensive strategy. At a general meeting held at the London Tavern on April 9, 1789, attended by 282 men, members resolved that Caribbean sugar cultivation would "immediately decline without the importation of Negro Labourers from Africa." At a general meeting attended by 160 members the following month, on May 19, 1789, the society further clarified its reasoning by returning to inherited racial characteristics, resolving, "That the constitution of Europeans has been found by experience to be unequal to the Labours of Agriculture in the West Indies and consequently if sufficient supplies of Negroes cannot be procured for that purpose, cultivation cannot proceed."[35]

The society claimed that "Negro" constitutions, unlike white bodies, were well adapted to agricultural labor in the tropics. Yet members also admitted that, owing to "natural causes and accidental calamities to which the West Indies are subject, there is a constant and rapid decrease in the numbers of negroes, which cannot be provided against by births." Even with the introduction of ameliorative measures to encourage slave breeding, "to depend on an internal population of negroes is an experiment that if it fails will ruin planters, creditors, merchants, et al., destroying a system long established in the colonies and sanctioned by many different acts of parliament." Moreover, the slaves purchased by British merchants, they claimed, consisted of prisoners of war, who would otherwise be massacred or sacrificed by their captors; criminals, "whose Punishments are commuted from Death to Slavery"; and those born into slavery or sold to cover their debts. Why should misguided concern for the alleged mistreatment of heathen aliens, naturally suited to slavery and hard labor, cripple the West Indian colonies? If merchants, manufacturers, and planters could no longer place their faith in the validity of royal charters, proclamations, and parliamentary statutes to uphold the national interest and protect the property rights of imperial subjects of British origin, what would become of the English constitutional inheritance?[36]

The West India interest identified inherited racial differences—principally, the physiological suitability of bodies descended from African stock to labor in hot climates—as the crucial motivating factor for retaining the transatlantic slave trade in perpetuity. As a result of hereditary characteristics deemed intrinsic to black and white bloodlines, only the continuous importation of African slaves could generate the requisite manpower to satisfy the voracious consumer demand for sugar in Britain and Europe. According to this logic, the maintenance of the African trade was not simply a matter of assuring a continuous supply of laborers, any laborers, to work the fields, it was a matter of supplying the *right kind* of laborers suited to the arduous task of sugar cultivation in the West Indies. By presenting whites and blacks as inherently fit for different climates and tasks, the West India interest popularized a modified version of George Best's Elizabethan-era fringe theory about African hereditary infection. Britons could colonize distant climes without losing their essential nature, as Best had argued, but they would need Africans to labor for them. Not even extended exposure to a harsh climate over multiple generations could alter the fixed, separate racial essences of whites and blacks. "The Climate is hot indeed," confirmed Reverend John Lindsay, "but that heat is to them [Africans] their Nature—it will no doubt in Different degrees affect both Blacks and Whites, but will never make a White man Black, nor a Black man a White one, no not even to gain the Indian clay colour or tawney." In recognition of the distinct natures of Britons and Africans, the property rights of subjects, as the Jamaica assembly had announced in a formal remonstrance to the Crown in December 1789, "are interwoven with the fundamental constitutions of the empire, and which constitutions do not give omnipotence to a British parliament." Hence, meddling with the slave trade or enslaved property without West Indian consent constituted "an unconstitutional assumption of power, subversive of all public faith and confidence, as applied to the colonists."[37]

Ultimately, the abolition debate turned on competing responses to two pressing, interrelated questions. First, and most important, were African slave trading and slavery constitutive of or repugnant to the ancient constitution and the fundamental principles of English law? Second, did the inherited nature of Africans predispose them to bondage rather than freedom, irrespective of the answer to the former question? Abolitionists took the opposite stance of the West India interest. In a letter to William Wilberforce dated June 4, 1795, for instance, Granville Sharp posited slaveholding as "contrary to the first principles of the English Constitution, an oppression which no limited Legislature can tolerate without Treason to the State." Sharp decried both slave trading and slavery as contradictory to English law. He argued that "some general Plan ought to be adopted as soon as possible, for the general enfranchisement of all the other slaves throughout the British colonies." By extending the rights of subjects to slaves, "the British government in those parts may be rendered constitutional and legal, by a total abolition not only of the slave trade but of slavery itself, that we may save our Nation and happy establishment by putting away the accursed thing before it is too late." Abolitionists agreed that imperial officials had long acted in dereliction of duty by not pronouncing slavery repugnant. In contrast, proslavery writers contended that Caribbean planters held a constitutional right to human property; moreover, slave birth or ancestry marked one as inherently ineligible for the full exercise of the liberties of the subject. Abolitionists and the West India interest thus formulated and sought to defend two fundamentally different interpretations of the English constitution and the nature and extent of British imperial subjecthood. They disagreed vehemently over the significance of bloodline in determining who held a right to claim the English birthright inheritance and be accounted an equal subject under the law.[38]

CHALLENGING AN EXCLUSIVE INHERITANCE

The wave of revolutionary violence unleashed by the French Revolution and the 1791 Saint-Domingue slave revolt disrupted and dramatically altered the tenor of Britain's slavery debate. Revolutionary activity in the French Empire provoked conservative reactions on both sides of the British Atlantic, as imperial officials and Caribbean colonists and administrators closed ranks and viewed racial outsiders with increased suspicion. In contrast to Jamaica, where Tacky's Revolt in 1760 provoked a repressive crackdown on African slaves and their free descendants and sharpened the lines of distinction between fungible colonial racial classes, in the nearby French sugar powerhouse of Saint-Domingue administrators had begun regulating manumissions and constricting the rights of freed slaves and people of mixed ancestry well before the eruption of bloodshed in 1791. Although the 1685 *Code noir,* which followed Roman legal doctrine, granted manumitted slaves all the rights of French citizenship without the need to obtain letters of naturalization, by the 1770s French colonial officials in Saint-Domingue had politically disenfranchised free people of African and mixed descent on the basis of their slave ancestry. Royal opinion had likewise evolved. "Whatever distance they may be from their origin, they always keep the stain of slavery, and are declared incapable of all public functions. Even gentlemen who descend to any degree from a woman of color cannot enjoy the prerogatives of nobility. This law is harsh, but wise and necessary," concluded Louis XVI in 1777.[39]

From the perspective of Saint-Domingue's free people and their supporters, colonial administrators not only refused to enforce the protections of the *Code noir* but also disregarded the shared bloodlines of French colonists and people of mixed lineage. To the disgrace of the French constitution, proclaimed the Abbé Grégoire, Bishop of Loire and Cher, deputy of the National Assembly, in a June 1791 letter to the citizens of color and free blacks in Saint-Domingue, white planters had cruelly ignored "the complaints of the unhappy people of mixed blood; who, notwithstanding, are their own children." Consequently, "the unnatural cruelty of their fathers" had "defrauded" free people of their "sacred inheritance": the full rights of French citizenship. "There was no law, nor custom, that allowed the privileges of a white person to any descendant from an African, however remote the origin. The taint in the blood was incurable, and spread to the latest posterity," commented Bryan Edwards in his 1797 history of revolutionary activity in Saint-Domingue. Employing the language of sanguinary inheritance, free men of mixed ancestry appealed for equal rights on the eve of the revolution, describing Saint-Domingue's white colonists as "the fathers, the brothers of the citizens of color; it is their blood, French blood, that runs in our veins, and the whites want to demean their children." Yet their claim to a shared lineage went unheeded.[40]

While the turmoil of the Saint-Domingue revolution halted sugar production, drove up prices, and temporarily diffused the abolition movement to the benefit of the British West Indian planters, the prospect of violent revolt and collusion between free people of color and slaves terrified Jamaican colonists. As the assembly declared, "Whatever temporary advantage our staples may derive from the calamities of that island, the tenure both of our properties and our lives is precarious, while our slaves have such a precedent of the triumph of savage anarchy over all order and government." Throughout the 1790s, Jamaican legislators pointed repeatedly to revolutionary activity in Saint-Domingue as evidence that "wild and enthusiastic doctrines," such as abolition and the equality of man, could annihilate government and society, transforming an island, "every class and colour of whose inhabitants (so far as their state of civilization will admit) possess the blessings of a mild and equitable government," into a "general scene of horror and confusion" characterized by "murder, robbery, [and] rape." In Jamaica, wrote Robert Hibbert, the Kingston-based agent of James Brydges, third Duke of Chandos, radical outside agitation held the power "to raise commotions amongst a set of People naturally peaceable and harmless, but who if they knew their Power have our Lives and property entirely at their mercy." Simon Taylor hoped that European troops would speedily retake Saint-Domingue and "the poor Deluded Wretches of Negroes may lay down their arms and submit to the Mercy of their Masters" before the contagion of rebellion spread to Jamaica. But not only did Saint-Domingue remain in turmoil, the French legislature also granted free people of color full citizenship in April 1792—only weeks before the British Commons approved a gradual abolition of the slave trade. Worse still for the slave cause, the revolutionary government in France, worried its Caribbean colonies would fall prey to Britain, abolished slavery in the French colonies in February 1794.[41]

The anticipated internal challenge to white hegemony in Jamaica officially began, as the assembly saw it, in the fall of 1792. Seeking to use the legal system to gain the privileges acquired by free people in Saint-Domingue, a group of mixed-race free men petitioned the legislature to remove restrictions on their ability to testify against whites in court and inherit property. Branding the petitioners' attempt "to be put upon an equal footing with the

White Inhabitants" as both dangerous and "expressed in the language of fanaticism," the assembly rejected their petition as an act of revolutionary defiance. The violent upheaval in Saint-Domingue intensified fears that enlarging the privileges of free people of mixed blood would provoke unrest among the enslaved population at a time when colonial officials sought to maintain the racial status quo. "The African black soon finds he has exchanged Barbarian slavery for a far less galling yoke, under civilized Christians," council members emphasized in an address to Lieutenant Governor Adam Williamson on November 26, 1792. "An obligation to vassalage is not felt as a calamity 'till discontent attaches. Whosoever disseminates the seeds of the discontent is, in fact, the Tyrant." The free colored petitioners, led astray by the "visionary theories" of abolitionists and rebels in Saint-Domingue, were sowing the seeds of revolution in home soil. Writing to Stephen Fuller in a letter marked "Most Secretive and Confidential" on December 5, 1792, the assembly noted, "We have every reason to believe that these free people of colour have it in their power to lead our slaves into rebellion by false representations. Their object would not be to make them free but to distress us and thereby oblige us to comply with their demands to be put upon an equal footing with the white Inhabitants."[42]

Privately, the British government encouraged Jamaican officials to consider the possibility that concessions to free people might eventually become necessary. If French colonial proprietors extended privileges to free people of color as a result of negotiations, argued Henry Dundas, the British war secretary, prudence suggested authorities take similar steps in Jamaica. However, he recognized that "the privileges enjoyed by the Mulattoes in Jamaica are of a more beneficial nature than those heretofore enjoyed by the same description of persons in the French colony," specifically that "at a certain degree of distance from his origin, the distinction between a person of Mulatto extraction and a white inhabitant ceases in Jamaica." In an age of revolutionary racial fervor, Jamaica's long-held whitening policy offered a potential olive branch to the descendants of slaves, or so government officials assumed. In a report entitled "The state of mulattoes in Jamaica," submitted to the British government in May 1793, Bryan Edwards observed that in consequence of "the boundary which the law has drawn between the perfect white, and the man of colour," gradations of blood and their corresponding casts determined the treatment of Jamaican subjects before the law, "according as they participate more or less of a white origin." Yet Jamaica's demographic situation diminished each generation's prospect of acquiring a sufficient portion of white blood to exercise the full privileges of whiteness. For most free people with slave ancestors, attaining white status in law was an illusory prospect; only the rights associated with British subjecthood lay within reach.[43]

Convincing the colonial government to extend British liberties to persons classified as nonwhite in Jamaica would prove an uphill battle. Although freedmen of African and mixed ancestry composed over a quarter of ordinary rank-and-file soldiers by the 1790s, the Jamaican legislature's growing reliance on nonwhite militiamen did not alter their treatment of free people. The complete subordination of blacks and browns to whites remained a crucial aspect of colonial policy. Brutally exploiting slave labor, erecting and policing legal and social boundaries between racial castes, and denying full civil rights to free people of African and mixed ancestry had enabled Jamaica's planter elites to maximize profits and power for well over a century. Yet renewed conflict with the Maroons in the mid-1790s forced their hand. In July 1795, the Trelawny Maroons, who numbered approximately 660 men, women, and children, revolted following the summary flogging of two of their members for theft based on white evidence. Rumors that the Trelawny Maroons, inspired by the "example of St. Domingo," wanted to rule the island and "could command the Aid of the Plantation Negroes at Pleasure" swept through Jamaica. Additional reports that Jamaica "swarmed with multitudes of French People of Colour" intent on inciting a general insurrection, and that "half the Negroes on every estate were ready to revolt," magnified officials' fears. Black and mixed-race militiamen aided the pursuit of the rebels and proved instrumental in the suppression of the rebellion. In 1796, in recognition of the "zeal and prompt obedience" exhibited by freedmen, the legislature granted free people the right to give evidence in cases of violent assault, but only if they presented valid certificates of freedom and baptism in court.[44]

The following year, the Jamaica assembly fervidly opposed the Crown's proposal to deploy a regular company of black and colored troops to defend the island, irrespective of the heavy losses faced by British forces in the West Indies. The British government outlined "the formation of a regular Negroe Force in the West Indies" as a strategic point of imperial policy, "which shall be suitable to the Climate and sufficient for the defence and security of the Island," as "mixing troops composed of negroes and men of colour with our European forces is intended to give strength and efficacy to both." The assembly refused to support this line of reasoning or cover any expenses incurred by such troops. Members countered with an offer to foot the entire bill for two thousand European troops. "Nothing but a scheme to massacre the white inhabitants, could have put it into the Heads of those that Advised government to raise Black and Mullatoe Troops for the West Indies," wrote Simon Taylor in disgust in December 1797. Jamaican colonial officials, after articulating a proslavery defense rooted in Africans' suitability for tropical labor, denounced the imperial government's call to arm slaves or free people, regardless of the "universal abhorrence" of colonists, as both unconstitutional and hypocritical. Furthermore, they asserted, "those who consider the African best adapted for the drudgery of the army" must admit "that he is also so for the most laborious work to be done on West-Indian plantations. And that the necessary number of negroes wanted for the various purposes of agriculture, also can only be obtained by a continuation of the importation from Africa." To arm slaves and free people in the context of abolitionist agitation invited disaster. Free of notions of colonial subordination, and supplied with weapons by the British government, black and colored troops would align themselves with disaffected slaves and together plot to overthrow minority white control.[45]

The passage of the Abolition Act in 1807, despite the misgivings of George III, sharply magnified fears of a general insurrection and convinced governing elites in Jamaica that Parliament had dealt a fatal blow to colonists' inherent birthright as British subjects, thereby sealing the island's fate as a failed British settler society. Without a necessary supply of slave labor from Africa, many "industrious and enterprising settlers" would abandon their plantations, the assembly predicted, leaving them to be overrun by "rebellious negroes, whose minds, having been poisoned by the fanatical doctrine of the day, will conspire to the total extermination of the race of white inhabitants." If the mother country had refrained from meddling unconstitutionally in the internal affairs of the West Indian colonies, Jamaican settlers would not have to face the imminent destruction of their "rights, properties, and lives" by slaves swayed to believe they were owed the precious inheritance of Englishmen. For "as the original settlers of this island were free British subjects," the assemblymen reiterated, "it is manifest that they brought with them all the rights and privileges of Britons," and "the legislature of this island has, and ever had, the exclusive and absolute right to enact its own laws, and to regulate entirely its internal government and affairs." Hence, they reiterated, "it is our duty, by all constitutional means in our power, to resist the attempt that has been, and every attempt that may be, made to destroy or to abridge that right." Despite the impassioned protests of West Indians and George III's long-held view that the British legislature had no "right from ideas of false phylanthropy to affect the property of British settlers," the Abolition Act remained in effect. Caribbean colonists anticipated a rebellion would occur at any moment, as the majority slave population sought to, in the words of Governor Coote of Jamaica, "regain that liberty, the British legislature has told them they have the right to as British subjects."[46]

THE BLOOD OF FREE SUBJECTS

In early nineteenth-century Jamaica a resounding demographic defeat paralleled the legislative defeat of the West India interest in Parliament. Free people, now close to equaling whites in numbers and strength, took collective action to improve their marginalized position at the bottom of the colonial racial hierarchy. The assembly's discontinuation of private privilege bills in 1802 provided additional impetus to individual freemen to work together for the benefit of the whole body of free people of mixed descent. In November 1813, over twenty-four hundred freedmen petitioned for an expansion of their privileges, arguing that their inability to testify against whites or inherit property beyond a limited amount undercut their inherited liberties as free imperial subjects. Although the assembly proclaimed that "free people of colour in this island have no right or claim whatever to political power," it nevertheless conceded the major points listed in the petition. Free people would be allowed to give evidence in all the courts of the island, to inherit property without restrictions, and to "save deficiency"—no longer incurring fines for themselves or their employers for being mixed-race rather than white. Secret correspondence between Lieutenant Governor Edward Morrison and Earl Bathurst reveals that the assembly contemplated enlarging the privileges of "that class of the coloured population which approaches nearest to the white inhabitants . . . designated Mestizoes," or the offspring of white-quadroon unions, "and whom it is difficult to distinguish by their complexion from the White inhabitants." Seeking the Crown's opinion, Morrison urged Bathurst to approach the question with great caution, "as it is extremely important that this subject should not be agitated"; the slightest whiff of such a measure "could be attended here with serious consequences." His Majesty (the prince regent), Bathurst wrote in response, wholeheartedly approved extending "mestizoes" all the privileges of white subjects. Under pressure, the assembly reluctantly passed a more inclusive measure removing some of the restrictions placed on all free people of slave ancestry, not just those perceived to hold the greatest share of white blood.[47]

Governor Manchester cast the new legislation in a positive light as an example of the colonial government's "liberality." The measures would diffuse racial tensions, he argued, and, more importantly, "produce in the minds of the
coloured population a proper sense of gratitude for the considerate attention
with which their claims have been admitted, and attach them more strongly
to His Majesty's Government, and a Country in which they now possess
an increased interest." White colonists nevertheless responded with outrage.
Alterations to the restrictions on free people met with sharp resistance from
whites in Kingston, who protested that these "sudden innovations" threatened to erase "an essential part of the constitution of Jamaica": the "marked
distinction between the white inhabitants and the free persons of colour and
free blacks." White colonial autonomy would take another hit in 1816, when
the British government forced the West Indian colonies to submit to a slave
registry designed to thwart illegal slave trading. Jamaican colonists attacked
the Slave Registry Bill as another misguided metropolitan intrusion and railed
against the predominance of fanatics in Parliament more concerned with
"black heathen woolly aliens" than preserving the lives of "the children of
Great Britain, her own precious Blood." The assembly had passed "humane"
and "highly favorable" legislation respecting both slaves and free people since
the Abolition Act went into effect, yet Parliament still accused colonists of
criminal behavior and denied them the right to govern their own affairs.[48]

In November 1816, seizing on the continued push for slave amelioration
in Britain, twenty-seven hundred free men of color petitioned for the removal
of all remaining restrictions on their civil and political rights "so they may
participate in the full enjoyment of the benefits of the British constitution
equally and in common with their fellow subjects." Rejecting their request as
a thinly veiled attempt to sow "anarchy and confusion," the assembly committee charged with examining the petition chastised those involved for opposing "that system of laws which it is as much their interest as their duty to
maintain." The committee's report also praised the conduct of the majority
of free people who did not sign the document, inspiring a counterpetition
submitted during the same session by seventy-one free men expressing satisfaction with their current privileges and gratitude for earlier concessions.
The assembly's stance and the obsequious tone of the counterpetitioners
prompted John Campbell, a propertied freeman of mixed ancestry and advo-
cate for equal treatment under the law, to submit a memorial directly to Earl
Bathurst. Campbell emphasized the loyalty of Jamaica's free people of mixed

blood to the British Crown and their "wish that the degradation under which they labour may be removed as far as possible" in a manner satisfactory to all involved—whites included. He detailed the severe disabilities crippling free people's civil liberties and socioeconomic advancement until as recently as 1813 and the remaining indignities to which they were still subject. These included poor employment prospects and compensation; an inability to hold positions of public trust, vote, or educate their children in the island's free schools; and an absence of legal recourse for "the seduction of their wives or daughters," who were looked upon and treated "as the prey and prostitutes of the white males." The free people of Jamaica, Campbell argued, "although they have sprung from the whites," were "exposed to every indignity, to every illiberality; so much so, that the white parent in public will scarce notice his coloured son or daughter, which in private are perhaps his only care and companion." Racial prejudice and subjugation had loosened the natural ties of blood and affection between white colonists and their mixed descendants, exacerbating the degraded status of free people as a result of the statutory restrictions placed upon them.[49]

Beginning in the early 1820s, as the British imperial government adopted an official amelioration policy to prepare enslaved men and women for freedom, members of Jamaica's Jewish community joined free people of mixed ancestry to protest against the violation of their rights as British subjects by the colonial government. Working separately, both groups invoked the ancient constitution and professed their unwavering allegiance to the Crown in an attempt to challenge their status as an alien people undeserving of the common law birthright of natural-born subjects. On July 5, 1820, Levy Hyman, an affluent Jewish merchant in Kingston and owner of a number of plantations and slaves in St. Andrew parish, tried to cast his vote for an assembly representative. After the deputy marshal overseeing polling, Joseph Geoghegan, rejected his vote, Hyman filed a lawsuit declaring that Geoghegan had contravened his rights as a British subject. While Hyman's lawsuit failed to produce immediate results, it indicated the lengths legally marginalized individuals would go to force recognition of their shared claim to British rights and liberties. If imperial authorities in Britain found the prospect of slave emancipation palatable as a result of renewed attacks by antislavery campaigners, then Jamaican Jews and free people would likewise vocalize their grievances and demand equal treatment with the Crown's rights-bearing white Protestant subjects.[50]

Free Jamaicans of mixed lineage regarded themselves as the rightful descendants of the first English settlers, unlawfully denied their common law inheritance as a result of prejudicial local policy. In 1823, coinciding with the foundation of a new Anti-Slavery Society in England, they appealed simultaneously to the colonial legislature and the imperial government for equal rights with whites. Leading free men of color organized an island-wide petition and collected nearly three thousand signatures, calling for the assembly to extend to free people the right to vote, serve as jurors, and have free access to public spaces, including schools and baths, heretofore preserved for whites alone. As it had in 1816, the assembly rejected the petition and branded its stated aims "subversive of the constitution and prejudicial to the interests of the colony"; yet it resumed granting private privilege bills on an individual basis as a means of diffusing tension. Undaunted, the Kingston Committee of Free People of Colour appointed an Englishman, Michael Hanly, to appeal directly to the Crown on their behalf. "The many restrictions under which they have so long suffered in consequence of local regulations, which had their origin in times far remote, and under circumstances of peculiar emergency, the coloured people now pray may be terminated," Hanly wrote to Lord Bathurst on May 23, 1823, in one of several appeals to the British government to intervene in colonial affairs and dissolve "that imaginary distinctive line" arbitrarily drawn between free men by local prejudice. "Whatever the original intention of the colonial legislature might have been in framing such regulations," he continued, "it never could have been to make their effects so injurious to posterity, thus visiting, not the sins of the fathers, but the misfortune of the mothers, upon the children into the third and fourth generation." Now they hoped that "under the benevolent auspices of his present most gracious Majesty, when it is even in contemplation to grant manumission to slaves, the free coloured inhabitants of Jamaica may be admitted into the full participation of the rights of British subjects, in common with their European brethren."[51]

Jamaica's Jewish community embraced a line of attack focused not on inherited liberties passed down over the generations but rather on unwarranted colonial departures from inclusive common law definitions of British subjecthood based on birthplace and allegiance. The Jews "have always behaved with loyalty to their King," argued a writer under the pen name JUSTICE in the *Kingston Chronicle* in May 1820; "and may fearlessly demand what they have a right to expect, in common with all his Majesty's natural born subjects—the darling privilege of elective franchise." In Jamaica, "nothing has as yet been produced against the eligibility of a Jew's voting, but these resolutions and *custom*," agreed a writer under the pen name A JEW later that month. "As no *law* can be pronounced against them, I must think they are entitled to the privileges as well as any other British subjects." In 1826, chiefly as a result of the efforts of Moses Delgado, a Kingston Jewish merchant of Portuguese ancestry, the assembly relented to local and imperial pressure and passed an act extending the franchise to Jamaican Jews. Delgado justified his efforts on behalf of the Jewish people in Jamaica by declaring "that the doctrine of exclusion," as formulated by the colonial legislature, "was at variance with the principles of the British Constitution" and therefore invalid.[52]

Although arguments based on local departures from the British constitution proved effective in extending the franchise to Jamaica's Jewish population in 1826, that same year the assembly again rejected petitions for equal rights presented by free men of color from the parishes of St. James and St. Elizabeth. Sharing the birthright of Englishmen with free individuals of mixed lineage in whose veins flowed the blood of slave ancestors met with unceasing resistance. The legislature's refusal to grant their request struck the petitioners as a grievous personal insult, given that the assembly had extended to the Jews "those privileges which they had refused to the freemen of colour, who were Christians; and who, even in point of complexion, could scarcely be distinguished from the whites themselves." At the same time that imperial administrators in Britain grew more receptive to the extension of civil and political liberties to a diverse array of subjects in the expanding, multiethnic, religiously plural empire, Jamaican officials dug in their heels. They continued to view free people through the lens of slave criminality and rebellion, even though free Jamaicans of mixed descent held in bondage roughly 50,000 slaves out of a total population of 310,000, and many were invested in the slave system. "The dominion of whites is founded on opinion," the assembly had admitted to the Crown in 1815; "unsettle those opinions, and the physical force is on the opposite side, and must soon preponderate." The fragility of white mastery could no longer be denied, and the numerical vulnerability of whites terrified colonial officials. With a population composed almost entirely of enslaved Africans, and an expanding population of free people convinced of their inherent equality with whites, Jamaica appeared destined for total Africanization, a change that would mark the loss of Britain's most valuable Atlantic possession.[53]

The apprehension that emancipation and the extension of common law rights to free people of African and mixed descent would lead to racial and social disorder was not confined to the colonial Caribbean. The possibility that the renewed agitations of abolitionists and radical black liberators to incorporate Africans and their descendants into the British imperial polity as free and equal subjects might introduce sociopolitical disorder and racial contagion in the mother country drew heavy censure in the era of amelioration. George Cruikshank's *The New Union-Club* (1819), for example, which creatively reimagines James Gillray's focus on a riotous Whig celebration following the Irish union in *The Union Club* (1801), depicts the radical black preacher Robert Wedderburn presiding over a chaotic scene of interracial drunkenness, debauchery, and violence (figure 24). Meanwhile, William Wilberforce sits on a commode and toasts the assembly: "Brothers I'll give you the Black Joke!! With three times three!!! Upstanding and uncovered!!" Grotesque black women with enormous breasts, thick lips, garish smiles, and sharp teeth

24. George Cruikshank, *The New Union-Club* (London, 1819).
Courtesy of The Lewis Walpole Library, Yale University.

kiss and caress white men and brutally beat one another as hordes of plebian black men fight, drink, and vomit. In the foreground, black children wrestle a dog named Mungo for a bone, while a plump black woman sits on the abolitionist Zachary Macaulay's lap as he gazes uncomfortably at her breasts. She strokes his chin delicately and comments, "I say massa' Cauley why you nebber look a body in the face?" In the far left middle ground, a white woman wearing a cross necklace stands serenely next to a smiling black man; between them they display a half-white, half-black infant divided vertically. A scrawny Quaker, held tightly by a large black woman, stands behind the couple saying, "Hail! piebald pledge of Love." Biblical scenes with black and white figures and parodies of graphic prints paper the wall. In *The Apotheosis of W. W.* in the upper left corner, modeled on Gillray's attack on revolutionary France in *The Apotheosis of Hoche,* black angels carry a nude Wilberforce, his wings too puny to bear his emaciated frame, to heaven. Underneath, a spotted baby suckles a black breast thrown over the shoulder of a woman smoking a pipe while an interracial couple engage in a lewd embrace.[54]

By the late 1820s, the imperial government's intervention into colonial affairs in response to the appeals of free people of mixed descent for the full rights of subjects had accelerated the push toward civil and political equality for free people, underscoring the extent to which white colonists' exclusive interpretation of Jamaica's constitution rested on notions of blood heredity. Even the planter and assembly member Richard Barrett, who supported solidary across racial classes of free men as a means of delaying emancipation, nevertheless argued that blood mixture had justly blocked free people of color from claiming British liberties by birthright. Jamaican colonists, Barrett proclaimed in the House of Commons on June 12, 1827, "love the pure blood of our English countrymen better than the mixed stream that flows in the veins of the other descendants of the negro." Although the British government sought to extend to free people "the privileges of Britons" to which the "children of slaves by the King's natural born subjects of England" claimed to be entitled by the proclamation of Charles II, Barrett protested that the descendants of African slaves "have no father. They follow the condition of the mother. The charter of King Charles could not contemplate the manumission of the children of Africans." "The father being unknown in the eyes of the law," the people of mixed ancestry "inherit no right to the privileges they claim." Furthermore, by undermining the authority of colonial administrators, "who are the constitutional arbitrators of the rights and claims of all persons within their limits," the British government, he prophesied, must soon "be satisfied to behold the English colonies denuded of their English inhabitants, and in the possession of a class of persons who know not England, and have no ties of consanguinity; to bind them to Great Britain beyond what they have to connect them with Africa and St. Domingo."[55]

To defend the ongoing subjugation of free people of African and mixed descent, slaveholders in Jamaica returned time and again to the matter of legitimacy and bloodline. In the absence of Christian marriage rites, blood ties between Britons and Africans simply did not exist, these commentators asserted; colonial law took no notice of such connections. Without official acknowledgment to the contrary, individuals of servile, alien extraction, descended from slaves "only one degree removed from savage life," held no inherited title to English liberties as their constitutional birthright. "You cannot," stated Barrett pointedly, "deprive persons of what they never possessed." Free people of mixed blood had long "demanded admission to the privileges of freehold suffrages," maintained the Reverend George Bridges, rector of St. Ann parish, yet considered it "an unnecessary degradation to be obliged to produce evidence of their conversion to Christianity, before they were permitted to bind themselves by a Christian oath." Prudence dictated against extending the historic birthright of freeborn Britons to the descendants of slaves "while the blood of pagan Africa still flowed thickly and darkly in their veins." For white elites in colonial Jamaica, both the rule of matrilineal descent for assigning slave status and the determinative power of blood heredity post manumission had judiciously prevented African-descended peoples from exercising British liberties in Jamaica without legislative mediation. Protecting the birthright of Englishmen in a slave society to the benefit of the public welfare and the empire as a whole meant allowing the colonial legislature to uphold the inherited rights and privileges of the few while simultaneously legislating over matters purely of local concern, including slavery and legal disabilities to which marginalized racial classes were subject. The result was a hybrid mix of common law governance for the white Protestant minority population alongside local practices intended to preserve the slave system and police racial boundaries.[56]

Faced with transatlantic agitation for slave emancipation and calls for the civil and political equality of free people, Jamaican colonists—including planters, merchants, lawyers, overseers, and administrators—stressed that local labor practices and racial divisions remained vital to the stability of Britain's Atlantic empire and to the preservation of whiteness. As former attorney general of Jamaica William Burge remarked before the House of Lords in the summer of 1832, West Indian planters "only desire the Negro's fitness for free-dom" and pronounced themselves alone qualified to render judgment con-cerning both the fitness of the enslaved for emancipation and the readiness of free people of African and mixed ancestry for civil and political equality with white subjects. Just as enslaved Africans had not yet demonstrated the intellectual capacity and moral responsibility necessary for freedom, so, too, did many free people of slave descent remain ill equipped to comprehend the complexities of common law rights and responsibilities.[57]

The arguments put forward in support of the proslavery cause on the eve of emancipation show how legal and moral issues regarding slavery and racial subordination in colonial Jamaica were enmeshed in another constitutional question: to what extent would the imperial government's eradication of pro-vincial customs—such as property rights in persons and hereditary blood status as a determinant for individual rights and obligations—transform the constitutional relationship between the colony of Jamaica and the Crown? What had once, fleetingly, been a conquered island settled by Englishmen seeking to plant a flourishing agricultural colony populated by white set-tlers was now a slave society chiefly inhabited by enslaved Africans and free men and women of servile, heathen ancestry. As Jamaican officials saw it, for Parliament to extend not only freedom but also the inherited liberties and privileges of Englishmen to slaves and their free descendants against the grave concerns and express wishes of the colonial legislature constituted a radical modification of Jamaica's constitution. For free Jamaicans of mixed ancestry, however, such an extension heralded the restoration of their common law birthright as the children of freeborn Englishmen and a long-awaited return to first principles.

Conclusion

In December 1830, the Jamaican colonial legislature passed an act declaring that "all the free brown and black population of this Island shall be entitled to have and enjoy all the rights, privileges, immunities and advantages whatsoever to which they would have been entitled if born and descended from white ancestors." While it was a momentous achievement, accomplished in no small measure due to the persistence of free people of African and mixed descent, the 1830 act granting the rights of British subjects to all free Jamaicans regardless of ancestry retuned to the contested issue of the English inheritance. By bestowing legal and political equality on the free community in language intentionally designed to set the descendants of slaves apart from Jamaican residents "born and descended from white ancestors," the colonial government retained control over official racial classifications and reaffirmed hereditary blood status as the most enduring categorical legacy of slavery. Although members of the Jamaica assembly, under the pressure of mounting local and imperial appeals, had relented, dissolving century-old statutory divisions erected between those of "pure" ancestry who could claim the common law as their birthright and those who could not, they framed the wording of the 1830 law with care. Free people of African and mixed lineage, the act signaled, would retain their social status as a discrete and inferior subset of the colonial population. Furthermore, the extension of British liberties to the free descendants of slaves did not constitute the restoration of a pretended birthright, long denied, but rather established a privilege conferred by the grace and favor of the colonial state.[1]

Since the late seventeenth century, colonial officials in Jamaica had fought to preserve the English legal inheritance for the island's shrinking population of white Protestant subjects while subjecting the growing enslaved African majority to punitive measures outside the common law and Jews to extraordinary taxation. The prerogative framework of the early Anglo-Atlantic empire, which facilitated legal decentralization with a strong emphasis on local self-government and selective reception of common law doctrines, both allowed for the development of hereditary slave regimes and permitted the divergent treatment of free subjects and slaves, with minimal oversight from the Crown. This evolving constitutional relationship also led to the creation of localized, distinct legal categories of colonial subjects, some of whom were simultaneously barred from exercising the rights of British subjects on the basis of alien, servile, and/or non-Christian ancestry and assigned additional duties. In Jamaica, beginning in the early eighteenth century, the assembly wrestled with the question of how to determine who qualified for the rights and privileges of British identity in a slave society, but only once "others" (initially free blacks and Jewish men) began to articulate their own claim to the liberties of the subject.

The idea that a colonial elective assembly should protect the common law inheritance of all freeborn Englishmen and pass statutes based on local conditions and needs resulted in the construction of an explicitly exclusionary definition of British subjecthood at the provincial level. Colonial officials in Jamaica privileged his "His Majesty's white subjects" above all others and legally institutionalized racial distinctions in such a way as to make those classes "appear to be naturally discrete subsets of the population" or "naturally distinct 'kinds of humans'"—identified as such rather than ascribed and mandated by the colonial government. Using blood ancestry as a marker of difference separating free colonial subjects into distinct racial classes in Jamaica, a tactic increasingly deployed throughout the European Atlantic empires but originating in the Spanish colonies, proved an effective boundary at first and raised virtually no concerns "in point of law" in England. Despite the Board of Trade's professed qualms about the denial of basic rights to propertied Christian freedmen descended from slave ancestors, the Privy Council was reluctant to pronounce colonial statutes repugnant and thus unlawful, given the prevalence of such acts in the Anglo-American mainland and Caribbean slave societies and the prudent provincial explanations put forward to justify them. By the early 1730s, Barbados (1721), South Carolina (1721), Virginia (1723), and Jamaica (1733) had legal strictures in place to deny free people of African, Indian, and mixed ancestry the right to vote, serve on juries, hold elective office, and testify in court cases involving whites—regardless of their property qualifications or religious identity—and Georgia followed suit in 1761. In matters relating to slave law and the marginalization of racialized colonial subjects, as Philip Hamburger notes, "whereas Englishmen tended to see repugnancy, Americans" (and West Indians as well) "tended to see only difference—a necessary local difference."[2]

In mid-eighteenth-century Jamaica, racial classifications based on heredity status soon created new challenges, and opened up new possibilities, as a result of two key local developments: pervasive sexual relations between white men and enslaved women of African descent and the manumission of enslaved individuals, mostly women and their mixed offspring, with blood ties to the white community. Provincial legislation specifying the official boundaries of whiteness based on genealogical succession and Christian conversion ("three degrees removed from the Negro ancestor") allowed for the possibility of gradual legal whitening over the generations and encouraged the assembly to make ad hoc exceptions for elite, Protestant mixed-blood individuals related to or known by members. A declining white settler population, sporadic conflicts with the Maroons, and ongoing fears of external French and Spanish attacks placed enormous strain on Jamaica's inadequate militia system and colonial treasury, fostering an experimental approach to local priorities. Yet the transformation of persons of mixed lineage into white subjects under the law, though always a matter of some local controversy, became increasingly problematic in Jamaica after Tacky's Revolt in 1760. As colonial officials began to doubt the loyalty of the island's growing population of free people of African and mixed descent, they drew tighter legal and financial barriers between whites and free people descended from slave ancestors, with individual exceptions still possible but strictly limited. Furthermore, as awareness of what some deemed aberrant colonial sexual practices and tastes became more widespread in metropolitan Britain, even the most fortunate freemen and women of mixed lineage with affluent paternal benefactors grappled with social and professional constraints as a result of their slave origins and "black blood."[3]

By the end of the eighteenth century, the popularity of the abolition movement in Britain prompted West Indian slaveholders to articulate a defense of slavery based on hereditary blood distinctions for a metropolitan audience.

At the same time, free people of mixed ancestry joined together collectively to protest their treatment by the colonial legislature and draw attention to their subjugated status as blood heirs unlawfully disinherited from the constitutional birthright of British subjects. Local definitions of British subjecthood, rooted in fictions of blood rather than birth and allegiance, lay at the heart of the unfolding tensions between colonial authorities and free people in Jamaica, and so, too, did competing understandings of Jamaica's constitutional relationship with the Crown. While white colonial elites looked to the 1661 proclamation of Charles II as a foundational charter confirming the traditional English rights and privileges they regarded as their special birthright, free people pointed to this same historic document as evidence of their own entitlement to equal treatment under the law as natural-born subjects of the British sovereign. After August 1791, the slave revolution in Saint-Domingue profoundly influenced the abolition debate in Britain and reignited disputes over the hereditary status and rights of free people in Jamaica, and not only in terms of shaping the responses of colonial and imperial administrators and metropolitan commentators.

In Jamaica, free people's repeated professions of loyalty to the Crown, faithful military service, Protestant faith, and inherited stake in the white colonial order represented a concerted attempt to achieve civil and political equality within the existing parameters of the Jamaican constitution rather than through rupture, bloodshed, and severance. Other historians have described what took place in Saint-Domingue both prior to and as a consequence of the rebellion in masterful detail, and I will not cover that well-trod ground here. But there are striking commonalities worth addressing. Although the *Code noir* of 1685 carried the weight of royal sovereignty and provided a systematic jurisprudence of slavery based on Roman legal principles lacking in the British Atlantic, local authorities in Saint-Domingue still took matters into their own hands. Beginning in the early eighteenth century, colonial administrators chipped away at articles of the *Code noir* granting masters full discretionary power over manumission and permitting manumitted slaves to enjoy the full rights of other natural-born French subjects in the colony without the need for naturalization. By the 1760s, at the same time colonial authorities in Jamaica attempted to tighten racial restrictions, a Saint-Domingue ministerial directive announced that the "first stain" of slavery carried by persons of African ancestry "extends to all their descendants, and . . . cannot be erased by the gift of freedom." This directive, and other legal moves to set limits on the rights of free people descended from slave ancestors, signified the new colonial racism of the post–Seven Years' War period that historians argue ultimately contributed to the alliance between the *gens de couleur* and slaves. Like free people in Jamaica, the gens de couleur in Saint-Domingue appealed to abolitionists and government ministers in France, insisting that local officials had denied them rights guaranteed in the *Code noir*, and embraced the rebellion's aims and universalist rhetoric only once it became clear that their appeals to the metropole had failed.[4]

Neither free people of mixed descent in Jamaica nor the gens de couleur in Saint-Domingue relied solely on Enlightenment principles of universal rights to challenge their subordinate position within their respective colonial racial orders. Both groups repeatedly referenced blood connections to whites and a shared constitutional and racial inheritance. Yet, in the wake of the Saint-Domingue revolution, slaveholders in Jamaica feared that any appeal for equal treatment by free people bore the stamp of radical revolutionary ideals and the prospect of violent upheaval. In this international political context, and with the example of Saint-Domingue before them, free Jamaicans of mixed ancestry reiterated their allegiance to Britain and insisted, now more than ever, that they sought only the inherited rights of British subjects denied to them by unconstitutional local policies. Claiming the English common law inheritance as their birthright as British subjects and emphasizing their blood connection to the early English settlers was thus a strategic move that helped to pave the way for the full incorporation of all free people of African descent into the British imperial polity. By the end of the 1820s, Jamaica's free population was twice as large as the white settler community and increasingly educated, Christian, and propertied. In 1829, two mixed-race booksellers in Kingston, Edward Jordan and Robert Osborn, the former a prominent voice in the campaign for equality for free people, established the *Watchman and Jamaica Free Press*, the first newspaper written solely by freemen of color. Their objective, as the *Anti-Slavery Monthly Reporter* put it, was "to vindicate before the public their full title to those civil and political rights of British subjects of which they are at present unjustly denied." But on what basis did this title rest? Was their claim to British liberties part of a calculated revolutionary campaign, "with a view of destroying lawful authority," as one white commentator saw it, or was it grounded in an inherited birthright secured by the Jamaican constitution? Opinions remained divided.[5]

The abolition movement in Britain had triggered a groundswell of opposition from West Indian slaveholders and their metropolitan allies focused on the divergent inherited natures of Europeans and Africans as a defense of

colonial slave regimes and racial categories. British antislavery reformers challenged these notions, arguing that colonial slaveholders had failed to let go of
racial prejudices born of slavery rather than innate hereditary traits. "As the
African race only can be enslaved," argued James Stephen, a member of the
African Institution, a British abolitionist group formed in 1807, "the abject and
vicious character known to be commonly produced by the state itself, is naturally associated and confounded, in the imaginations of the superior class, with
the disgusting exterior of that enslaved people, as if it were generated rather
by their blood, than by their degraded and brutalized condition." Stephen and
others saw the extension of British liberties to free people as the duty of a civilized, Christian nation to its imperial subjects. Additionally, unless both slaves
and free people descended from slave ancestors attained equality before the
law, illicit sexual relations between white men and women of African descent
would continue unabated. "As such intermixtures are never by lawful marriage,
which would be ineffably disgraceful to the European party, the attainder of
African blood is purged only by impure cohabitation; and the enfranchisement
of the progeny is a premium on concubinage," wrote Stephen. However, he
emphasized, "I know of no act of parliament that has excluded the children
and posterity of imported Africans from the birthright of British subjects, and
ordained that they shall for ever be the property of the man by whom their
mother or ancestress was bought." To deny a share of the English legal inheritance to colonial subjects descended from slave ancestors, once subject to "the
barbarous institutions of Africa" yet now governed by the laws of a civilized,
Christian society, demonstrated not only the inhumanity of West Indians but
also the callous disregard of the British people for universal human rights.[6]

Behind the surefooted rhetoric of the metropolitan-based humanitarian
campaign to expand the rights of free people and ultimately eradicate slavery in the British Empire simmered a lingering ambivalence about extending the birthright of Britons to the descendants of slaves. The rising tide
of proemancipation sentiment in Britain carried with it a disquieting sense
that black freedom would foster conditions conducive to widespread racial
mixture throughout the British polity, infecting future generations with the
purportedly inferior physical, mental, and moral traits of Africans. Against
this cultural backdrop, J. Lewis Marks's satirical print *Every Man in His Humour* (1824) offered an interracial twist on Ben Jonson's comedic Elizabethan
play of the same name (first performed in 1598), in which a merchant named
Thomas Kitely fears his wife cannot control her sexual appetites and is cuck-
olding him (figure 25). As Kitely exclaims,

25. J. Lewis Marks, *Every Man in His Humour,* from *Illustrations of Plays,*
no. 17 (London, 1824). © The Trustees of the British Museum.

> beware
> When mutuall pleasure swayes the appetite,
> And spirits of one kinde and qualitie,
> Do meete to parlee in the pride of blood.

Kitely appoints himself an "Iron Barre," intent on blocking the fulfillment of
his wife's unlawful desire and returning her to her duty:

> Yea euery looke or glaunce mine eye objects,
> Shall cheke occasion, as one doth his slaue,
> When he forgets the limit of prescription.[7]

Marks's print envisions the destructive consequences of disorderly interracial passions barred by neither law nor private mastery. A woman with coal-
black skin and brutish features sits astride a rosy-cheeked white man within
the privacy of intimate domestic space. The room contains a bed and a table

strewn with pipes, tobacco, and a pewter mug of beer; the walls are bare except for a mirror and a portrait of the Hottentot Venus. To the couple's lower right sits a half-white, half-black child playing with a black doll resembling her mother. In this intimate domestic scene, white male lust for the black female has effectively eroded the central pillars of British racial and national identity: familial legitimacy, purity of blood, Protestant civility, and whiteness.

Continued contests over interracial sex and its lasting consequences on the eve of emancipation show how the question of incorporating freed slaves and their descendants, as well as other racially marginalized peoples, into the British polity as free and equal subjects remained a particularly divisive issue. In colonial Jamaica, attempts by provincial administrators to legislate statutory racial classifications rooted in ideologies of blood had originated in apprehensions regarding the preservation of freeborn white Protestant subjects' exclusive birthright as Britons in a slave society. By the early 1830s, concerns about imagined threats to white racial purity were no longer simply those of minority white settlers in distant Caribbean slave colonies but rather were seen as integral to broader questions about the changing boundaries of Britishness and the rights and obligations conferred by imperial citizenship.

Abbreviations

BL   British Library, London.
BOD   Bodleian Library, Oxford University.
CO   Colonial Office Series, National Archives, Kew.
CSPC   *Calendar, State Paper: Colonial Series: America and the West Indies,*
            1574–1739. 45 vols. London: HMSO, 1860–1994.
HL   Henry E. Huntington Library, San Marino, CA.
ICS   Institute of Commonwealth Studies, Senate House, University of
            London.
JA   Jamaica Archives, Spanish Town.
JAJ   *Journals of the Assembly of Jamaica.* 14 vols. Kingston: Alexander
            Aikman, 1792–1809. Cited by volume number.
PFP, HSP   Powel Family Papers, Historical Society of Pennsylvania, Philadelphia.
RL   David M. Rubenstein Library, Duke University.
UASCA   University of Aberdeen Special Collections and Archives, Aberdeen.
WCL   William Clements Library, University of Michigan, Ann Arbor.
WMQ   *The William and Mary Quarterly: A Magazine of Early American History*
            and Culture. Third series.

Notes

INTRODUCTION

1. Campbell to Hill, December 1825, CO 318/76, f. 47; Gad Heuman, *Between Black and White: Race, Politics, and the Free Coloreds in Jamaica, 1792–1865* (Westport, CT: Greenwood Press, 1981), 37; Great Britain, *First Report of the Commissioners of Inquiry into the Administration of Civil and Criminal Justice in the West Indies: Jamaica* (London, 1827), 5–6, 114; Walter Adolphe Roberts, *Six Great Jamaicans: Biographical Sketches* (Kingston: Pioneer Press, 1957), 6; *Hansard's Parliamentary Debates*, 2nd ser., 25 vols. (London, 1820–1830), 10: 1113.

2. Campbell to Hill, CO 318/76, ff. 47, 52, 55, 59. Between 1774 and 1812, freemen of African descent expanded from 20 percent to 46 percent of Jamaica's militia; see Jamaica Census, 1774, CO 137/70, ff. 88–98; Return of militia of 1812, CO 137/137, f. 7.

3. Sympson to Hill, CO 318/76, ff. 51, 59.

4. Sympson to Hill, CO 318/76, ff. 60–61.

5. The commissioners of legal inquiry traveled throughout the British Caribbean in the 1820s, charged by the Colonial Office to report on the constitution and laws of each colony as part of a larger program of imperial legislative review. See Lauren Benton and Lisa Ford, *Rage for Order: The British Empire and the Origins of International Law, 1800–1850* (Cambridge, MA: Harvard University Press, 2016), 56–84; A. Wood Renton, "The Work of the West Indian Commissioners," *Juridical Review: A Journal of Legal and Political Science* 2, no. 4 (Edinburgh, 1890): 357–65. For the questions and answers relative to free people of color in Jamaica, see Great Britain, *First Report of the Commissioners of Inquiry*, 81, 114–15, appendix A: no. 14, 155.

6. Jack P. Greene, *Creating the British Atlantic: Essays on Transplantation, Adaptation, and Continuity* (Charlottesville: University of Virginia Press, 2013), 162. See "An Act for

the Better Ordering and Governing of Negroes," Barbados, 1661, CO 30/2, ff. 16–26. Antigua's 1644 "Act against Carnall Coppulation between Christian and Heathen" demonstrates both the initial association of Africans and Indians with heathen ancestry and the perceived need to prevent the intermixture of Christian and heathen bloodlines. See CO 154/1, ff. 49–51. By the 1670s, *Whites* and *Negroes* had begun to replace *Christians* and *Heathens* in English Caribbean legislation, yet the religious aspects of these identities remained crucial. See, for example, Nevis's 1675 statute "White Men Not to Keep Company with Negroes," with its emphasis on the "unchristian like association of white people with negroes," CO 154/2, f. 36.

7. Early modern English notions of heritable blood and mixture are detailed in Mary Floyd-Wilson, *English Ethnicity and Race in Early Modern Drama* (Cambridge: Cambridge University Press, 2003), 1–22; Declan Downey, "Purity of Blood and the Purity of Faith in Early Modern Ireland," in *The Origins of Sectarianism in Early Modern Ireland*, ed. Alan Ford and John McCaefferty (Cambridge: Cambridge University Press, 2005), 216–28; Jean Feerick, *Strangers in Blood: Relocating Race in the Renaissance* (Toronto: University of Toronto Press, 2010); Wolfram Schmidgen, *Exquisite Mixture: The Virtues of Impurity in Early Modern England* (Philadelphia: University of Pennsylvania Press, 2012), 1–23; Jean Feerick, "'Rude Uncivill Blood': The Pastoral Challenge to Hereditary Race in Fletcher and Milton," in *The Cultural Politics of Blood, 1500–1900*, ed. Kimberly Anne Coles et al. (New York: Palgrave Macmillan, 2015), 65–83. Quoted in Michel Foucault, *The History of Sexuality: An Introduction* (1978; repr., New York: Random House, 1990), 149.

8. Scholarship on the origins of racial slavery in the early British Atlantic is substantial and focused overwhelmingly on North America, particularly the Chesapeake. Influential works include Oscar Handlin and Mary F. Handlin, "Origins of the Southern Labor System," *WMQ* 7 (1950): 199–222; Carl N. Degler, "Slavery and the Genesis of American Race Prejudice," *Comparative Studies in Society and History* 2 (1959): 49–56; Winthrop Jordan, *White over Black: American Attitudes toward the Negro, 1550–1812* (1968; repr., Chapel Hill: University of North Carolina Press, 2012); Alden T. Vaughan, "The Origins Debate: Slavery and Racism in Seventeenth-Century Virginia," *Virginia Magazine of History and Biography* 97, no. 3 (1989): 1–54; Ira Berlin, *Many Thousands Gone: The First Two Centuries of Slavery in North America* (Cambridge, MA: Harvard University Press, 1998); Philip D. Morgan, *Slave Counterpoint: Black Culture in the Eighteenth-Century Chesapeake and Lowcountry* (Chapel Hill: University of North Carolina Press, 1998). For a useful summary of the debate and its limitations, see Rebecca Anne Goetz, "Rethinking the Unthinking Decision: Old Questions and New Problems in the History of Slavery and Race in the Colonial South," *Journal of Southern History* 25, no. 3 (2009): 599–612.

9. Works focused on gender, class, and sexuality include Kathleen M. Brown, *Good Wives, Nasty Wenches, and Anxious Patriarchs: Gender, Race, and Power in Colonial Virginia* (Chapel Hill: University of North Carolina Press, 1996); Kirsten Fischer, *Suspect Relations: Sex, Race, and Resistance in Colonial North Carolina* (Ithaca, NY: Cornell University Press, 2002); Jennifer L. Morgan, *Laboring Women: Reproduction and Gender in New World Slavery* (Philadelphia: University of Pennsylvania Press, 2004). The

role of religion in constructing race is explored in Colin Kidd, *The Forging of Races: Race and Scripture in the Protestant Atlantic World, 1600–2000* (Cambridge: Cambridge University Press, 2006); Rebecca Anne Goetz, *The Baptism of Early Virginia: How Christianity Created Race* (Baltimore: Johns Hopkins University Press, 2012). Early modern practices of slavery and their influence on the English are analyzed in Michael Guasco, *Slaves and Englishmen: Human Bondage in the Early Modern Atlantic World* (Philadelphia: University of Pennsylvania Press, 2014).

10. Catherine Adams and Elizabeth H. Pleck, *Love of Freedom: Black Women in Colonial and Revolutionary New England* (New York: Oxford University Press, 2010), 46.

11. Quoted in Joyce Chaplin, *Subject Matter: Technology, the Body, and Science on the Anglo-American Frontier, 1500–1676* (Cambridge, MA: Harvard University Press, 2009), 22. Important discussions of race and lineage in the British Atlantic include Nicholas Hudson, "From 'Nation' to 'Race': The Origin of Racial Classification in Eighteenth-Century Thought," *Eighteenth-Century Studies* 29, no. 3 (1996): 247–64; Joyce E. Chaplin, "Race," in *The British Atlantic World, 1500–1800*, ed. David Armitage and Michael J. Braddick (Basingstoke: Palgrave Macmillan, 2002), 154-72; Goetz, *Baptism of Early Virginia*; Feerick, *Strangers in Blood;* Holly Brewer, "Subjects by Allegiance to the King? Debating Status and Power for Subjects--and Slaves--through the Religious Debates of the Early British Atlantic," in *State and Citizen: British America and the Early United States,* ed. Peter Thompson and Peter S. Onuf (Charlottesville: University of Virginia Press, 2013): 25–51. Brewer's newest work, published while this book was in production, promises to bring issues of slavery and hereditary status in early America to the forefront of scholarly attention. See Holly Brewer, "Slavery, Sovereignty, and 'Inheritable Blood': Reconsidering John Locke and the Origins of American Slavery," *American Historical Review* 122, no. 4 (2017): 1038–78.

12. On the paradoxes of empire, see Ann Laura Stoler and Frederick Cooper, "Between Metropole and Colony: Rethinking a Research Agenda," in *Tensions of Empire: Colonial Cultures in a Bourgeois World,* ed. Frederick Cooper and Ann Laura Stoler (Berkeley: University of California Press, 1997), 1–56. On Jamaica's demography and value to Britain, see Trevor Burnard, "A Failed Settler Society: Marriage and Demographic Failure in Early Jamaica," *Journal of Social History* 28, no. 1 (1994): 63–82; Trevor Burnard, "Not a Place for Whites? Demographic Failure and Settlement in Comparative Context: Jamaica, 1655–1780," in *Jamaica in Slavery and Freedom: History, Heritage and Culture,* ed. Kathleen E. A. Monteith and Glen Richards (Kingston: University of the West Indies Press, 2002), 73–88; Trevor Burnard, "'A Prodigious Mine': The Wealth of Jamaica before the American Revolution Once Again," *Economic History Review* 54, no. 3 (2001): 505–23. Quoted in Vincent Brown, *The Reaper's Garden: Death and Power in the World of Atlantic Slavery* (Cambridge, MA: Harvard University Press, 2008), 8; Kathleen Wilson, *The Island Race: Englishness, Empire, and Gender in the Eighteenth Century* (London: Routledge, 2003), 130.

13. Jack P. Greene, *The Constitutional Origins of the American Revolution* (Cambridge: Cambridge University Press, 2010), 1–18; Michal Jan Rozbicki, *Culture and Liberty in the Age of the American Revolution* (Charlottesville: University of Virginia Press, 2011), 87–97; Henry Care, *British Liberties; or, The Freeborn Subject's Inheritance* (London,

1766), 2; Burke quoted in John Phillip Reid, *Constitutional History of the American Revolution: The Authority of Rights* (Madison: University of Wisconsin Press, 2003), 105–6.

14. For the tension between English liberties as universal rights and as an inheritance exclusive to certain kinds of subjects, see Craig Yirush, *Settlers, Liberty, and Empire: The Roots of Early American Political Theory, 1675–1775* (New York: Cambridge University Press, 2011), 29–50; Jack P. Greene, "Introduction: Empire and Liberty," and Elizabeth Mancke, "Languages of Liberty in British North America, 1607–1776," in *Exclusionary Empire: English Liberty Overseas, 1600–1900,* ed. Jack P. Greene (Cambridge: Cambridge University Press, 2010), 1–24, 25–49; Paul D. Halliday, *Habeas Corpus: From England to Empire* (Cambridge, MA: Harvard University Press, 2010), 177–212; Henry Horwitz, "Liberty, Law, and Property, 1689–1776," in *Liberty Secured? Britain before and after 1688,* ed. J. R. Jones (Stanford, CA: Stanford University Press, 1992), 265–98.

15. John Collier, *An Essay on Charters* (London, 1777), 1, 2. Jonathan A. Bush's persuasive argument that the problem of colonial slavery in the British empire was constitutional rather than political in nature has influenced my thinking on this issue. See Jonathan A. Bush, "Free to Enslave: The Foundations of Colonial American Slave Law," *Yale Journal of Law and the Humanities* 5, no. 2 (1993): 417–70; Jonathan A. Bush, "The British Constitution and the Creation of American Slavery," in *Slavery and the Law,* ed. Paul Finkelman (Madison, WI: Madison House, 1997), 379–418.

16. Melanie J. Newton, *The Children of Africa in the Colonies: Free People of Color in Barbados in the Age of Emancipation* (Baton Rouge: Louisiana State University Press, 2008), 87.

17. On allegiance and British subjecthood, see Rieko Karatani, *Defining British Citizenship: Empire, Commonwealth and Modern Britain* (London: Routledge, 2003), 40–45; Halliday, *Habeas Corpus,* 70–71, 203–4; Hannah Weiss Muller, *Subjects and Sovereign: Bonds of Belonging in the Eighteenth-Century British Empire* (Oxford: Oxford University Press, 2017), 23–27. For Spanish American racial hierarchies, see esp. María Elena Martínez, *Genealogical Fictions: Limpieza de Sangre, Religion, and Gender in Colonial Mexico* (Stanford, CA: Stanford University Press, 2008); P. B. Villella, "'Pure and Noble Indians, Untainted by Inferior Idolatrous Races': Native Elites and the Discourse of Blood Purity in Late Colonial Mexico," *Hispanic American Historical Review* 91, no. 4 (2011): 633–63; Ann Twinam, *Purchasing Whiteness: Pardos, Mulattos, and the Quest for Social Mobility in the Spanish Indies* (Stanford, CA: Stanford University Press, 2015). Quoted in Twinam, *Purchasing Whiteness,* 45.

18. The legal pluralism of the early modern Atlantic is analyzed in Lauren Benton, *Law and Colonial Cultures: Legal Regimes in World History, 1400–1900* (Cambridge: Cambridge University Press, 2001), 31–79; Eliga H. Gould, "Zones of Law, Zones of Violence: The Legal Geography of the British Atlantic, circa 1772," *WMQ* 60 (2003): 471–510. On Britain's shift toward greater centralized control over imperial subjects, see Elizabeth Mancke, "Chartered Enterprises and the Evolution of the British Atlantic World," in *The Creation of the British Atlantic World,* ed. Elizabeth Mancke and Carole Shammas (Baltimore: Johns Hopkins University Press, 2005), 237–62; Elizabeth Mancke, "Negotiating an Empire: Britain and Its Overseas Peripheries, c. 1550–

1780," in *Negotiated Empires: Centers and Peripheries in the New World, 1500–1820,* ed. Christine Daniels and Michael V. Kennedy (New York: Routledge, 2002), 235–65; Benton and Ford, *Rage for Order.*

19. For Jewish political exclusion, see Todd M. Endelman, *The Jews of Georgian England, 1714–1830: Tradition and Change in a Liberal Society, 1714–1830* (Ann Arbor: University of Michigan Press, 1979), 86–117, 272–88; Dana Rabin, "The Jew Bill of 1753: Masculinity, Virility, and the Nation," *Eighteenth-Century Studies* 39, no. 2 (2006): 157–71. Catholic disabilities are discussed in Colin Haydon, *Anti-Catholicism in Eighteenth-Century England, c. 1714–80: A Political and Social Study* (Manchester: Manchester University Press, 1993), 1–21. For Protestant Nonconformists and Dissenters, see James Bradley, *Religion, Revolution and English Radicalism: Nonconformity in Eighteenth-Century Politics and Society* (Cambridge: Cambridge University Press, 1990). Michael Hechter explores the status of Highland Scots in *Internal Colonialism: The Celtic Fringe in British National Development, 1536–1966* (Berkeley: University of California Press, 1977), 79–126.

20. George Coningesby, *The Jewish Naturalization Considered* (London, 1753), 5. On British subjects in India, see P. J. Marshall, *The Making and Unmaking of Empires: Britain, India, and America c. 1750–1783* (New York: Oxford University Press, 2005); Sudipta Sen, "Imperial Subjects on Trial: On the Legal Identity of Britons in Late Eighteenth-Century India," *Journal of British Studies* 45, no. 3 (2006): 532–55; Muller, *Subjects and Sovereign,* 166–208. For Catholic imperial subjects, see Mary L. Sanderson, "'Our Own Catholic Countrymen': Religion, Loyalism, and Subjecthood in Britain and Its Empire, 1755–1829," (PhD diss., Vanderbilt University, 2010). For indigenous subjecthood, see Jenny Hale Pulsipher, *Subjects unto the Same King: Indians, English, and the Contest for Authority* (Philadelphia: University of Pennsylvania Press, 2014); Lisa Ford, *Settler Sovereignty: Jurisdiction and Indigenous People in America and Australia, 1788–1836* (Cambridge, MA: Harvard University Press, 2010). On slaves as subjects, see Christopher L. Brown, "From Slaves to Subjects: Envisioning an Empire without Slavery, 1772–1834," in *Black Experience and the Empire,* ed. Philip D. Morgan and Sean Hawkins (Oxford: Oxford University Press, 2004), 111–40.

21. Keechang Kim, *Aliens in Medieval Law: The Origins of Modern Citizenship* (Cambridge: Cambridge University Press, 2001), 142–44; Ralph Griffiths, *King and Country: England and Wales in the Fifteenth Century* (1964; repr., London: Hambledon Press, 1991), 40–41.

22. Jacob Selwood, *Diversity and Difference in Early Modern London* (Farnham, UK: Ashgate, 2010), 49; Frederick Clifford, *A History of Private Bill Legislation,* 2 vols. (London, 1885), 1:380; 7 Jam. I, c. 6 (1609) in *The Statutes at Large, from the Thirty-Ninth Year of Q. Elizabeth to the Twelfth Year of K. Charles Inclusive,* 24 vols., ed. Danby Pickering (Cambridge, 1763), 7:218.

23. Andrea Ruddick, *English Identity and Political Culture in the Fourteenth Century* (Cambridge: Cambridge University Press, 2013), 127–28; Kim, *Aliens in Medieval Law,* 158; Sir Edward Coke, *The Reports of Sir Edward Coke,* 6 vols. (London, 1826), 4:9.

24. Polly J. Price, "Natural Law and Birthright Citizenship in Calvin's Case (1608)," *Yale Journal of Law and the Humanities* 9, no. 1 (2013): 73–145; "The Case of Elizabeth Key,

1655/56," in *The Old Dominion in the Seventeenth Century: A Documentary History of Virginia, 1606–1689*, ed. Warren M. Billings (Chapel Hill: University of North Carolina Press, 1975), 165–69; Taunya Lovell Banks, "Dangerous Woman: Elizabeth Key's Freedom Suit--Subjecthood and Racialized Identity in Seventeenth Century Colonial Virginia," *Akron Law Review* 41, no. 3 (2008): 799–837, here 831; Annette Gordon-Reed, *The Hemingses of Monticello: An American Family* (New York: W. W. Norton, 2008), 45–47; Brown, *Good Wives, Nasty Wenches, and Anxious Patriarchs*, 132–33; Sir William Blackstone, *Commentaries on the Laws of England*, 2 vols. (London, 1783), 2:390.

25. For geohumoral interpretations of colonization, see Karen Ordahl Kupperman, "Fear of Hot Climates in the Anglo-American Colonial Experience," *WMQ* 41, no. 2 (1984): 213–40; Karen Kupperman, "Climate and Mastery of the Wilderness in the Seventeenth-Century New World," in *Seventeenth-Century New England History*, ed. David Hall et al. (Boston: Colonial Society of Massachusetts, 1984), 3–38; Michael Craton, "Reluctant Creole: The Planters' World in the British West Indies," in *Strangers within the Realm: Cultural Margins of the First British Empire*, ed. Bernard Bailyn and Philip D. Morgan (Chapel Hill: University of North Carolina Press, 1991), 314–62; Joyce Chaplin, "Climate and Southern Pessimism: The Natural History of an Idea, 1500–1800," in *The South as an American Problem*, ed. Larry Griffin and Don Doyle (Athens: University of Georgia Press, 1995), 57–82; R. R. Davies, *The First English Empire: Power and Identities in the British Isles 1093–1343* (New York: Oxford University Press, 2000), 142–71.

26. J. M. Ross, "English Nationality Law: Soli or Sanguinis?," in *Studies in the History of the Law of Nations*, ed. Charles Henry Alexandrowicz (The Hague: Martinus Nijhoff, 1972), 1–22; Karatani, *Defining British Citizenship*, 41; Jack P. Greene, "Liberty, Slavery, and the Transformation of British Identity in the Eighteenth-Century West Indies," *Slavery and Abolition* 21, no. 1 (2000): 1–31; Bush, "The British Constitution and the Creation of American Slavery," 398–99; Kunal M. Parker, *Making Foreigners: Immigration and Citizenship Law in America, 1600–2000* (Cambridge: Cambridge University Press, 2015), 1–21. Quoted in Marilyn C. Baseler, *"Asylum for Mankind": America, 1607–1800* (Ithaca, NY: Cornell University Press, 1998), 61; Sir William Blackstone, *Analysis of the Laws of England* (Oxford, 1756), 21.

27. James Robertson, "'Stories' and 'Histories' in Late Seventeenth-Century Jamaica," in Monteith and Richards, *Jamaica in Slavery and Freedom*, 40–44; David Barry Gaspar, "'Rigid and Inclement': Origins of the Jamaica Slave Laws of the Seventeenth Century," in *The Many Legalities of Early America*, ed. Christopher L. Tomlins and Bruce H. Mann (Chapel Hill: University of North Carolina Press, 2001), 78–97. Quoted in Morgan, *Laboring Women*, 3.

28. Mary Ann Mason, *From Father's Property to Children's Rights: The History of Child Custody in the United States* (New York: Columbia University Press, 1994), 24–25; Blackstone, *Commentaries*, 2:247, 249.

29. On Jamaica's Jewish community, see esp. Holly Snyder, "Rules, Rights, and Redemption: The Negotiation of Jewish Status in British Atlantic Port Towns, 1740–1831," *Jewish History* 20, no. 2 (2006): 147–70. Quoted in Mara Loveman, *National Colors: Racial Classification and the State in Latin America* (Oxford: Oxford University Press, 2014), 60–61.

30. George W. Roberts, *The Population of Jamaica* (1957; repr., Cambridge: Cambridge University Press, 2013), 36. On the Maroons, see Mavis Christine Campbell, *The Maroons of Jamaica, 1655–1796: A History of Resistance, Collaboration and Betrayal* (Granby, MA: Bergin and Garvy, 1988); Orlando Patterson, "Slavery and Slave Revolts: A Socio-historical Analysis of the First Maroon War, Jamaica 1655–1740," *Social and Economic Studies* 1, no. 19 (1970): 289–325; Kathleen Wilson, "The Performance of Freedom: Maroons in the Colonial Order in Eighteenth-Century Jamaica and the Atlantic Sound," *WMQ* 66, no. 1 (2009): 45–86. Jamaica Census, December 24, 1730, CO 137/19/part 2, f. 3.

31. Ruddick, *English Identity and Political Culture in the Fourteenth Century,* 152.

32. Martínez, *Genealogical Fictions,* esp. 227–65; Jennifer M. Spear, *Race, Sex, and Social Order in Early New Orleans* (Baltimore: Johns Hopkins University Press, 2009), 129–54; Ruth Hill, "The Blood of Others: Breeding Plants, Animals, and White People in the Spanish Atlantic," in Coles, *Cultural Politics of Blood,* 45–64.

33. French and Spanish models are detailed, respectively, in Guillaume Aubert, "'The Blood of France': Race and Purity of Blood in the French Atlantic World," and María Elena Martínez, "The Black Blood of New Spain: Limpieza de Sangre, Racial Violence, and Gendered Power in Early Colonial Mexico," *WMQ* 61, no. 3 (2004): 439–78, 479–520. See also Guillaume Aubert, "'To Establish One Law and Definite Rules': Race, Religion, and the Transatlantic Origins of the Louisiana Code Noir," and Cécile Vidal, "Caribbean Louisiana: Church, *Métissage,* and the Language of Race in the Mississippi Colony during the French Period," in *Louisiana: Crossroads of the Atlantic World,* ed. Cécile Vidal (Philadelphia: University of Pennsylvania Press, 2014), 31–43, 125–46.

34. Multiple English mainland colonies and two Caribbean colonies, Antigua (1644) and Bermuda (1663), banned fornication or marriage between "whites" and "negroes" (and in some cases "Indians"). See Virginia Bernhard, *Slaves and Slaveholders in Bermuda, 1616–1782* (Columbia: University of Missouri Press, 1999), 192; David Barry Gaspar, *Bondmen and Rebels: A Study of Master-Slave Relations in Antigua* (1985; repr., Durham, NC: Duke University Press, 1999), 167–68. For British America generally, see Brown, *Good Wives, Nasty Wenches, and Anxious Patriarchs,* 107–36, 187–211; A. Leon Higginbotham Jr. and Barbara K. Kopytoff, "Racial Purity and Interracial Sex in the Law of Colonial and Antebellum Virginia," in *Interracialism: Black-White Intermarriage in American History, Literature, and Law,* ed. Werner Sollors (Oxford: Oxford University Press, 2000), 81–139; Fischer, *Suspect Relations,* 131–58; Richard Godbeer, *Sexual Revolution in Early America* (Baltimore: Johns Hopkins University Press, 2002), 154–226. Quoted in Bryan Edwards, *The History, Civil and Commercial, of the British West Indies,* 3 vols. (London, 1793), 2:22.

35. "An Act for the better ordering and governing of Negroes," CO 30/2, f. 16; Orlando Patterson, *Slavery and Social Death: A Comparative Study* (Cambridge, MA: Harvard University Press, 1982), 5; Colin Dayan, *The Law Is a White Dog: How Legal Rituals Make and Unmake Persons* (Princeton, NJ: Princeton University Press, 2011), 45; Sympson to Hill, CO 318/76, f. 90.

36. Edward Brathwaite, *The Development of Creole Society in Jamaica, 1770–1820* (Oxford: Clarendon Press, 1971), 44; Sir Matthew Hale, *History of the Common-Law of*

England, Written by a Learned Hand (London, 1712), 3; Francis Plowden, *An Investigation of the Native Rights of British Subjects* (London, 1784), 88–89.

37. Orlando Patterson, "Three Notes of Freedom: The Nature and Consequences of Manumission," in *Paths to Freedom: Manumission in the Atlantic World,* ed. Rosemary Brana-Shute and Randy J. Sparks (Columbia: University of South Carolina Press, 2009), 18–20, 27; Sympson to Hill, CO 318/76, f. 60.

38. Edward Long, *The History of Jamaica,* 3 vols. (London, 1774), 2:320–21.

39. 6 Geo. II, c. 2 (April 25, 1733), CO 139/13, ff. 139–42; Edwards, *History, Civil and Commercial,* 2:17.

40. See esp. Anne McClintock, *Imperial Leather: Race, Gender and Sexuality in the Colonial Contest* (New York: Routledge, 1995); Ann Laura Stoler, *Carnal Knowledge and Imperial Power: Race and the Intimate in Colonial Rule* (Berkeley: University of California Press, 2010); Philippa Levine, *Prostitution, Race and Politics: Policing Venereal Disease in the British Empire* (New York: Routledge, 2003); Gwyn Campbell and Elizabeth Elbourne, eds., *Sex, Power, and Slavery* (Athens: Ohio University Press, 2014).

41. Daniel Livesay, "Emerging from the Shadows: New Developments in the History of Interracial Sex and Intermarriage in Colonial North America and the Caribbean," *History Compass* 13, no. 3 (2015): 122–33, here 128. For an analysis of the treatment of mixed-race Jamaicans emphasizing familial membership over exclusionary ideologies, see also Daniel Livesay, *Children of Uncertain Fortune: Mixed-Race Jamaicans in Britain and the Atlantic Family, 1733–1833* (Chapel Hill: University of North Carolina Press, 2018). Quoted in Stoler, *Carnal Knowledge and Imperial Power,* 39.

42. Winthrop D. Jordan, "American Chiaroscuro: The Status and Definition of Mulattoes in the British Colonies," *WMQ* 19 (1962): 183–200, here 199.

43. Andrew Jackson O'Shaughnessy, *An Empire Divided: The American Revolution and the British Caribbean* (Philadelphia: University of Pennsylvania Press, 2000), 175–81; Christopher Leslie Brown, *Moral Capital: Foundations of British Abolitionism* (Chapel Hill: University of North Carolina Press, 2006), 209–58; Maya Jasanoff, *Liberty's Exiles: American Loyalists in the Revolutionary World* (New York: Knopf, 2011), 71–73; Olwyn M. Blouet, "Bryan Edwards and the Haitian Revolution," in *The Impact of the Haitian Revolution in the Atlantic World,* ed. David P. Geggus (Columbia: University of South Carolina Press, 2001), 44–57.

44. David Armitage, "Three Concepts of Atlantic History," in Armitage and Braddick, *British Atlantic World,* 15.

45. Trevor Burnard, "The British Atlantic," in *Atlantic History: A Critical Reappraisal,* ed. Jack P. Greene and Philip D. Morgan (Oxford: Oxford University Press, 2009), 123.

CHAPTER 1. THE BIRTHRIGHT OF FREEBORN SUBJECTS

1. John Dryden, *Astraea Redux* (London, 1660), 6, 14–15; Robert M. Bliss, *Revolution and Empire: English Politics and the American Colonies in the Seventeenth Century* (New York: St. Martin's Press, 1990), 103; Nuala Zahedieh, *The Capital and the Colonies: London and the Atlantic Economy 1660–1700* (Cambridge: Cambridge University Press,

2010), 7; David Eltis, *The Rise of African Slavery in the Americas* (New York: Cambridge University Press, 2000), 114–36; T. H. Breen, *The Marketplace of Revolution: How Consumer Politics Shaped American Independence* (Oxford: Oxford University Press, 2004), 88–89.

2. Carla Pestana, *The English Conquest of Jamaica: Oliver Cromwell's Bid for Empire* (Cambridge, MA: Harvard University Press, 2017), 139, 153.

3. On the repugnancy principle, see Mary Sarah Bilder, *The Transatlantic Constitution: Colonial Legal Culture and the Empire* (Cambridge, MA: Harvard University Press, 2004), 31–50; Philip Hamburger, *Law and Judicial Duty* (Cambridge, MA: Harvard University Press, 2008), 255–80. The Privy Council preferred to let questionable legislation "lye by probationary," subject to future review if deemed inconvenient. See Elmer B. Russell, *The Review of American Colonial Legislation by the King in Council* (New York: Columbia University Press, 1915), 57.

4. John Phillip Reid, *Constitutional History of the American Revolution: The Authority of Rights* (Madison: University of Wisconsin Press, 2003), 98, 99–100; Jack P. Greene, "Liberty and Slavery: The Transfer of British Liberty to the West Indies, 1627–1865," in *Exclusionary Empire: English Liberty Overseas, 1600–1900*, ed. Jack P. Greene (Cambridge: Cambridge University Press, 2010), 51; William Style, *The Practical Register* (London, 1671), 232.

5. Christopher Tomlins, *Freedom Bound: Law, Labor, and Civic Identity in Colonizing English America* (Cambridge: Cambridge University Press, 2010), 417; Christopher Tomlins, "Atlantic Crossings," in *The Many Legalities of Early America*, ed. Christopher Tomlins and Bruce H. Mann (Chapel Hill: University of North Carolina Press, 2001), 22.

6. Quoted in Tomlins, *Freedom Bound,* 70.

7. Oliver Cromwell, Commission to the Commissioners for the West Indian Expedition, December 9, 1654, BL, Add MS 11410, f. 47. Reprinted in C. H. Firth, ed., *The Narrative of General Venables* (London: Royal Historical Society, 1900), appendix A, 109–10. On the ideological underpinnings of the Western Design, see S. A. G. Taylor, *The Western Design: An Account of Cromwell's Expedition to the Caribbean* (Kingston: Jamaica Historical Society, 1965); David Armitage, *The Ideological Origins of the British Empire* (Cambridge: Cambridge University Press, 2000), 134–39; Kristen Block, *Ordinary Lives in the Early Caribbean: Religion, Colonial Competition, and the Politics of Profit* (Athens: University of Georgia Press, 2012), 109–18.

8. Richard Blome, "Description of Jamaica," 1670–1680, BL, Sloane 1394, ff. 20; *A True Description of Jamaica with the Fertility, Commodities, and Healthfulness of the Place* (London, 1657), 1–2; proposals concerning Jamaica by James Earl of Marlborough, November 1660, *CSPC,* 1:491–92, no. 56; Agnes M. Whitson, *The Constitutional Development of Jamaica, 1660–1729* (Manchester: Manchester University Press, 1929), 8–9; Bliss, *Revolution and Empire,* 138; *By the King, a Proclamation Declaring the Cessation of Hostility, and Preserving an Entire Amity between His Majesty, and the King of Spain* (London, 1660).

9. W. L. Grant and James Munro, eds., *Acts of the Privy Council of England,* Colonial Series, vol. 1, *1613–1680* (Hereford: Wyman and Sons, 1908), 298–99, nos. 489, 491;

I. S., *A Brief and Perfect Journal of the Late Proceedings and Successe of the English Army in the West Indies, Cont'd until June 1655* (London, 1655), 4; *By the Protector: A Proclamation Giving Encouragement to Such as Shall Transplant Themselves to Jamaica* (London, 1655); Firth, *Narrative of General Venables*, 41; Barrington to [Sir John Barrington], July 14, 1655, in *Seventh Report of the Royal Commission on Historical Manuscripts*, pt. 1, *Report and Appendix* (London, 1879), appendix, 574; Venables to Thurloe, June 13, 1655, and [September] 1655, in *Interesting Tracts, Relating to the Island of Jamaica: Consisting of Curious State-Papers, Councils of War, Letters, Petitions, Narratives, &c.* (St. Jago de le Vega, 1800), 47–48, 68.

10. "Extracts from Henry Whistler's Journal of the West India Expedition," in Firth, *Narrative of General Venables*, 169; entries for January 7, 1656, and February 14, 1656, Journal of Edward D'Oyley, 1656–1662, Jamaica, BL, Add. MS 12423, ff. 3, 6; Brayne to Thurloe, March 12, 1656, in *A Collection of the State Papers of John Thurloe, Esq.; Secretary, First to the Council of State, and Afterwards to the Two Protectors, Oliver and Richard Cromwell*, ed. Thomas Birch, 7 vols. (London, 1742), 6:111; D'Oyley to Thurloe, November 10, 1658, in Birch, *Collection of the State Papers of John Thurloe*, 7:499.

11. Richard Price, ed., *Maroon Societies: Rebel Slave Communities in the Americas* (1979; repr., Baltimore: Johns Hopkins University Press, 1996), xii; BL, Add. MS 12423, ff. 17, 36, 81, 83.

12. Ysassi to the Duke of Alburquerque, Jamaica, August 29, 1657, in *Jamaica under the Spaniards Abstracted from the Archives of Seville*, ed. Frank Cundall and Joseph L. Pietersz (Kingston: Institute of Jamaica, 1919), 62; Mavis C. Campbell, *The Maroons of Jamaica, 1655–1796: A History of Resistance, Collaboration, and Betrayal* (Trenton, N. J.: Africa World Press, 1990), 17–20; David Buisseret and S. A. G. Taylor, "Juan De Bolas and His Pelinco," *Caribbean Quarterly* 24 (1978): 1–7; Michael Craton, *Testing the Chains: Resistance to Slavery in the British West Indies* (1982; repr., Ithaca, NY: Cornell University Press, 2009), 70–71; Edward D'Oyley, *A Narrative of the Great Success God Hath Been Pleased to Give His Highness Forces in Jamaica, Against the King of Spains Forces* (London, 1658), 5–6; John Speed, *An Epitome of Mr. John Speed's Theatre of the Empire of Great Britain* (London, 1676), 234; Burrough to [Commissioners of the Navy], June 20, 1660, Jamaica, *CSPC*, 1:482, no. 11; Ysassi to the Duke of Alburquerque, August 10, 1660, in Cundall and Pietersz, *Jamaica under the Spaniards*, 100.

13. Harvey Wheeler, "The Constitutional Ideas of Francis Bacon," *Western Political Quarterly* 9 (1956): 927–36; Daniel Lee, *Popular Sovereignty in Early Modern Constitutional Thought* (New York: Oxford University Press, 2016), 279; Thomas Poole, *Reason of State: Law, Prerogative and Empire* (Cambridge: Cambridge University Press, 2015), 27; Francis Bacon, *The Works of Francis Bacon, Baron of Verulam, Viscount St. Alban, Lord High Chancellor of England*, 4 vols. (London, 1740), 4:281.

14. Ian Williams, "Edward Coke," in *Constitutions and the Classics: Patterns of Constitutional Thought from Fortesque to Bentham*, ed. D. J. Galligan (Oxford: Oxford University Press, 2014), 86–107, here 95; speech of Sir Edward Coke, March 24, 1628, in William Cobbett, *Cobbett's Complete Collection of State Trials and Proceedings for High Treason and Other Crimes and Misdemeanors from the Earliest Period to the Present Time*, ed. Thomas Bayley Howell, 38 vols. (London, 1809), 3:68; Sir Edward Coke,

The Third Part of the Institutes of the Laws of England (London, 1680), 84; Sir Edward Coke, *The Fifth Part of the Reports of Sir Edward Coke* (London, 1738), iii. On Coke and the ancient constitution, see J. G. A. Pocock, *The Ancient Constitution and the Feudal Law: A Study of English Historical Thought in the Seventeenth Century* (1957; repr., Cambridge: Cambridge University Press, 1987), 30–55; Paul Christianson, "Ancient Constitutions in the Age of Sir Edward Coke and John Selden," in *The Roots of Liberty: Magna Carta, Ancient Constitution, and the Anglo-American Tradition of Rule of Law*, ed. Ellis Sandoz (Columbia: University of Missouri Press, 1993), 232–53.

15. Ken MacMillan, *Sovereignty and Possession in the English New World: The Legal Foundations of Empire, 1576–1640* (Cambridge: Cambridge University Press, 2006), 33–39; Craig Yirush, *Settlers, Liberty, and Empire: The Roots of Early American Political Theory, 1675–1775* (Cambridge: Cambridge University Press, 2011), 11; Sir Edward Coke, Calvin's Case (1608), in *The Seventh Part of the Reports of Sir Edward Coke Knt. Chief Justice of the Common Pleas* (Savoy, 1727), 17; Barbara Black, "The Constitution of Empire: The Case for the Colonists," *University of Pennsylvania Law Review* 124 (1976): 1157–1211, here 1181; Daniel J. Hulsebosch, "The Ancient Constitution and the Expanding Empire: Sir Edward Coke's British Jurisprudence," *Law and History Review* 21 (2003): 439–82, here 469–70.

16. James Robertson, "'Stories' and 'Histories' in Late-Seventeenth-Century Jamaica," in *Jamaica in Slavery and Freedom: History, Heritage and Culture*, ed. Kathleen E. A. Monteith and Glen Richards (Kingston: University of the West Indies Press, 2002), 36; account of the population of Jamaica, 1661, *CSPC*, 12:632, no. 2014; Taylor, *Western Design*, 91–92; Pestana, *English Conquest of Jamaica*, 228–29; Michael J. Jarvis, *In the Eye of All Trade: Bermuda, Bermudians, and the Maritime Atlantic World, 1680–1783* (Chapel Hill: University of North Carolina Press, 2010), 45; Edmund Hickeringill, *Jamaica Viewed* (London, 1661) 1, reader's epistle.

17. Order of the King in Council, November 28, 1660, *CSPC*, 1:491, no. 53; Whitson, *Constitutional Development of Jamaica*, 10; Abigail L. Swingen, *Competing Visions of Empire: Labor, Slavery, and the Origins of the British Atlantic Empire* (New Haven, CT: Yale University Press, 2015), 75; instructions to Edward D'Oyley, governor of Jamaica, February 8, 1661, *CSPC*, 5:6, no. 22. Quoted in Robert A. Williams Jr., *The American Indian in Western Legal Thought: The Discourses of Conquest* (New York: Oxford University Press, 1990), 215; Holly Brewer, "Subjects by Allegiance to the King? Debating Status and Power for Subjects--and Slaves--through the Religious Debates of the Early British Atlantic," in *State and Citizen: British America and the Early United States*, ed. Peter Thompson and Peter S. Onuf (Charlottesville: University of Virginia Press, 2013), 26, 30.

18. Irving Rouse, *The Tainos: Rise and Decline of the People Who Greeted Columbus* (New Haven, CT: Yale University Press, 1992), 18; Bartolomé de Las Casas, *The Spanish Colonie*, trans. M. M. S. (London, 1583); Bartolomé de Las Casas, *The Tears of the Indians: Being an Historical and True Account of the Cruel Massacres and Slaughters of Above Twenty Millions of Innocent People, Committed by the Spaniards in the Islands of Hispaniola, Cuba, Jamaica, &c.*, trans. John Phillips (London, 1656), 20; Margaret Ellen Newell, *Brethren by Nature: New England Indians, Colonists, and the Origins of*

American Slavery (Ithaca, NY: Cornell University Press, 2015), 45–47; Alan Gallay, *The Indian Slave Trade: The Rise of the English Empire in the American South, 1670–1717* (New Haven, CT: Yale University Press, 2002), 299–301; John Taylor, *Jamaica in 1687: The Taylor Manuscript at the National Library of Jamaica,* ed. David Buisseret (Kingston: University of the West Indies Press, 2008), 267; Richard Ligon, *A True and Exact History of the Island of Barbados* (London, 1657), 54.

19. Frederick H. Russell, *The Just War in the Middles Ages* (Cambridge: Cambridge University Press, 1975), 19; Bailey W. Diffie and George D. Winius, *Foundations of the Portuguese Empire, 1415–1580* (Minneapolis: University of Minnesota Press, 1977), 93–95; Pope Nicholas V, *Romanus pontifex,* January 8, 1455, in *Church and State through the Centuries: A Collection of Historic Documents with Commentaries,* ed. Sidney Z. Ehler and John B. Morrall (Westminster, MD: Newman Press, 1954), 149; James Muldoon, *The Americas in the Spanish World Order: The Justification for Conquest in the Seventeenth Century* (Philadelphia: University of Pennsylvania Press, 2015), 16–19.

20. Williams, *American Indian in Western Legal Thought,* 78–81; Robert J. Miller et al., *Discovering Indigenous Lands: The Doctrine of Discovery in the English Colonies* (Oxford: Oxford University Press, 2010), 11.

21. Francisco Morales Padrón, *Spanish Jamaica* (Kingston: Ian Randle, 2003), 153; Lawrence A. Clayton, *Bartolomé de Las Casas: A Biography* (New York: Cambridge University Press, 2012), 426; O. A. Sherrard, *Freedom from Fear: The Slave and His Emancipation* (1959; repr., Westport, CT: Greenwood Press, 1973), 33; Robin Blackburn, *The Making of New World Slavery: From the Baroque to the Modern, 1492–1800* (London: Verso, 1998), 136.

22. The Trans-Atlantic Slave Trade Database, http://slavevoyages.org/voyages/OJXQ 8bHH, accessed January 2, 2015; Gregory E. O'Malley, *Final Passages: The Intercolonial Slave Trade of British America, 1619–1807* (Chapel Hill: University of North Carolina Press, 2014), 119; P. E. H. Hair and Robin Law, "The English in Western Africa to 1700," in *The Oxford History of the British Empire,* vol. 1, *The Origins of Empire,* ed. Nicholas Canny (Oxford: Oxford University Press, 1998), 241–63; E. E. Rich, "The Slave Trade and National Rivalries," in *The Cambridge Economic History of Europe,* ed. E. E. Rich and C. H. Wilson (Cambridge: Cambridge University Press, 1967), 4:323–37; Richard Jobson, *The Golden Trade* (London, 1623), 89–90, 2–3.

23. *A True Declaration of the Troublesome Voyadge of M. Iohn Haukins to the Parties of Guynea and the West Indies, in the Yeares of Our Lord 1567 and 1568* (London, 1569); Harry Kelsey, *Sir John Hawkins: Queen Elizabeth's Slave Trader* (New Haven, CT: Yale University Press, 2003), 1–69; Swingen, *Competing Visions of Empire,* 58; George Frederick Zook, *The Company of Royal Adventurers Trading into Africa* (Lancaster: New Era, 1919), 12–13; James H. Sweet, "The Iberian Roots of American Racist Thought," *WMQ* 54, no. 1 (1997): 143–66.

24. Job [John] Hortop, *The Rare Trauailes of Iob Hortop, an Englishman, Who Was Not Heard of in Three and Twentie Yeeres Space* (London, 1591); Michael Guasco, *Slaves and Englishmen: Human Bondage in the Early Modern Atlantic World* (Philadelphia: University of Pennsylvania Press, 2014), 73.

25. Eltis, *Rise of African Slavery*, 54, 114; Swingen, *Competing Visions of Empire*, 59-62; England and Wales, Sovereign, *An Act for the Encouraging and Increasing of Shipping and Navigation* (London, 1660), 3; England and Wales, Parliament, *An Act for Increase of Shipping, and Encouragement of the Navigation of this Nation* (London, 1651), 1453.

26. Carla Gardina Pestana, *Protestant Empire: Religion and the Making of the British Atlantic World* (Philadelphia: University of Pennsylvania Press, 2009), 68–74; Richard Hakluyt, "Discourse on Western Planting, 1584," in *The Original Writings and Correspondence of the Two Richard Hakluyts*, ed. E. G. R. Taylor (London: Hakluyt Society, 1935), 2:318.

27. Rebecca Anne Goetz, *The Baptism of Early Virginia: How Christianity Created Race* (Baltimore: Johns Hopkins University Press, 2012), 6.

28. Yon-Gyong Kwon, *Eschatology in Galatians: Rethinking Paul's Response to the Crisis in Galatia* (Tübingen, Germany: Mohr Siebeck, 2004), 90–91; Leonard B. Glick, *Abraham's Heirs: Jews and Christians in Medieval Europe* (Syracuse, NY: Syracuse University Press, 1999), ix.

29. Richard Hooker, "Of the Laws of Ecclesiastical Politie," in *The Works of That Learned and Judicious Divine, Mr. Richard Hooker* (London, 1723), 209; Thomas Becon, *The Catechism of Thomas Becon*, ed. Rev. John Ayre (Cambridge, 1844), 214; William Sherlock, *A Resolution of Some Cases of Conscience Which Respect Church-Communion* (London, 1683), 8; Dennis Austin Britton, *Becoming Christian: Race, Reformation, and Early Modern English Romance* (New York: Fordham University Press, 2014), 57.

30. Quoted in Brian Cumming, ed., *The Book of Common Prayer: The Texts of 1549, 1559, and 1662* (Oxford: Oxford University Press, 2011), 412–13; Brewer, "Subjects by Allegiance to the King?," 33; H. L. A. Hart, *The Concept of Law*, intro. by Leslie Green (1961; repr., Oxford: Oxford University Press, 2012), 51; Thomas Becon, *Principles of Christen Religion* (London, 1560).

31. [William Duke], *Some Memoirs of the First Settlement of the Island of Barbados and Other Caribbee Islands* (London, 1743), 20; Lorena S. Walsh, *Motives of Honor, Pleasure, and Profit: Plantation Management in the Colonial Chesapeake, 1607–1763* (Chapel Hill: University of North Carolina Press, 2010), 117; Linda M. Heywood and John K. Thornton, *Central Africans, Atlantic Creoles, and the Foundation of the Americas, 1585–1660* (New York: Cambridge University Press, 2007), 323; Sir Edward Coke, *The First Part of the Institutes of the Lawes of England* (London, 1628), 128. Quoted in James H. Sweet, "Spanish and Portuguese Influences on Racial Slavery in British North America, 1492–1619," in *Collective Degradation: Slavery and the Construction of Race: Proceedings of the Fifth Annual Gilder Lehrman Center International Conference at Yale University*, November 6–7, 2003, Gilder Lehrman Center, New Haven, CT.

32. "An act for the liberties of the people," Assembly Proceedings, February–March 1639, in Archives of Maryland, *Proceedings and Acts of the General Assembly of Maryland, January 1637/8-September 1664*, ed. William Hand Browne (Baltimore, 1883), 1:41.

33. Joyce Lee Malcolm, *To Keep and Bear Arms: The Origins of an Anglo-American Right* (Cambridge, MA: Harvard University Press, 1994), 141; Vicki Hsueh, *Hybrid Constitutions: Challenging Legacies of Law, Privilege, and Culture in Colonial America* (Durham, NC: Duke University Press, 2010), 47.

34. Kathleen M. Brown, *Good Wives, Nasty Wenches, and Anxious Patriarchs: Gender, Race, and Power in Colonial Virginia* (Chapel Hill: University of North Carolina Press, 1996), 116–18; "An Act against Carnall Coppulation between Christian and Heathen," November 20, 1644, CO 154/1, f. 55.

35. "An act for mulatto children, being bond or free, according to the condition of the mother," December 23, 1662, CO 5/1376, f. 28; Tomlins, *Freedom Bound*, 456–57; Anthony S. Parent Jr., *Foul Means: The Formation of a Slave Society in Virginia, 1660–1740* (Chapel Hill: University of North Carolina Press, 2003), 115–16; Virginia Bernhard, *Slaves and Slaveholders in Bermuda, 1616–1782* (Columbia: University of Missouri Press, 1999), 91–92.

36. Assembly Proceedings, September 1664, *Archives of Maryland*, 1:526–27, 533–34; "Negroes not to Sport or absent themselues on the Lords day, and White men not to keep Company with Negroes," May 26, 1675, CO 154/2, ff. 32, 36.

37. "Extracts from Henry Whistler's Journal of the West India Expedition," in Firth, *Narrative of General Venables*, appendix E, 146; Winthrop D. Jordan, *White over Black: American Attitudes toward the Negro, 1550–1812* (1968; repr., Chapel Hill: University of North Carolina Press, 2012), 64–65; Jonathan A. Bush, "Free to Enslave: The Foundations of Colonial American Slave Law," *Yale Journal of Law and the Humanities* 5, no. 2 (1993): 417–70, here 421, 434.

38. "An act for the better ordering and gouerning of Negroes," 1661, Barbados Acts, CO 30/2, ff. 16–26; Simon Newman, *A New World of Labor: The Development of Plantation Slavery in the British Atlantic* (Philadelphia: University of Pennsylvania Press, 2013), 74; Jerome S. Handler, "Custom and Law: The Status of Enslaved Africans in Seventeenth-Century Barbados" *Slavery and Abolition* 37, no. 2 (2016): 233–55, here 234.

39. CO 30/2, f. 16; Edward B. Rugemer, "The Development of Mastery and Race in the Comprehensive Slave Codes of the Greater Caribbean during the Seventeenth Century," *WMQ* 70, no. 3 (2013): 429–58, here 438–39; Russell R. Menard, *Sweet Negotiations: Sugar, Slavery, and Plantation Agriculture in Early Barbados* (Charlottesville: University of Virginia Press, 2006), 25. On French concerns with punishing slaves, see Malick W. Ghachem, *The Old Regime and the Haitian Revolution* (Cambridge: Cambridge University Press, 2012), 58–63.

40. "Report of the Council for Foreign Plantations to his Majesty," [July] 1661, *CSPC*, 5:47, no. 132; King Charles II, "A Proclamation for the Encouraging of Planters in his Majesties Island of Jamaica in the West Indies," December 14, 1661, CO 139/1, f. 18; Charter to Sir Walter Raleigh (1584), and The First Charter of Virginia (1606), in Francis Newton Thorpe, ed., *The Federal and State Constitutions, Colonial Charters, and Other Organic Laws of the States, Territories, and Colonies Now or Heretofore Forming the United States of America* (Washington, D.C.: Government Printing Office, 1909), 1:53–57, 7:3786; Tomlins, *Freedom Bound*, 72–73; Lloyd G. Barnett, *The Constitutional Law of Jamaica* (Oxford: Oxford University Press, 1977), 2.

41. Sir Robert L'Estrange, *The Free-Born Subject; or, The Englishman's Birthright Asserted against All Tyrannical Vsurpations either in Church or State* (London, 1679), 1; William Penn, *The Excellent Priviledge of Liberty and Property Being the Birth-Right of the Free-*

Born Subjects of England (Philadelphia, 1687), epistle to reader; *The Laws of Jamaica* (London, 1684), iii.

42. "A Journal kept by Coll William Beeston from his first comeing to Jamaica," BL, Add MS 12430, ff. 23, 27; Treaty with Juan Lubola's Palenque, February 1, 1662, CO 139/1, ff. 38–39; Campbell, *Maroons of Jamaica*, 17–18.

43. BL, Add. MS 12430, f. 29; Order by the Deputie Governor and the Council, October 23, 1663, and Council of Warr, held at St. Jago de la Vega, August 15, 1665, CO 140/1, ff. 85–86, ff. 135–42; Craton, *Testing the Chains*, 70–75.

44. Modyford to Bennet, June 30, 1664, *CSPC*, 5:219–20, no.767; *A Discourse Concerning the Signification of Allegiance, as It Is to Be Understood in the New Oath of Allegiance* (London, 1689), 7; "Act For the Better Ordering and Governing of Negro Slaves, and For the good Governing of Servants, and ordering the Rights between Masters and Servants," CO 139/1, ff. 66–69, 71–75; Philip D. Curtin, *The Atlantic Slave Trade: A Census* (Madison: University of Wisconsin Press, 1972), 58–59. The transformation of feudal understandings of the relation of subject and sovereign in seventeenth-century England is detailed in Victoria Kahn, *Wayward Contracts: The Crisis of Political Obligation in England, 1640–1674* (Cambridge: Cambridge University Press, 2009). On the redevelopment of feudal principles in early America, see Holly Brewer, "Entailing Aristocracy in Colonial Virginia: 'Ancient Feudal Restraints' and Revolutionary Reform," WMQ 54 (1997): 307–46.

45. CO 139/1, ff. 66–69; Susan Amussen, *Caribbean Exchanges: Slavery and the Transformation of English Society, 1640–1700* (Chapel Hill: University of North Carolina Press, 2007), 140–41; Phil Withington, *The Politics of Commonwealth: Citizens and Freemen in Early Modern England* (Cambridge: Cambridge University Press, 2005), 10.

46. [Sir Charles Lyttelton], "An account of the state of Jamaica," October 1664, *CSPC*, 5:240, no. 812.

47. Heads of the treaty between Charles II of England and Charles II of Spain relating to the West Indies, July 18, 1670, BOD, MS Rawl. A 478, ff. 11–12; Propositions of Mr. Kendall concerning the settling of Jamaica, 1664, *CSPC*, 5:253, no. 842; Handasyd to Board of Trade, September 24, 1708, CO 137/8, f. 96; Trevor Burnard, *Planters, Merchants, and Slaves: Plantation Societies in British America, 1650–1820* (Chicago: University of Chicago Press, 2015), 65.

48. "Act For the Better Ordering and Governing of Negro Slaves," 1672, CO 139/2, ff. 46–55; the revised 1674 Slave Act is in CO 139/1, ff. 121–25. The rights commonly associated with allegiance to the English Crown are detailed in Ken MacMillan, *The Atlantic Imperial Constitution: Center and Periphery in the English Atlantic World* (New York: Palgrave Macmillan, 2011), 27.

49. Geoffrey V. Scammell, *The First Imperial Age: European Overseas Expansion 1500–1715* (1989; repr., New York: Routledge, 1991), 136; Paper on the advantages of the trade of the English plantations, BOD, MS. Rawl. A478, f. 67; Long quoted in Whitson, *Constitutional Development of Jamaica*, 267.

50. Journal of the Lords of Trade and Plantations, April 30, 1677, and the King's Instructions to Charles, Earl of Carlisle, Governor of Jamaica, March 30, 1678, *CSPC*, 10:67–68, no. 200, and 230–31, no. 641.

51. Journal of the Lords of Trade and Plantations, April 4, 1679, *CSPC,* 10:348–49, no. 960; *JAJ,* 1:32–33, 35.

52. Richard S. Dunn, "Imperial Pressures on Massachusetts and Jamaica, 1675–1700," in *Anglo-American Political Relations, 1675–1775,* ed. Alison G. Olson and Richard M. Brown (New Brunswick, NJ: Rutgers University Press, 1970), 52–75; Bliss, *Revolution and Empire,* 186; Letter from Major General Handasyd, May 19, 1711, CO 137/9, f. 101.

53. William Salkeld, *Report of Cases in the Court of Kings Bench, from the Fifth Year of King William and Queen Mary, to the Tenth Year of Queen Anne,* 4 vols. (London, 1718), 2:411–12; Raymond and York, opinions, on revenue act, to lords, rec'd May 22, 1723, CO 137/14/part 2, ff. 194–95; Whitson, *Constitutional Development of Jamaica,* 145; Paul D. Halliday, *Habeas Corpus: From England to Empire* (Cambridge, MA: Harvard University Press, 2010), 274.

54. Whitson, *Constitutional Development of Jamaica,* 107; Richard S. Dunn, *Sugar and Slaves: The Rise of the Planter Class in the English West Indies, 1624–1713* (1972; repr., Chapel Hill: University of North Carolina Press, 2000), 158–59, 165; Lords of Trade and Plantations to Lynch, February 17, 1683, *CSPC,* 11:386, no. 948.

55. "An Act for Regulating Servants," in *Acts of Assembly, Passed in the Island of Jamaica, from 1681 to 1737, Inclusive,* ed. John Baskett (London, 1738), 2, 4, 73–82; *JAJ,* 1:70; Robert Worthington Smith, "The Legal Status of Jamaican Slaves before the Antislavery Movement," *Journal of Negro History* 30, no. 3 (1945): 293–303.

56. Quoted in George Fobtottatos Judah, "The Jews' Tribute in Jamaica. Extracted from the Journals of the House of Assembly of Jamaica," *Publications of the American Jewish Historical Society,* no. 18 (Baltimore: Printed by the Society, 1909): 152; "An act for raising Money to discharge the Debts contracted in the late invasion of the French, 1695," and "An Act for the completing the payment of the Debts contracted during the late Invasion, and erecting and Finishing the Fortifications at Port-Morat," 1696, CO 139/9, ff. 1, 34; Bruno Feitler, "Jews and New Christians in Dutch Brazil, 1630–1654," in *Atlantic Diasporas: Jews, Conversos and Crypto-Jews in the Age of Mercantilism, 1500–100,* ed. Richard L. Kagan and Philip D. Morgan (Baltimore: Johns Hopkins University Press, 2009), 123–51; Jessica Roitman, "Creating Confusion in the Colonies: Jews, Citizenship, and the Dutch and British Atlantic," *Itinerario* 36, no. 2 (2012): 55–57; Eli Faber, *A Time for Planting: The First Migration, 1654–1820* (Baltimore: Johns Hopkins University Press, 1995), 15–16.

57. Eli Faber, *Jews, Slaves, and the Slave Trade: Setting the Record Straight* (New York: New York University Press, 2000), 45–46, 49; Judah, "The Jews' Tribute in Jamaica," 149–50; Oscar Reiss, *The Jews in Colonial America* (London: MacFarland, 2004), 9; Edward Long, *The History of Jamaica,* 3 vols. (London, 1774), 2:294.

58. Eltis, *Rise of African Slavery,* 240.

59. Baskett, *Acts of Assembly,* 79; January 30, 1708, *JAJ,* 1:437.

60. February 6 and 12, 1708, and May 1, 1675, *JAJ,* 1:8, 438, 439; 35 Car. 2, c. 3 (1684), in *The Laws of Jamaica, Pass'd by the Governour, Council, and Assembly in that Island, and Confirm'd by the Crown* (London, 1716), 139–41; 6 Ann., c. 5 (1709), and 9 Ann., c. 5 (1712) in *The Statutes at Large, from Magna Charta, to the Twenty-Fifth Year of the*

Reign of King George the Third, Inclusive, 14 vols., ed. Owen Ruffhead and Charles Runnington (London, 1786), 4:326, 495; James H. Kettner, *The Development of American Citizenship, 1608–1870* (1978; repr., Chapel Hill: University of North Carolina Press, 1984), 71–72; Francis Hare, *The Reception of the Palatines Vindicated* (London, 1711), 30.

61. February 19 and 28, 1708, *JAJ,* 1:446, 449.

62. Handasyd to the Lords Commissioners for Trade, March 31, 1708, CO 137/8, ff. 24–26; 10 Ann., c. 4 (May 19, 1711), in *The Laws of Jamaica: 1681–1759* (St. Jago de la Vega, 1802), 1:111–12.

63. 11 Ann., c. 3 (November 14, 1712), 2 Geo. I, c. 2 (November 10, 1716), 6 Geo. II, c. 2 (April 25, 1733), and 21 Geo. II, c. 7 (August 13, 1748), in *The Laws of Jamaica,* 1:122–23, 127, 206, 340.

64. Hunter to the Council of Trade and Plantations, May 10, 1730, *CSPC,* 37:107, no. 225; November 25, 1715, December 7, 1715, *JAJ,* 2:152–53, 157; Gad Heuman, *Between Black and White: Race, Politics, and the Free Coloreds in Jamaica, 1792–1865* (Westport, CT: Greenwood Press, 1981), 5; September 28, 1716, *JAJ,* 2:206; "Mr. Attorney General's report upon an act passed in Jamaica in November 1716 to prevent negroes being evidence against Dorothy Williams et al., rec'd April 17, 1717," CO 137/12, f. 131; Yirush, *Settlers, Liberty, and Empire,* 42–43.

65. West to the Lords Commissioners of Trade and Plantations, January 10, 1724, CO 5/1323, f. 177.

66. Vincent Caretta, "Who Was Francis Williams?," *Early American Literature* 38, no. 2 (2003): 213–37; Brooke N. Newman, "Contesting 'Black' Liberty and Subjecthood in the Anglophone Caribbean, 1730s–1780s," *Slavery and Abolition* 32, no. 2 (2011): 169–83.

67. November 19 and 21, 1724, *JAJ,* 2:510, 512.

68. November 2, 1721, November 2, 1722, and October 23, 1725, *JAJ,* 2:392, 431, 547.

CHAPTER 2. BLOOD OF THE FATHER

1. 3 Geo. II, c. 6 (March 28, 1730), CO 139/12, ff. 76–79. The law was first proposed on November 21, 1724; see *JAJ,* 2:512.

2. 4 Geo. II, c. 21 (1731), in Owen Ruffhead and Charles Runnington, eds., *The Statutes at Large, from Magna Charta to the Twenty-Fifth Year of the Reign of King George the Third, Inclusive,* 14 vols. (London, 1786), 5:573.

3. Jennifer M. Spear, *Race, Sex, and Social Order in Early New Orleans* (Baltimore: Johns Hopkins University Press, 2009), 61–67; Alan Watson, *Slave Law in the Americas* (Athens: University of Georgia Press, 1989), 40–62, 83–90.

4. 10 Ann., c. 4 (May 19, 1711), and 11 Ann., c. 3 (November 14, 1712), in *The Laws of Jamaica* (London, 1716), 146, 425. Beginning in 1715, deficiency legislation prescribed a minimum number of white laborers on estates and barred free people from holding supervisory positions on plantations. See Gad Heuman, "The Free Coloreds in Jamaican Slave Society," in *The Slavery Reader,* ed. Gad Heuman and James Walvin (London: Routledge, 2003), 655–56; June 24, 1730, and November 12, 1730, *JAJ,* 2:712, 714.

5. A Short Case of Francis Williams of Jamaica, rec'd June 30, 1731, CO 137/19, ff. 29–30.

6. "Fane's Report on Six Acts Passed there in 1730," March 22, 1731, and Delafaye to Popple, July 17, 1731, CO 137/19/part 1, ff. 31, 73–74; Popple to Delafaye, July 30, 1731, State Papers Domestic 36/23, f. 248, National Archives, Kew; Hunter to the Council of Trade and Plantations, May 10, 1730, CO 137/18, ff. 112–16; St James's Court, November 25, 1731, CO 137/20, f. 33.

7. Orlando Patterson, "Slavery and Slave Revolts: A Socio-historical Analysis of the First Maroon War in Jamaica, 1655–1740," *Social and Economic Studies* 1, no. 19 (1970): 289–325; David Barry Gaspar, "A Dangerous Spirit of Liberty: Slave Rebellion in the West Indies in the 1730s," in *Origins of the Black Atlantic,* ed. Laurent Dubois and Julius S. Scott (New York: Routledge, 2010), 11–23.

8. George W. Roberts, *The Population of Jamaica* (1957; repr., Cambridge: Cambridge University Press, 2013), 36–37; Trevor Burnard, "A Failed Settler Society: Marriage and Demographic Failure in Early Jamaica," *Journal of Social History* 28, no. 1 (1994): 63–82; Jamaica Census, December 24, 1730, CO 13/19/part 2, f. 1; August 5, 1729, *JAJ,* 2:685.

9. Patterson, "Slavery and Slave Revolts"; CO 13/19/part 2, f. 3; March 17, 1730, *JAJ,* 2:701–2; 3 Geo. II, c. 14 (November 20, 1730), CO 139/12, ff. 102–7.

10. Michael Craton, *Testing the Chains: Resistance to Slavery in the British West Indies* (1982; repr., Ithaca, NY: Cornell University Press, 2009), 83–84; Col. Hayes to Major Sowle, February 14, 1731, Extract of a Letter from Col. Cornwallis, March 10, 1731, and March 20, 1731, and letter from Governor Hunter, October 8, 1731, and November 13, 1731, CO 137/19/part 1, ff. 25, 26, 105, 108–9; January 8, 1732, and January 12, 1732, *JAJ,* 3:51, 53.

11. March 30, 1733, *JAJ,* 3:328.

12. March 30, 1733, and April 4, 1733, *JAJ,* 3:122, 130; 6 Geo. II, c. 2 (April 25, 1733), CO 139/13, ff. 139–42; "An Act for the better ordering and gouerning of Negroes," Barbados, 1661, CO 30/2, f. 16. Quoted in Wayne A. Meeks, *The Origins of Christian Morality: The First Two Centuries* (New Haven, CT: Yale University Press, 1993), 18.

13. Patricia Crawford, *Blood, Bodies and Families in Early Modern England* (2004; repr., Abingdon: Routledge, 2014), 113–15; Jacques Guillemeau, *The Nursing of Children* (London, 1635), preface. For Spanish and French concerns about blood purity, see María Elena Martínez, *Genealogical Fictions: Limpieza de Sangre, Religion, and Gender in Colonial Mexico* (Stanford, CA: Stanford University Press, 2008); Guillaume Aubert, "'The Blood of France': Race and Purity of Blood in the French Atlantic World," *WMQ* 61, no. 3 (2004): 439–78.

14. Colin Dayan, *The Law Is a White Dog: How Legal Rituals Make and Unmake Persons* (Princeton, NJ: Princeton University Press, 2011), 46–47; Edward Phillips, *The New World of English Words* (London, 1658).

15. John Cowell, *The Interpreter of Words and Terms, Used Either in the Common or Statute Laws of This Realm, and in Tenures and Jocular Customs* (London, 1701); Dayan, *The Law Is a White Dog,* 46, 49; Carla Pestana, *The English Atlantic in an Age of Revolution, 1640–1661* (Cambridge, MA: Harvard University Press, 2009), 166; Edward Long, *The History of Jamaica,* 3 vols. (London, 1774), 2:492; Andrew T. Fede, *Homicide Justified: The Legality of Killing Slaves in the United States and the Atlantic World* (Athens: Uni-

versity of Georgia Press, 2017), 53–54; "An act continuing the tax on negro women," September 17, 1668, Virginia, CO 5/1376, f. 56.

16. Richard Ligon, *A True and Exact History of the Island of Barbadoes* (London, 1657), 53; CO 30/2, f. 71; Gooch to Popple, May 18, 1736, *CSPC,* 42:207–8, no. 308.

17. Colin Kidd, *The Forging of Races: Race and Scripture in the Protestant Atlantic World, 1600–2000* (Cambridge: Cambridge University Press, 2006), 72–73; Jonathan Schorsch, *Jews and Blacks in the Early Modern World* (Cambridge: Cambridge University Press, 2004), 137–38, 157; Mary Floyd-Wilson, *English Ethnicity and Race in Early Modern Drama* (Cambridge: Cambridge University Press, 2003), 85–86.

18. George Best, "A True Discourse of the Three Voyages of Discoverie, for the Finding of a Passage to Cathaya, by the North-west, Under the Conduct of Martin Frobisher Generall" (1578), in *The Three Voyages of Martin Frobisher,* ed. Richard Collinson (London, 1867), 54–57; David M. Whitford, *The Curse of Ham in the Early Modern Era: The Bible and the Justifications for Slavery* (Farnham, UK: Ashgate, 2009), 105–9; Rebecca Anne Goetz, *The Baptism of Early Virginia: How Christianity Created Race* (Baltimore: Johns Hopkins University Press, 2012), 28–29.

19. Virginia Bernhard, *Slaves and Slaveholders in Bermuda, 1616–1782* (Columbia: University of Missouri Press, 1999), 92; "An act concerning Negroes and other Slaves," Maryland, September 1664, in *Proceedings and Acts of the General Assembly of Maryland, January 1637/8–September 1664,* ed. William Hand Browne (Baltimore, 1883), 1:533–34.

20. *The Digest of Justinian,* ed. Alan Watson (1985; repr., Philadelphia: University of Pennsylvania Press, 1998), 1:15, 17; *Las siete partidas,* vol. 4, *Family, Commerce, and the Sea: The Worlds of Women and Merchants,* trans. Samuel Parsons Scott, ed. Robert I. Burns (Philadelphia: University of Pennsylvania Press, 2001), 977; Joseph C. Dorsey, "Women without History: Slavery, Jurisprudence, and the International Politics of Partus Sequitur Ventrem in the Spanish Caribbean," *Journal of Caribbean History* 28, no. 2 (1994): 165–207; Camillia Cowling, *Conceiving Freedom: Women of Color, Gender, and the Abolition of Slavery in Havana and Rio de Janeiro* (Chapel Hill: University of North Carolina Press, 2013), 53–54; Doris L. Garraway, *The Libertine Colony: Creolization in the Early French Caribbean* (Durham, NC: Duke University Press, 2005), 202–3; "An Act Encouraging the Baptizing of Negro, Indian, and Mulatto Slaves," October 1706, in *Acts of Assembly Passed in the Province of New-York: From 1691 to 1725* (London, 1726), 65; "Act for the better ordering and governing of Negroes and other Slaves in this Province," May 1740, in *The Statutes at Large of South Carolina,* ed. David J. McCord (Columbia, S.C.: Johnston, 1840), 7:397.

21. Thomas Aquinas, *The Summa Theologica,* 3rd pt., supplement, trans. the Dominican Fathers (New York: Benziger Brothers, 1922), 180–82; David Brion Davis, *The Problem of Slavery in Western Culture* (New York: Oxford University Press, 1966), 96–97; Alan Watson, "Seventeenth-Century Jurists, Roman Law, and Slavery," in *Slavery and the Law,* ed. Paul Finkelman (Madison, WI: Madison House, 1997), 373–74; Hugo Grotius, *The Illustrious Hugo Grotius of the Law of Warre and Peace* (London, 1654), 567, 569.

22. "An Act concerning Negroes and slaves," September 1681, *Archives of Maryland,* 203–5; "An Act for suppressing out-lying Slaves," Virginia, April 16, 1691, CO 5/1380,

ff. 95; Anthony S. Parent Jr., *Foul Means: The Formation of a Slave Society in Virginia, 1660–1740* (Chapel Hill: University of North Carolina Press, 2003), 116–17.

23. "An Act for the Better Preventing of a Spurious and Mixt issue," Massachusetts, October 24, 1705, State Library of Massachusetts, http://archives.lib.state.ma.us/actsResolves/1705/1705acts0010.pdf, accessed February 7, 2016; Jack D. Forbes, *Africans and Native Americans: The Language of Race and the Evolution of Red-Black Peoples* (Urbana: University of Illinois Press, 1993), 195; *Acts and Resolves, Public and Private, of the Province of the Massachusetts Bay* (Boston, 1869), 1:580; Kelly A. Ryan, *Regulating Passion: Sexuality and Patriarchal Rule in Massachusetts, 1700–1830* (Oxford: Oxford University Press, 2014), 79; "An Act Concerning Servants and Slaves," October 23, 1705, CO 5/1380, f. 166; Kathleen Brown, *Good Wives, Nasty Wenches, and Anxious Patriarchs: Gender, Race, and Power in Colonial Virginia* (Chapel Hill: University of North Carolina Press, 1996), 130–34, 196–97. Quoted in Kristen Fischer, *Suspect Relations: Sex, Race, and Resistance in Colonial North Carolina* (Ithaca, NY: Cornell University Press, 2002), 85.

24. Thomas Tryon, *Friendly Advice to the Gentlemen-Planters of the East and West Indies* (London, 1684), 114, 128–30; Goetz, *Baptism of Early Virginia*, 108.

25. "Journal, March 1715: Journal Book R," in *Journals of the Board of Trade and Plantations*, vol. 3, *March 1715–October 1718*, ed. K. H. Ledward (London: His Majesty's Stationery Office, 1924), 1–15; January 12, 1732, and January 13, 1732, *JAJ*, 3:53, 54.

26. April 4, 1733, and April 6, 1733, *JAJ*, 3:129, 130; "An Act to Intitle John Golding Senior of the Parish of Vere planter and his family to the Rights and priviledges of English men born of White Ancestors," April 14, 1733, CO 139/13, f. 126; Inventory of John Golding, senior, JA, 1B/11/3/39, f. 74.

27. June 23, 1730, *JAJ*, 2:712; Edward Southwell, "The Jews Case in Jamaica," 1721, CO 137/14/part 1, f. 51; "No Jew shall stand for a deficiency excepting upon his own Estate," February 1730, CO 139/13, f. 14; "Journal, June 1731: Journal Book H. H.," in *Journals of the Board of Trade and Plantations*, vol. 6, *January 1729–December 1734*, ed. K. H. Ledward (London: His Majesty's Stationary Office, 1928), 204–16.

28. August 21, 1734, *JAJ*, 3:265; "The Humble Petition and Representation of several Traders to Jamaica and others in behalf of the Jews who are Inhabitants of that Island," [1735], William Wood, "Answers to several Queries relating to the Jews and Taxes laid on them in Jamaica," February 18, 1735, and Gregory to Lords, October 23, 1735, CO 137/22, ff. 30–32, 35–36, 37–38.

29. May 4 and November 9, 1732, *JAJ*, 3:87, 101; "An Act for Manumission of the Wife and Children of a Free Negro Man Sambo and of other Negroes and for recompensing their respective owners," April 14, 1733, CO 139/13, ff. 121–24, 126.

30. "A short state of Jamaica," rec'd October 8, 1730, CO 137/18, ff. 104–6.

31. Fane to the Lords Commissioners, March 28, 1734, CO 137/21, ff. 79–80.

32. March 29, 1733, *JAJ*, 3:111; letter from Robert Hunter, December 24, 1733, CO 137/21, ff. 16–17; "Petition to the council from the Inhabitants of the Parish of Portland," read January 8, 1734, and "Council Meeting in St. Jago de la Vega," April 20, 1734, JA, 1B/5/3/12b, ff. 34, 41.

33. "At a council held at St Iago de la Vega," August 17, 1733, CO 137/20, f. 171; "Address of the Honorable John Ayscough to the Assembly," and "Address of the Assembly to the Honorable John Ayscough," October 3, 1734, CO 137/21, ff. 186, 187; February 25, 1734, *JAJ*, 3:229; Craton, *Testing the Chains*, 85–87.

34. June 20, 1735, March 9 and 25, 1736, *JAJ*, 3:328, 330, 339.

35. "The Humble Memorial and proposal of the merchants of London, Bristol, and Liverpool, and others trading to and interested in your majesty's island of Jamaica," October 27, 1735, CO 137/22, ff. 20–27.

36. Johnson to Lords of Trade and Plantations, April 20, 1689, *CSPC*, 13:25–29, no. 83.

37. Richard Hall, *Acts, Passed in the Island of Barbados* (London, 1764), 252–53, 256, 323; *A Collection of All the Acts of Assembly, Now in Force, in the Colony of Virginia* (Williamsburg, VA, 1733), 474.

38. Gooch to Popple, May 18, 1736, and Council of Trade and Plantations to Gooch, October 15, 1736, *CSPC*, 42:207–8, no. 308, 42:301, no. 409; Matthew Bacon, *A New Abridgment of the Law*, 5 vols. (London, 1736), 1:671.

39. David J. McCord, ed., *The Statutes at Large of South Carolina*, 11 vols. (Columbia, SC: Johnston, 1840), 7:384; Bernhard, *Slaves and Slaveholders in Bermuda*, 212; Trevor Burnard, "Not a Place for Whites? Demographic Failure and Settlement in Comparative Context: Jamaica, 1655–1780," in *Jamaica in Slavery and Freedom: History, Heritage and Culture*, ed. Kathleen E. A. Monteith and Glen Richards (Kingston: University of the West Indies Press, 2002), 82.

40. Trelawny to Lords of Trade, March 30, 1739, and Treaty with Capt. Cudjoe, March 1, 1739, CO 137/23, ff. 5–6, 7–10.

41. The Jewish tax debate is detailed in Trelawny to Lords of Trade, May 10, 1739, CO 137/23, ff. 48–51; April 29, 1741, *JAJ*, 3:566.

42. Charles Leslie, *A New and Exact Account of Jamaica* (Edinburgh, 1740), 50–51.

43. Brooke N. Newman, "Gender, Sexuality, and the Formation of Racial Identities in the Eighteenth-Century Anglo-Caribbean World," *Gender and History* 22, no. 3 (2010): 585–602, here 587; James Lewis, Clerk to the Assembly, [1763], CO 137/33, ff. 46–47; Lucille Mathurin Mair, *A Historical Study of Women in Jamaica: 1655–1844*, ed. Hilary McD. Beckles and Verene A. Shepherd (Kingston: University of the West Indies Press, 2006), 91; CO 139/15, f. 20.

44. Inventory of Susannah Augier, Jamaica Inventories, JA, 1B/11/3/39, f. 99; Marisa J. Fuentes, *Dispossessed Lives: Enslaved Women, Violence, and the Archive* (Philadelphia: University of Pennsylvania Press, 2016), 68–69; "Table of Acts, Private Acts—1747," in *The Laws of Jamaica: 1681–1759*, vol. 1 (St. Jago de la Vega, 1802); April 11 and 28, May 1 and 5, 1747, Minutes of Assembly, March 17, 1747, to December 14, 1751, CO 140/34, nf.

45. Samuel J. Hurwitz and Edith F. Hurwitz, "A Token of Freedom: Private Bill Legislation for Free Negroes in Eighteenth-Century Jamaica," *WMQ* 24 (1967): 423–31; Edward Long, *The History of Jamaica*, 3 vols. (London, 1774), 3:320. The privilege acts are listed in full in CO 139/13–51 and tabled in *The Laws of Jamaica*.

46. Winthrop D. Jordan, "American Chiaroscuro: The Status and Definition of Mulattoes in the British Colonies," *WMQ* 19 (1962): 183–200; Arnold A. Sio, "Colour and

Miscegenation: The Free Coloureds of Jamaica and Barbados," *Caribbean Studies* 16, no. 1 (1976): 17–18; July 13, 1738, *JAJ*, 3:450.

47. July 15 and 18, 1738, *JAJ*, 3:453, 455; Inventory of William Cunningham, senior, April 27, 1750, Jamaica Inventories, JA, 1B/11/3/29, f. 157; Daniel Livesay, "The Decline of Jamaica's Interracial Households and the Fall of the Planter Class, 1733–1823," *Atlantic Studies* 9, no. 1 (2012): 109–10.

48. Warwick Anderson, *The Cultivation of Whiteness: Science, Health, and Racial Destiny in Australia* (Durham, NC: Duke University Press, 2006), 255.

49. John Patrick Montaño, *The Roots of English Colonialism in Ireland* (Cambridge: Cambridge University Press, 2011), 14–16; Davies quoted in Steven G. Ellis, "Civilizing the Natives: State Formation and the Tudor Monarchy, c. 1400–1603," in *Imagining Frontiers, Contesting Identities*, ed. Steven G. Ellis and Luďa Klusáková (Pisa: Pisa University Press, 2007), 85; Jean Feerick, *Strangers in Blood: Relocating Race in the Renaissance* (Toronto: University of Toronto Press, 2010), 23–25.

50. Edmund Burke, *The Annual Register; or, A View of the History, Politics, and Literature for the Year 1772* (London, 1786), 238; White quoted in Nicholas Canny, "Identity Formation in Ireland: The Emergence of the Anglo-Irish," in *Colonial Identity in the Atlantic World, 1500–1800*, ed. Nicholas Canny and Anthony Pagden (Princeton, NJ: Princeton University Press, 1989), 166.

51. William Petty, *Essays in Political Arithmetick* (London, 1711), 247, 252; William Petty, *Tracts; Chiefly Relating to Ireland* (Dublin, 1769), 321–22; Ted McCormick, *William Petty and the Ambitions of Political Arithmetic* (Oxford: Oxford University Press, 2010), 10; Coleman A. Dennehy, *Restoration Ireland: Always Settling and Never Settled* (Aldershot, UK: Ashgate, 2008), 131.

52. Christer Petley, "'Home' and 'This Country': Britishness and Creole Identity in the Letters of a Transatlantic Slaveholder," *Atlantic Studies* 6, no. 1 (2009): 43–61; Kathleen Wilson, *The Island Race: Englishness, Empire and Gender in the Eighteenth Century* (London: Routledge, 2003), 154.

53. April 26, 1739, *JAJ*, 3:481; Fane to the Lords, May 12, 1740, CO 137/23, ff. 60–61; Trevor Burnard, "'A Matron in Rank, a Prostitute in Manners': The Manning Divorce of 1741 and Class, Gender, Race, and the Law in Eighteenth-Century Jamaica," in *Working Slavery, Pricing Freedom: Perspectives from the Caribbean, Africa and the African Diaspora*, ed. Verene Shepherd (New York: St. Martin's Press, 2002), 133–52.

54. Feerick, *Strangers in Blood*, 8; Dennehy, *Restoration Ireland*, 131.

55. Edmund Spenser, *The Works of Mr. Edmund Spenser*, 6 vols., ed. Theodore Bathurst (London, 1715), 6:1569, 1572–73; Andrew Hadfield, "Irish Colonies and the Americas," in *Envisioning an English Empire: Jamestown and the Making of North America*, ed. Robert Appelbaum and John Sweet (Philadelphia: University of Pennsylvania Press, 2005), 188–89.

56. Bryan Edwards, *The History, Civil and Commercial, of the British West Indies*, 3 vols. (London, 1793), 2:18–20; September 2, 1756, *JAJ*, 4:584.

57. July 3, 1745, *JAJ*, 3:701.

58. April 23, May 5, 8, and 22, 1747, *JAJ*, 4:72, 84, 87, 99.

59. October 11 and 17, 1753, *JAJ*, 4:414, 417.

60. October 4 and 12, 1750, *JAJ*, 4:238, 246–47.

61. "Debate in the Commons on the Jews naturalization Bill," May 7, 1753, in *Parliamentary History of England, from the Earliest Period to the Year 1803*, vol. 14, *1747–1753* (London, 1813), 1366–67, 1369, 1372, 1377–78, 1380; Thomas W. Perry, *Public Opinion, Propaganda, and Politics in Eighteenth-Century England* (Cambridge, MA: Harvard University Press, 1962), 1–2, 147–48.

CHAPTER 3. WHITENESS AND HEREDITARY BLOOD STATUS

1. Moore to the Board, April 19, 1760, CO 137/32, f. 1. For representative examples of British accounts of Tacky's Revolt, see *British Magazine*, July 1760, 443–44; *London Magazine*, July 1760, 366–67; *Scots Magazine*, July 1760, 378–79.

2. Vincent Brown, *The Reaper's Garden: Death and Power in the World of Atlantic Slavery* (Cambridge, MA: Harvard University Press, 2008), 148–49; *Universal Magazine*, August 1760, 109; [Edward Trelawny], *An Essay Concerning Slavery, and the Danger Jamaica Is Expos'd to from the Too Great Number of Slaves, and the Too Little Care That Is Taken to Manage Them* (London, 1746), intro.; Trelawny's responses to queries, November 21, 1741, CO 137/23, f. 153; Jack P. Greene, *Evaluating Empire and Confronting Colonialism in Eighteenth-Century Britain* (New York: Cambridge University Press, 2013), 161. The impact of the Seven Years' War in the West Indies is detailed in Trevor Burnard and John Garrigus, *The Plantation Machine: Atlantic Capitalism in French Saint-Domingue and British Jamaica* (Philadelphia: University of Pennsylvania Press, 2016), 82–92.

3. *Royal Magazine*, September 1760, 144–48; Edward Long, *The History of Jamaica*, 3 vols. (London, 1774), 2:458, 462; *Leeds Intelligencer*, September 30, 1760; *Caledonian Mercury*, March 13, 1762; Burnard and Garrigus, *Plantation Machine*, 139.

4. October 23, 1761, *JAJ*, 5:273; "Table of Public Acts," in *The Laws of Jamaica*, vol. 2 (Kingston, 1802), act 22.

5. 1 Geo. 3, c. 22 (December 18, 1760), CO 139/21, f. 47; Diana Paton, *The Cultural Politics of Obeah* (Cambridge: Cambridge University Press, 2014), 17–18. For the register format, see, for example, Register of Free Persons, St. Catherine, Jamaica, 1789–1828, JA, 2/2/28A.

6. Knowle's responses to queries, 1755, CO 137/28, f. 228; Fuller to Germain, December 24, 1778, Stephen Fuller Papers, RL, f. 92; Jamaica Census, 1774, CO 137/70, f. 94; "Table of Negroes imported from Africa, 1702–1775," CO 137/38, f. 5.

7. November 5, 1761, *JAJ*, 5:281.

8. Private petitions presented on behalf of free people of mixed lineage to the assembly between 1733 and 1760 are recorded in *JAJ*, vols. 3–5.

9. November 5, 1761, *JAJ*, 5:281; 2 Geo. 3, c. 8 (December 19, 1761), in *The Laws of Jamaica: 1760–1792* (St. Jago de la Vega, 1802), 23–26; December 16, 1768, *JAJ*, 6:152.

10. Lamb to the Commissioners for Trade and Plantations, November 8, 1762, CO 137/33, f. 18.

11. Vera Copia, James Lewis, Clerk to the Assembly, CO 137/33, ff. 46–49. See also November 16, 1762, *JAJ*, 5:376; Herbert Henry Cousins, *History of the Hope Farm* (Washington, D.C.: U.S. Government Printing Office, 1933), 4.

12. CO 137/33, ff. 46–49; Daniel Livesay, "The Decline of Jamaica's Interracial Households and the Fall of the Planter Class, 1733–1823," *Atlantic Studies* 9, no. 1 (2012): 107–23.

13. Stanhope to Pownallyn, and Stanhope to the Board of Trade, June 13, 1763, CO 137/33, ff. 32–33, 34–43.

14. Stanhope, "Reasons in support of the Bill to restrain exorbitant Grants to Negroes, and Answers to the Protest of three of the Members of the Council in Jamaica," June 13, 1763, CO 137/33, ff. 34–43; Michael Craton, "Property and Propriety: Land Tenure and Slave Property in the Creation of a British West Indian Plantocracy, 1612–1740," in *Early Modern Conceptions of Property*, ed. John Brewer and Susan Staves (London: Routledge, 1996), 512.

15. CO 137/33, ff. 37–38.

16. CO 137/33, ff. 38, 42. Settlers in the British North American colonies made similar arguments during the crises of the 1770s; see Jack P. Greene, *The Constitutional Origins of the American Revolution* (New York: Cambridge University Press, 2011), 139–40.

17. CO 137/33, f. 40.

18. Rose Fuller to Pownall, May 11, 1763, CO 137/33, ff. 24–25; Lewis Namier and John Brooke, eds., *The History of Parliament: The House of Commons, 1754–1790* (London: Secker and Warburg, 1985), 478.

19. CO 137/33, ff. 24–25; S. D. Smith, *Slavery, Family, and Gentry Capitalism in the British Atlantic: The World of the Lascelles* (Cambridge: Cambridge University Press, 2006), 24; Perry Gauci, *William Beckford: First Prime Minister of the London Empire* (New Haven, CT: Yale University Press, 2013), 79, 263.

20. December 8 and December 17, 1763, *JAJ*, 5:431, 443–44. Morris's estate was valued slightly higher than the average for a Kingstonian merchant's estate (£3,715) but much higher than the average white woman's estate (£727) during this period. See Trevor Burnard, "'The Grand Mart of the Island': The Economic Function of Kingston, Jamaica in the Mid-eighteenth Century," in *Jamaica in Slavery and Freedom: History, Heritage, and Culture*, ed. Kathleen E. A. Monteith and Glen Richards (Kingston: University of the West Indies Press, 2002), 230.

21. Alan J. Karras, *Sojourners in the Sun: Scottish Migrants in Jamaica and the Chesapeake, 1740–1800* (Ithaca, NY: Cornell University Press, 1992), 72; Douglas Hamilton, *Scotland, the Caribbean, and the Atlantic World, 1750–1820* (Manchester: Manchester University Press, 2005), 76; Trevor Burnard, "Kingston, Jamaica: Crucible of Modernity," in *The Black Urban Atlantic in the Age of the Slave Trade*, ed. Jorge Cañizares-Esguerra, Matt Childs, and James Sidbury (Philadelphia: University of Pennsylvania Press, 2013), 143; Jamaica Church of England Parish Register Transcripts, 1664–1880, Baptisms 1722–1792, vol. 1, Island Record Office, Spanish Town, Jamaica, f. 145; December 8, 1763, *JAJ*, 5:431. Legally, Morris was a "mulatto."

22. In December 1763 the assembly received a total of thirty petitions on behalf of free people requesting white privileges, two of which specified that the petitioner, or the

petitioner's children, were "half Indian." Only one other petition, that of Stephen Lost in 1756, was made on behalf of "quadroons"; the rest were presented by or for "mulattoes."

23. Burnard, "Kingston, Jamaica: Crucible of Modernity," 122–46; Kingston Parish Tax List, 1765, Kingston Vestry Book, JA, 2/6/4; Simon Taylor to George Hibbert, January 14, 1804, Simon Taylor Papers, ICS, 1/F/42.

24. Trevor Burnard and Emma Hart, "Kingston, Jamaica, and Charleston, South Carolina: A New Look at Comparative Urbanization in Plantation Colonial British America," *Journal of Urban History* 39, no. 2 (2013): 214–34; quoted in Jack Greene, *Settler Jamaica in the 1750s: A Social Portrait* (Charlottesville: University of Virginia Press, 2016), 208; Charles Leslie, *A New and Exact Account of Jamaica* (Edinburgh, 1740), 15; "Journal of an Officer who travelled over part of the West Indies, and of North America, in the course of 1764–1765," BL, MS Kings 213, f. 9; *The History of Miss Katty N——* (London, 1757), 206.

25. JA, 2/6/4; Burnard, "'Grand Mart of the Island,'" 225–41; Colin G. Clarke, *Kingston, Jamaica: Urban Development and Social Change, 1692–1962* (Kingston: Ian Randle, 1975), 5–28; "Table of Private Acts," in *The Laws of Jamaica*, vol. 2.

26. November 23, and 24, 1784, *JAJ*, 8:26, 27; Kingston Parish Tax List, 1780, Kingston Vestry Book, JA, 2/6/103. Morris now leased a property worth fifty pounds per annum.

27. Kingston Parish Tax List, 1791, Kingston Vestry Book, JA, 2/6/104.

28. *The Register Book of Marriages Belonging to the Parish of St. George, Hanover Square, in the County of Middlesex*, ed. John H. Chapman (London, 1886), 1:213; Anne M Powers, *A Parcel of Ribbons: Letters of the 18th-Century Lee Family in London and Jamaica* (London: Lulu, 2012), 111, 151, 183.

29. Petition of Robert Cooper Lee, November 16, 1776, CO 140/56; November 16, 19, and 22, 1776, *JAJ*, 6:649–50, 654; Fuller to the Board of Trade, June 3, 1777, CO 137/37, f. 154.

30. A total of twenty private acts were passed between 1768 and 1797 allowing William Patrick Browne (1768), George Brooks (1775), Robert Cooper Lee (1776), John Williams (1777), John Hiatt (1780), William Wright (1783), Thomas Wynter (1783), Patrick Duncan (1783), Thomas Roper (1784), Sarah Morris (1784), John Angwin (1787), Samuel Laing (1788), John Russell (1788), George Lesslie (1789), George Bedward (1790), Ebenezer Edie (1791), John Hiatt (1791), Edward Brown (1792), James Craggs (1796), and William Wright (1797) to devise their estates as they wished or to inherit property, notwithstanding the 1761 Devises Act. Brooks and Duncan petitioned twice before the assembly granted their appeals, and a faction opposing exemptions for illegitimate mixed-race devisees contested bills passed in favor of Browne and Brooks. The debate attending Browne's bill is in *JAJ*, 6:148, 156–58, 165, 170. George Brooks's petitions are detailed in *JAJ*, 6:183, 610, 613–15. Patrick Duncan's petitions are recorded in *JAJ*, 7:632, 8:50–52, 56, 62, 93.

31. "Table of Private Acts," in *The Laws of Jamaica*; CO 137/37, f. 27. Donaldson's first petition, in 1772, was rejected, probably owing to his middling social position; his second petition, in 1774, resulted in a private bill in his favor. See *JAJ*, 6:414–16, 523.

32. October 23 and December 18, 1773, *JAJ*, 6:448, 486; "Inhabitants in Jamaica, 1773, from Sir Basil Keith," Stephen Fuller Papers, RL. The Kingston register lists roughly 3,285 individuals (some pages are torn); the St. Catherine register records 830 names. See "Register of free people for Kingston," 1760–93, Local Government Records, 2/6/277, JA; and "Register of free people for St. Catherine," Local Government Records, 2/2/28A, JA.

33. Long, *History of Jamaica*, 2:337; Bryan Edwards, *The History, Civil and Commercial, of the British West Indies*, 3 vols. (London, 1793), 2:204; Gad Heuman, *Between Black and White: Race, Politics, and the Free Coloreds in Jamaica, 1792–1865* (Westport, CT: Greenwood Press, 1981), 7.

34. November 18/19 and November 26, 1774, *JAJ*, 6:526, 528, 531. The tax on bachelors was hotly contested, with fourteen members voting against it, including one of the island's wealthiest and most powerful bachelors: Simon Taylor. See November 27, 1776, *JAJ*, 6:660.

35. Ewers's petition was presented on November 13, 1782, and approved five days later. See *JAJ*, 7:601, 604.

36. Return of militia, 1788, CO 137/87, f. 32. The assembly first considered forming companies of rangers on November 28, 1766, *JAJ*, 6:10. See also December 2, 1774, *JAJ*, 6:536; April 12, 1782, *JAJ*, 7:467–68.

37. Benjamin Franklin, "Observations Concerning the Increase of Mankind, Peopling of Countries, &c.," in William Clarke, *Observations on the Late and Present Conduct of the French, with Regard to their Encroachments upon the British Colonies in North America* (London, 1775), 10.

38. Thomas Jefferson, *Notes on the State of Virginia* (London, 1787), 229, 239–40; Thomas Jefferson to James Monroe, November 24, 1801, in *The Writings of Thomas Jefferson*, ed. H. A. Washington, 9 vols. (New York, 1854), 4:420–21.

39. Andrea Ruddick, *English Identity and Political Culture in the Fourteenth Century* (Cambridge: Cambridge University Press, 2013), 127–28, 140; William Camden, *Britain; or, A Chorographicall Description of the Most Flourishing Kingdomes, England, Scotland, and Ireland* (London, 1610), 8, 88; Mary Floyd-Wilson, *English Ethnicity and Race in Early Modern Drama* (Cambridge: Cambridge University Press, 2003), 15–16; Wolfram Schmidgen, *Exquisite Mixture: The Virtues of Impurity in Early Modern England* (Philadelphia: University of Pennsylvania Press, 2013), 5.

40. Lisa Zunshine, *Bastards and Foundlings: Illegitimacy in Eighteenth-Century England* (Columbus: Ohio State University Press, 2005), 1–22.

41. Karen Ordahl Kupperman, "Fear of Hot Climates in the Anglo-American Colonial Experience," *WMQ* 41, no. 2 (1984): 213–40.

42. Cecily Jones, *Engendering Whiteness: White Women and Colonialism in Barbados and North Carolina, 1627–1865* (Manchester: Manchester University Press, 2005); Hilary Beckles, *Centering Woman: Gender Discourses in Caribbean Slave Societies* (Kingston: Ian Randle Publishers, 1999); Wylie Sypher, "The West-Indian as a 'Character' in the Eighteenth Century," *Studies in Philology* 36, no. 3 (1939): 503–20. Quoted in Mary Fissell, *Vernacular Bodies: The Politics of Reproduction in Early Modern England* (New York: Oxford University Press, 2004), 194.

43. Samuel Foote, *The Patron: A Comedy in Three Acts* (London, 1764), 13; Mrs. [Elizabeth] Bonhote, *The Rambles of Mr. Frankly,* 4 vols. (London, 1772), 1:49; Richard Cumberland, *The West Indian: A Comedy* (London, 1771), 7, 45, 78; *Critical Review* 18 (London, 1764): 53.

44. Sarah Scott, *The History of Sir George Ellison,* 2 vols. (London, 1766), 1:24, 18.

45. Isaac Bickerstaff, *Love in the City: A Comic Opera as It Is Performed at the Theatre-Royal in Covent-Garden* (Dublin, 1767), 8, 10.

46. Bickerstaff, *Love in the City,* 32, 52. Londoners apparently disliked the opera, which ran for only four nights before being withdrawn, but enjoyed the character of the "Creolian girl." See Peter A. Tasch, *The Dramatic Cobbler: The Life and Works of Isaac Bickerstaff* (Cranbury, NJ: Associated University Presses, 1971), 105–8; *Monthly Catalogue* 36 (London, 1767): 164.

47. John Gilmore, "'Too oft allur'd by Ethiopic charms'? Sex, Slaves and Society in John Singleton's *A General Description of the West-Indian Islands* (1767)," *Ariel* 38 (2007): 75–95; John Singleton, *A General Description of the West-Indian Islands* (London, 1767), 151–53; Roxann Wheeler, "Colonial Exchanges: Visualizing Racial Ideology and Labour in Britain and the West Indies," in *An Economy of Colour: Visual Culture and the Atlantic World, 1660–1830,* ed. Geoff Quilley and Kay Dian Kriz (Manchester: Manchester University Press, 2003), 37.

48. Singleton, *General Description,* 147.

49. Long, *History of Jamaica,* 2:274, 278–79, 330; J. B. Moreton, *West India Customs and Manners: Containing Strictures on the Soil, Cultivation, Produce, Trade, Officers, and Inhabitants; with the Method of Establishing and Conducting a Sugar Plantation* (London, 1793), 120–21.

50. Robert Young, *Colonial Desire: Hybridity in Theory, Culture, and Race* (New York: Routledge, 1995), 90–117; Long, *History of Jamaica,* 2:327.

51. Moreton, *West India Customs and Manners,* 78; Long, *History of Jamaica,* 2:433.

52. Edwards, *History, Civil and Commercial,* 2:4, 16; Long, *History of Jamaica,* 2:276; Jennifer M. Spear, *Race, Sex, and Social Order in Early New Orleans* (Baltimore: Johns Hopkins University Press, 2009), 76; Sean X. Goudie, *Creole America: The West Indies and the Formation of Literature and Culture in the New Republic* (Philadelphia: University of Pennsylvania Press, 2006), 70; Lucille Mathurin Mair, *A Historical Study of Women in Jamaica: 1655–1844,* ed. Hilary McD. Beckles and Verene A. Shepherd (Kingston: University of the West Indies Press, 2006), 119; *The True Flower of Brimstone: Extracted from the Briton, North Briton, and Auditor* (London, 1763), 8–9.

53. Long, *History of Jamaica,* 2:332; Edwards, *History, Civil and Commercial,* 2:26.

54. Hellena Wells, *Constantia Neville; or, The West Indian,* 3 vols. (London, 1800), 1:322, 110, 326. See also Sypher, "West-Indian as a 'Character'."

55. Moreton, *West India Customs and Manners,* 123; Long, *History of Jamaica,* 2:274.

56. Long, *History of Jamaica,* 2:333.

CHAPTER 4. BLOOD TIES IN THE COLONIAL SEXUAL ECONOMY

1. John Tailyour to Simon Taylor, January 3, 1782, and September 12, 1782, John Tailyour Letterbook, 1781–1785, Tailyour Papers, WCL. For another interpretation of Tailyour's treatment of his enslaved mistress and mixed-race offspring, see Daniel Livesay, "Extended Families: Mixed-Race Children and the Scottish Experience, 1770–1820," *International Journal of Scottish Literature*, no. 4 (2008): 1–17.

2. On Tailyour's slave-trading career and personal profits, see Nicholas Radburn, "Guinea Factors, Slave Sales, and the Profits of the Transatlantic Slave Trade in Late Eighteenth-Century Jamaica: The Case of John Tailyour," *WMQ* 72, no. 2 (2015): 243–86.

3. The WCL collection guide describes Polly Graham as Tailyour's "common-law wife," but there is no evidence that anyone used this phrase to describe her.

4. For Jamaica's high mortality rate, see Trevor Burnard, "'The Countrie Continues Sicklie': White Mortality in Jamaica, 1655–1780," *Social History of Medicine* 12, no. 1 (1999): 45–72; Vincent Brown, *The Reaper's Garden: Death and Power in the World of Atlantic Slavery* (Cambridge, MA: Harvard University Press, 2008), 16–20. On informal sexual relations in imperial spaces, see esp. Durba Ghosh, *Sex and the Family in Colonial India: The Making of Empire* (Cambridge: Cambridge University Press, 2006); Kathleen Wilson, *The Island Race: Englishness, Empire and Gender in the Eighteenth Century* (London: Routledge, 2003); Felicity Nussbaum, *Torrid Zones: Maternity, Sexuality, and Empire in Eighteenth-Century English Narratives* (Baltimore: Johns Hopkins University Press, 1995).

5. *Anti-Slavery Monthly Reporter*, vol. 1 (London, 1827), 6.

6. Isaac Grant to James Stothert, June 10, 1799, James Stothert Papers, WCL.

7. In defense of the 1761 Devises Act, for instance, the assembly cited Lucius Levermore, "who bequeathed to his housekeeper, Elizabeth, reputed free," the use of a livestock pen and three slaves for life, "and the residue to four mulatto Children, Eleanor, Ann, Lucius, and William, in tail, while free; and his Executor and Trustee to purchase their freedom if it could be obtained, otherwise to his sister." Vera Copia, James Lewis, clerk to the assembly, included in Stanhope to Board of Trade, June 13, 1763, CO 137/33, f. 48.

8. John Tailyour to Hercules Tailyour, June 7, 1783, John Tailyour Letterbook, Tailyour Papers, WCL.

9. James Hakewell, *A Picturesque Tour of the Island of Jamaica* (London, 1825); B. W. Higman, *Plantation Jamaica, 1750–1850: Capital and Control in a Colonial Economy* (Mona: University of the West Indies Press, 2005), 139–40; John Tailyour to Hercules Tailyour, June 7, 1783, John Tailyour Letterbook, Tailyour Papers, WCL.

10. Simon Taylor to Chaloner Arcedeckne, September 2, 1765, Taylor Family Papers, reel 1, ICS.

11. Simon Taylor to Benjamin Cowell, July 25, 1768, Taylor Family Papers, reel 1, ICS; Trevor Burnard, "Not a Place for Whites? Demographic Failure and Settlement in Comparative Context: Jamaica, 1655–1780," in *Jamaica in Slavery and Freedom: History, Heritage and Culture*, ed. Kathleen E. A. Monteith and Glen Richards (Kingston: University of the West Indies Press, 2002), 77.

12. Olwyn M. Blouet, "Bryan Edwards, F.R.S., 1743–1800," *Notes and Records of the Royal Society of London* 54, no. 2 (2000): 215–22; Bryan Edwards, *An Abridgment of Mr. Edwards's Civil and Commercial History of the British West Indies*, 2 vols. (London, 1794), 2:349.

13. Copy of Simon Taylor's will, January 27, 1783, Taylor Family Papers, ICS, 2/B/36; Simon Taylor to Sir John Taylor, January 27, 1783, Taylor Family Papers, ICS, 1/A/27.

14. Simon Taylor to George Hibbert, January 14, 1804, 1/F/42, Taylor Family Papers, ICS; Lady Maria Nugent, *Lady Nugent's Journal*, ed. Frank Cundall (London: Institute of Jamaica, 1907), 93.

15. Will of Simon Taylor of Saint Thomas, Jamaica, September 24, 1813, PROB 10/7400/7, ff. 2–4, 58–59, National Archives, Kew; Charlotte Taylor christening, March 14, 1798, Jamaica, Church of England Parish Register Transcripts, 1664–1880, St. Thomas in the East, "Baptisms, marriages, burials, 1708–1821," vol. 1, f. 230, FamilySearch, https://familysearch.org/ark:/61903/1:1:VHDZ-H54, accessed November 11, 2014; Richard B. Sheridan, "Simon Taylor, Sugar Tycoon of Jamaica, 1740–1813," *Agricultural History* 45 (1971): 285–96; Christer Petley, "'Home' and 'This Country': Britishness and Creole Identity in the Letters of a Transatlantic Slaveholder," *Atlantic Studies* 6, no. 1 (2009): 43–61; Christer Petley, "Plantations and Homes: The Material Culture of the Early Nineteenth-Century Jamaican Elite," *Slavery and Abolition* 35, no. 3 (2014): 440.

16. 53 Geo. III, c. 19 (December 4, 1813), *The Laws of Jamaica* (St. Jago de la Vega, 1817), 247. The repeal of the 1761 Devises Act generated considerable debate; see November 5, 16, and 25, 1813, *JAJ*, 12:506, 519, 530; Alexander Lindsay to Coote, May 15, 1805, box 8, item 12, Eyre Coote Papers, WCL; John Tailyour to Hercules Tailyour, June 7, 1783, John Tailyour Letterbook, Tailyour Papers, WCL.

17. John Tailyour to Hercules Tailyour, June 7, 1783, John Tailyour to J. Truland, May 30, 1784, John Tailyour to Messrs Okland, Anderson, July 12, 1784, and John Tailyour to Okland and Anderson, July 18, 1785, John Tailyour Letterbook, Tailyour Papers, WCL.

18. James Taylor christening, November 9, 1786, and Simon Taylor and John Taylor christenings, February 24, 1791, Kingston, Jamaica, Church of England Parish Register Transcripts, 1664–1880, Registrar General, Spanish Town, (mf 1291763), ff. 371, 425; Radburn, "Guinea Factors, Slave Sales, and the Profits of the Transatlantic Slave Trade," 244; Jean Tailyour to John Tailyour, August 14, 1787, and November 20, 1789, and Robert Tailyour to John Tailyour, November 2, 1788, and February 9, 1790, Tailyour Papers, WCL.

19. Simon Taylor to Chaloner Arcedeckne, January 3, 1790, and July 9, 1790, Taylor Family Papers, reel 3, ICS; Robert Tailyour to John Tailyour, July 24, 1791, November 2, 1791, and April 4, 1792, Tailyour Papers, WCL.

20. John Tailyour to Simon Taylor, January 3, 1790, Taylor Family Papers, reel 15, ICS; Edward Long, *The History of Jamaica*, 3 vols. (London, 1774), 2:332; Benjamin Vaughan to Charles Vaughan, October 24, 1777, Benjamin Vaughan Papers, series 2: General Correspondence, American Philosophical Society, Philadelphia; Andrew Hamilton, "Benjamin Vaughan on Commerce and International Harmony in the Eighteenth Century," in *Sociability and Cosmopolitanism: Social Bonds on the Fringes*

of the Enlightenment, ed. Scott Breuniger and David Burrow (Oxford: Routledge, 2012), 103–5; Robert Charles Dallas, *A Short Journey in the West Indies, in Which Are Interspersed, Curious Anecdotes and Characters*, 2 vols. (London, 1790), 2:56–57.

21. Trevor Burnard, *Mastery, Tyranny, and Desire: Thomas Thistlewood and His Slaves in the Anglo-Jamaican World* (Chapel Hill: University of North Carolina Press, 2004), 156; Douglas Hall, *In Miserable Slavery: Thomas Thistlewood in Jamaica, 1750–86* (1989; repr., Kingston: University of West Indies Press, 1999), 314; Simon Taylor to Chaloner Arcedeckne, December 3, 1771, in *Travel, Trade, and Power in the Atlantic, 1765–1884*, ed. Betty Wood and Martin Lynn (Cambridge: Cambridge University Press, 2002), 107–8; John F. Campbell, "How Free Is Free? The Limits of Manumission for Enslaved Africans in Eighteenth-Century British West Indian Sugar Society," in *Paths to Freedom: Manumission in the Atlantic World*, ed. Rosemary Brana-Shute and Randy J. Sparks (Columbia: University of South Carolina Press, 2009), 143–60.

22. Roger Hope Elletson to [Mr. Poole], February 1, 1771, and Anna Elizabeth Elletson to Poole and East, January 17, 1776, Letters to Jamaica, vol. 2, ST 14, Stowe MS, HL. On Anna Elletson, see Linda L. Sturtz, "The 'Dimduke' and the Duchess of Chandos: Gender and Power in Jamaican Plantation Management—A Case Study or a Different Story of 'A Man [and His Wife] from a Place Called Hope," *Revista/Review Interamericana* 29 (1999), http://cai.sg.inter.edu/revista-ciscla/volume29/sturtz.pdf, accessed October 9, 2014.

23. John Tailyour to Simon Taylor, January 3, 1790, and John Tailyour to Simon Taylor, August 12, 1790, Taylor Family Papers, reel 15, ICS.

24. Richard Tailyour to John Tailyour, August 22, 1791, and February 1, 1792, Tailyour Papers, WCL; Ghosh, *Sex and the Family in Colonial India*, 127.

25. Catherine Taylor christening, November 20, 1792, Kingston, Jamaica, Church of England Parish Register Transcripts, 1664–1880, Registrar General, Spanish Town, (mf 1291763), f. 454; Robert Tailyour to John Tailyour, January 4, 1792, John McCall to John Tailyour, May 12, 1793, and September 8, 1793, and David Dick to John Tailyour, April 11, 1798, Tailyour Papers, WCL.

26. George Robertson, *A General View of Kincardineshire; or, The Mearns; Drawn up and Published by Order of the Board of Agriculture* (London, 1810), 129, 171, 135; John Tailyour to John McCall, November 25, 1807, and John Tailyour to John Orr, October 28, 1809, Tailyour Papers, WCL.

27. Journal of Jonathan Troup, 1788–1790, MS 2070, UASCA, f. 107v; Stephen Fuller to the Earl of Shelburne, April 2, 1782, Shelburne Papers, vol. 78, WCL, ff. 121–24; "A Few Conjectural Considerations upon the Creation of the Humane Race, Occasioned by the Present British Quixottical Rage of setting the Slaves from Africa at Liberty, by the Reverend Dr. Lindsay," 1788, BL, Add MS 12439, f. 171.

28. Ann Storrow to Mrs. Brown, September 12, 1792, Ann Appleton Storrow Papers, 1790–1794, P-772 (microfilm), Massachusetts Historical Society, Boston; Laura J. Rosenthal, *Infamous Commerce: Prostitution in Eighteenth-Century British Literature and Culture* (Ithaca, NY: Cornell University Press, 2006); Dallas, *Short Journey in the West Indies*, 2:55–56.

29. John Stewart, *An Account of Jamaica, and Its Inhabitants* (London, 1808), 296–97, 301, 304.

30. Nugent, *Lady Nugent's Journal*, 104–5, 131–32 .

31. Simon Tailyour's attendance at Bowman's school is noted in John Bowman to John Tailyour, St. Vigeans, January 22, 1803, and September 9, 1803, Tailyour Papers, WCL; Catherine is mentioned in James Tailyour to John Tailyour, March 15, 1810, Tailyour Papers, WCL. Confirmation of John Tailyour Jr.'s appointment as a captain's clerk on a vessel headed to the East Indies is recorded in Robert Tailyour to John Tailyour, November 27, 1811, Tailyour Papers, WCL.

32. Robert Tailyour to John Tailyour, March 8, 1805, Tailyour Papers, WCL.

33. Robert Tailyour to John Tailyour, April 6, 1805, April 11, 1805, Tailyour Papers, WCL; quoted in Christopher J. Hawes, *Poor Relations: The Making of a Eurasian Community in British India, 1773–1833* (London: Curzon Press, 1996), 64. This policy may have also stemmed from the perceived lack of respect accorded to "half-castes" in India boasting "a colour more black than any of the natives themselves." See *Minutes of Evidence Taken before the Select Committee of the House of Lords Appointed to Enquire into the Present State of the Affairs of the East-India Company* (London, 1830), 369.

34. Robert Tailyour to John Tailyour, May 8, 1805, July 29, 1806, and August 21, 1806, James Taylor to John Tailyour, November 29, 1805, and June 27, 1810, Tailyour Papers, WCL.

35. Alexander Johnston to John Johnston, June 24, 1783, folder 10, box 54, PFP, HSP. The Johnston family papers are included as a subset of the Powel Family Papers at the HSP.

36. Alan Karras, "The World of Alexander Johnston: The Creolization of Ambition, 1762–1787," *Historical Journal* 30, no. 1 (1987): 54–55; Richard Sheridan, *Doctors and Slaves: A Medical and Demographic History of Slavery in the British West Indies, 1680–1834* (Cambridge: Cambridge University Press, 1985), 44.

37. Alan L. Karras, *Sojourners in the Sun: Scottish Migrants in Jamaica and the Chesapeake, 1740–1800* (Ithaca, NY: Cornell University Press, 1992), 167–68; William Smalling to Joseph Foster Barham, May 3, 1775, Jamaica Correspondence, 1760–1808, Barham Family Papers, MSS Clare dep c357, BOD.

38. Alexander Johnston's Medical Record, 1768–1773, vol. 342, PFP, HSP. For a sample of charges to Tucker, see ff. 80, 102, 127, 155, 164, 203, 209.

39. January 2, 1772, January 15, 1773, and February 26, 1773, Alexander Johnston Daybook and Ledger, 1767–1777, vol. 334, PFP, HSP; Karras, "World of Alexander Johnston," 65–66.

40. Certificate of Marriage, February 7, 1773, and Philip Pinnock to Alexander Johnston, June 5, 1775, folder 8, box 54, PFP, HSP; Karras, "World of Alexander Johnston," 68, 71.

41. October 29, 1774, Alexander Johnston Daybook and Ledger, 1767–77, vol. 334, and August 27, 1786, October 11, 1786, Alexander Johnston's Notebook, 1783–86, vol. 341, PFP, HSP.

42. A. Johnson to James Johnston, September 14, 1783, folder 10, box 54, PFP, HSP; Milburn and Ludlow to Johnston, March 21, 1776, folder 1, and "Estimate value of

the property of Dr. A. Johnston, St. Ann," July 7, 1784, folder 2, box 55, PFP, HSP; November 12, 1786, and December 1, 1786, Alexander Johnston's Notebook, 1783–86, vol. 341, PFP, HSP.

43. Copy of the will of Alexander Johnston, undated, folder 8, box 55, PFP, HSP; "A Bequest from A. Johnston to Jenny and Jemmy Johnston his reputed children at Richmond," September 1, 1786, Alexander Johnston's Legal Records, 1773–1782, ff.342, PFP, HSP.

44. William Robertson to James Johnston, June 25, 1787, September 25, 1787, July 4, 1788, and Elizabeth Johnston to James Johnston, June 2, 1787, folder 10, box 55, PFP, HSP.

45. William Robertson to James Johnston, May 19, 1789, November 5, 1789, folder 10, box 55, PFP, HSP; Robert Grant to James Johnston, January 19, 1794, September 12, 1794, folder 12, box 55, PFP, HSP; Robert Grant to John Johnston, August 18, 1797, folder 13, box 55, PFP, HSP.

46. John Johnston to James Johnston, September 30, 1799, Robert Grant to John Johnston, April 26, 1798, and William Robertson to James Johnston, November 25, 1799, folder 13, box 55, PFP, HSP.

47. James Johnston to James Johnston, June 7, 1802, and December 9, 1802, folder 13, box 55, PFP, HSP; James Johnston to Robert Johnston, December 9, 1802, folder 1, box 44, PFP, HSP.

48. James Johnston to Robert Johnston, April 22, 1804, March 10, 1804, and August 26, 1805, folder 1, box 44, PFP, HSP.

49. James Johnston to Robert Johnston, June 19, 1806, folder 1, box 44, PFP, HSP; Journal of Jonathan Troup, 1788–1790, MS 2070, UASCA, f. 133v.

50. Receipt, Lauren Hall, St. Ann, April 25, 1813, folder 3, box 57, PFP, HSP; James Johnston to Robert Johnston, May 25, 1814, folder 5, box 44, PFP, HSP.

51. James Johnston to Robert Johnston, March 30, 1814, September 24, 1814, and November 9, 1814, folder 5, box 44, PFP, HSP; James Johnston to Robert Johnston, October 6, 1815, folder 7, box 44, PFP, HSP.

52. James Johnston to Robert Johnston, December 27, 1815, folder 7, box 44, PFP, HSP; James Johnston to Robert Johnston, March 27, 1817, folder 11, box 44, PFP, HSP.

53. Robert Johnston, Miscellaneous, 1800–39, folder 10, box 52, and Robert Johnston's Jamaica Journal, June 25, 1818, folder 7, box 49, PFP, HSP.

54. Robert Johnston was involved in a proslavery West Indian group based in Edinburgh. See Robert Johnston, correspondence, folder 9, box 44, and Commonplace Book, 1811, Robert Johnston Writings, folder 1, box 49, PFP, HSP.

55. Robert Johnston's Jamaica Journal, June 25, 1818, folder 7, box 49, PFP, HSP.

56. Published letter to the editor of the *New Times,* signed A Patriot, February 19, Robert Johnston Writings, folder 3, box 49, PFP, HSP; Mary Turner, *Slaves and Missionaries: The Disintegration of Jamaican Slave Society, 1787–1834* (Kingston: University Press of the West Indies, 1982), 148; R. Johnston to William Wilberforce, October 16, 1832, folder 11, box 45, PFP, HSP; public advertisement, March 1832, folder 8, box 45, PFP, HSP.

57. James Johnston to Robert Johnston, October 17, 1824, folder 4, box 45, PFP, HSP; 1830 Case for the Advice and Opinion of Fitzherbert Batty, folder 1, box 57, PFP, HSP.

58. 1830 Case for the Advice and Opinion of Fitzherbert Batty, 1830, folder 1, box 57, PFP, HSP.

CHAPTER 5. ENSLAVED WOMEN AND BRITISH COMIC CULTURE

1. David Alexander, *Richard Newton and English Caricature in the 1790s* (New York: St. Martin's, 1998), 23; Kay Dian Kriz, *Slavery, Sugar, and the Culture of Refinement* (New Haven, CT: Yale University Press, 2008), 232n125; Steve O. Buckridge, *The Language of Dress: Resistance and Accommodation in Jamaica, 1760–1890* (Mona: University of the West Indies Press, 2004), 94; Cindy McCreery, "True Blue and *Black, Brown and Fair*: Prints of British Sailors and Their Women during the Revolutionary and Napoleonic Wars," *British Journal for Eighteenth-Century Studies* 23, no. 2 (2000): 135–52, here 144.

2. Robert Darnton, *The Great Cat Massacre and Other Episodes in French Cultural History* (1984; repr., New York: Basic Books, 2009), 78; John Ash, *The New and Complete Dictionary of the English Language,* 2 vols. (London, 1775), 1:x; Francis Grose, *A Classical Dictionary of the Vulgar Tongue* (London, 1788); Roger F. Buckley, "The Frontier in the Caricatures of Abraham James," *Yale University Library Gazette* 58 (1984): 153; Linda Colley, *Britons: Forging the Nation, 1707–1837* (New Haven, CT: Yale University Press, 1992), 358.

3. Vic Gatrell, *City of Laughter: Sex and Satire in Eighteenth-Century London* (New York: Walker, 2007), 9–10; Eirwen E. C. Nicholson, "Consumers and Spectators: The Public of the Political Print in Eighteenth-Century England," *History* 81 (1996): 5–21, here 14; Sheila O'Connell, *The Popular Print in England, 1550–1850* (London: British Museum Press, 1999), 12; Diana Donald, *The Age of Caricature: Satirical Prints in the Reign of George III* (New Haven, CT: Yale University Press, 1996), 19–20.

4. Srividhya Swaminathan, *Debating the Slave Trade: Rhetoric of British National Identity, 1759–1815* (Surrey, UK: Ashgate, 2009), 171–202; J. R. Oldfield, *Popular Politics and British Anti-slavery: The Mobilisation of Public Opinion* (Manchester: Manchester University Press, 1995), 96–124; Christopher Leslie Brown, *Moral Capital: Foundations of British Abolitionism* (Chapel Hill: University of North Carolina Press, 2006), 391–450.

5. Quoted in Alex Potts, *Flesh and the Ideal: Winckelmann and the Origins of Art History* (New Haven, CT: Yale University Press, 2000), 3; Geoffrey Cubitt, "Atrocity Materials and the Representation of Transatlantic Slavery: Problems, Strategies and Reactions," in *Representing Enslavement and Abolition in Museums: Ambiguous Engagements,* ed. Laurajane Smith et al. (New York: Routledge, 2011), 240.

6. Marcus Wood, *Blind Memory: Visual Representations of Slavery in England and America, 1780–1865* (Manchester: Manchester University Press, 2000); Kriz, *Slavery, Sugar, and the Culture of Refinement;* Catherine Molineux, *Faces of Perfect Ebony: Encountering Atlantic Slavery in Imperial Britain* (Cambridge, MA: Harvard University Press, 2012). See also Trevor Burnard, "'A Compound Mongrel Mixture': Racially Coded Humor, Satire, and the Denigration of White Creoles in the British West Indies, 1780–1834," in *Seeing Satire in the Eighteenth Century,* ed. Elizabeth C. Mansfield and Kelly Malone (Oxford: Voltaire Foundation, 2013), chap. 7; Keith Sandiford,

"Envisioning the Colonial Body: The Fair, the Carnivalesque, and the Grotesque," in *An Economy of Colour: Visual Culture and the Atlantic World, 1660–1830,* ed. Geoff Quilley and Kay Dian Kriz (Manchester: Manchester University Press, 2003), 28. White male fixation on African women's physical appearance is detailed in Jennifer Morgan, "'Some Could Suckle Over Their Shoulder': Male Travelers, Female Bodies, and the Gendering of Racial Ideology," *WMQ* 54, no. 1 (1997): 167–92. I have borrowed the phrase "property rights in pleasure" from Hilary Beckles, "Property Rights in Pleasure: The Marketing of Enslaved Women's Sexuality," in *West Indies Accounts: Essays on the History of the British Caribbean and the Atlantic Economy, in Honour of Richard Sheridan,* ed. Roderick A. McDonald (Kingston: University of the West Indies Press, 1996), 169–87.

7. Richard Ligon, *A True and Exact History of the Island of Barbados* (London, 1657), 55; Richard Steele, "The History of Inkle and Yarico," *Spectator,* no. 11 (March 13, 1711). Lawrence M. Price, in *The Inkle and Yarico Album* (Berkeley: University of California Press, 1937), catalogs forty-five eighteenth-century versions of the Inkle and Yarico story, some of which are discussed in Wylie Sypher, *Guinea's Captive Kings* (Chapel Hill: University of North Carolina Press, 1942), 122–37. William J. Burling, *Summer Theatre in London, 1661–1820, and the Rise of the Haymarket Theatre* (Madison, NJ: Fairleigh Dickinson University Press, 2000), 150, table 5.6; Frank Felsenstein, *English Trader, Indian Maid: Representing Gender, Race, and Slavery in the New World: An Inkle and Yarico Reader* (Baltimore: Johns Hopkins University Press, 1999), 167–68; Errol Hill, *The Jamaican Stage, 1655–1900: Profile of a Colonial Theatre* (Amherst: University of Massachusetts Press, 1992), 80; *Monthly Review, or Literary Journal* 77 (London, 1787), 384; David Brion Davis, *The Problem of Slavery in Western Culture* (New York: Oxford University Press, 1966), 12.

8. George Colman, the Younger, *Inkle and Yarico: An Opera, in Three Acts* (London, 1787), 18–19, 23–25.

9. Daniel O'Quinn, *Entertaining Crisis in the Atlantic Imperium, 1770–1790* (Baltimore: Johns Hopkins University Press, 2011), 299; Colman, *Inkle and Yarico,* 33, 47, 57.

10. Colman, *Inkle and Yarico,* 68, 69.

11. Colman, *Inkle and Yarico,* 54–55; Jenna M. Gibbs, *Performing the Temple of Liberty: Slavery, Theater, and Popular Culture in London and Philadelphia, 1760–1850* (Baltimore: Johns Hopkins University Press, 2014), 3; Felicity Nussbaum, *The Limits of the Human: Fictions of Anomaly, Race, and Gender in the Long Eighteenth Century* (Baltimore: Johns Hopkins University Press, 2003), 153; Colman, *Inkle and Yarico,* 62–63. On the early modern grotesque, see Mikhail Bakhtin, *Rabelais and His World,* trans. Helene Iswolsky (1965; repr., Bloomington: Indiana University Press, 2008), chap. 5; Peter Stallybrass and Allon White, *The Politics and Poetics of Transgression* (Ithaca, NY: Cornell University Press, 1986), chap. 2; Gail Kern Paster, *The Body Embarrassed: Drama and the Disciplines of Shame in Early Modern England* (Ithaca, NY: Cornell University Press, 1993), chaps. 2–3.

12. Mark M. Smith, *How Race Is Made: Slavery, Segregation, and the Senses* (Chapel Hill: University of North Carolina Press, 2006), 18; Aphra Behn, *Oroonoko; or, The Royal Slave* (London, 1688), 23; Felicity Nussbaum, "Women and Race: 'A Difference of

Complexion,'" in *Women and Literature in Britain, 1700–1800,* ed. Vivien Jones (Cambridge: Cambridge University Press, 2000), 75; Ligon, *True and Exact History of Barbados,* 55; Colman, *Inkle and Yarico,* 19, 57, 74.

13. *New London Magazine* (London, August 1787), 438; Robert Richardson, *Travels along the Mediterranean and Parts Adjacent,* 2 vols. (London, 1822), 1:366; Nandini Bhattacharya, *Slavery, Colonialism, and Connoisseurship: Gender and Eighteenth-Century Literary Transnationalism* (Aldershot, UK: Ashgate, 2006), 27.

14. Address of the Council to Clarke, October 21, 1789, CO 137/88, f. 84; Prince William to the Prince Wales, May 20, 1787, and October 26, 1788, quoted in Philip Ziegler, *King William IV* (London: Collins, 1971), 58–59, 69; Correspondence to and from, and also papers re, the Duke of Clarence, 1779–1830, and Prince William to the Duke of York, July 4, 1787, GEO/MAIN/44789–90, Royal Archives, Windsor Castle; Doctor's report, March 2, 1788, GEO/MAIN/44823–4, Royal Archives, Windsor Castle; entry for May 15, 1789, Journal of Dr. Jonathan Troup, 1788–1790, MS 2070, UASCA, ff. 11v, 162.

15. *Rambler's Magazine* 6 (April 1788), 104; [Elizabeth] Inchbald, *The British Theatre; or, A Collection of Plays,* 25 vols. (London, 1808) 21:4; R. P. Forster, *A Collection of the Most Celebrated Voyages and Travels, from the Discovery of America to the Present Time,* 4 vols. (London, 1818), 2:59.

16. Jenny Uglow, *William Hogarth: A Life and a World* (London, 2011), 457–58; David Dabydeen, *Hogarth's Blacks: Images of Blacks in Eighteenth-Century English Art* (Manchester: Manchester University Press, 1987), 97.

17. Dabydeen, *Hogarth's Blacks,* 97; Helen M. Burke, *Riotous Performances: The Struggle for Hegemony in Irish Theater, 1712–1784* (South Bend, IN: University of Notre Dame Press, 2003), 106; Gordon Williams, *A Dictionary of Sexual Language and Imagery in Shakespearean and Stuart Literature* (1994; repr., London: Bloomsbury, 2001), 110–11; John Donne, *The Poems of John Donne,* ed. Herbert J. C. Grierson, 2 vols. (Oxford: Clarendon Press, 1912), 1:461.

18. Gatrell, *City of Laughter,* 298; Edgar V. Roberts, "An Unrecorded Meaning of 'Joke' (or 'Joak') in England," *American Speech* 37, no. 2 (1962): 137–40; Paul Dennat, "The 'Barbarous Old English Jig': The 'Black Joke' in the Eighteenth and Nineteenth Centuries," *Folk Music Journal* 10, no. 3 (2013): 298–318, here 305; Charles Coffey, *The Beggar's Wedding* (London, 1729), 17–18; Joseph Donohue, *The Cambridge History of British Theatre* (Cambridge: Cambridge University Press, 2004), 2:138; *The London Miscellany* (London, 1730), 32; John Gay, *Calista* (London, 1731), 25; *Gentleman's Magazine* (London, May 1732), 781; British Museum, BM Satires 2188.

19. In Henry Carey's farcical *Chrononhotonthologos,* for example, the Queen of Queerummunie commands her fiddler to play the "Black Joak." Henry Carey, *The Tragedy of Chrononhotonthologos* (Edinburgh, 1734), 6. Quoted in Dennat, "Barbarous Old English Jig," 302; *The Musical Miscellany; or, Songster's Pocket Companion* (London, 1760), 53–55; "Tune, *Black-Joke,*" in Anon., *A Collection of Songs with Some Originals* (Dublin, 1769), 95–96; *The Convivial Songster, Being a Select Collection of the Best Songs in the English Language* (London, 1788), 76–78.

20. Grose, *Classical Dictionary of the Vulgar Tongue;* William Shakespeare, *The Works of Mr Shakespear* (Oxford, 1743), 3:84–85.

21. John Nichols, *Biographical Anecdotes of William Hogarth* (London, 1785), 440–41; Wendy Doniger, *The Bedtrick: Tales of Sex and Masquerade* (Chicago: University of Chicago Press, 2000), 176.

22. Sir Walter Scott, *The Journal of Sir Walter Scott,* ed. W. E. K. Anderson (Oxford: Clarendon, 1972), 471–72; Charles James Fox, *Memorials and Correspondence of Charles James Fox,* 2 vols., ed. Lord John Russell (London, 1853), 1:94.

23. Nineteenth-century critics noted the connection between Fox's alleged disgrace and Foote's *The Cozeners.* See John Forster, *Oliver Cromwell, Daniel De Foe, Sir Richard Steele, Charles Churchill, Samuel Foote: Biographical Essays* (London, 1860), 448–49; John Timbs, *Anecdote Lives of the Later Wits and Humourists* (London, 1872), 228; Samuel Foote, *The Cozeners, a Comedy, of Three Acts, as It Was Performed at the Theatre Royal in the Hay-Market* (London, 1778), 55, 62–63.

24. Scott, *Journal of Sir Walter Scott,* 472; Foote, *The Cozeners,* 67–68; Samuel Foote, *The Works of Samuel Foote, Esq.,* 3 vols. (London, 1830), 3:304.

25. Marliss C. Desens, *The Bed-Trick in English Renaissance Drama: Explorations in Gender, Sexuality, and Power* (Newark: University of Delaware Press, 1994), 99; Kim F. Hall, *Things of Darkness: Economies of Race and Gender in Early Modern England* (Ithaca, NY: Cornell University Press, 1995), 115–16; Doniger, *The Bedtrick;* Virginia Mason Vaughan, *Performing Blackness on English Stages, 1500–1800* (Cambridge: Cambridge University Press, 2005), 74–92; Louise Denmead, "The Discovery of Blackness in the Early Modern Bed-Trick," in *The Invention of Discovery,* ed. James Dougal Fleming (Aldershot, UK: Ashgate, 2011), 153–66.

26. John Fletcher, *Monsievr Thomas* (London, 1639), 49–53, 55–62, 66–67; Vaughan, *Performing Blackness on English Stages,* 81.

27. Denmead, "Discovery of Blackness," 156; Anu Korhonen, "Washing the Ethiopian White: Conceptualising Black Skin in Renaissance England," in *Black Africans in Renaissance Europe,* ed. T. F. Earle and K. J. P. Lowe (Cambridge: Cambridge University Press, 2005), 106; Francis Beaumont and John Fletcher, *The Works of Mr. Francis Beaumont and Mr. John Fletcher,* 10 vols. (London, 1711), 5:2600–2601; Isaac Teale, *The Sable Venus* (Kingston, 1765), 9.

28. Beaumont and Fletcher, *Works of Mr. Francis Beaumont and Mr. John Fletcher,* 5:2659; Vaughan, *Performing Blackness on English Stages,* 75; Molineux, *Faces of Perfect Ebony,* 18–60; Susan Amussen, *Caribbean Exchanges: Slavery and the Transformation of English Society, 1640–1700* (Chapel Hill: University of North Carolina Press, 2007), 286–308. Quoted in Roxann Wheeler, *The Complexion of Race: Categories of Difference in Eighteenth-Century British Culture* (Philadelphia: University of Pennsylvania Press, 2000), 3.

29. Daniel Livesay, "The Decline of Jamaica's Interracial Households and the Fall of the Planter Class, 1733–1823," *Atlantic Studies* 9, no. 1 (2012): 107–23; Brooke N. Newman, "Gender, Sexuality, and the Formation of Racial Identities in the Eighteenth-Century Anglo-Caribbean World," *Gender and History* 22, no. 3 (November 2010): 585–602; Georgianna Ziegler, "My Lady's Chamber: Female Space, Female Chastity in Shakespeare," *Textual Practice* 4 (1990): 73–90; Peter Stallybrass, "Patriarchal Ter-

ritories: The Body Enclosed," in *Rewriting the Renaissance: The Discourses of Sexual Difference in Early Modern Europe,* ed. Margaret Ferguson et al. (Chicago: University of Chicago Press, 1986), 123–42.

30. Nathan Bailey, *Dictionarium Britannicum* (London, 1736).

31. Gatrell, *City of Laughter,* 166, 276.

32. Imtiaz H. Habib, *Black Lives in the English Archives, 1500–1677: Imprints of the Invisible* (Aldershot, UK: Ashgate, 2008), 107; Gretchen Holbrook Gerzina, *Black London: Life before Emancipation* (New Brunswick, NJ: Rutgers University Press, 1995), 21–22; Norma Myers, *Reconstructing the Black Past: Black People in Britain, 1780–1830* (1996; repr., Portland, OR: Frank Cass, 2013), 18–37.

33. John Gay, *The Beggar's Opera* (London, 1728), 2; Grose, *Classical Dictionary of the Vulgar Tongue;* Bradford K. Mudge, *The Whore's Story: Women, Pornography, and the British Novel, 1684–1830* (Oxford: Oxford University Press, 2000), 51; Dabydeen, *Hogarth's Blacks,* 101.

34. Seymour Drescher, *Capitalism and Antislavery: British Mobilization in Comparative Perspective* (Oxford: Oxford University Press, 1987), 30; Peter Fryer, *Staying Power: The History of Black People in Britain* (1984; repr., London: Pluto Press, 1988), 76; Nussbaum, *Limits of the Human,* 165; Tony Henderson, *Disorderly Women in Eighteenth-Century London: Prostitution and Control in the Metropolis, 1730–1830* (New York: Pearson, 1999), 178–79; William Winstanley, *Old Poor Robin* (London, 1793), 38; *The Bacchanalian Songster* (London, 1783), 39; Grose, *Classical Dictionary of the Vulgar Tongue;* William Shakespeare, *The Tragoedy of Othello, the Moore of Venice* (London, 1622), 91. See also Roxanne But, "The Role of Context in the Meaning Specification of Cant and Slang Words in Eighteenth-Century English," in *Meaning in the History of English: Words and Texts in Context,* ed. Andreas H. Jucker et al. (Philadelphia: John Benjamins, 2013), 129–56.

35. James De-La-Cour, *Poems by the Revd. James De-La-Cour* (Cork, 1778), 98. Thais, an "expensive Greek courtesan," was a stock character in Greco-Roman comedies. See Alison Keith, "Naming the Elegiac Mistress: Elegiac Onomastics in Roman Inscriptions," in *Roman Literary Cultures: Domestic Politics, Revolutionary Poetics, Civic Spectacle,* ed. Alison Keith and Jonathan Edmondson (Toronto: University of Toronto Press, 2016), 62–63.

36. Matthew J. Kinservik, *Disciplining Satire: The Censorship of Satiric Comedy on the Eighteenth-Century London Stage* (Cranbury, NJ: Associated University Presses, 2002), 255.

37. Lois Peters Agnew, *Outward, Visible Propriety: Stoic Philosophy and Eighteenth-Century British Rhetorics* (Columbia: University of South Carolina Press, 2008), 86; *The Art of Beauty; or, A Companion for the Toilet* (London, 1760), 2, 7.

38. Georges Louis Leclerc, Comte de Buffon, *Natural History, General and Particular, by the Count de Buffon, Translated into English* (London, 1785), 84–85; Thomas Jefferson, *Notes on the State of Virginia* (Boston, 1801), 205; Jean-Jacques Rousseau, *Discourse upon the Origin and Foundation of the Inequality among Mankind* (London, 1761), 222, 224; Sarah Salih, "Filling Up the Space between Mankind and Ape: Racism, Speciesism and the Androphilic Ape," *Ariel* 38, no. 1 (2007): 95–111; William B. Cohen,

The French Encounter with Africans: White Response to Blacks, 1530–1880 (1980; repr., Bloomington: Indiana University Press, 2003), 88; Andrew S. Curran, *The Anatomy of Blackness: Science and Slavery in an Age of Enlightenment* (Baltimore: Johns Hopkins University Press, 2011), 130; Edward Long, *The History of Jamaica*, 3 vols. (London, 1774), 2:375.

39. Jennifer L. Morgan, *Laboring Women: Reproduction and Gender in New World Slavery* (Philadelphia: University of Pennsylvania Press, 2004), 49; "A Few Conjectural Considerations upon the Creation of the Humane Race, Occasioned by the Present British Quixottical Rage of setting the Slaves from Africa at Liberty, by the Reverend Dr. Lindsay," 1788, BL, Add MS 12439, f. 108; Saugnier, *Voyages to the Coast of Africa* (London, 1792), 98–99; Richard Newton, *The Full Moon in Eclipse* (London, 1797), Andrew Edmunds Collection, London. Quoted in Clifton C. Crais and Pamela Scully, *Sara Baartman and the Hottentot Venus: A Ghost Story and a Biography* (Princeton, NJ: Princeton University Press, 2009), 80.

40. Hector Macneil, *Observations on the Treatment of the Negroes, in the Island of Jamaica* (London, 1788), 40; Charles Leslie, *A New and Exact Account of Jamaica* (Edinburgh, 1740), 36.

41. Captain Charles Johnson, *A General History of the Pyrates, from Their First Rise and Settlement in the Island of Providence to the Present Time* (London, 1724), 199; J. Hector St. John de Crèvecoeur, *More Letters from the American Farmer: An Edition of the Essays in English Left Unpublished*, ed. Dennis D. Moore (Athens: University of Georgia Press, 1995), 107; Robert Charles Dallas, *A Short Journey in the West Indies, in Which Are Interspersed, Curious Anecdotes and Characters*, 2 vols. (London, 1790), 1:51–52, 54; Forster, *Collection of the Most Celebrated Voyages*, 2:59–60.

42. Adriana Craciun, *British Women Writers and the French Revolution: Citizens of the World* (Basingstoke, UK: Palgrave, 2005), 171–78; Charlotte Smith, *Desmond*, 3 vols. (London, 1792), 3:163–64.

43. Royal Navy of Great Britain, *Statement Respecting the Prevalence of Certain Immoral Practices in His Majesty's Navy* (London, 1821), 1, 3.

44. McCreery, "True Blue and *Black, Brown and Fair*," 135–52; Saunders Welch, *A Proposal to Render Effectual a Plan, to Remove the Nuisance of Common Prostitutes from the Streets of the Metropolis* (London, 1758), 15.

45. Quoted in McCreery, "True Blue and *Black, Brown and Fair*," 144.

46. Roger Norman Buckley, *The British Army in the West Indies: Society and the Military in the Revolutionary Age* (Gainesville: University Press of Florida, 1998), 160. On female lodge keepers renting out slaves for sexual purposes, see Beckles, "Property Rights in Pleasure," 169–87; Paulette Kerr, "Victims or Strategists? Female Lodging-House Keepers in Jamaica," in *Engendering History: Caribbean Women in Historical Perspective*, ed. Verene Shepherd, Bridget Brereton, and Barbara Bailey (Kingston: Ian Randle, 1995), 197–212; Marisa J. Fuentes, "Power and Historical Figuring: Rachel Pringle Polgreen's Troubled Archive," *Gender and History* 22, no. 3 (2010): 564–84.

47. Peter Marshall, "The Anti Slave Trade Movement in Bristol," in *Bristol in the Eighteenth Century*, ed. Patrick McGrath (Newton Abbot, 1972), 206–11; Srividhya Swa-

minathan, "Reporting Atrocities: A Comparison of the Zong and the Trial of Captain John Kimber," *Slavery and Abolition* 31 (2010): 483–99.

48. Oldfield, *Popular Politics and British Anti-slavery,* 76; Donald, *Age of Caricature,* 171–83; Wood, *Blind Memory,* 260–61.

49. Marcus Wood, *Black Milk: Imagining Slavery in the Visual Cultures of Brazil and America* (Oxford: Oxford University Press, 2013), 86.

50. *Rochester's Jests: or, The Quintessence of Wit* (London, 1766), 96. I am grateful to Catherine Ingrassia for alerting me to this passage.

51. Christer Petley, "Gluttony, Excess and the Fall of the Planter Class in the British Caribbean," *Atlantic Studies* 9, no. 1 (2012): 85–106; Richard Cumberland, *The West Indian: A Comedy* (London, 1771), prologue, 90; Dallas, *Short Journey in the West Indies,* 1:54.

52. J. B. Moreton, *West India Customs and Manners: Containing Strictures on the Soil, Cultivation, Produce, Trade, Officers, and Inhabitants; with the Method of Establishing and Conducting a Sugar Plantation* (London, 1793), 105–6.

53. Charles Horne, *Serious Thoughts on the Miseries of Seduction and Prostitution* (London, 1783), 32; Jack Harris, *Harris's List of Covent-Garden Ladies; or, Man of Pleasure's Kalendar, for the Year, 1788* (London, 1788), 133; Elizabeth Campbell Denlinger, "The Garment and the Man: Masculine Desire in *Harris's List of Covent-Garden Ladies,* 1764–1793," *Journal of the History of Sexuality* 11, no. 3 (2002): 357–94.

54. Cindy McCreery, *The Satirical Gaze: Prints of Women in Late Eighteenth-Century England* (Oxford: Oxford University Press, 2008), 39; William Woodfall, *The Parliamentary Register* (London, 1800), 2:304; *London Chronicle* 87 (1800): 493; Robert Huish, *The History of the Life and Reign of William the Fourth, the Reform Monarch* (London, 1837), 417; *Substance of the Speech of His Royal Highness the Duke of Clarence in the House of Lords, on the Motion for the Recommitment of the Slave Trade Limitation Bill, on the Fifth Day of July, 1799* (London, 1799); Prince of Wales to Duke of York, Carlton House, April 14, 1793, in *The Correspondence of George Prince of Wales, 1770–1812,* vol. 2, *1789–1794,* ed. A. Aspinall (London: Cassell, 1969), 350.

55. Long, *History of Jamaica,* 2:328–29; Mrs. Charles Matthews, *Memoirs of a Scots Heiress,* 3 vols. (London, 1791), 2:208, 236, 238.

56. Amelia Opie, *Adeline Mowbray; or, The Mother and Daughter,* 3 vols. (London, 1805), 2:157; Cora Kaplan, "Imagining Empire: History, Fantasy, Literature," in *At Home with the Empire: Metropolitan Culture and the Imperial World,* ed. Catherine Hall and Sonya Rose (Cambridge: Cambridge University Press, 2006), 191–211, here 196; Anon., *The Woman of Colour: A Tale,* 2 vols. (London, 1808).

CHAPTER 6. INHERITABLE BLOOD AND
THE IMPERIAL BODY POLITIC

1. Fuller to the Committee of Correspondence, January 30, 1788, Stephen Fuller Papers, RL. Stephen Fuller, a London-based merchant and the brother of Rose Fuller, served as Jamaica's agent in London from 1764 to 1794. See L. M. Penson, *The Colonial Agents*

of the British West Indies: A Study in Colonial Administration, Mainly in the Eighteenth Century (London: 1924), 164, 228. On the West India lobby, see L. M. Penson, "The London West India Interest in the Eighteenth Century," *English Historical Review* 30 (1921): 373–92; Andrew J. O'Shaughnessy, "The Formation of a Commercial Lobby: The West India Interest, British Colonial Policy and the American Revolution," *Historical Journal* 40, no. 1 (1997): 71–95; David Beck Ryden, *West Indian Slavery and British Abolition, 1783–1807* (New York: Cambridge University Press, 2009).

2. Paul E. Lovejoy, *Transformations in Slavery: A History of Slavery in Africa* (1983; repr., Cambridge: Cambridge University Press, 2000), 52; Kenneth Morgan, *Slavery, Atlantic Trade and the British Economy, 1660–1800* (Cambridge: Cambridge University Press, 2000), 50–51; Trevor Burnard and John Garrigus, *The Plantation Machine: Atlantic Capitalism in French Saint-Domingue and British Jamaica* (Philadelphia: University of Pennsylvania Press, 2016), 244–45.

3. Fuller to the Committee of Correspondence, January 30, 1788, and Fuller to Sydney, January 29, 1788, Stephen Fuller Papers, RL.

4. Seymour Drescher, *Capitalism and Antislavery: British Mobilization in Comparative Perspective* (Oxford: Oxford University Press, 1987), 82; Kenneth Morgan, *Slavery and the British Empire: From Africa to America* (Oxford: Oxford University Press, 2007), 157; Thomas Clarkson, *The History of the Rise, Progress, and Accomplishment of the Abolition of the African Slave-Trade by the British Parliament*, 2 vols. (Philadelphia, 1808) 1:455.

5. Fuller to the Committee of Correspondence, May 16, 1788, Stephen Fuller Papers, RL.

6. Ibid.

7. On the impact of the abolition debate on British racial constructs, see esp. David Lambert, *White Creole Culture, Politics and Identity during the Age of Abolition* (Cambridge: Cambridge University Press, 2005), 10–40; Srividhya Swaminathan, *Debating the Slave Trade: Rhetoric of British National Identity, 1759–1815* (2009; repr., Oxford: Routledge, 2016), 127–70; Catherine Hall, "Reconfiguring Race: The Stories the Slave-Owners Told," in *Legacies of British Slave-Ownership: Colonial Slavery and the Formation of Victorian Britain*, ed. Catherine Hall et al. (Cambridge: Cambridge University Press, 2014), 163–202.

8. Jack P. Greene, *Evaluating Empire and Confronting Colonialism in Eighteenth-Century Britain* (New York: Cambridge University Press, 2013), 169–70; [John] Wynne, *A General History of the British Empire in America*, 2 vols. (London, 1770), 2:541.

9. Christopher Leslie Brown, *Moral Capital: Foundations of British Abolitionism* (Chapel Hill: University of North Carolina Press, 2006), 212–19; William Knox, *Three Tracts Respecting the Conversion and Instruction of the Free Indians and Negroe Slaves in the Colonies* (London, 1768), 19.

10. Granville Sharp, *Extract from "A Representation of the Injustice and Dangerous Tendency of Tolerating Slavery; or, Of Admitting the Least Claim of Private Property in the Persons of Men, in England"* (Philadelphia, 1769), 45, 21; Justin Buckley Dyer, *Natural Law and the Antislavery Constitutional Tradition* (Cambridge: Cambridge University Press, 2012), 53; Greene, *Evaluating Empire and Confronting Colonialism*, 171–75.

11. *Somerset v. Stewart,* March 14, 1772, *Reports of Cases Adjudged in the Court of King's Bench* (Dublin, 1790), 17, 18; Ruth Paley, "Imperial Politics and English Law: The Many Contexts of Somerset," *Law and History Review* 24, no. 3 (Fall 2006): 659–64; Dana Rabin, "'In a Country of Liberty?': Slavery, Villeinage, and the Making of Whiteness in the Somerset Case (1772)" *History Workshop Journal* 72, no. 1 (2011): 5–29; James Oldham, *English Common Law in the Age of Mansfield* (Chapel Hill: University of North Carolina Press, 2004), 314–15; Paul D. Halliday, *Habeas Corpus: From England to Empire* (Cambridge, MA: Harvard University Press, 2010), 8.

12. Edward Long, *Candid Reflections upon the Court of King's Bench in Westminster-Hall on What Is Commonly Called the Negro-Cause* (London, 1772), 4; Samuel Estwick, *Considerations on the Negro Cause Commonly So Called* (London, 1772), viii–ix; Travis Glasson, *Mastering Christianity: Missionary Anglicanism and Slavery in the Atlantic World* (New York: Oxford University Press, 2012), 86.

13. Long, *Candid Reflections,* 5–6, 10, 12–13; Edward Long, "Draft of a discourse on the subject of slavery in Jamaica," BL, Add. MS 18271, f. 6; *Smith v. Brown and Cooper* (1702), *English Reports* (London, 1705), 91:567; Holt quoted in Jonathan A. Bush, "The British Constitution and the Creation of American Slavery," in *Slavery and the Law,* ed. Paul Finkelman (Madison, WI: Madison House, 1997), 388.

14. Estwick, *Considerations on the Negro Cause,* 39–40, 50–51.

15. Estwick, *Considerations on the Negro Cause,* 81, 84, 90–91; James Walvin, *Questioning Slavery* (London: Routledge, 1996), 85–88.

16. Long, *Candid Reflections,* 48–49; 157; Philip Thicknesse, *A Year's Journey through France, and Part of Spain,* 2 vols. (London, 1778), 2:103–4, 110; quoted in Peter Fryer, *Staying Power: The History of Black People in Britain* (1984; repr., London: Pluto Press, 1988), 164. For satirical depictions of lower-class white women and black men, see Catherine Molineux, *Faces of Perfect Ebony: Encountering Atlantic Slavery in Imperial Britain* (Cambridge, MA: Harvard University Press, 2012).

17. Robert H. Webking, *The American Revolution and the Politics of Liberty* (Baton Rouge: Louisiana State University Press, 1988), 16–17; James Otis, *The Rights of the British Colonies Asserted and Proved* (London, 1764), 36–37.

18. Jamaica Census of 1788, CO 137/87, f. 173; Trevor Burnard, "European Migration to Jamaica, 1655–1780," *WMQ* 53, no. 4 (1996): 772; Maya Jasanoff, *Liberty's Exiles: American Loyalists in the Revolutionary World* (New York: Knopf, 2012), 357; Elsa V. Goveia, *Slave Society in the British Leeward Islands at the End of the Eighteenth Century* (New Haven, CT: Yale University Press, 1965), 85, 96; Jerome Handler, *The Unappropriated People: Freedmen in the Slave Society of Barbados* (Baltimore: Johns Hopkins University Press, 1974), 18–19; Melanie J. Newton, *The Children of Africa in the Colonies: Free People of Color in Barbados in the Age of Emancipation* (Baton Rouge: Louisiana State University Press, 2008), 39–40.

19. Henrice Altink, "Deviant and Dangerous: Proslavery Representations of Jamaican Slave Women's Sexuality, ca. 1780–1834," *Slavery and Abolition* 26 (2005): 271–88; William Smalling to Joseph Foster Barham, February 2, 1774, MSS Clare dep c357, Barham Family Papers, BOD; East to Elletson, September 12, 1780, folder 8, box 26, Brydges Correspondence, Stowe Collection, STB, HL.

20. James Ramsay, *An Essay on the Treatment and Conversion of African Slaves in the British Sugar Colonies* (London, 1784), 83–84, 85.

21. James Tobin, *Cursory Remarks upon the Reverend Mr. Ramsay's "Essay on the Treatment and Conversion of African Slaves in the Sugar Colonies"* (London, 1785), 29, 37–38.

22. Tobin, *Cursory Remarks upon the Reverend Mr. Ramsay's "Essay,"* 116–19; Rev. Lyndsay, "A Few Conjectural Considerations upon the Creation of the Humane Race, Occasioned by the Present British Quixottical Rage of setting the Slaves from Africa at Liberty," 1788, BL, Add. MS 12439, f. 17; William Beckford, *A Descriptive Account of the Island of Jamaica*, 2 vols. (London, 1790), 2: 331; Bryan Edwards, *The History, Civil and Commercial, of the British Colonies in the West Indies*, 3 vols. (London, 1793), 2:17; BL, Add. MS 18271, f. 60.

23. Edward Long, "Collections relating to Jamaica," BL Add. MS 18959, ff. 19, 21, 35.

24. Beckford, *Descriptive Account of the Island of Jamaica*, 2; BL, Add. MS 12439, f. 160.

25. Seymour Drescher, *The Mighty Experiment: Free Labor versus Slavery in British Emancipation* (Oxford: Oxford University Press, 2002), 34–35; William Belsham, *An Essay on the African Slave Trade* (Philadelphia, 1790), 12, 13; James Ramsay, *Objections to the Abolition of the Slave Trade, with Answers* (London, 1788), 31.

26. Clarke to Sydney, April 22, 1788, CO 137/87, f. 81; Brydges to Hibbert, April 1, 1788, folder 62, and Brydges to Hibbert, August 5, 1788, folder 64, Brydges Correspondence, Stowe Collection, STB, box 27, HL; Clarke to Sydney, August 1, 1788, CO 137/87, ff. 121–22. The Consolidated Slave Act sent by Clarke is in CO 137/87, ff. 126–45.

27. October 16, 1788, *JAJ*, 8:409–11; Fuller to the Committee of Correspondence, May 10, 1788, Stephen Fuller Papers, RL; Simon Taylor to John Tailyour, January 4, 1792, Tailyour Papers, WCL.

28. October 16, 1788, *JAJ*, 8:409–11.

29. Consolidated Slave Act, December 6, 1788, CO 139/44, ff. 60–66; November 12, 1788, *JAJ*, 8:427–36; Fuller to the Committee of Correspondence, September 2, 1788, and December 3, 1788, Stephen Fuller Papers, RL.

30. November 12, 1788, and December 2, 1789, *JAJ*, 8:409–11, 427–36, 524–25; BL, Add MS 12439, f. 114; Jesse Foot, *A Defence of the Planters in the West-Indies; Comprised in Four Arguments on Comparative Humanity, on Comparative Slavery, on the African Slave Trade, and on the Condition of Negroes in the West-Indies* (London, 1792), 32.

31. *An Abstract of the Evidence Delivered before a Select Committee of the House of Commons in the Years 1790, and 1791; On the Part of the Petitioners for the Abolition of the Slave-Trade* (London, 1792), 52–53; Sasha Turner, *Contested Bodies: Pregnancy, Childrearing, and Slavery in Jamaica* (Philadelphia: University of Pennsylvania Press, 2017), 91.

32. Barham to Wedderburn and Graham, September 8, 1789, June 23, 1792, and July 6, 1797, Barham Papers, c428, BOD; Council Committee Report, March 23, 1800, CO 137/104, ff. 52–56. For a sustained analysis of Mesopotamia, see Richard Dunn, *A Tale of Two Plantations: Slave Life and Labor in Jamaica and Virginia* (Cambridge, MA: Harvard University Press, 2014).

33. Barham to Webb, December 15, 1809, Barham to Grant and Blyth, June 20, 1813, Barham to Ridgard, June 1, 1825, and Barham to Blyth, September 2, 1829, c428, BOD; Barham to William Smith, August 29, 1806, William Smith Letters, 1800–1806, RL.

34. Fuller to the Committee of Correspondence, May 16, 1788, Stephen Fuller Papers, RL; *The New Act of Assembly of the Island of Jamaica . . . Commonly Called the New Consolidated Act . . . Being the Present Code Noir of that Island* (London, 1789); Fuller to the Committee of Correspondence, June 2, 1789, and Sugar and Rum imported from March 25, 1787 to March 25, 1788, Stephen Fuller Papers, RL; Fuller to Sydney, November 13, 1790, CO 137/87, f. 260.

35. General Meeting, June 30, 1788, April 9, 1789, and May 19, 1789, West India Committee Minutes, May 1785–December 1792, reel 3, M915, ICS.

36. General Meeting, May 19, 1789, reel 3, M915, ICS.

37. BL, Add. MS 12439, f. 112; December 10, 1789, *JAJ*, 8:536.

38. Sharp to Wilberforce, June 4, 1795, folder 2: 1790–95, box 1, William Wilberforce Letters, 1782–1837, RL.

39. J. R. Oldfield, *Transatlantic Abolitionism in the Age of Revolution: An International History of Anti-slavery, c. 1787–1820* (New York: Cambridge University Press, 2013), 8–9; John D. Garrigus, "Color, Class and Identity on the Eve of the Haitian Revolution: Saint-Domingue's Free Colored Elite as *Colons américains,*" *Slavery and Abolition* 17 (1996): 20–43; Louis XVI quoted in Darcy Grimaldo Grigsby, *Extremities: Painting Empire in Post-revolutionary France* (New Haven, CT: Yale University Press, 2002), 20.

40. Quoted in *An Historical Account of the Black Empire of Hayti,* ed. Marcus Rainsford et al. (Durham, NC: Duke University Press, 2013), 221–26; Bryan Edwards, *An Historical Survey of the French Colony in the Island of St. Domingo* (London, 1797), 9; John D. Garrigus, *Before Haiti: Race and Citizenship in French Saint-Domingue* (New York: Palgrave Macmillan, 2006), 257.

41. March 14, 1792, *JAJ*, 9:100; December 22, 1797, *JAJ*, 10:99; Hibbert to Brydges, May 20, 1788, Brydges Correspondence, folder 69, STB, box 26, Stowe Collection, HL; Simon Taylor to John Tailyour, March 2, 1792, Tailyour Papers, WCL; Seymour Drescher, *Abolition: A History of Slavery and Antislavery* (Cambridge: Cambridge University Press), 161–62, 222.

42. Petition of Free People of Colour, 1792, CO 137/91, ff. 39–41; Council Address to Williamson, November 26, 1792, CO 137/90, f. 50; Assembly to Fuller, December 5, 1792, CO 137/91, f. 37.

43. Secret and Separate, Dundas to Williamson, June 5, 1793, CO 137/91, ff. 142–45; Bryan Edwards, "The state of mulattoes in Jamaica," May 16, 1793, CO 137/50, ff. 220–25.

44. Return of militia, January 13, 1792, CO 137/90, f. 79; Return of militia, April 18, 1808, Eyre Coote Papers, box 12, item 41, WCL; Return of militia, November 1812, CO 137/137, f. 7; Michael Craton, *Testing the Chains: Resistance to Slavery in the British West Indies* (1982; repr., Ithaca, NY: Cornell University Press, 1982), 214; Vaughan to Cuthbert, August 3, 1795, Headquarters, Vaughan's Field, August 14, 1795, and Balcarres to Portland, May 23, 1796, Hardwicke Papers, vol. 567, BL, Add. MS 35916, ff. 157–59, 170–71, 200–201; 36 Geo. 3, c. 23 (March 25, 1796), *The Laws of Jamaica* (St. Jago de la Vega, 1802), 3:150–52.

45. Portland to Balcarres, January 10, 1797, and August 1797, CO 137/98, f. 232; Simon Taylor to John Tailyour, December 5, 1797, Tailyour Papers, WCL; November 28,

1797, *JAJ*, 10:36; Balcarres to Portland, May 24, 1800, CO 137/104, ff. 80–84; December 15, 1803, December 14, 1804, and October 15, 1807, *JAJ*, 11:156–57, 280, 575.

46. November 11, 1807, *JAJ*, 11:611; Hallam to Coote, June 11, 1807, CO 137/120, ff. 133–34; His Majesty George III to Earl Camden, May 1, 1805, in *The Later Correspondence of George III*, vol. 4, *1802–1807*, ed. A. Aspinall (Cambridge: Cambridge University Press, 1968), 516; Coote to Castlereagh, June 27, 1807, CO 137/119, f. 61.

47. November 5, 1813, and November 16, 1813, *JAJ*, 12:506, 519; 54 Geo. 3, c. 19 and c. 20 (December 4, 1813), CO 139/60, ff. 110–11; Secret, Morrison to Bathhurst, February 20, 1813, and Secret, Bathhurst to Morrison, May 13, 1813, CO 137/136, ff. 86–87, 88–89.

48. Manchester to Bathhurst, December 10, 1813, CO 137/136, ff. 195–97; November 25, 1813, *JAJ*, 12:530; Letter to His Majesty's Cabinet, July 10, 1816, CO 137/43, f. 213; *Brief Remarks on the Slave Registry Bill* (London, 1816), 17, 18.

49. "A petition of certain free persons to house of assembly," November 19, 1816, and November 29, 1816, and extract from assembly report, December 20, 1816, in Hibbert to Bathurst, CO 137/148, ff. 147–49, 145; Campbell to Bathurst [1816], CO 137/145, ff. 270–72.

50. Petition of Joseph Samuel Geoghegan, October 31, 1820, *JAJ*, 13:433; Holly Snyder, "Rules, Rights, and Redemption: The Negotiation of Jewish Status in British Atlantic Port Towns, 1740–1831," *Jewish History* 20, no. 2 (2006): 147–70.

51. Gad Heuman, *Between Black and White: Race, Politics, and the Free Coloreds in Jamaica, 1792–1865* (Westport, CT: Greenwood Press, 1981), 34; Hanly to Bathurst, September 22, 1823, CO 137/155, ff. 67–68. Bathurst also received counternarratives from West Indian agents strongly opposed to emancipation and racial equality; see Memorial of West India Agents to Bathurst, May 3, 1823, and Hibbert to Bathurst, October 18, 1823, CO 137/155, ff. 174–76, 188–89.

52. *Narrative of the Proceedings of the Jews, in Their Attempt to Establish Their Right to the Elective Franchise in Jamaica* (Belfast, 1828), 19, 22–23; Delgado quoted in Snyder, "Rules, Rights, and Redemption," 163.

53. Great Britain, *The Parliamentary Debates* 2nd series, 25 vols. (London, 1827), 17:1246; H. V. Bowen, "British Conceptions of Global Empire, 1756–1783," *Journal of Commonwealth History*, 26 (1998): 1–27; December 20, 1815, *JAJ*, 12:798.

54. Robert L. Patten, *George Cruikshank's Life, Times, and Art: 1792–1835* (New Brunswick, NJ: Rutgers University Press, 1996), 196–98; Jenna M. Gibbs, *Performing the Temple of Liberty: Slavery, Theater, and Popular Culture in London and Philadelphia, 1760–1850* (Baltimore: Johns Hopkins University Press, 2014), 123–24.

55. [Richard] Barrett, *A Reply to the Speech of Dr. Lushington, in the House of Commons, on the 12th of June, 1827, on the Condition of the Free-Coloured People of Jamaica* (London, 1828), 17–19, 48, 57–58.

56. Barrett, *Reply to the Speech of Dr. Lushington*, 18, 31; George Bridges, *The Annals of Jamaica*, 2 vols. (London, 1828), 2:371.

57. *Abstract of the Report of the Lords Commitees on the Condition and Treatment of the Colonial Slaves, and of the Evidence Taken by Them on That Subject* (London, 1833), 77.

CONCLUSION

1. Quoted in Christer Petley, *Slaveholders in Jamaica: Colonial Society and Culture during the Era of Abolition* (2009; repr., Oxford: Routledge, 2016), 74; Gad Heuman, *Between Black and White: Race, Politics, and the Free Coloreds in Jamaica, 1792–1865* (Westport, CT: Greenwood Press, 1981), 23–34.

2. Mara Loveman, *National Colors: Racial Classification and the State in Latin America* (Oxford: Oxford University Press, 2014), 13, 14; Elmer B. Russell, *The Review of American Colonial Legislation by the King in Council* (New York: Columbia University Press, 1915), 63; *Barbados Acts, from 1643 to 1762* (London, 1764), 256; *The Statutes at Large of South Carolina* (Columbia, SC, 1833), 136; William Hening, *Statutes at Large of Virginia* (Richmond, VA, 1820), 4:133; *Abridgement of the Laws of Jamaica* (St. Jago de la Vega, 1793), 273; *A Digest of the Laws of the State of Georgia* (Philadelphia, 1800), 67; Philip Hamburger, *Law and Judicial Duty* (Cambridge, MA: Harvard University Press, 2008), 261.

3. Michael Craton, "Property and Propriety: Land Tenure and Slave Property in the Creation of a British West Indian Plantocracy, 1612–1740," in *Early Modern Conceptions of Property*, ed. John Brewer and Susan Staves (London: Routledge, 1996), 510.

4. See esp. Sue Peabody, *"There Are No Slaves in France": The Political Culture of Race and Slavery in the Ancien Régime* (Oxford: Oxford University Press, 1996); Laurent Dubois, *Avengers of the New World: The Story of the Haitian Revolution* (Cambridge, MA: Harvard University Press, 2004); John Garrigus, *Before Haiti: Race and Citizenship in French Saint-Domingue* (New York: Palgrave Macmillan, 2006); Malick W. Ghachem, *The Old Regime and the Haitian Revolution* (Cambridge: Cambridge University Press, 2012); Trevor Burnard and John Garrigus, *The Plantation Machine: Atlantic Capitalism in French Saint-Domingue and British Jamaica* (Philadelphia: University of Pennsylvania Press, 2016).

5. Petley, *Slaveholders in Jamaica*, 83; *Anti-slavery Monthly Reporter* 3 (London, 1831): 162.

6. James Stephen, *The Slavery of the British West India Colonies Delineated, as It Exists Both in Law and Practice, and Compared with the Slavery of Other Countries, Ancient and Modern* (London, 1824), 30, 122–23, 71.

7. Ben Jonson, *Every Man in His Humour* (London, 1601), D3.

Index